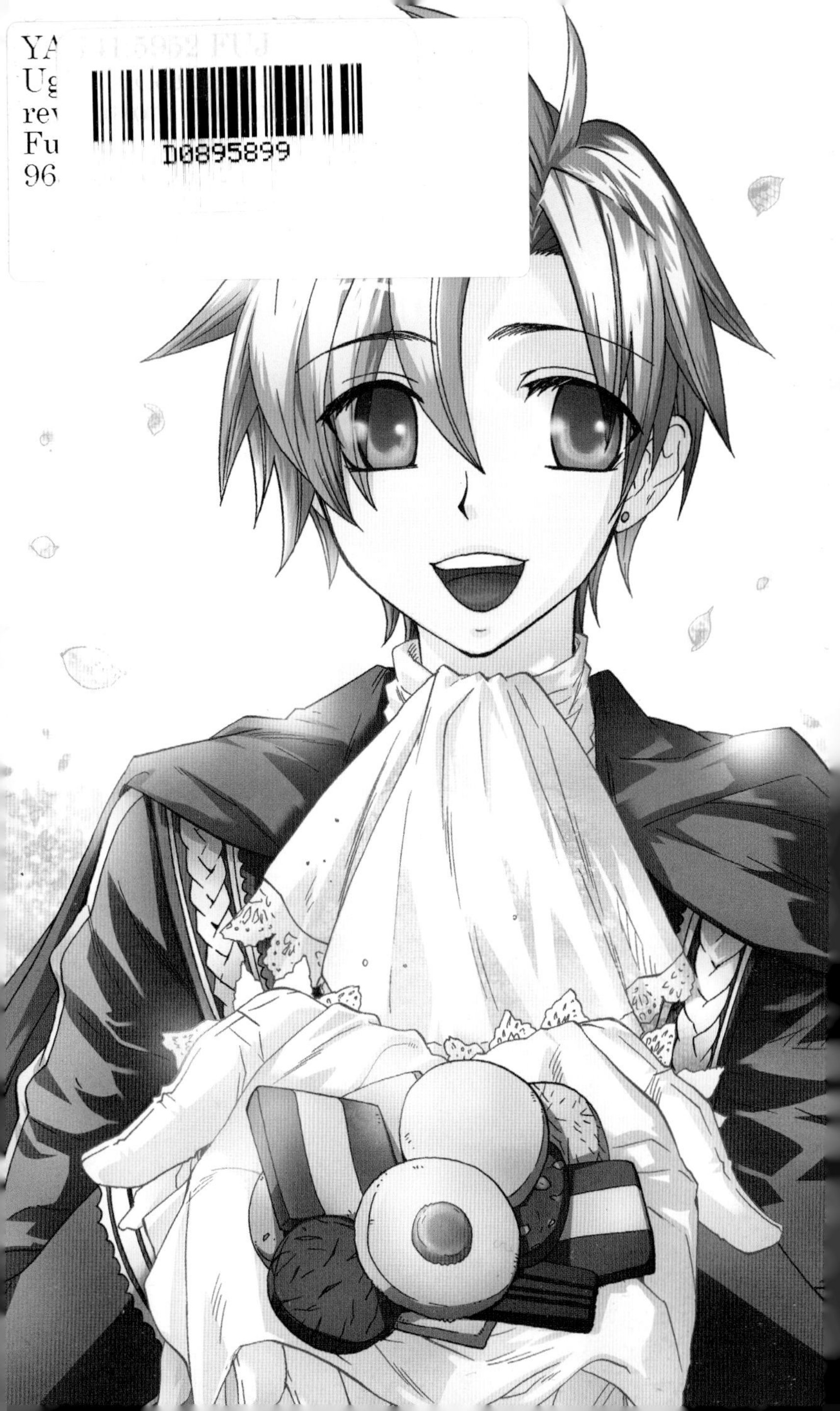

UGLY DUCKLING'S LOVE REVOLUTION

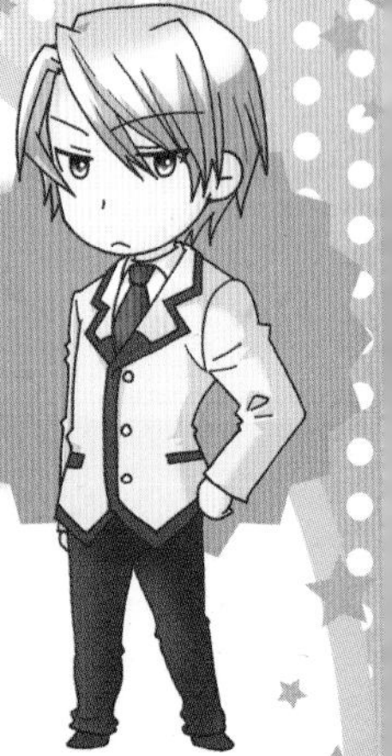

②

CONTENTS

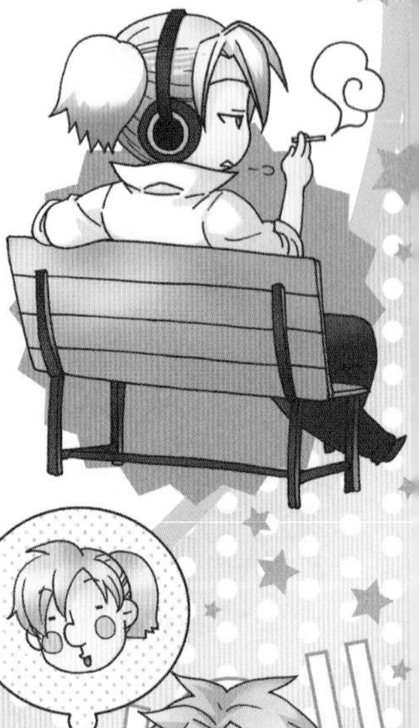

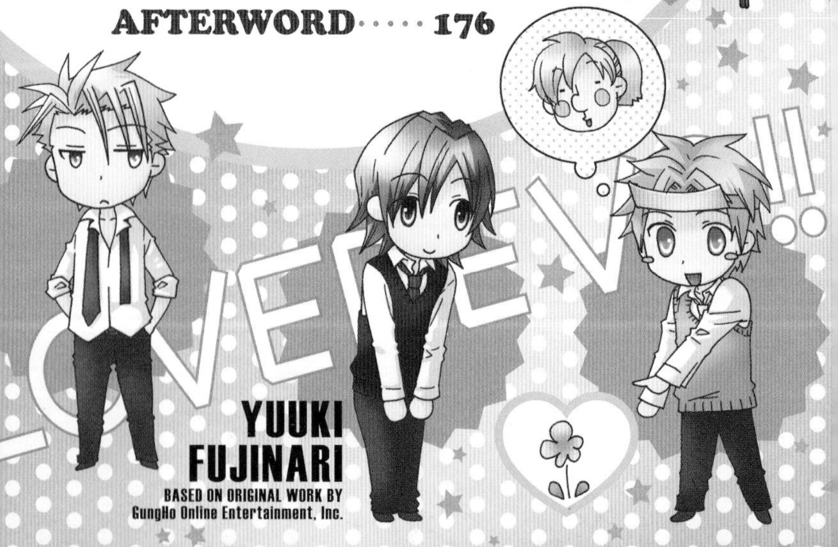

YUUKI FUJINARI

BASED ON ORIGINAL WORK BY GungHo Online Entertainment, Inc.

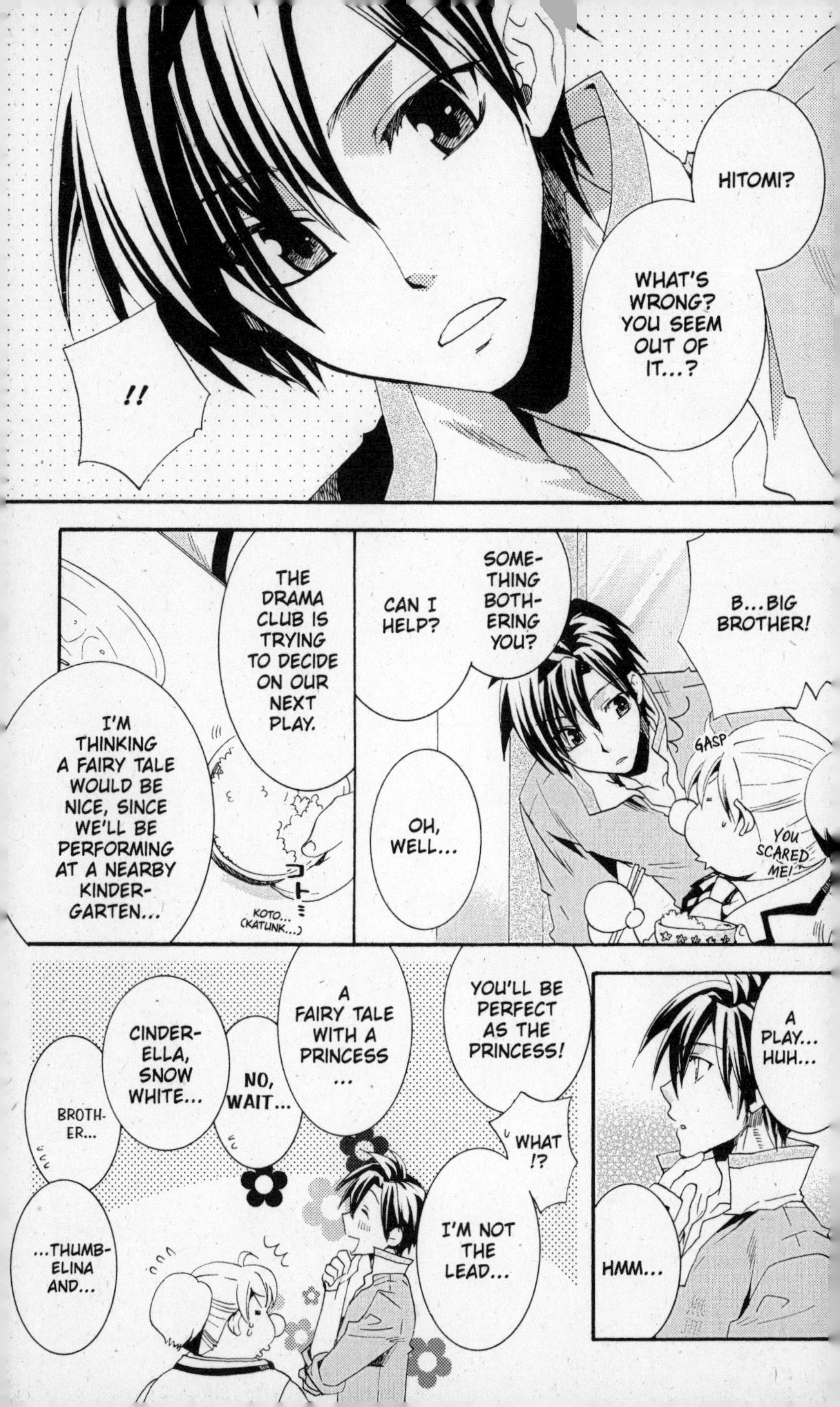
HITOMI?
WHAT'S WRONG? YOU SEEM OUT OF IT...?
!!
B...BIG BROTHER!
GASP
YOU SCARED ME!
SOMETHING BOTHERING YOU?
CAN I HELP?
OH, WELL...
THE DRAMA CLUB IS TRYING TO DECIDE ON OUR NEXT PLAY.
KOTO... (KATUNK...)
I'M THINKING A FAIRY TALE WOULD BE NICE, SINCE WE'LL BE PERFORMING AT A NEARBY KINDERGARTEN...
A PLAY... HUH...
HMM...
YOU'LL BE PERFECT AS THE PRINCESS!
WHAT!?
I'M NOT THE LEAD...
A FAIRY TALE WITH A PRINCESS...
NO, WAIT...
CINDERELLA, SNOW WHITE...
BROTHER...
...THUMBELINA AND...

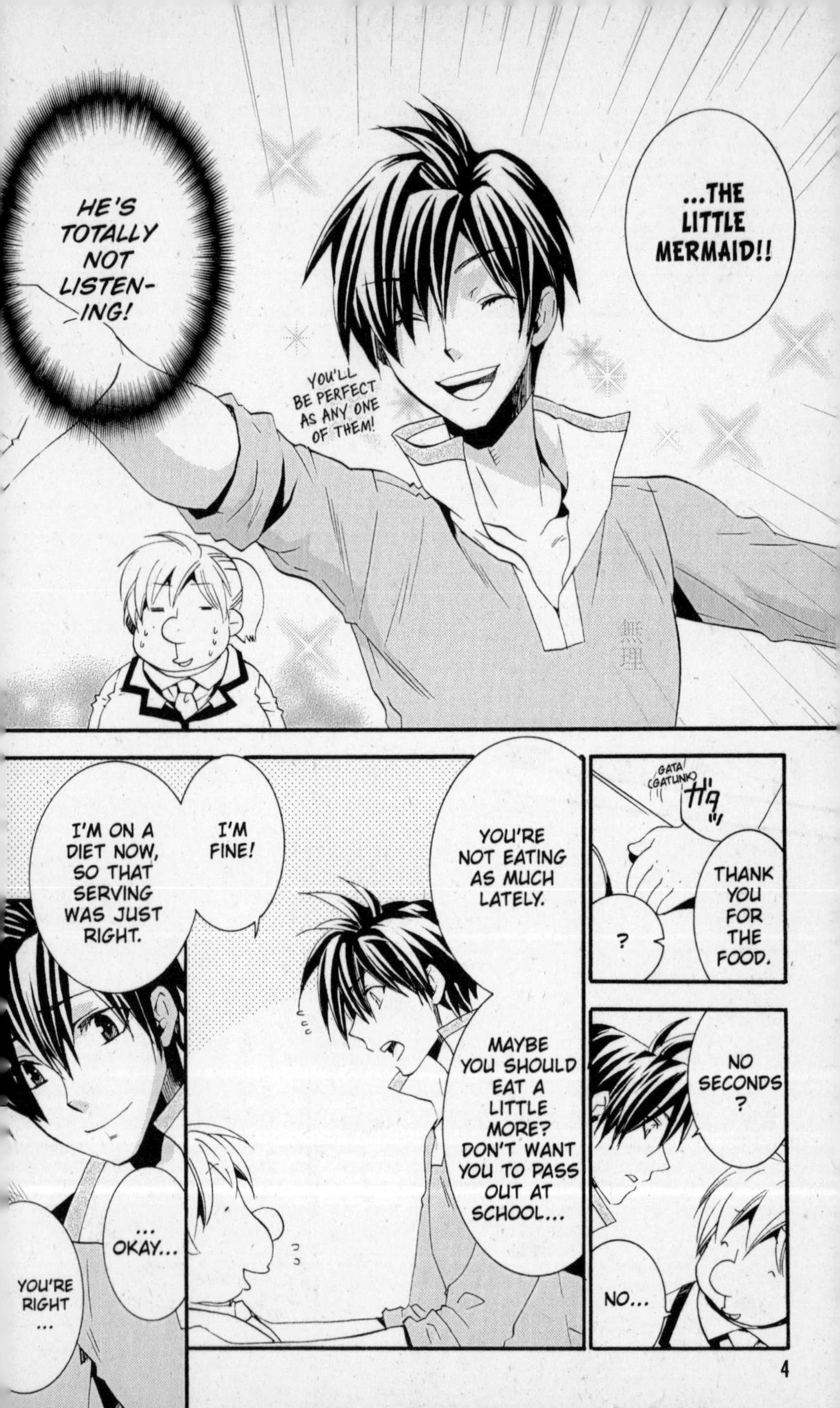

...THE LITTLE MERMAID!!
YOU'LL BE PERFECT AS ANY ONE OF THEM!
HE'S TOTALLY NOT LISTENING!
無理
GATA (GATUNK)
ガタ
THANK YOU FOR THE FOOD.
?
NO SECONDS?
NO...
YOU'RE NOT EATING AS MUCH LATELY.
MAYBE YOU SHOULD EAT A LITTLE MORE? DON'T WANT YOU TO PASS OUT AT SCHOOL...
I'M FINE!
I'M ON A DIET NOW, SO THAT SERVING WAS JUST RIGHT.
...OKAY...
YOU'RE RIGHT...

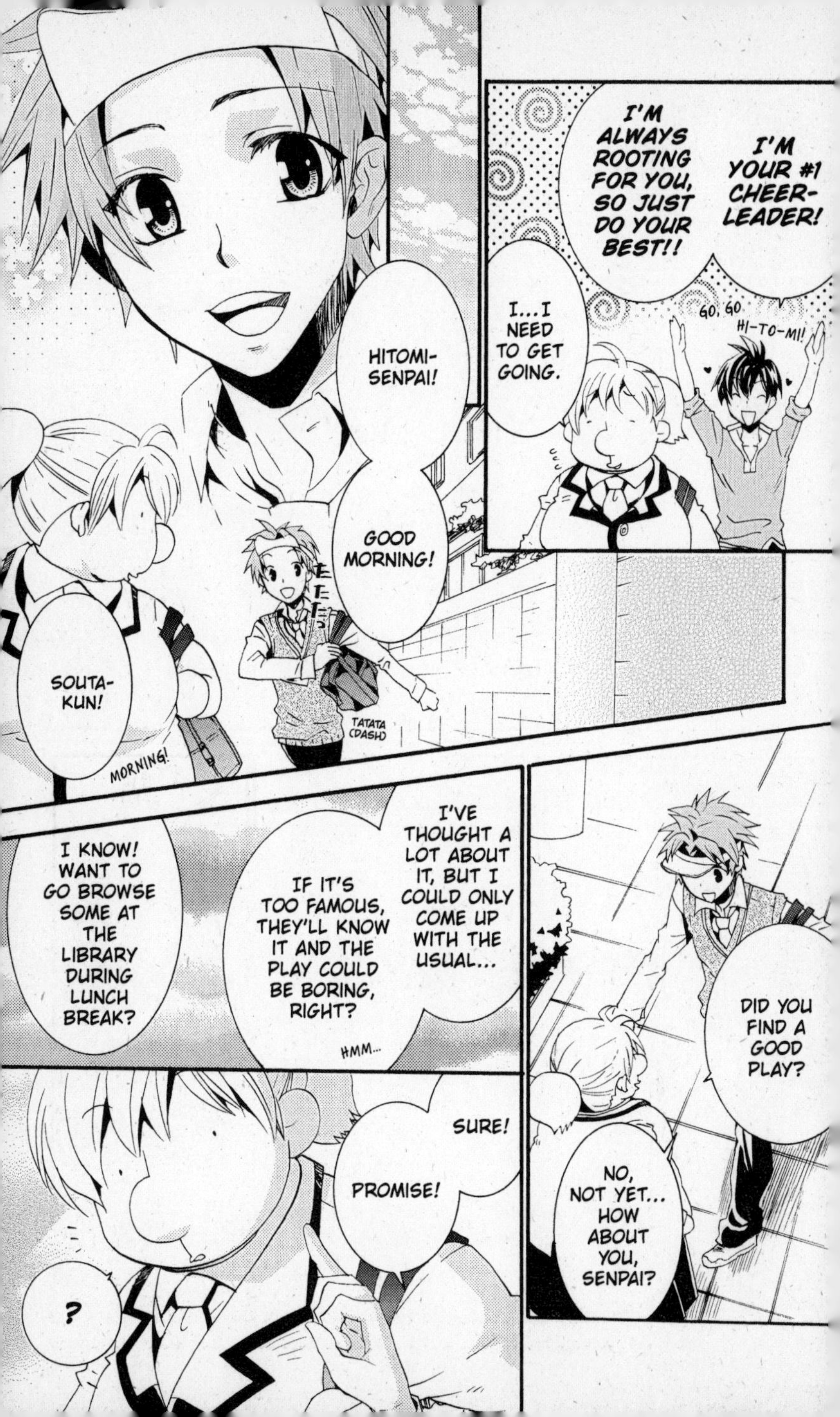
I'M YOUR #1 CHEER-LEADER!
I'M ALWAYS ROOTING FOR YOU, SO JUST DO YOUR BEST!!
GO, GO HI-TO-MI!
I...I NEED TO GET GOING.
HITOMI-SENPAI!
GOOD MORNING!
TATATA (DASH)
SOUTA-KUN!
MORNING!
DID YOU FIND A GOOD PLAY?
NO, NOT YET... HOW ABOUT YOU, SENPAI?
I'VE THOUGHT A LOT ABOUT IT, BUT I COULD ONLY COME UP WITH THE USUAL...
IF IT'S TOO FAMOUS, THEY'LL KNOW IT AND THE PLAY COULD BE BORING, RIGHT?
HMM...
I KNOW! WANT TO GO BROWSE SOME AT THE LIBRARY DURING LUNCH BREAK?
SURE!
PROMISE!
?

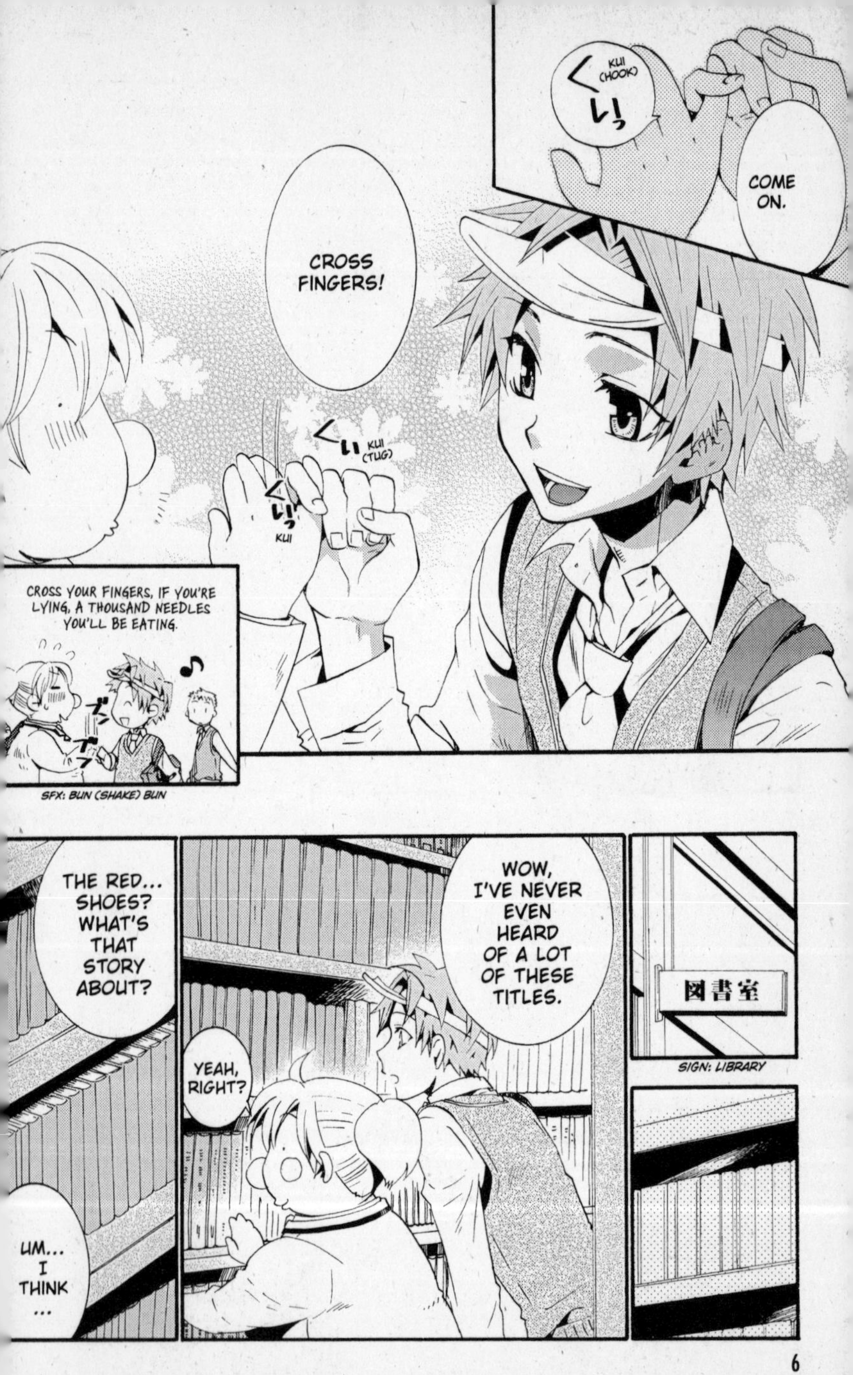
くいっ
KUI (HOOK)
COME ON.
CROSS FINGERS!
くい
KUI (TUG)
くいっ
KUI
CROSS YOUR FINGERS, IF YOU'RE LYING, A THOUSAND NEEDLES YOU'LL BE EATING.
SFX: BUN (SHAKE) BUN
図書室
SIGN: LIBRARY
WOW, I'VE NEVER EVEN HEARD OF A LOT OF THESE TITLES.
YEAH, RIGHT?
THE RED... SHOES? WHAT'S THAT STORY ABOUT?
UM... I THINK ...

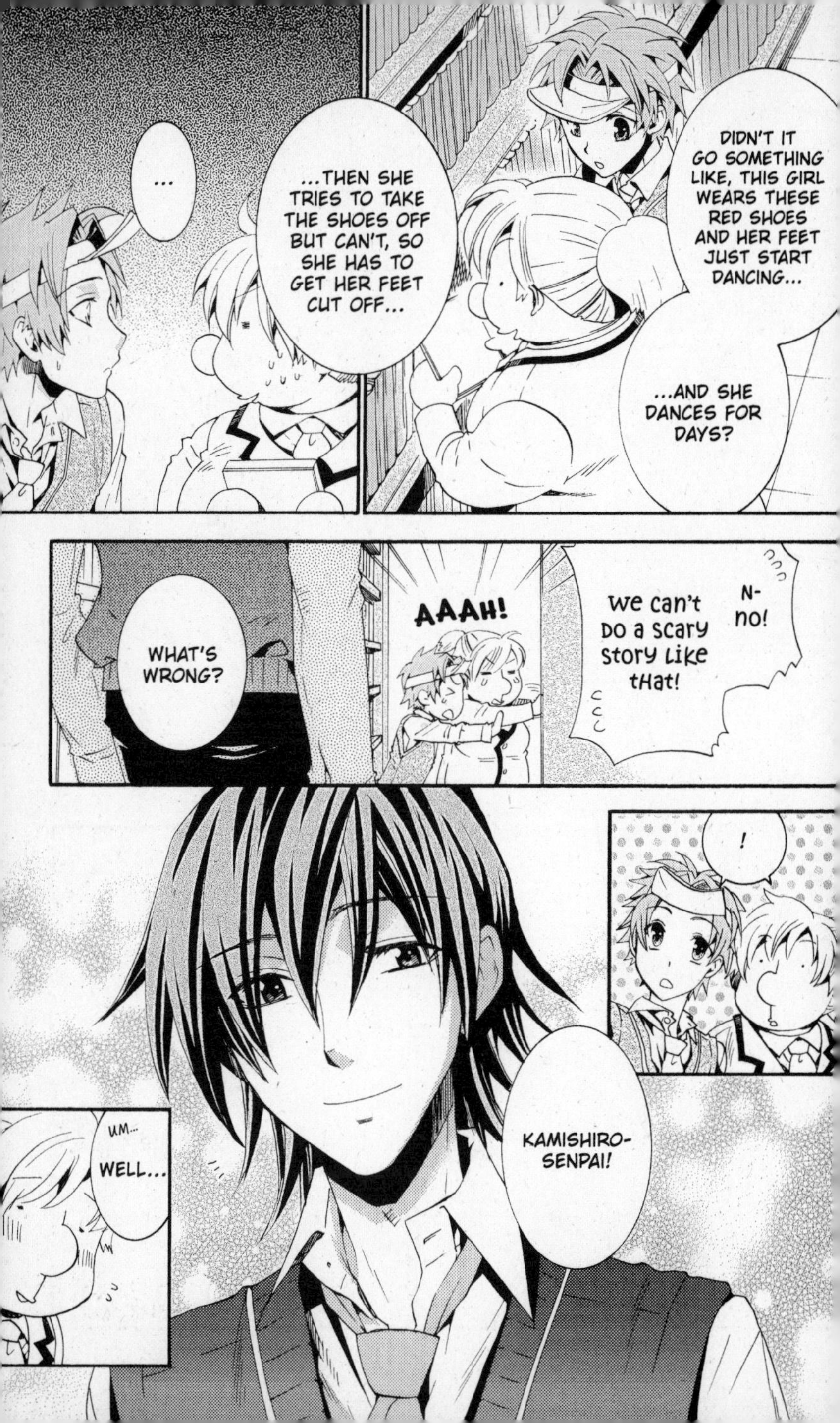
DIDN'T IT GO SOMETHING LIKE, THIS GIRL WEARS THESE RED SHOES AND HER FEET JUST START DANCING...
...AND SHE DANCES FOR DAYS?
...THEN SHE TRIES TO TAKE THE SHOES OFF BUT CAN'T, SO SHE HAS TO GET HER FEET CUT OFF...
...
N-no!
We can't do a scary story like that!
AAAH!
WHAT'S WRONG?
!
KAMISHIRO-SENPAI!
UM... WELL...

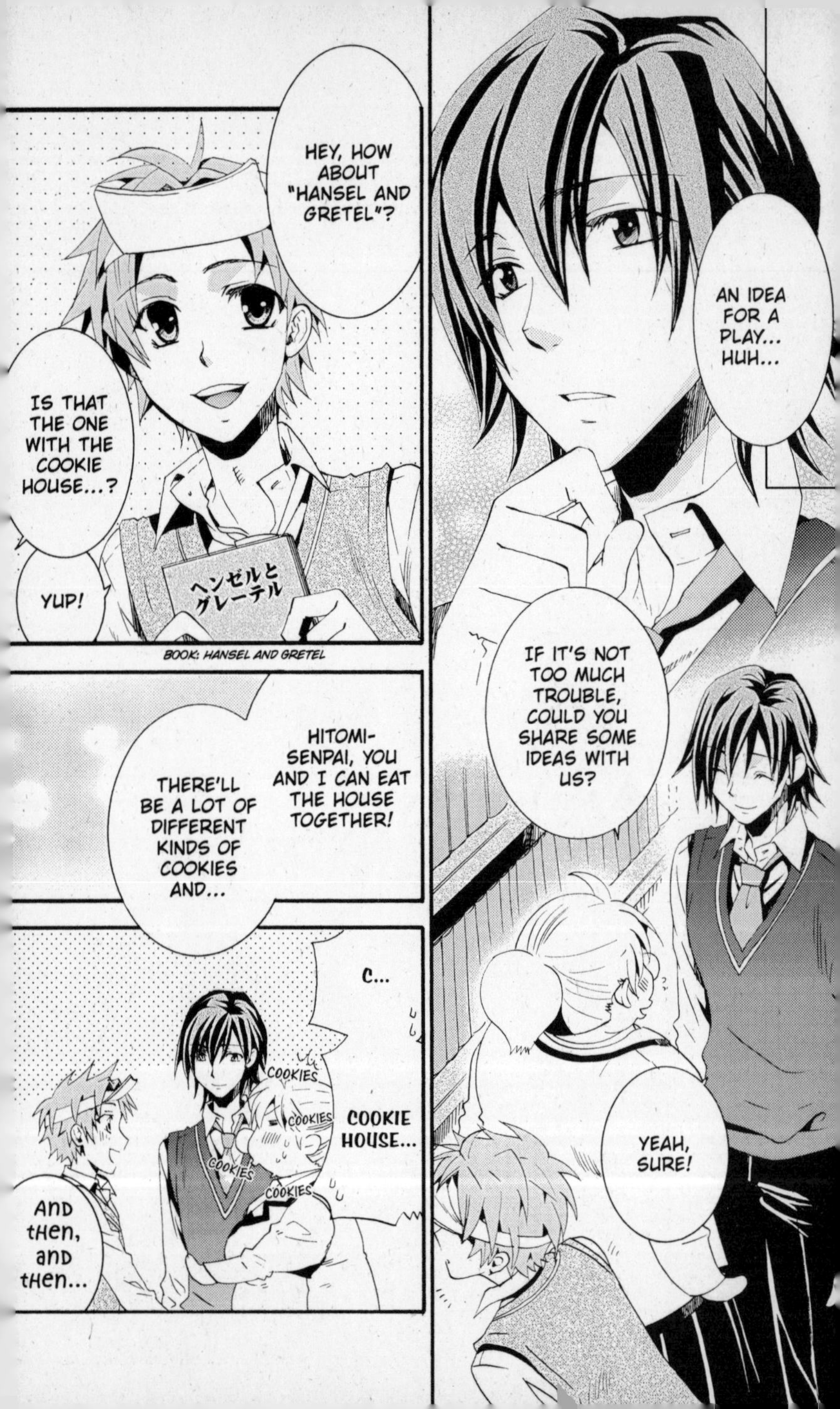
AN IDEA FOR A PLAY... HUH...
IF IT'S NOT TOO MUCH TROUBLE, COULD YOU SHARE SOME IDEAS WITH US?
YEAH, SURE!
HEY, HOW ABOUT "HANSEL AND GRETEL"?
IS THAT THE ONE WITH THE COOKIE HOUSE...?
YUP!
ヘンゼルとグレーテル
BOOK: HANSEL AND GRETEL
HITOMI-SENPAI, YOU AND I CAN EAT THE HOUSE TOGETHER!
THERE'LL BE A LOT OF DIFFERENT KINDS OF COOKIES AND...
C...
COOKIE HOUSE...
COOKIES
COOKIES
COOKIES
COOKIES
And then, and then...

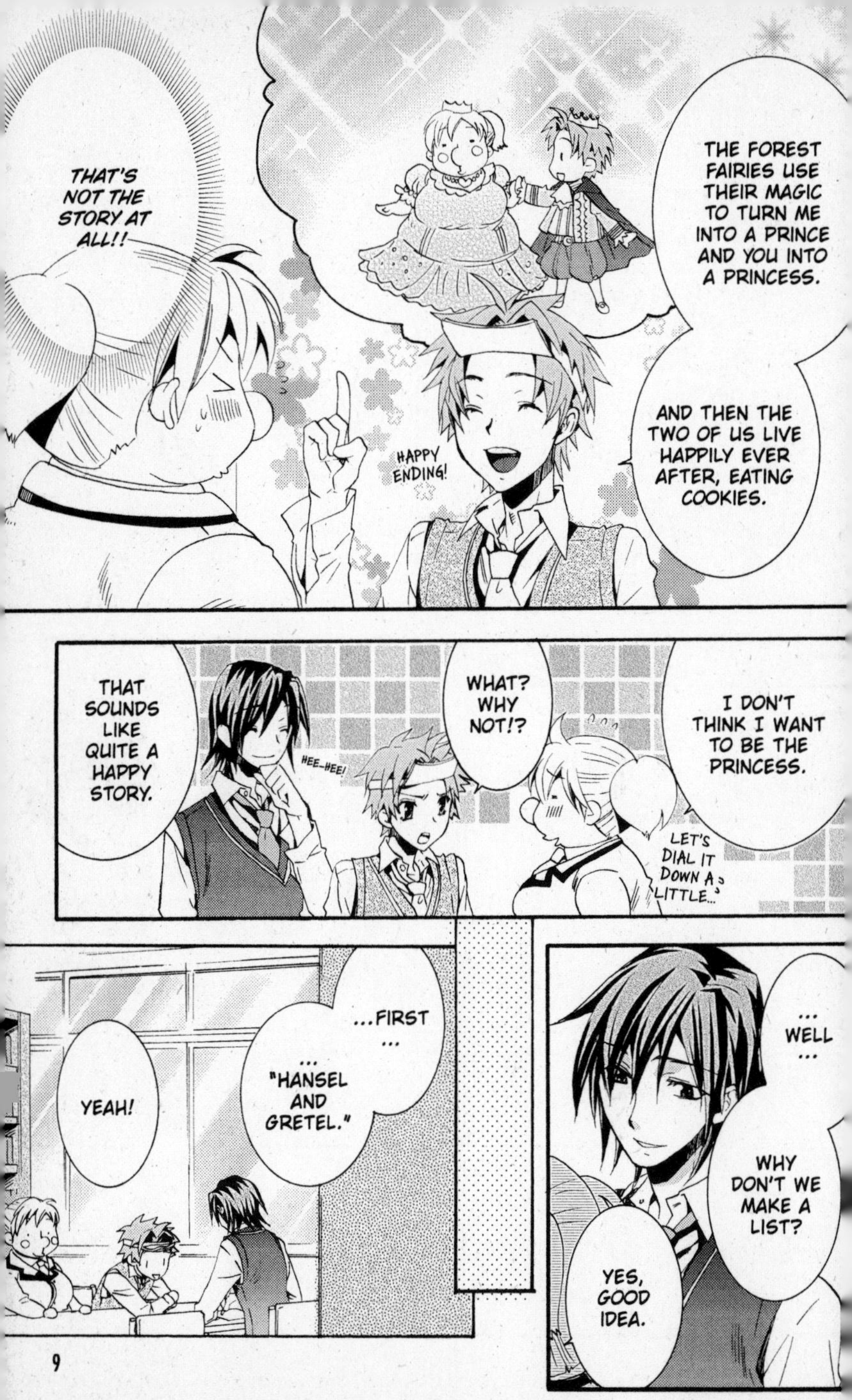
THE FOREST FAIRIES USE THEIR MAGIC TO TURN ME INTO A PRINCE AND YOU INTO A PRINCESS.
AND THEN THE TWO OF US LIVE HAPPILY EVER AFTER, EATING COOKIES.
HAPPY ENDING!
THAT'S NOT THE STORY AT ALL!!
I DON'T THINK I WANT TO BE THE PRINCESS.
LET'S DIAL IT DOWN A LITTLE...
WHAT? WHY NOT!?
THAT SOUNDS LIKE QUITE A HAPPY STORY.
HEE-HEE!
...WELL...
WHY DON'T WE MAKE A LIST?
YES, GOOD IDEA.
...FIRST...
..."HANSEL AND GRETEL."
YEAH!

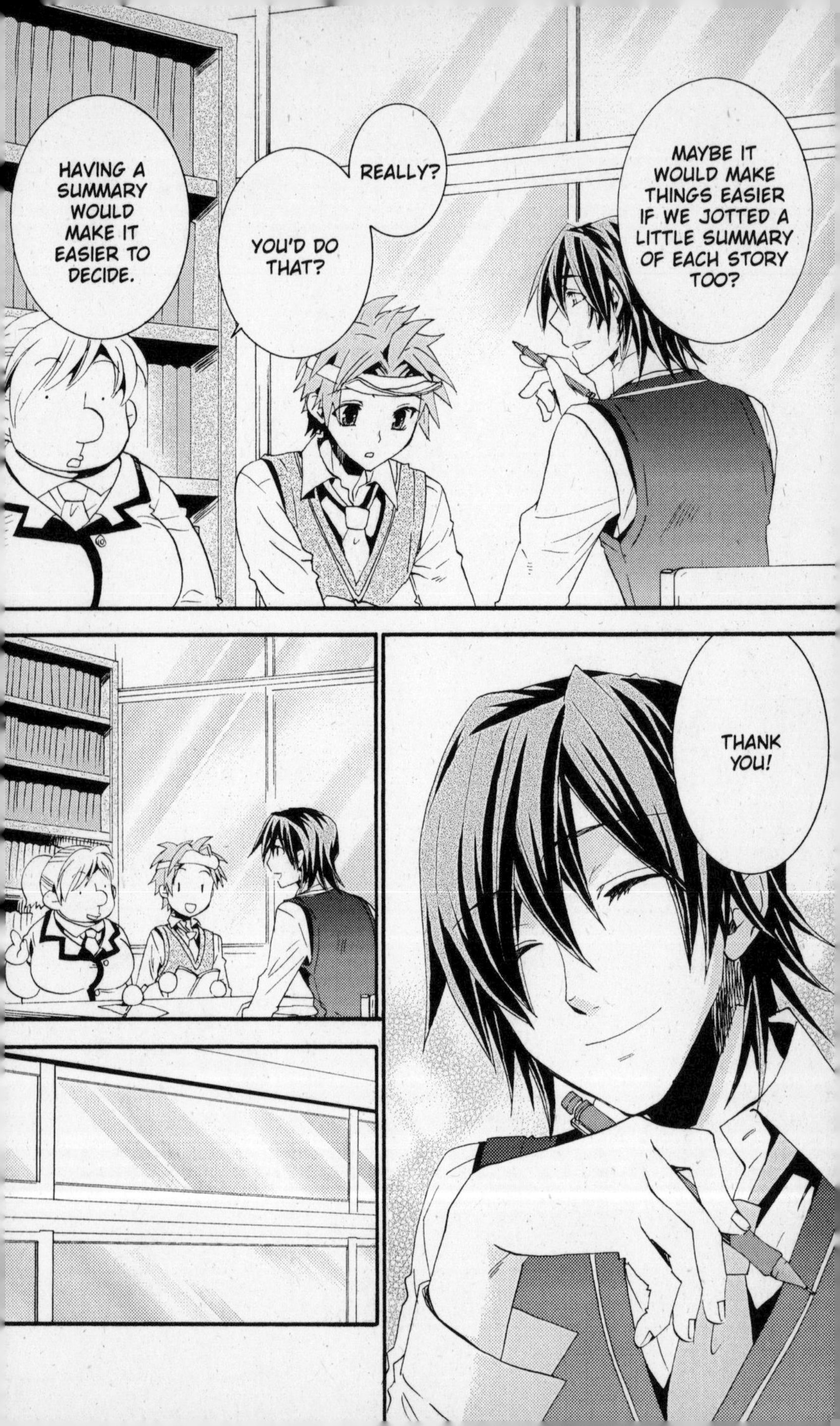
MAYBE IT WOULD MAKE THINGS EASIER IF WE JOTTED A LITTLE SUMMARY OF EACH STORY TOO?
REALLY?
YOU'D DO THAT?
HAVING A SUMMARY WOULD MAKE IT EASIER TO DECIDE.
THANK YOU!

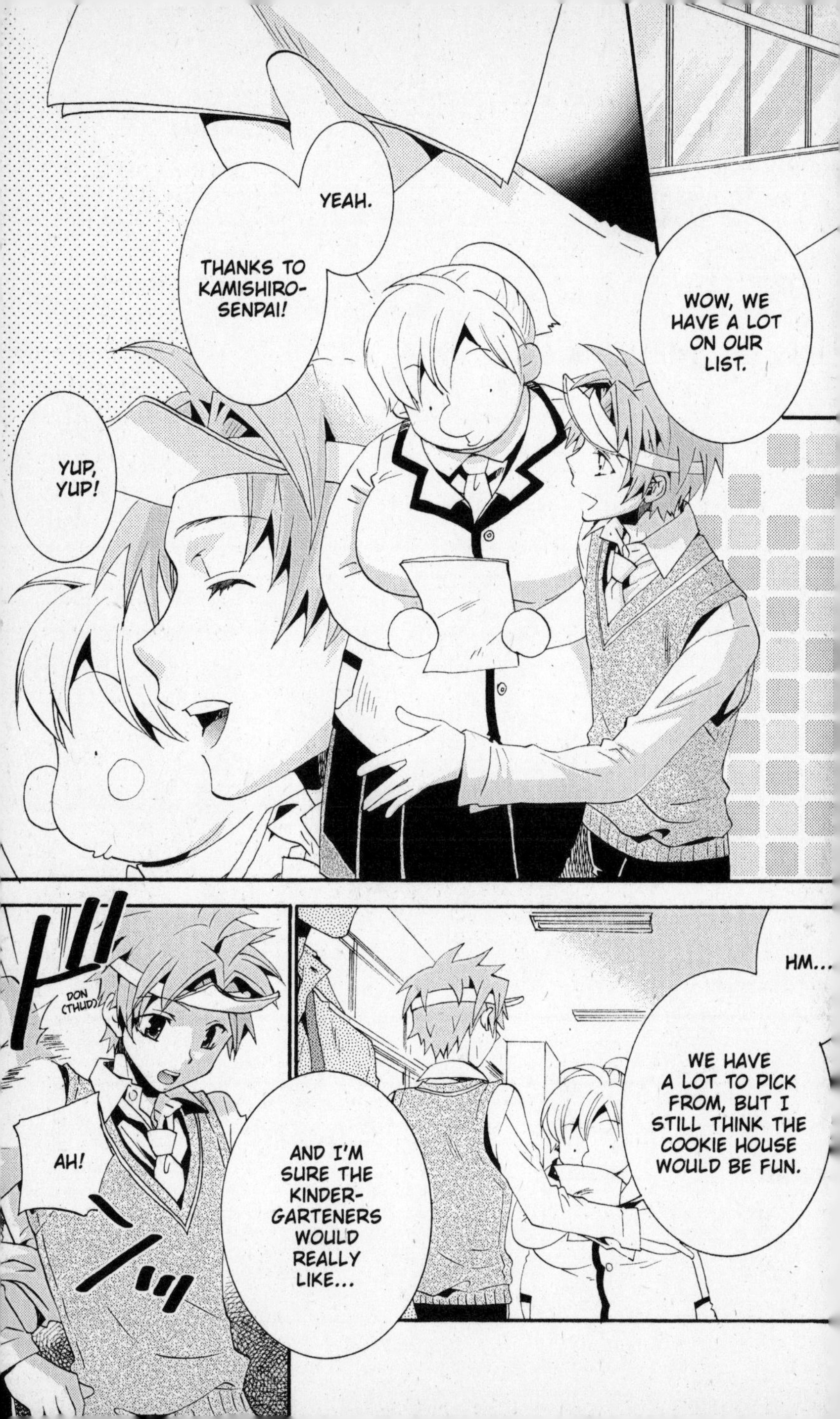
WOW, WE HAVE A LOT ON OUR LIST.
YEAH.
THANKS TO KAMISHIRO-SENPAI!
YUP, YUP!
HM...
WE HAVE A LOT TO PICK FROM, BUT I STILL THINK THE COOKIE HOUSE WOULD BE FUN.
AND I'M SURE THE KINDERGARTENERS WOULD REALLY LIKE...
DON (THUD)
AH!

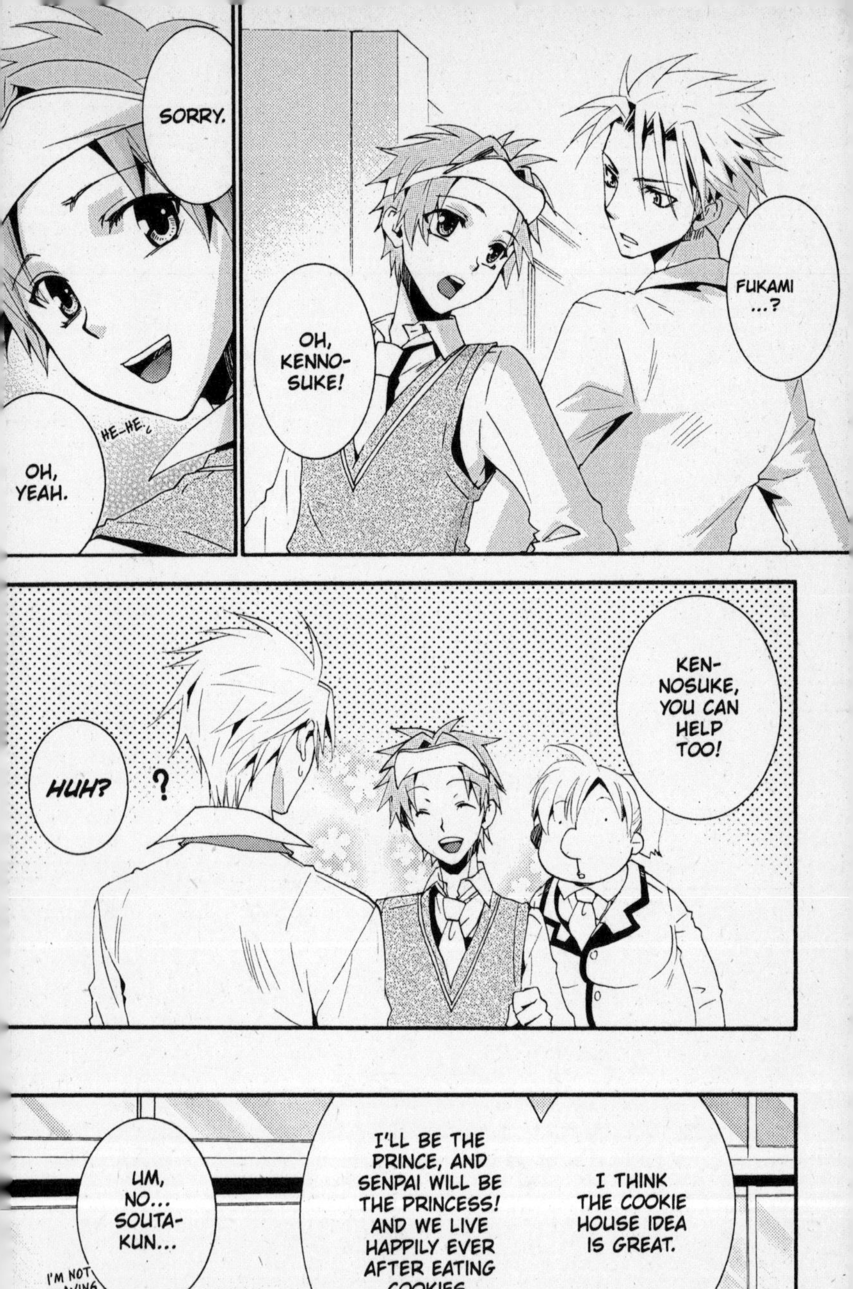
FUKAMI ...?
OH, KENNO-SUKE!
SORRY.
HE-HE.
OH, YEAH.
KEN-NOSUKE, YOU CAN HELP TOO!
HUH?
?
I THINK THE COOKIE HOUSE IDEA IS GREAT.
I'LL BE THE PRINCE, AND SENPAI WILL BE THE PRINCESS! AND WE LIVE HAPPILY EVER AFTER EATING COOKIES.
UM, NO... SOUTA-KUN...
I'M NOT PLAYING THE HEROINE...

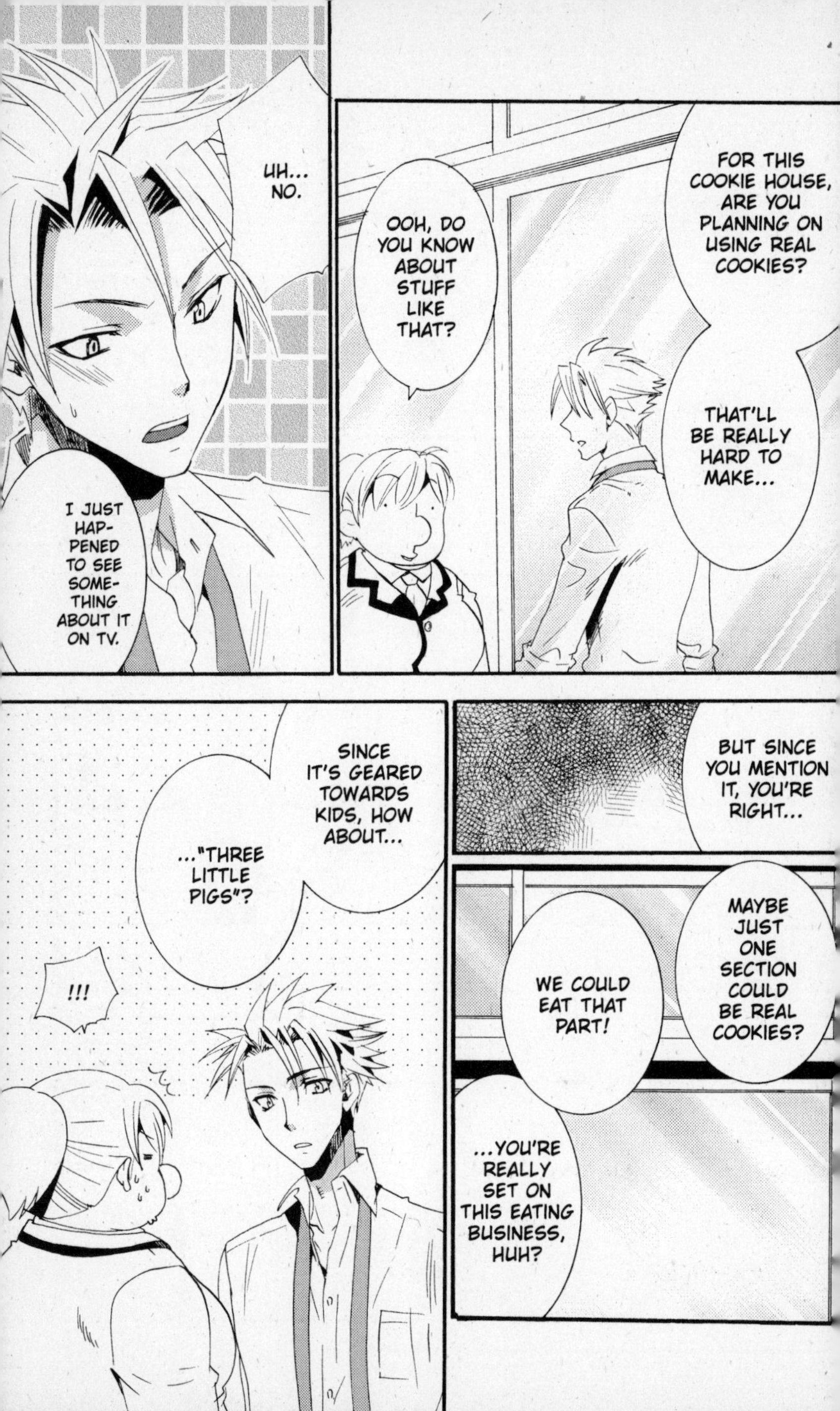
FOR THIS COOKIE HOUSE, ARE YOU PLANNING ON USING REAL COOKIES?
THAT'LL BE REALLY HARD TO MAKE...
OOH, DO YOU KNOW ABOUT STUFF LIKE THAT?
UH... NO.
I JUST HAP-PENED TO SEE SOME-THING ABOUT IT ON TV.
BUT SINCE YOU MENTION IT, YOU'RE RIGHT...
MAYBE JUST ONE SECTION COULD BE REAL COOKIES?
WE COULD EAT THAT PART!
...YOU'RE REALLY SET ON THIS EATING BUSINESS, HUH?
SINCE IT'S GEARED TOWARDS KIDS, HOW ABOUT...
..."THREE LITTLE PIGS"?
!!!

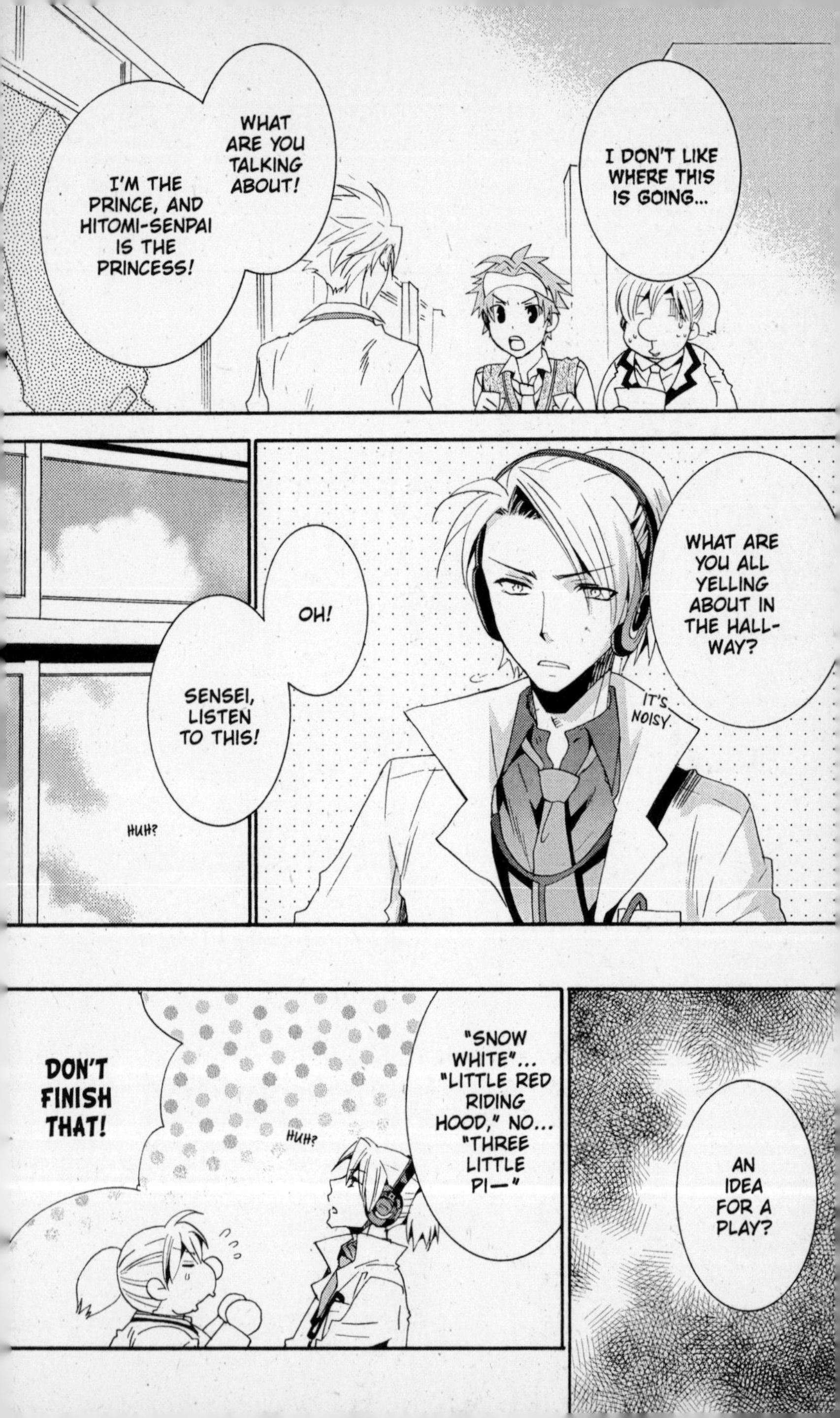
I DON'T LIKE WHERE THIS IS GOING...
WHAT ARE YOU TALKING ABOUT!
I'M THE PRINCE, AND HITOMI-SENPAI IS THE PRINCESS!
WHAT ARE YOU ALL YELLING ABOUT IN THE HALL-WAY?
IT'S NOISY.
OH!
SENSEI, LISTEN TO THIS!
HUH?
AN IDEA FOR A PLAY?
"SNOW WHITE"... "LITTLE RED RIDING HOOD," NO... "THREE LITTLE PI—"
HUH?
DON'T FINISH THAT!

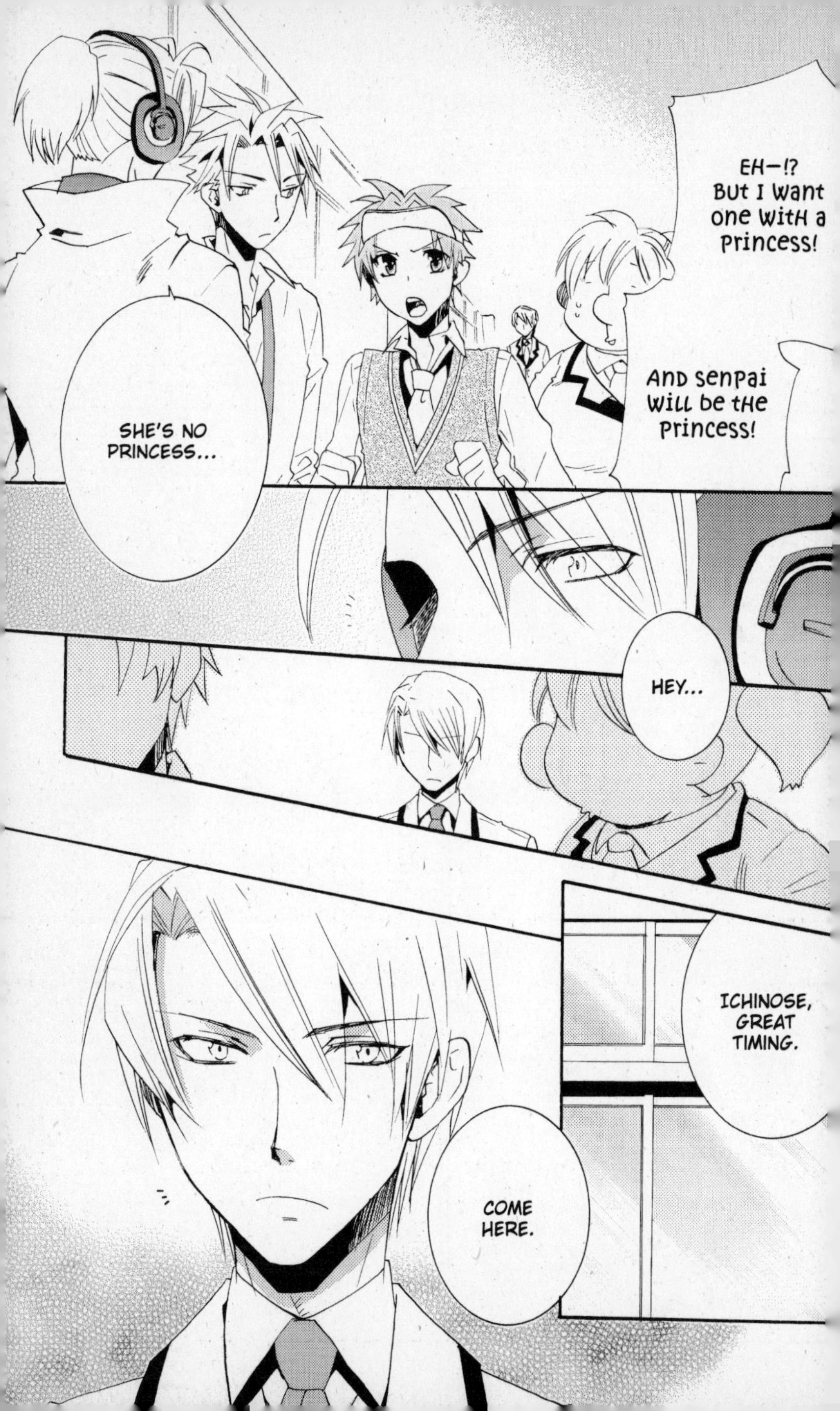
EH—!? But I want one with a princess!
And senpai will be the princess!
SHE'S NO PRINCESS...
HEY...
ICHINOSE, GREAT TIMING.
COME HERE.

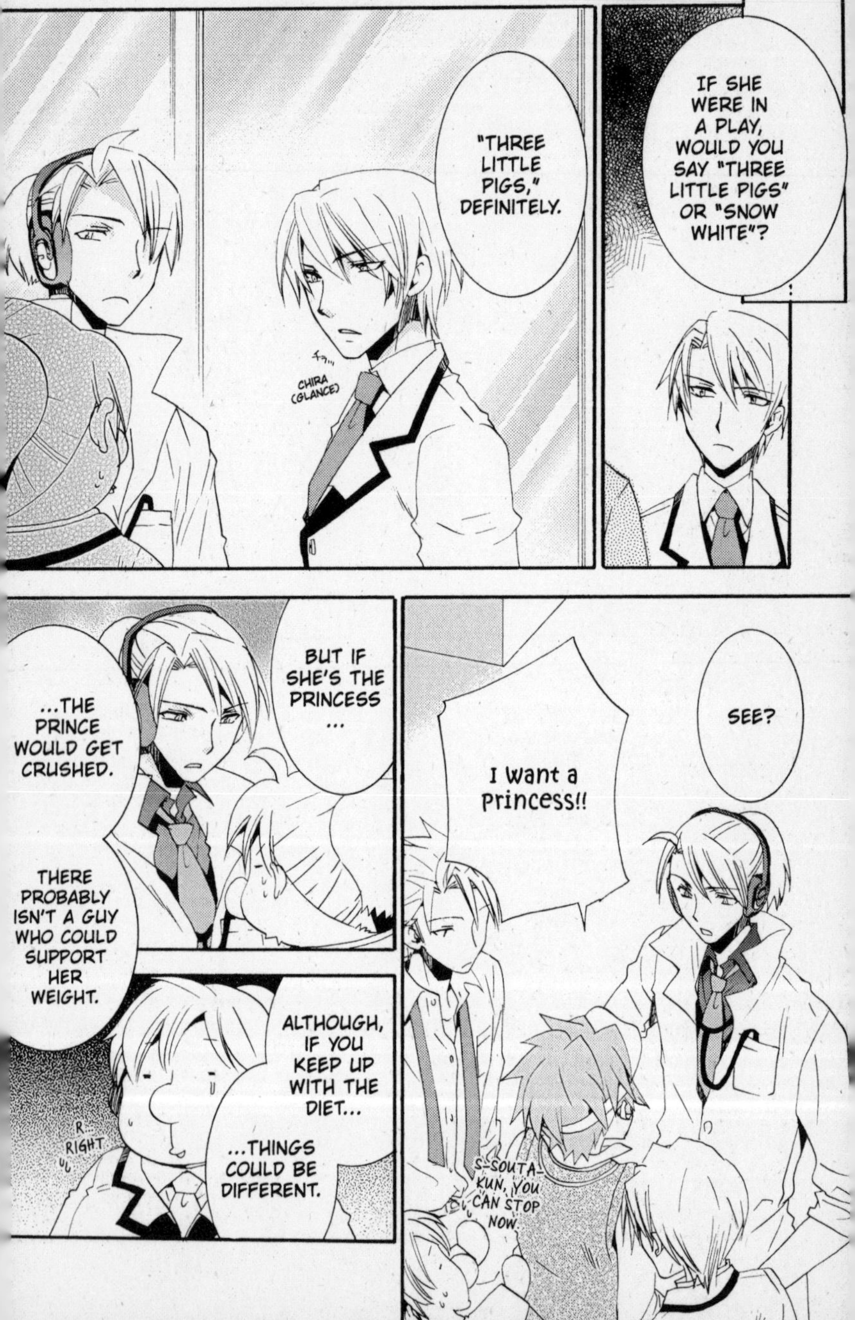
IF SHE WERE IN A PLAY, WOULD YOU SAY "THREE LITTLE PIGS" OR "SNOW WHITE"?
"THREE LITTLE PIGS," DEFINITELY.
CHIRA (GLANCE)
SEE?
I want a Princess!!
S-SOUTA-KUN, YOU CAN STOP NOW.
BUT IF SHE'S THE PRINCESS...
...THE PRINCE WOULD GET CRUSHED.
THERE PROBABLY ISN'T A GUY WHO COULD SUPPORT HER WEIGHT.
ALTHOUGH, IF YOU KEEP UP WITH THE DIET...
...THINGS COULD BE DIFFERENT.
R-RIGHT

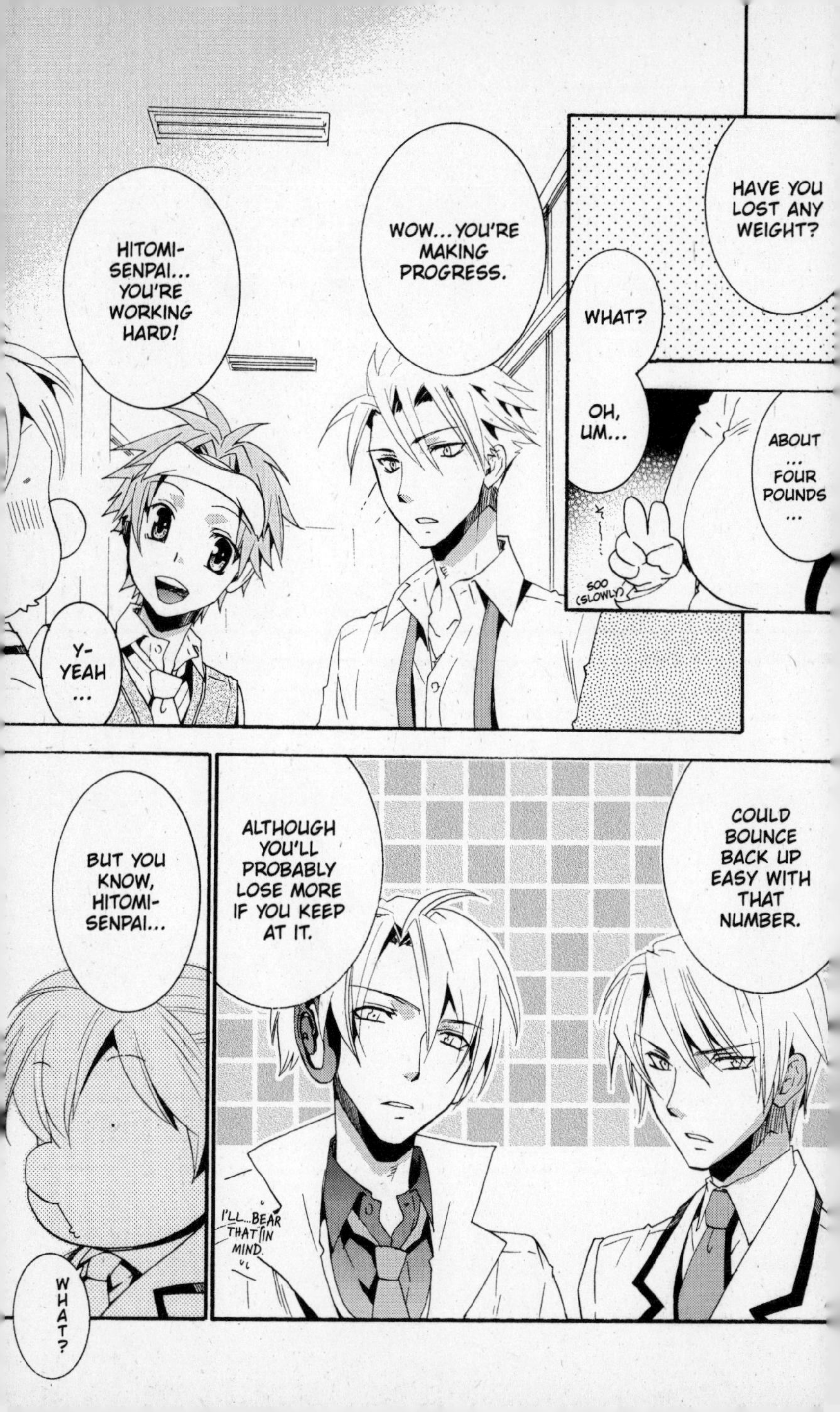
HAVE YOU LOST ANY WEIGHT?
WHAT?
OH, UM...
ABOUT ... FOUR POUNDS ...
SOO (SLOWLY)
WOW...YOU'RE MAKING PROGRESS.
HITOMI-SENPAI... YOU'RE WORKING HARD!
Y-YEAH ...
COULD BOUNCE BACK UP EASY WITH THAT NUMBER.
ALTHOUGH YOU'LL PROBABLY LOSE MORE IF YOU KEEP AT IT.
I'LL...BEAR THAT IN MIND.
BUT YOU KNOW, HITOMI-SENPAI...
WHAT?

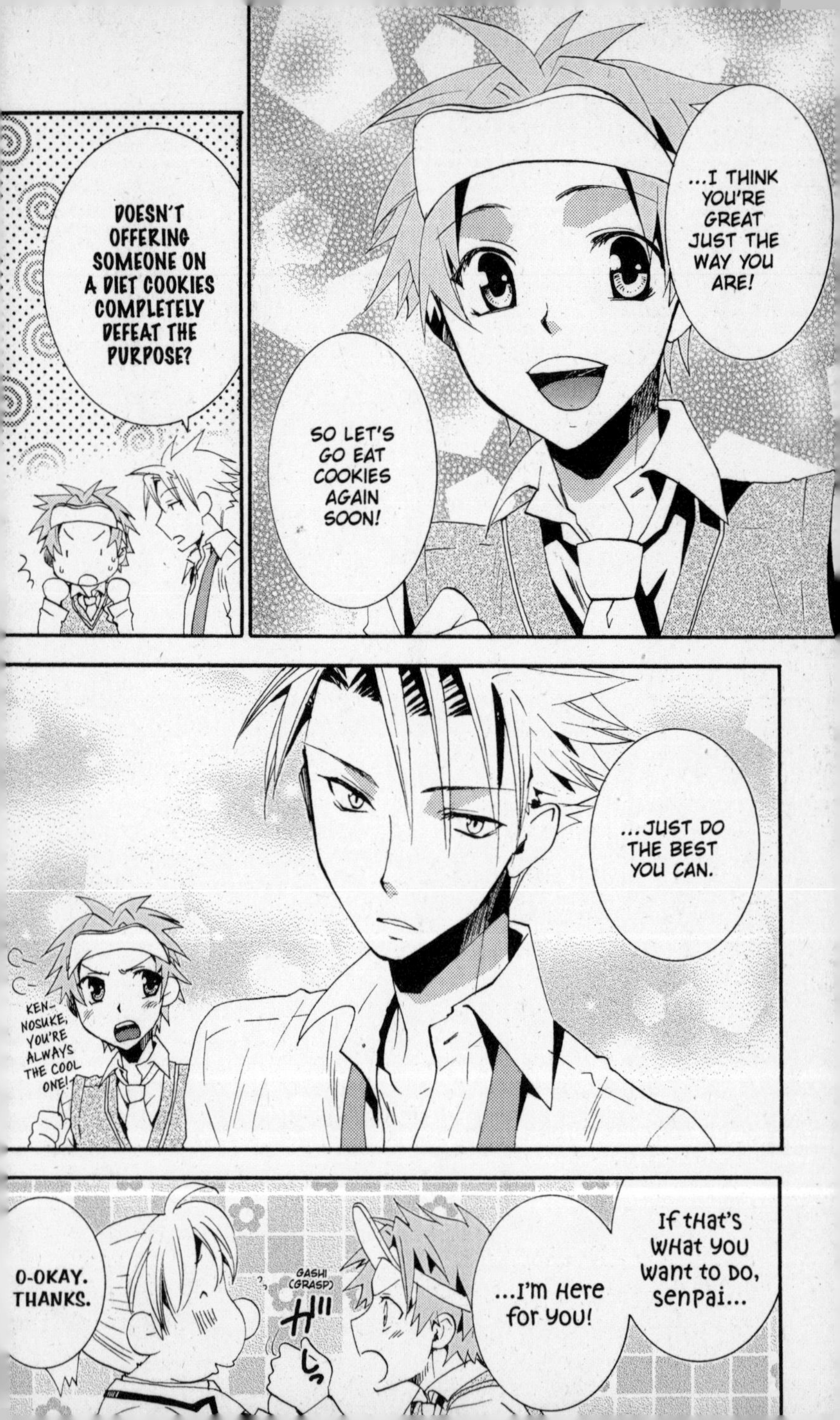
...I THINK YOU'RE GREAT JUST THE WAY YOU ARE!
SO LET'S GO EAT COOKIES AGAIN SOON!
DOESN'T OFFERING SOMEONE ON A DIET COOKIES COMPLETELY DEFEAT THE PURPOSE?
...JUST DO THE BEST YOU CAN.
KEN-NOSUKE, YOU'RE ALWAYS THE COOL ONE!
If that's what you want to do, senpai...
...I'm here for you!
GASHI (GRASP)
O-OKAY. THANKS.

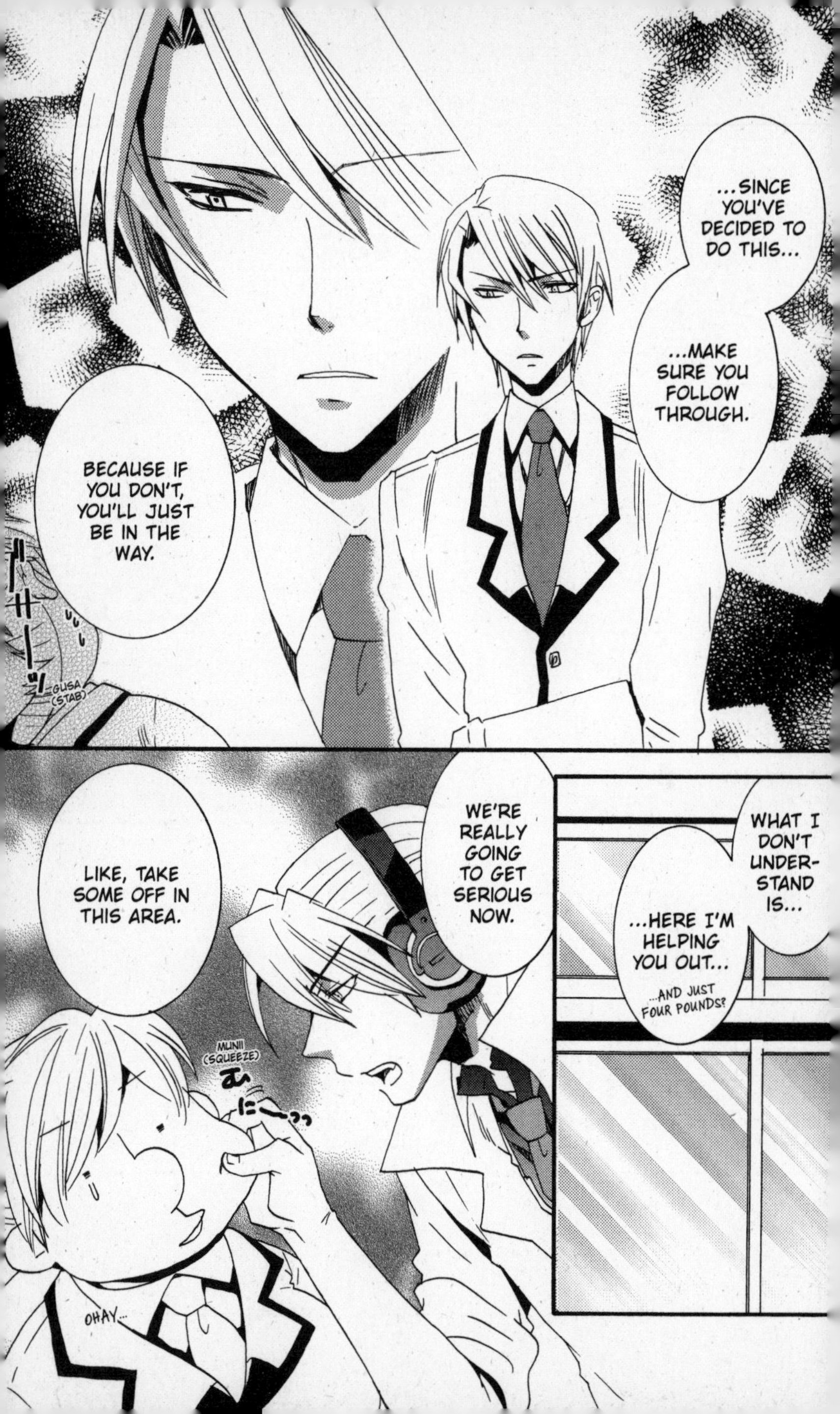
...SINCE YOU'VE DECIDED TO DO THIS...
...MAKE SURE YOU FOLLOW THROUGH.
BECAUSE IF YOU DON'T, YOU'LL JUST BE IN THE WAY.
GUSA (STAB)
WHAT I DON'T UNDER-STAND IS...
...HERE I'M HELPING YOU OUT...
...AND JUST FOUR POUNDS?
WE'RE REALLY GOING TO GET SERIOUS NOW.
LIKE, TAKE SOME OFF IN THIS AREA.
MUNII (SQUEEZE)
OKAY...

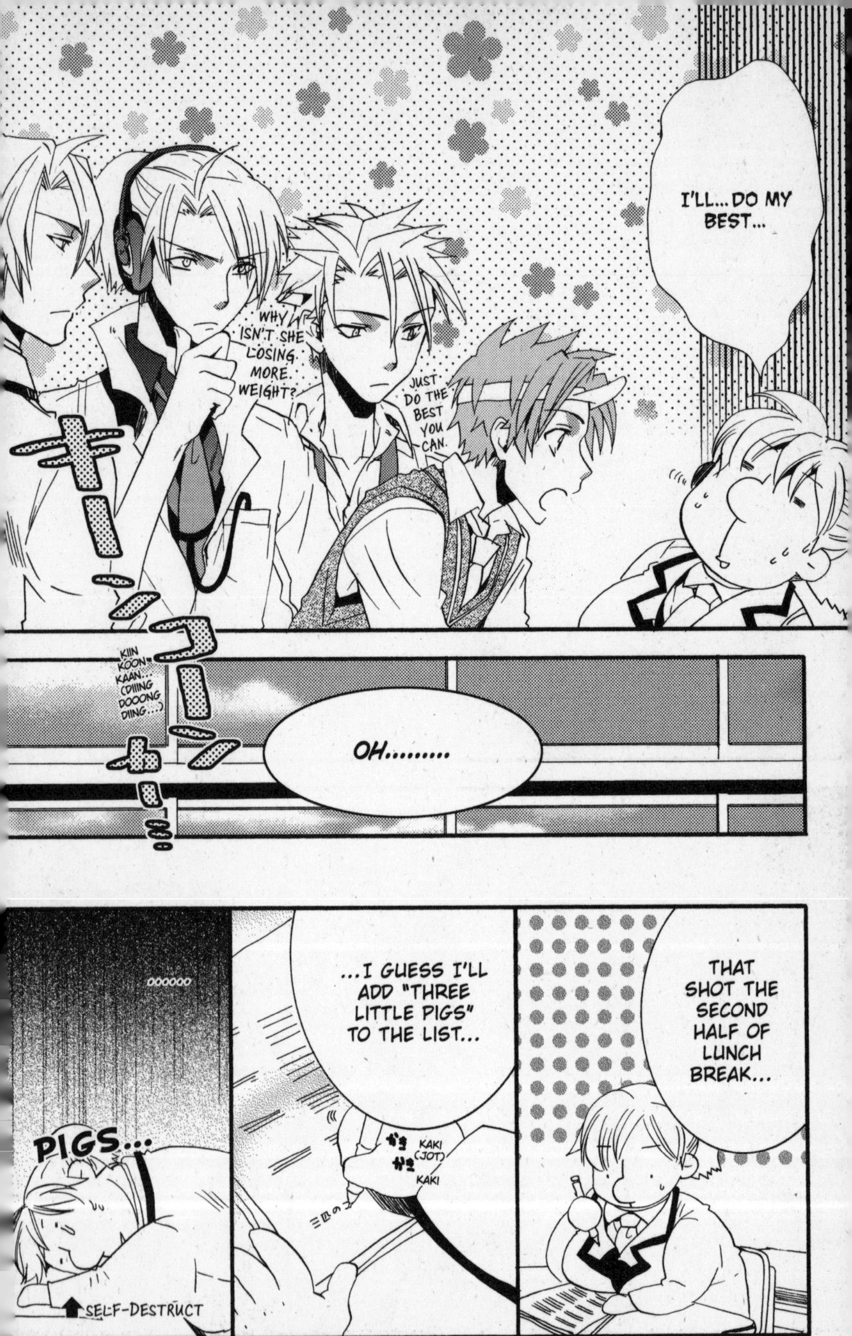
I'LL... DO MY BEST...
JUST DO THE BEST YOU CAN.
WHY ISN'T SHE LOSING MORE WEIGHT?
KIIN KOON KAAN... (DIIING DOOONG DIING...)
OH.........
THAT SHOT THE SECOND HALF OF LUNCH BREAK...
...I GUESS I'LL ADD "THREE LITTLE PIGS" TO THE LIST...
KAKI (JOT) KAKI
PIGS...
SELF-DESTRUCT
PAPER: "THREE LITTLE..."

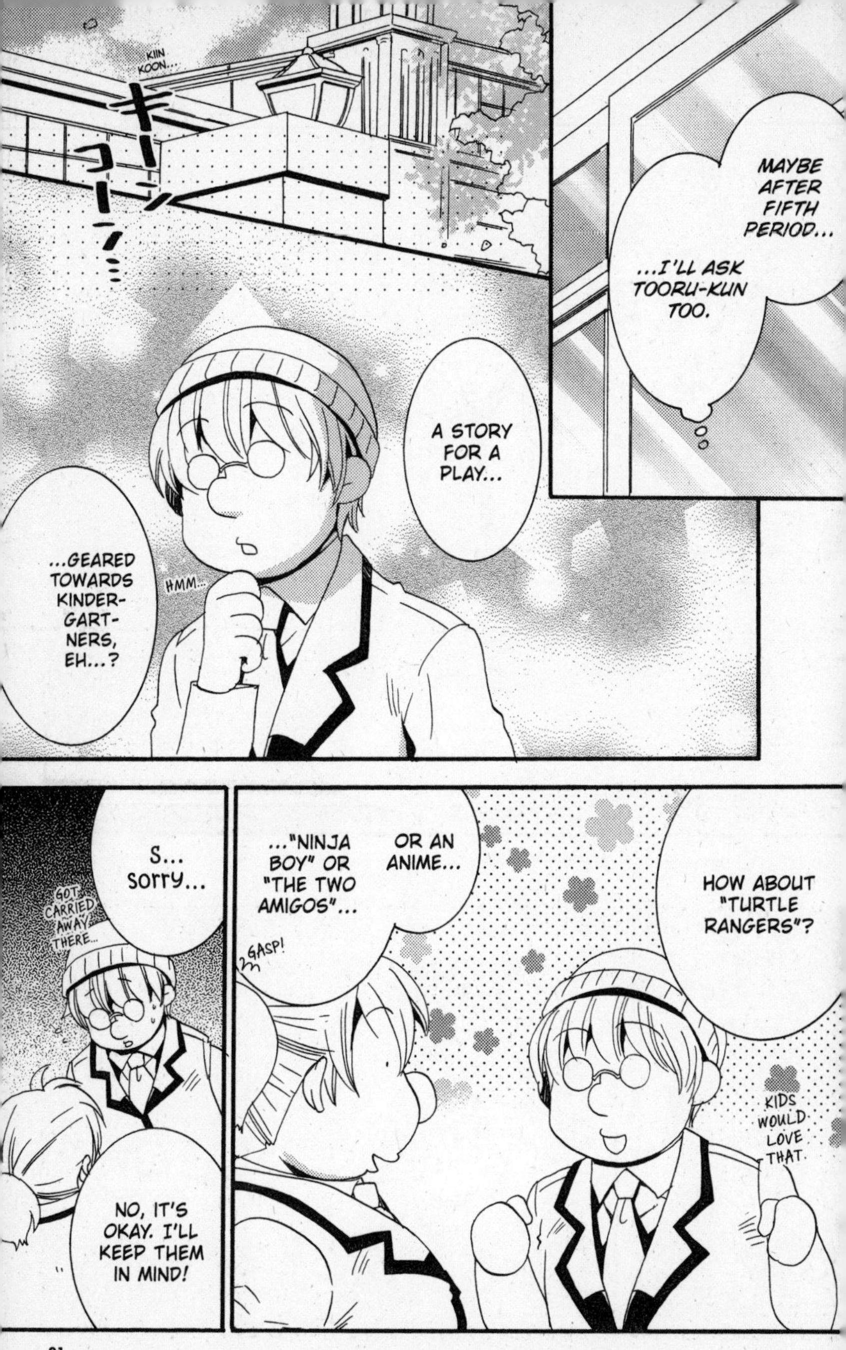
MAYBE AFTER FIFTH PERIOD...
...I'LL ASK TOORU-KUN TOO.
キーンコーン
KIIN KOON...
A STORY FOR A PLAY...
HMM...
...GEARED TOWARDS KINDER-GART-NERS, EH...?
HOW ABOUT "TURTLE RANGERS"?
KIDS WOULD LOVE THAT.
OR AN ANIME...
..."NINJA BOY" OR "THE TWO AMIGOS"...
GASP!
S... sorry...
GOT CARRIED AWAY THERE...
NO, IT'S OKAY. I'LL KEEP THEM IN MIND!

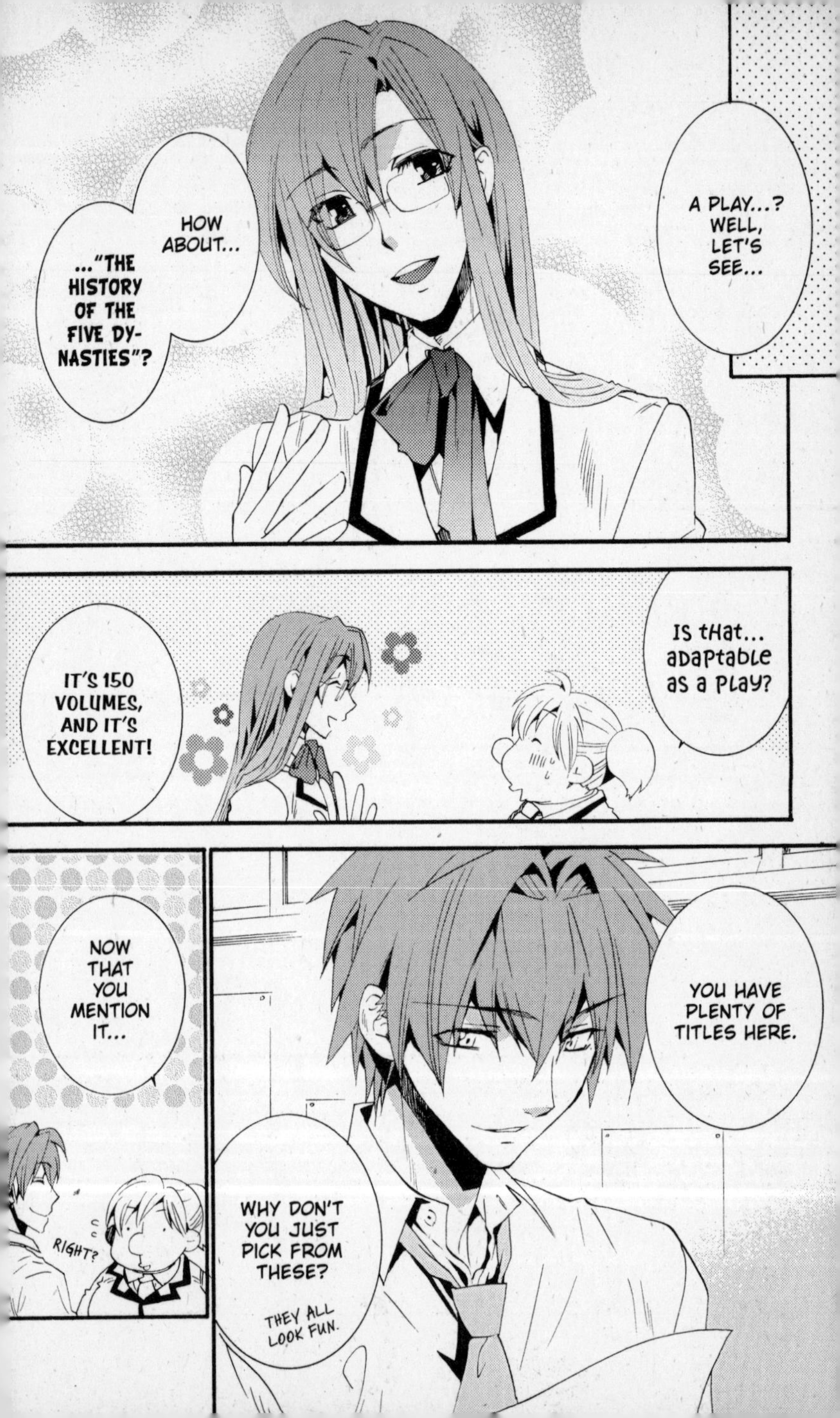
A PLAY...? WELL, LET'S SEE...
HOW ABOUT...
..."THE HISTORY OF THE FIVE DY-NASTIES"?
IS THAT... ADAPTABLE AS A PLAY?
IT'S 150 VOLUMES, AND IT'S EXCELLENT!
YOU HAVE PLENTY OF TITLES HERE.
WHY DON'T YOU JUST PICK FROM THESE?
THEY ALL LOOK FUN.
NOW THAT YOU MENTION IT...
RIGHT?

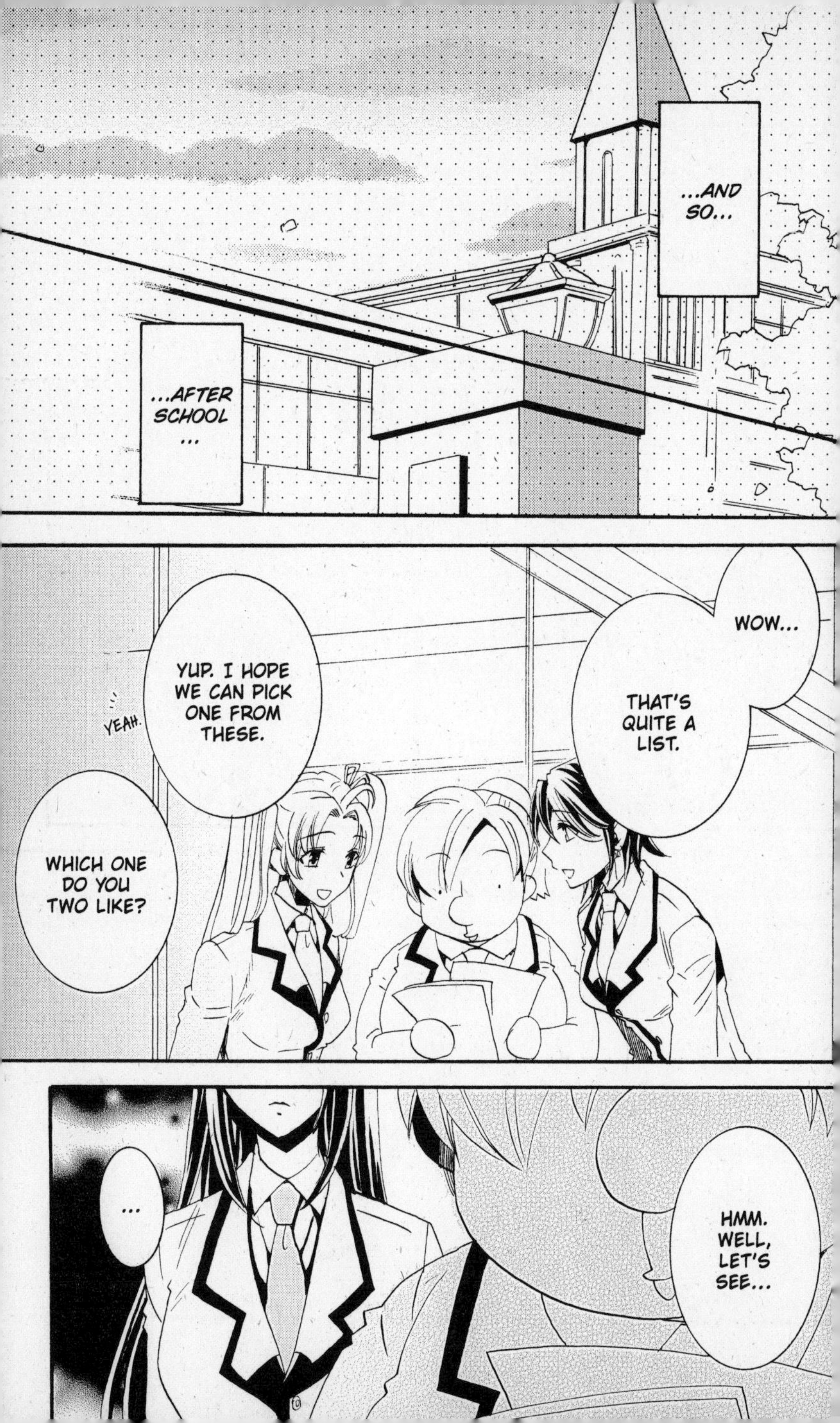
...AND SO...
...AFTER SCHOOL ...
WOW...
THAT'S QUITE A LIST.
YUP. I HOPE WE CAN PICK ONE FROM THESE.
YEAH.
WHICH ONE DO YOU TWO LIKE?
HMM. WELL, LET'S SEE...
...

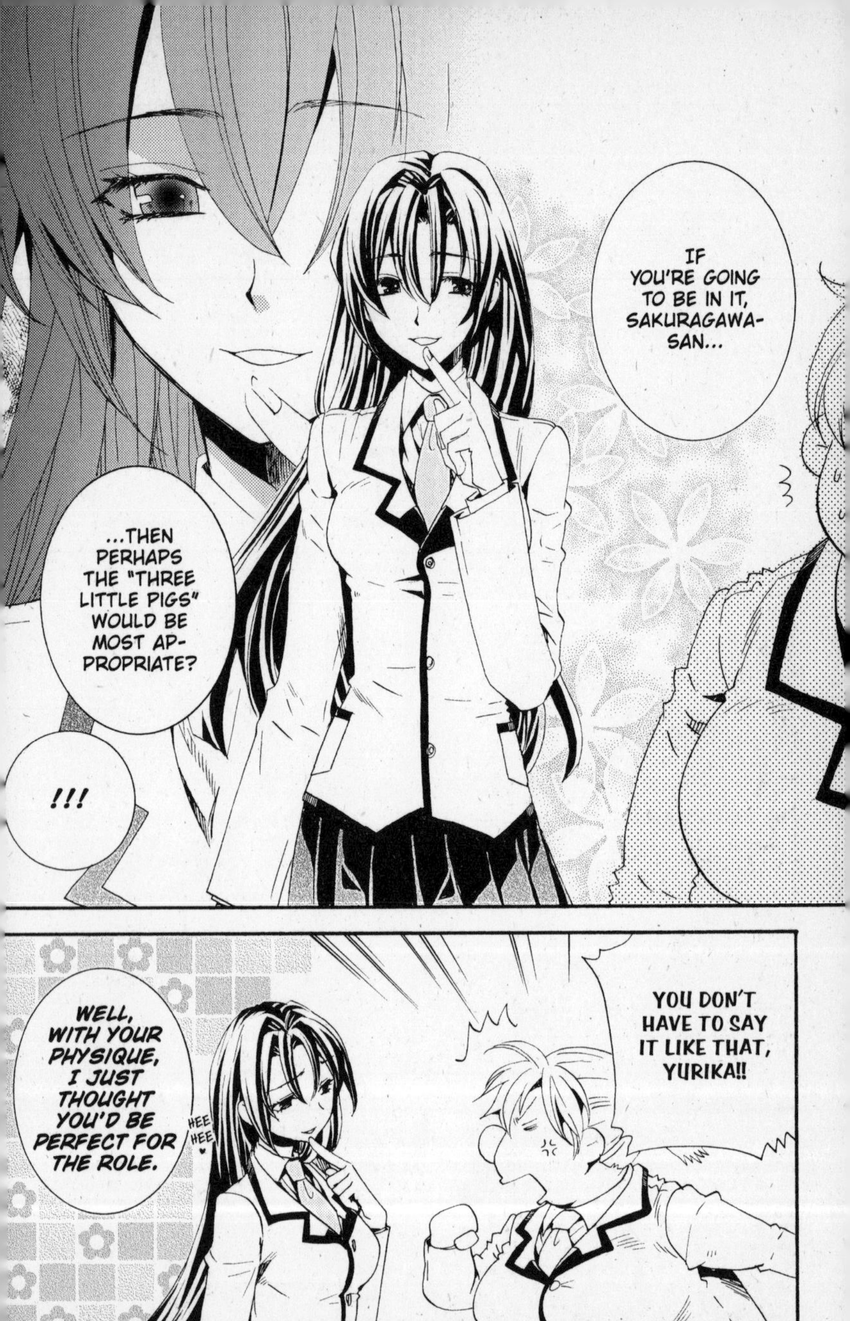
IF YOU'RE GOING TO BE IN IT, SAKURAGAWA-SAN...
...THEN PERHAPS THE "THREE LITTLE PIGS" WOULD BE MOST AP-PROPRIATE?
!!!
YOU DON'T HAVE TO SAY IT LIKE THAT, YURIKA!!
HEE HEE
WELL, WITH YOUR PHYSIQUE, I JUST THOUGHT YOU'D BE PERFECT FOR THE ROLE.

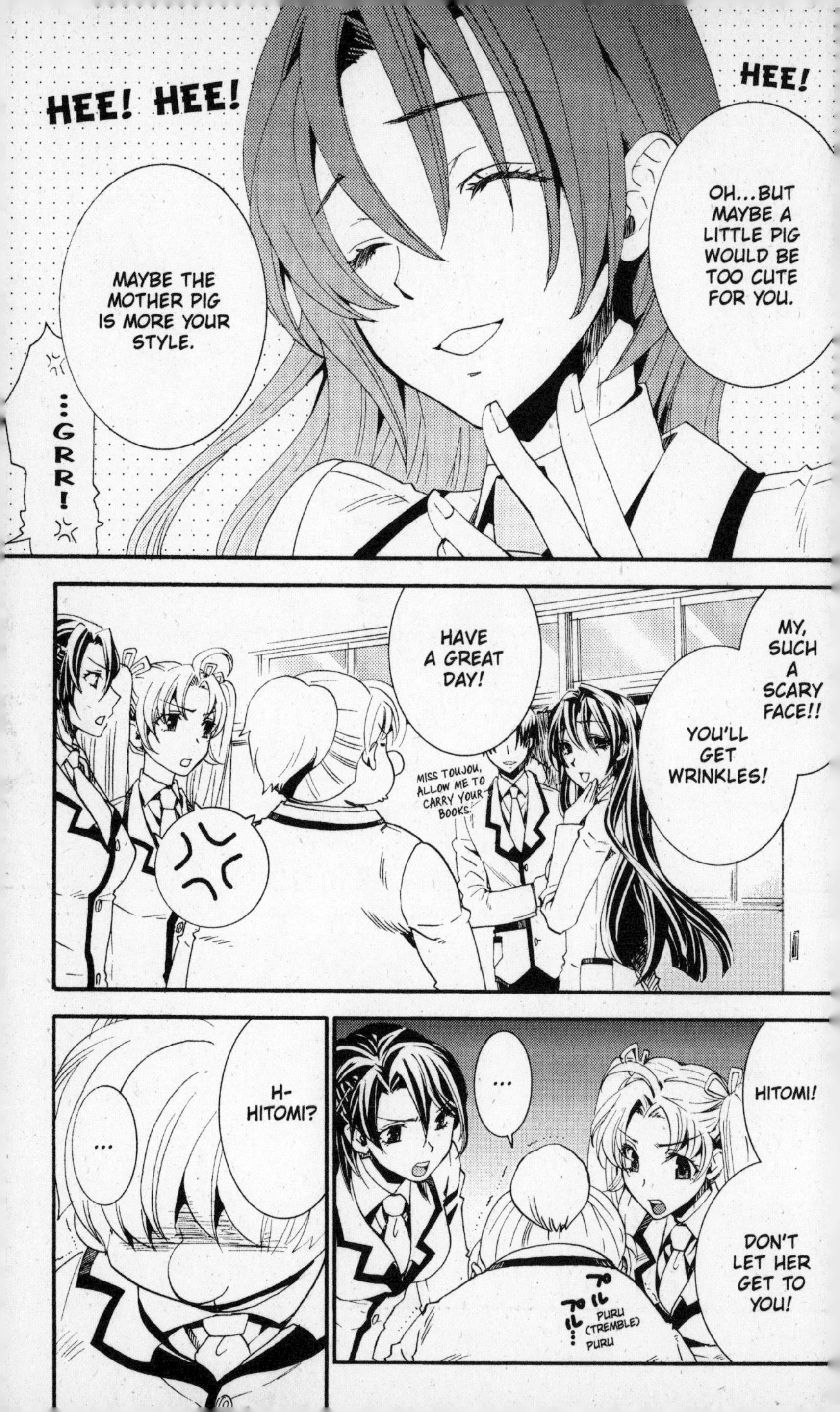
HEE!
OH...BUT MAYBE A LITTLE PIG WOULD BE TOO CUTE FOR YOU.
HEE! HEE!
MAYBE THE MOTHER PIG IS MORE YOUR STYLE.
...GRR!
MY, SUCH A SCARY FACE!!
YOU'LL GET WRINKLES!
HAVE A GREAT DAY!
MISS TOUJOU, ALLOW ME TO CARRY YOUR BOOKS.
HITOMI!
DON'T LET HER GET TO YOU!
...
プルプル…
PURU (TREMBLE) PURU
H- HITOMI?
...

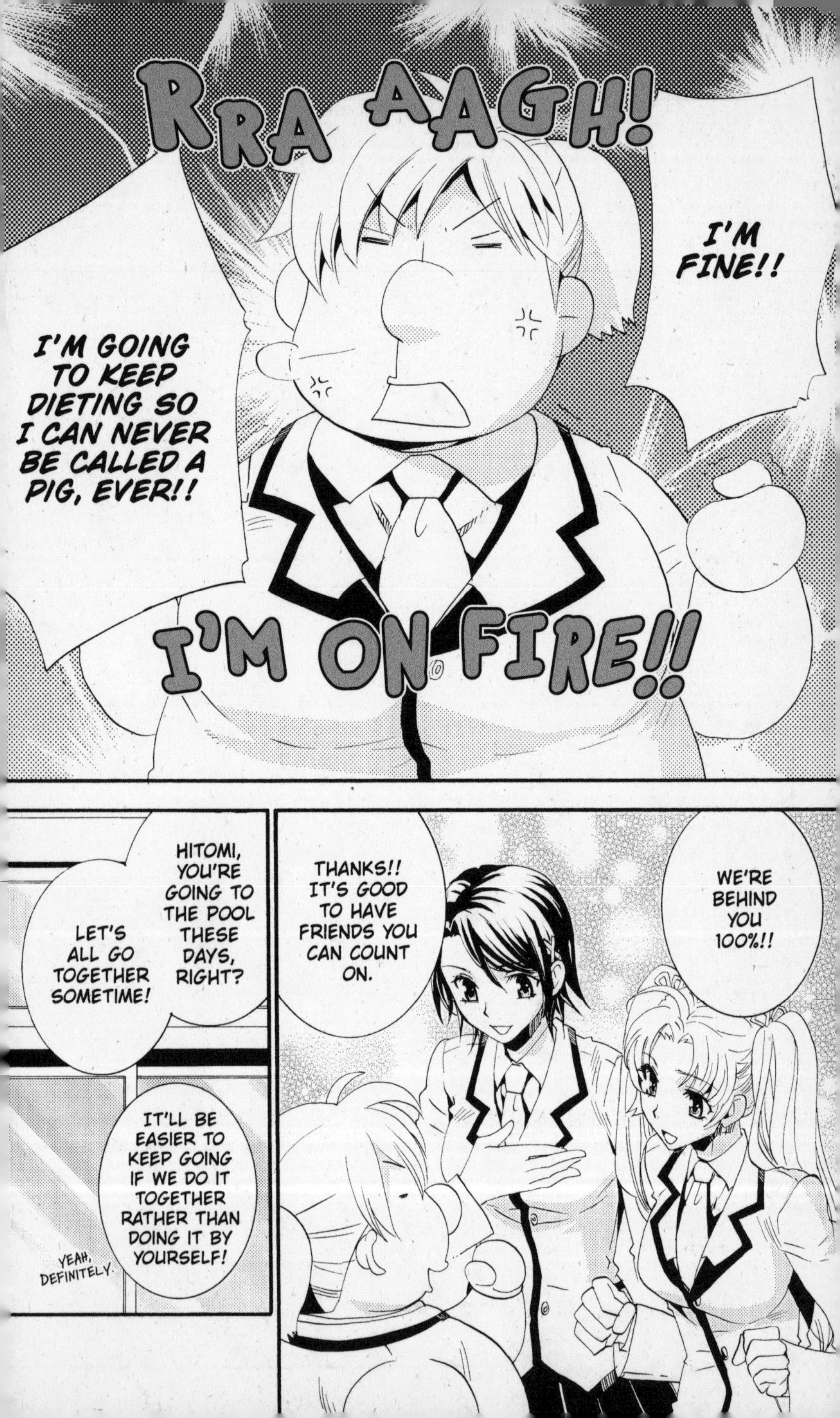
RRAAAGH!
I'M FINE!!
I'M GOING TO KEEP DIETING SO I CAN NEVER BE CALLED A PIG, EVER!!
I'M ON FIRE!!
WE'RE BEHIND YOU 100%!!
THANKS!! IT'S GOOD TO HAVE FRIENDS YOU CAN COUNT ON.
HITOMI, YOU'RE GOING TO THE POOL THESE DAYS, RIGHT?
LET'S ALL GO TOGETHER SOMETIME!
IT'LL BE EASIER TO KEEP GOING IF WE DO IT TOGETHER RATHER THAN DOING IT BY YOURSELF!
YEAH, DEFINITELY.

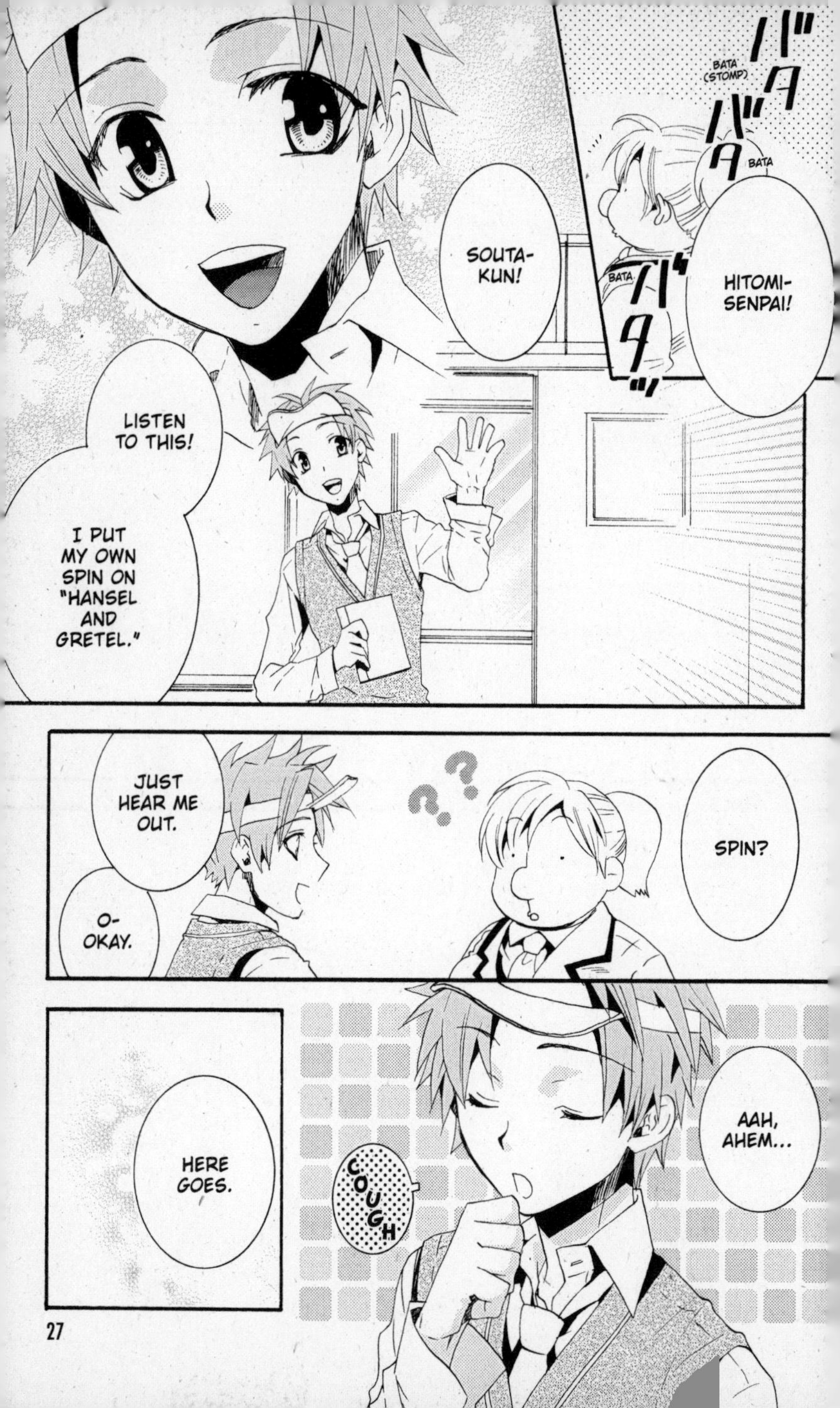
BATA (STOMP)
BATA
BATA
HITOMI-SENPAI!
SOUTA-KUN!
LISTEN TO THIS!
I PUT MY OWN SPIN ON "HANSEL AND GRETEL."
SPIN?
JUST HEAR ME OUT.
O-OKAY.
AAH, AHEM...
COUGH
HERE GOES.

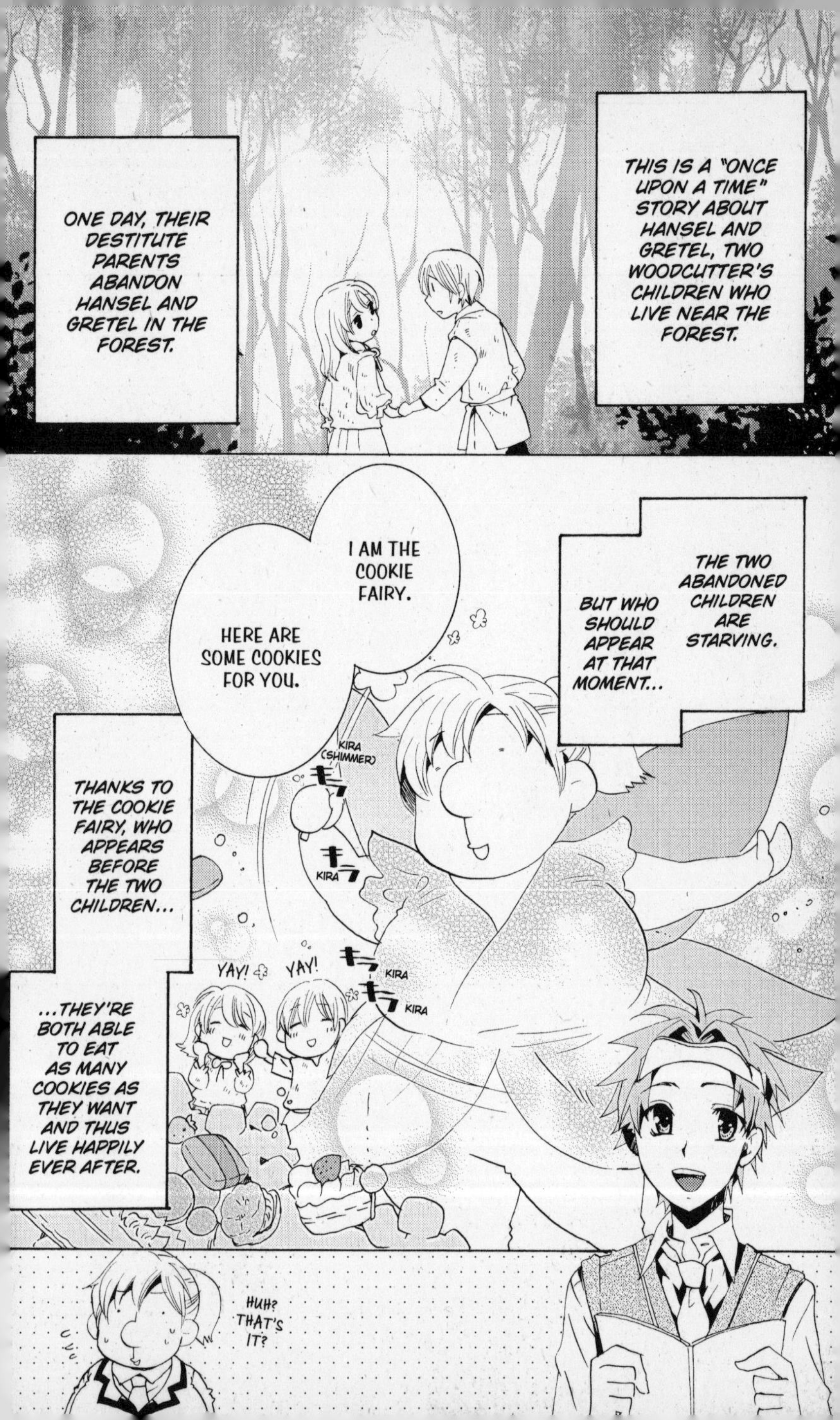
THIS IS A "ONCE UPON A TIME" STORY ABOUT HANSEL AND GRETEL, TWO WOODCUTTER'S CHILDREN WHO LIVE NEAR THE FOREST.
ONE DAY, THEIR DESTITUTE PARENTS ABANDON HANSEL AND GRETEL IN THE FOREST.
THE TWO ABANDONED CHILDREN ARE STARVING.
BUT WHO SHOULD APPEAR AT THAT MOMENT...
I AM THE COOKIE FAIRY.
HERE ARE SOME COOKIES FOR YOU.
KIRA (SHIMMER)
KIRA
THANKS TO THE COOKIE FAIRY, WHO APPEARS BEFORE THE TWO CHILDREN...
KIRA
KIRA
YAY!
YAY!
...THEY'RE BOTH ABLE TO EAT AS MANY COOKIES AS THEY WANT AND THUS LIVE HAPPILY EVER AFTER.
HUH? THAT'S IT?

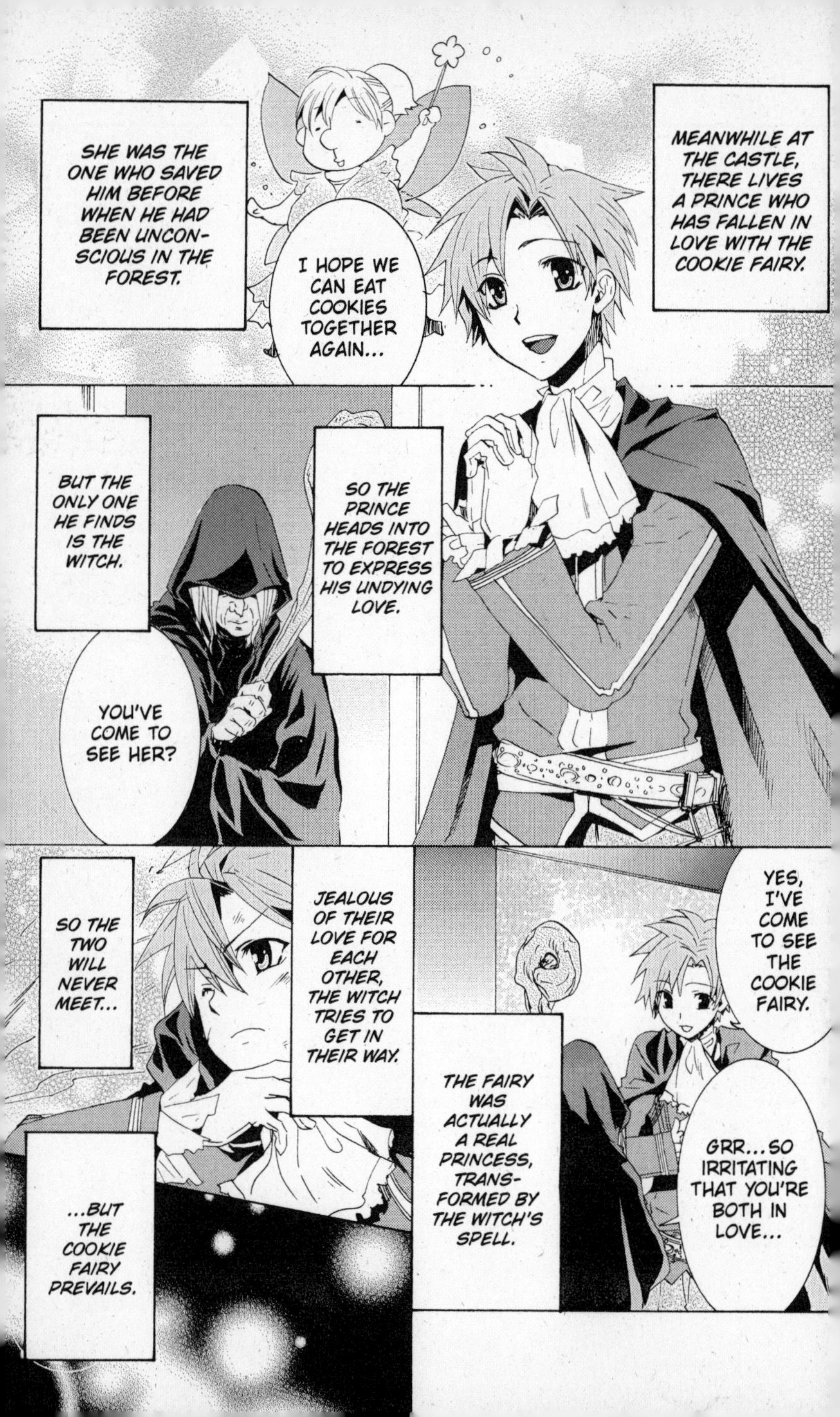
MEANWHILE AT THE CASTLE, THERE LIVES A PRINCE WHO HAS FALLEN IN LOVE WITH THE COOKIE FAIRY.
SHE WAS THE ONE WHO SAVED HIM BEFORE WHEN HE HAD BEEN UNCON-SCIOUS IN THE FOREST.
I HOPE WE CAN EAT COOKIES TOGETHER AGAIN...
SO THE PRINCE HEADS INTO THE FOREST TO EXPRESS HIS UNDYING LOVE.
BUT THE ONLY ONE HE FINDS IS THE WITCH.
YOU'VE COME TO SEE HER?
YES, I'VE COME TO SEE THE COOKIE FAIRY.
THE FAIRY WAS ACTUALLY A REAL PRINCESS, TRANS-FORMED BY THE WITCH'S SPELL.
GRR...SO IRRITATING THAT YOU'RE BOTH IN LOVE...
JEALOUS OF THEIR LOVE FOR EACH OTHER, THE WITCH TRIES TO GET IN THEIR WAY.
SO THE TWO WILL NEVER MEET...
...BUT THE COOKIE FAIRY PREVAILS.

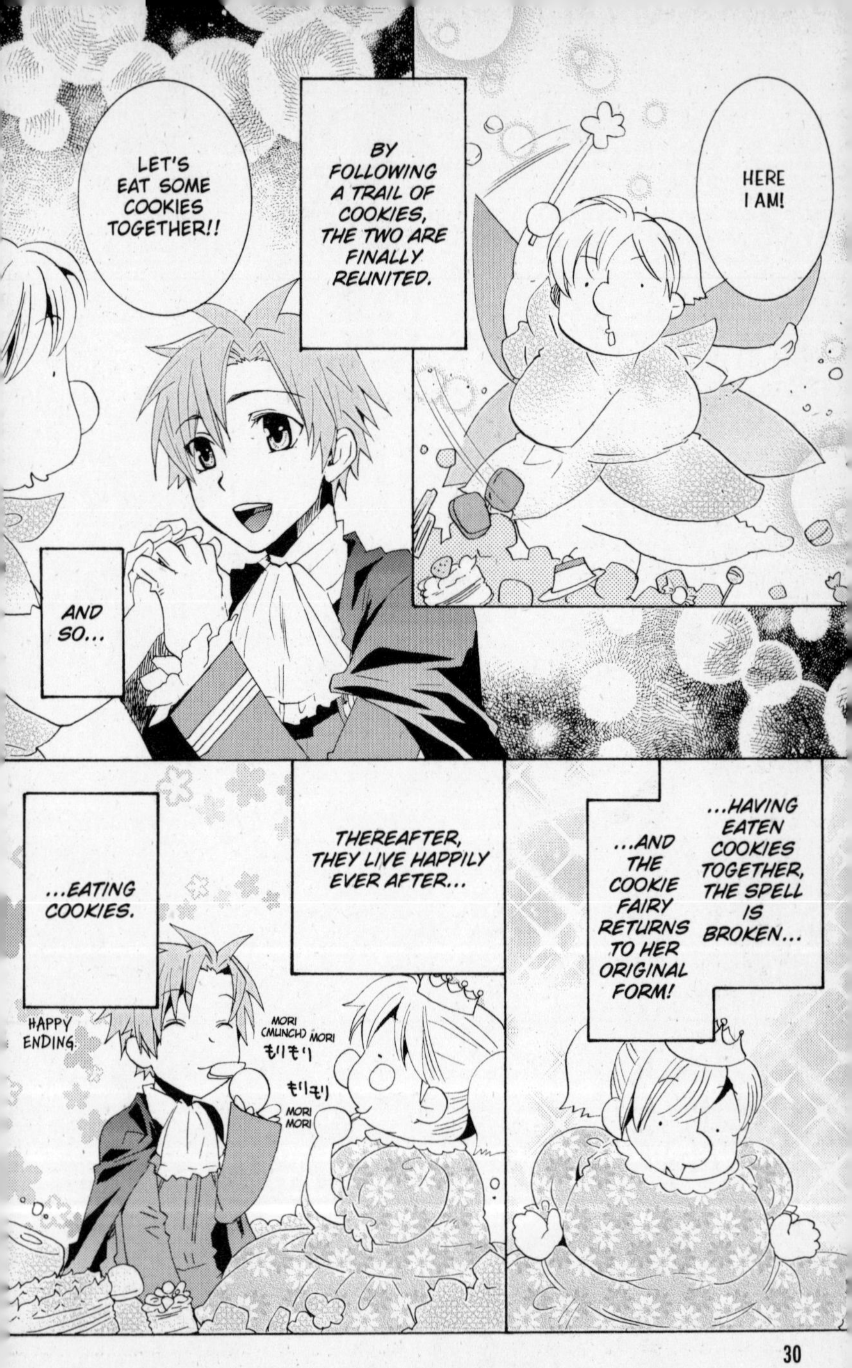
HERE I AM!
BY FOLLOWING A TRAIL OF COOKIES, THE TWO ARE FINALLY REUNITED.
LET'S EAT SOME COOKIES TOGETHER!!
AND SO...
...HAVING EATEN COOKIES TOGETHER, THE SPELL IS BROKEN...
...AND THE COOKIE FAIRY RETURNS TO HER ORIGINAL FORM!
THEREAFTER, THEY LIVE HAPPILY EVER AFTER...
...EATING COOKIES.
MORI (MUNCH) MORI
もりもり
もりもり
MORI MORI
HAPPY ENDING

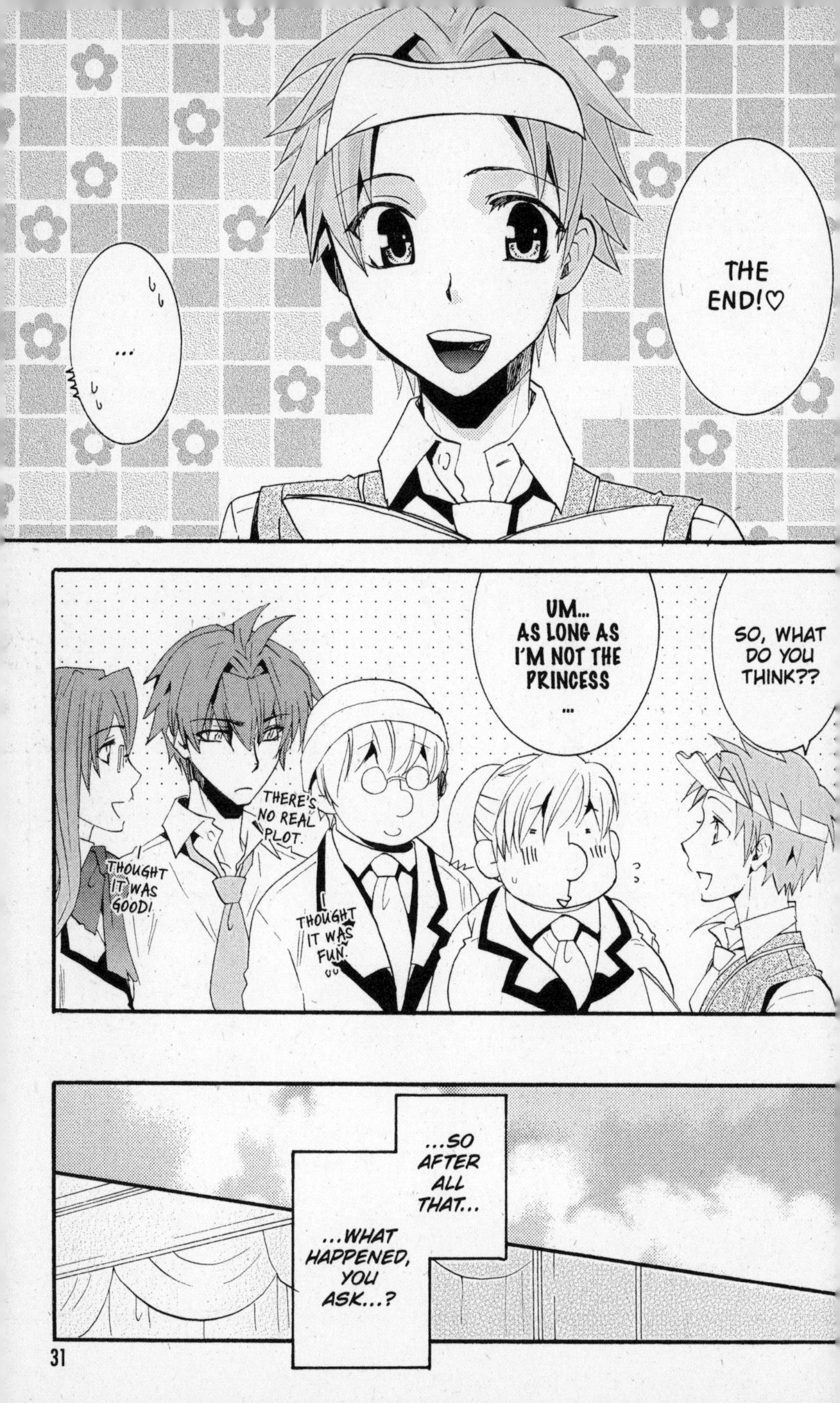
THE END!♡
...
SO, WHAT DO YOU THINK??
UM... AS LONG AS I'M NOT THE PRINCESS ...
THERE'S NO REAL PLOT.
I THOUGHT IT WAS FUN.
I THOUGHT IT WAS GOOD!
...SO AFTER ALL THAT...
...WHAT HAPPENED, YOU ASK...?

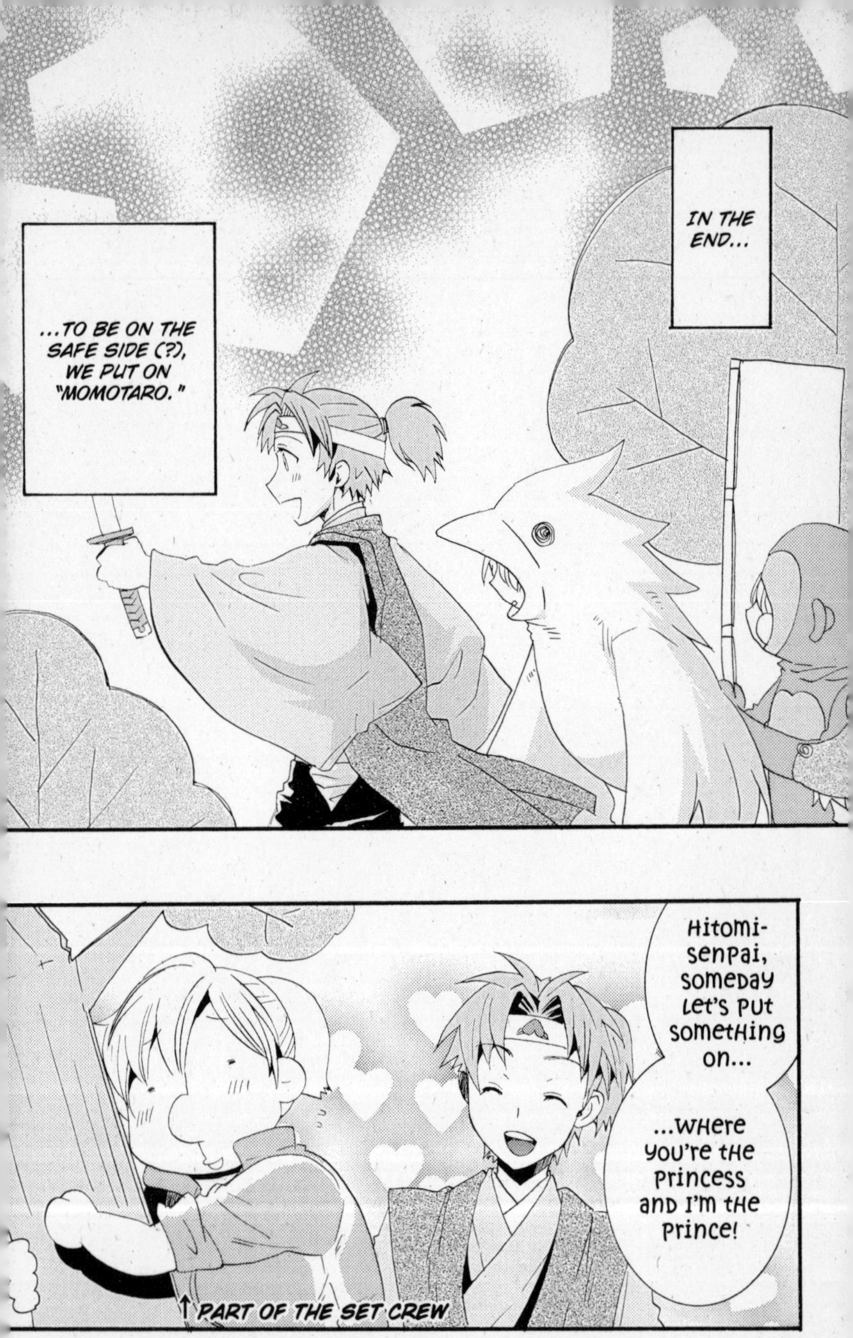
IN THE END...
...TO BE ON THE SAFE SIDE (?), WE PUT ON "MOMOTARO."
Hitomi-senpai, someday let's put something on...
...where you're the princess and I'm the prince!
↑PART OF THE SET CREW

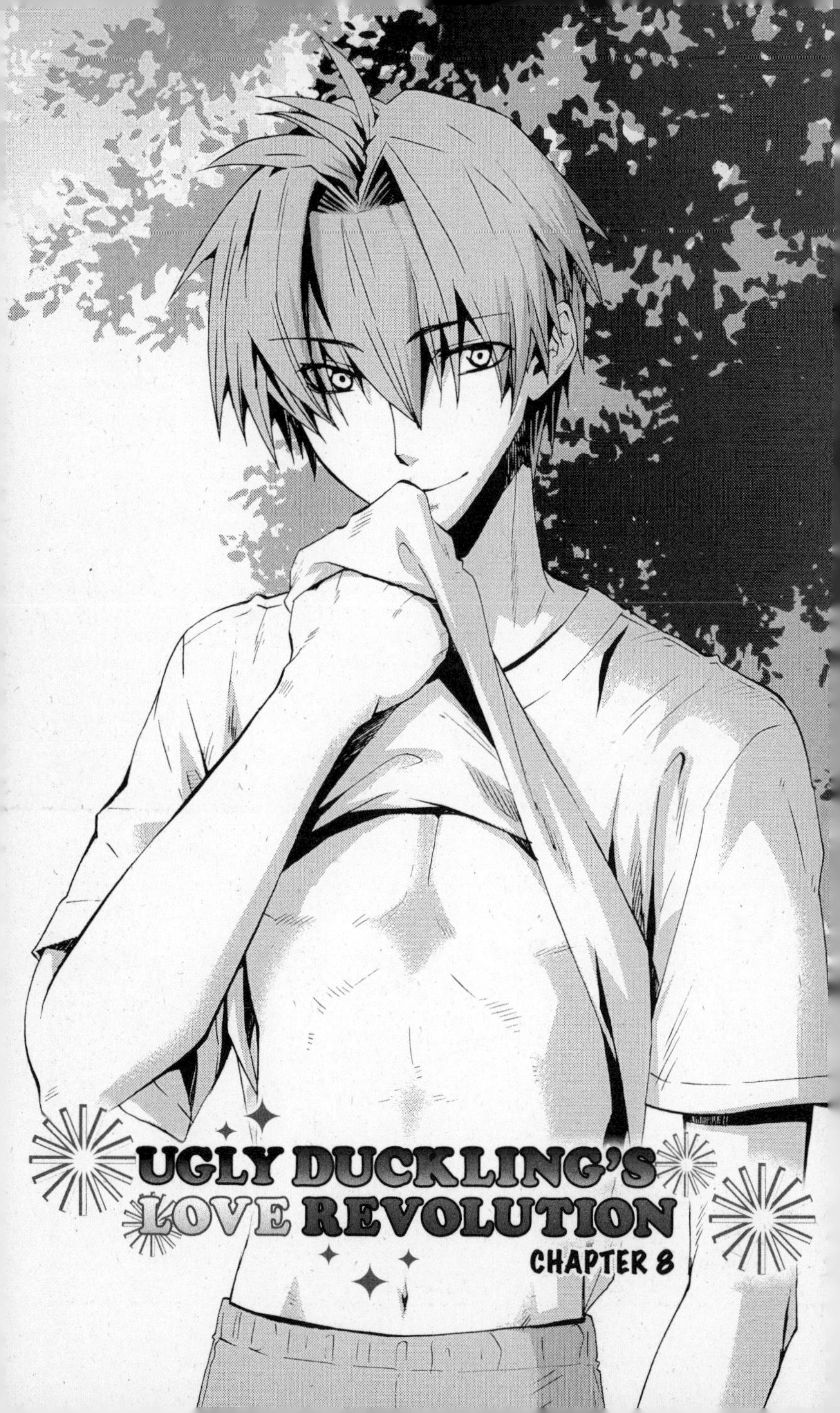
UGLY DUCKLING'S LOVE REVOLUTION
CHAPTER 8

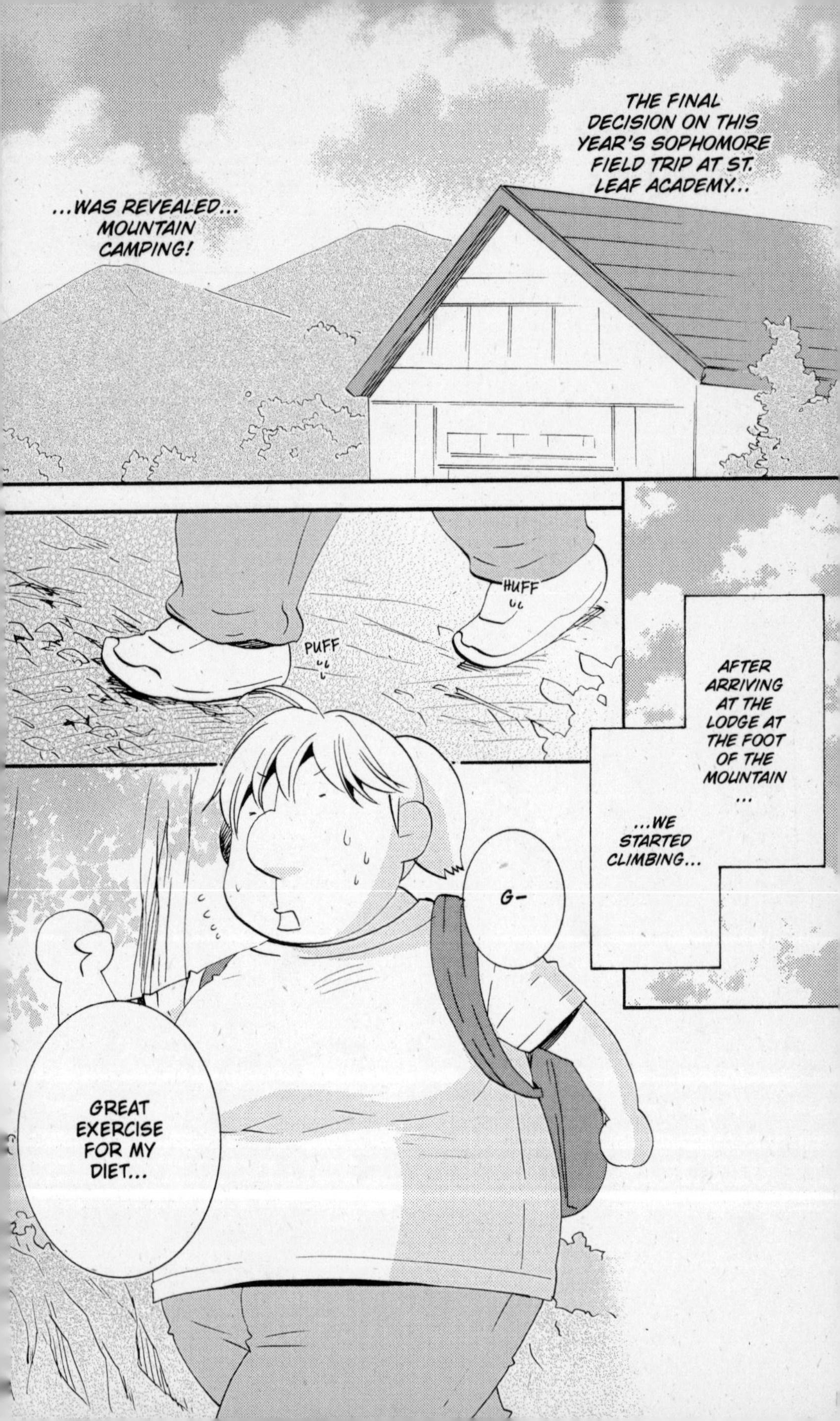
THE FINAL DECISION ON THIS YEAR'S SOPHOMORE FIELD TRIP AT ST. LEAF ACADEMY...
...WAS REVEALED... MOUNTAIN CAMPING!
AFTER ARRIVING AT THE LODGE AT THE FOOT OF THE MOUNTAIN...
...WE STARTED CLIMBING...
HUFF
PUFF
G-
GREAT EXERCISE FOR MY DIET...

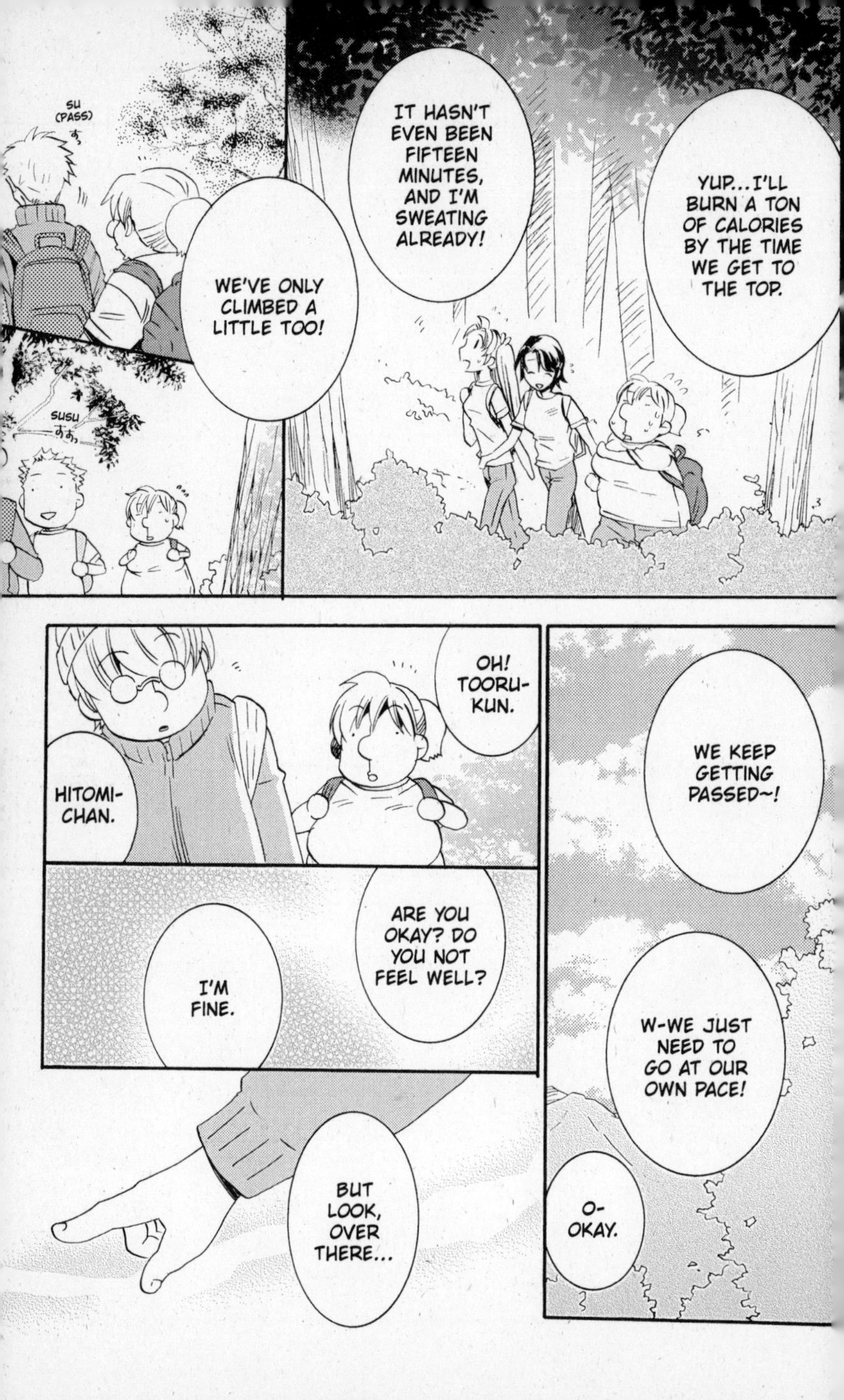
IT HASN'T EVEN BEEN FIFTEEN MINUTES, AND I'M SWEATING ALREADY!
YUP...I'LL BURN A TON OF CALORIES BY THE TIME WE GET TO THE TOP.
WE'VE ONLY CLIMBED A LITTLE TOO!
SU (PASS)
す
SUSU
すすっ
WE KEEP GETTING PASSED~!
W-WE JUST NEED TO GO AT OUR OWN PACE!
O-OKAY.
OH! TOORU-KUN.
HITOMI-CHAN.
ARE YOU OKAY? DO YOU NOT FEEL WELL?
I'M FINE.
BUT LOOK, OVER THERE...

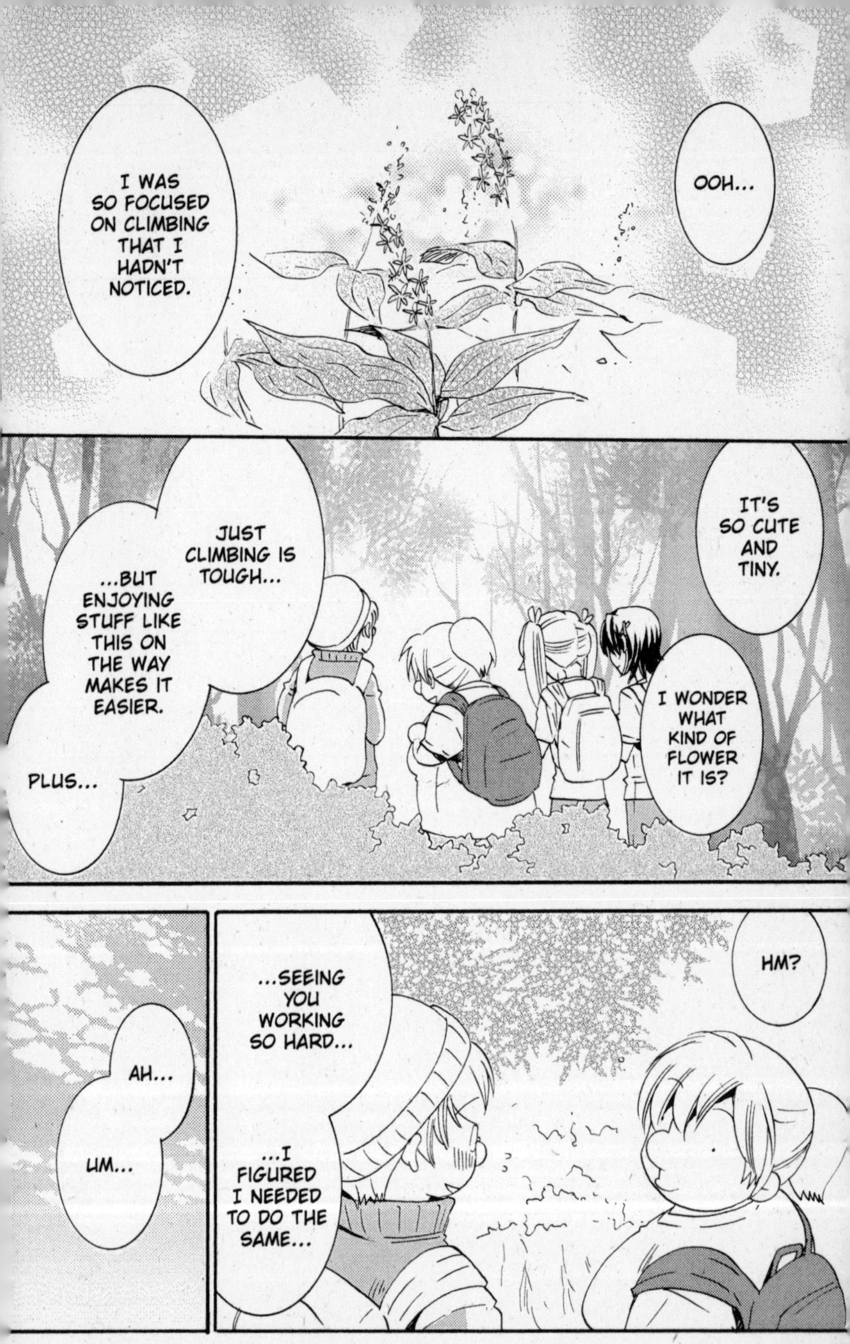
OOH...
I WAS SO FOCUSED ON CLIMBING THAT I HADN'T NOTICED.
IT'S SO CUTE AND TINY.
I WONDER WHAT KIND OF FLOWER IT IS?
JUST CLIMBING IS TOUGH...
...BUT ENJOYING STUFF LIKE THIS ON THE WAY MAKES IT EASIER.
PLUS...
HM?
...SEEING YOU WORKING SO HARD...
...I FIGURED I NEEDED TO DO THE SAME...
AH...
UM...

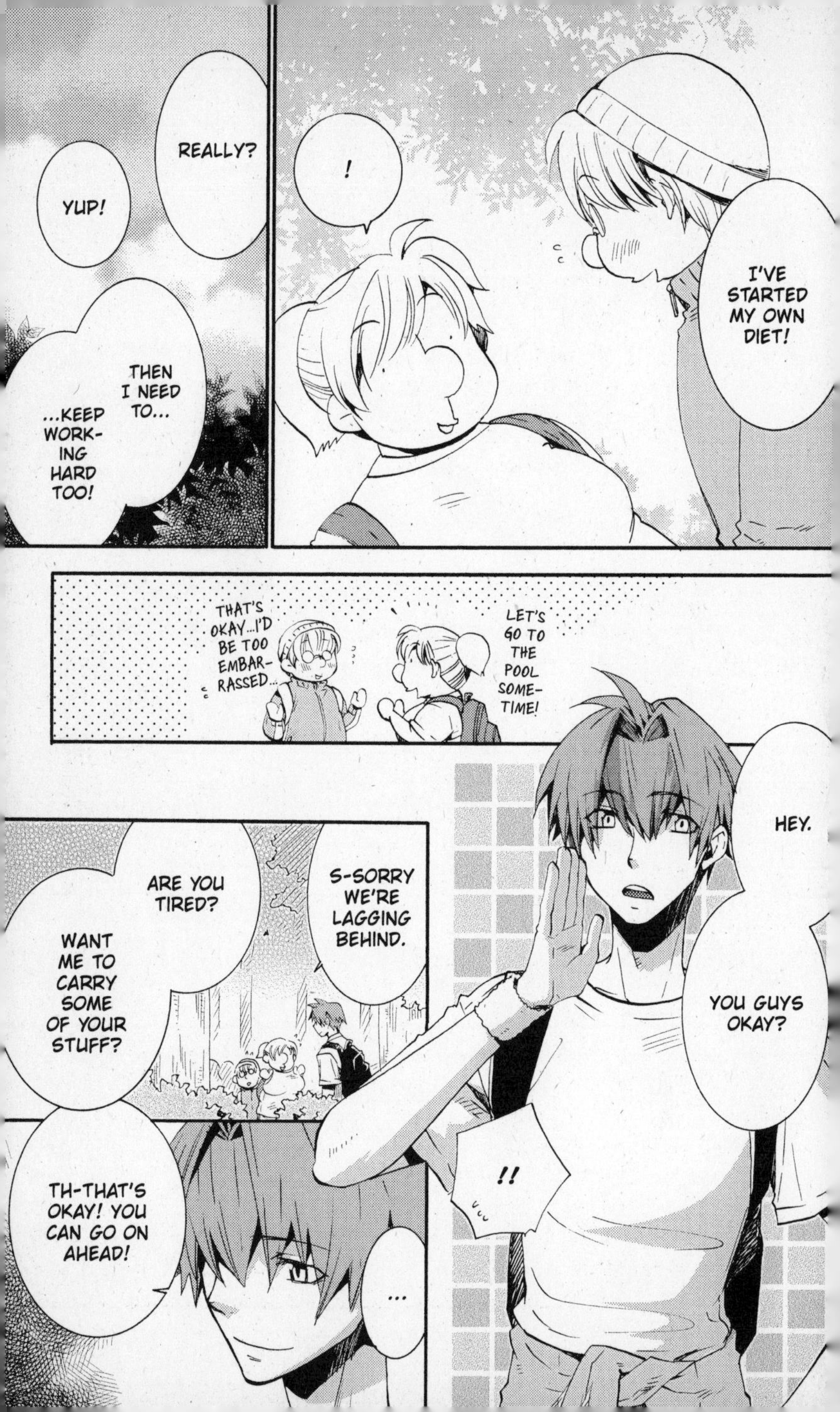
I'VE STARTED MY OWN DIET!
!
REALLY?
YUP!
THEN I NEED TO...
...KEEP WORKING HARD TOO!
LET'S GO TO THE POOL SOMETIME!
THAT'S OKAY...I'D BE TOO EMBARRASSED...
HEY.
YOU GUYS OKAY?
S-SORRY WE'RE LAGGING BEHIND.
ARE YOU TIRED?
WANT ME TO CARRY SOME OF YOUR STUFF?
!!
...
TH-THAT'S OKAY! YOU CAN GO ON AHEAD!

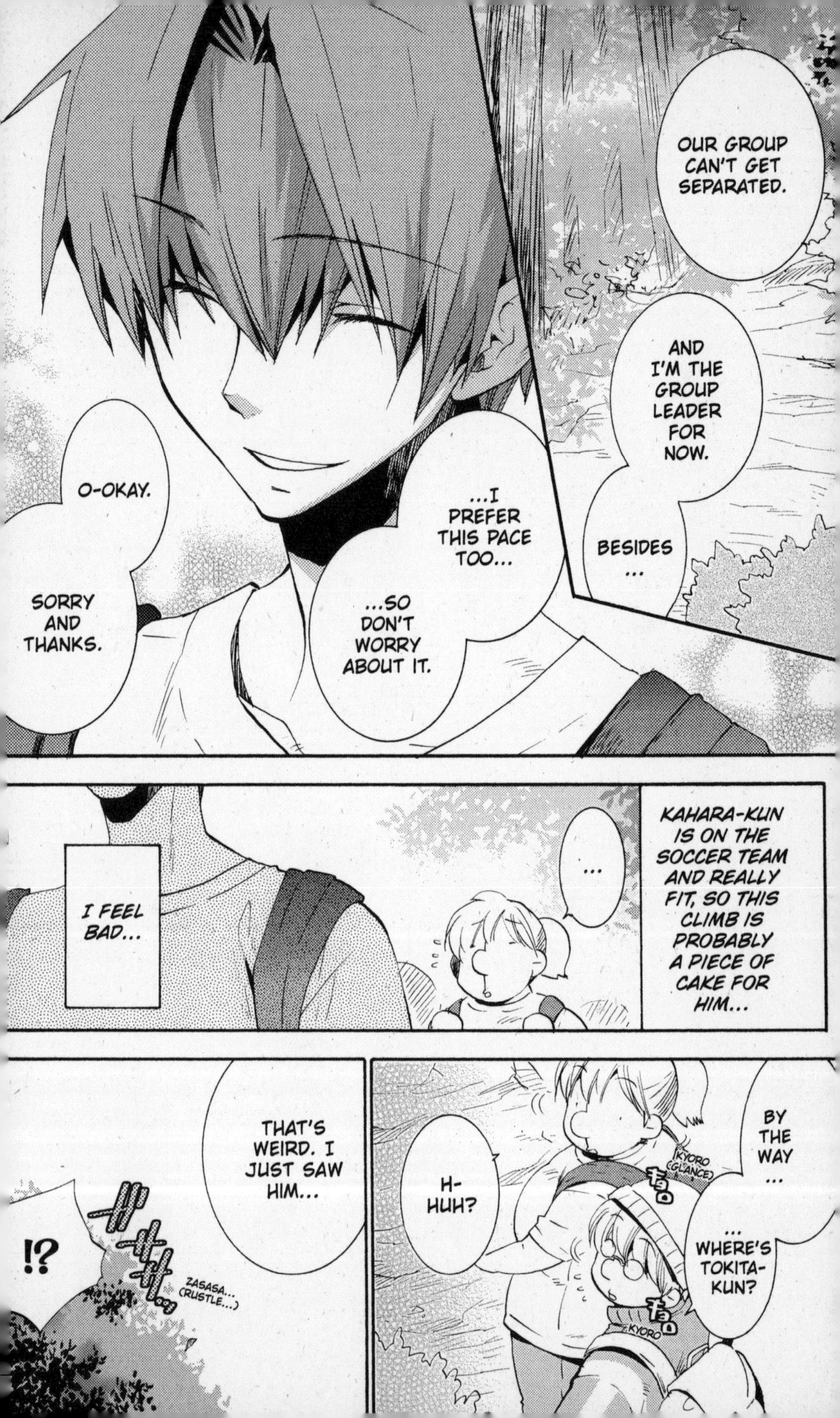
OUR GROUP CAN'T GET SEPARATED.
AND I'M THE GROUP LEADER FOR NOW.
BESIDES...
...I PREFER THIS PACE TOO...
...SO DON'T WORRY ABOUT IT.
O-OKAY.
SORRY AND THANKS.
KAHARA-KUN IS ON THE SOCCER TEAM AND REALLY FIT, SO THIS CLIMB IS PROBABLY A PIECE OF CAKE FOR HIM...
...
I FEEL BAD...
BY THE WAY...
...WHERE'S TOKITA-KUN?
KYORO (GLANCE)
KYORO
H-HUH?
THAT'S WEIRD. I JUST SAW HIM...
ZASASA... (RUSTLE...)
!?

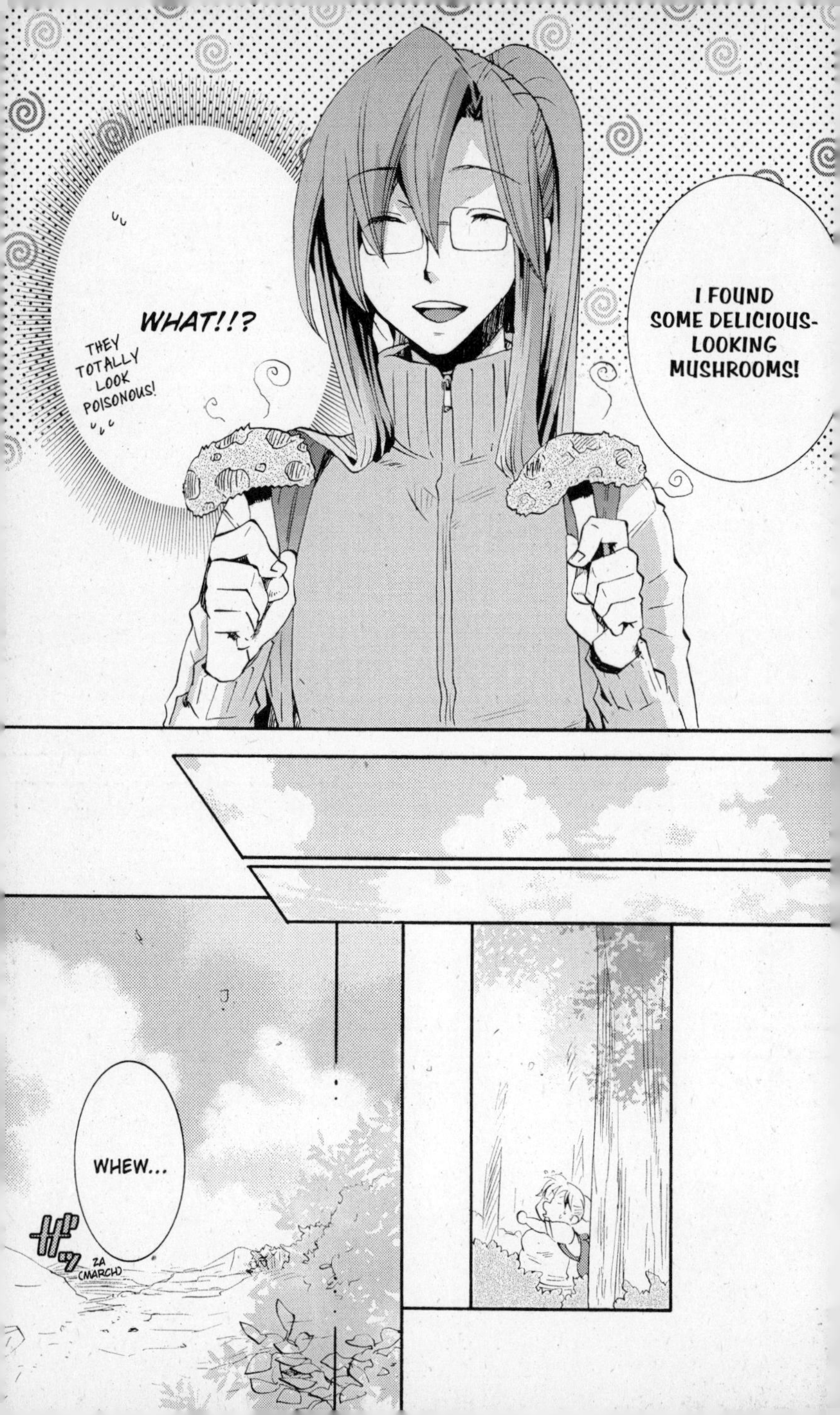
I FOUND SOME DELICIOUS-LOOKING MUSHROOMS!
WHAT!!?
THEY TOTALLY LOOK POISONOUS!
WHEW...
ZA (MARCH)

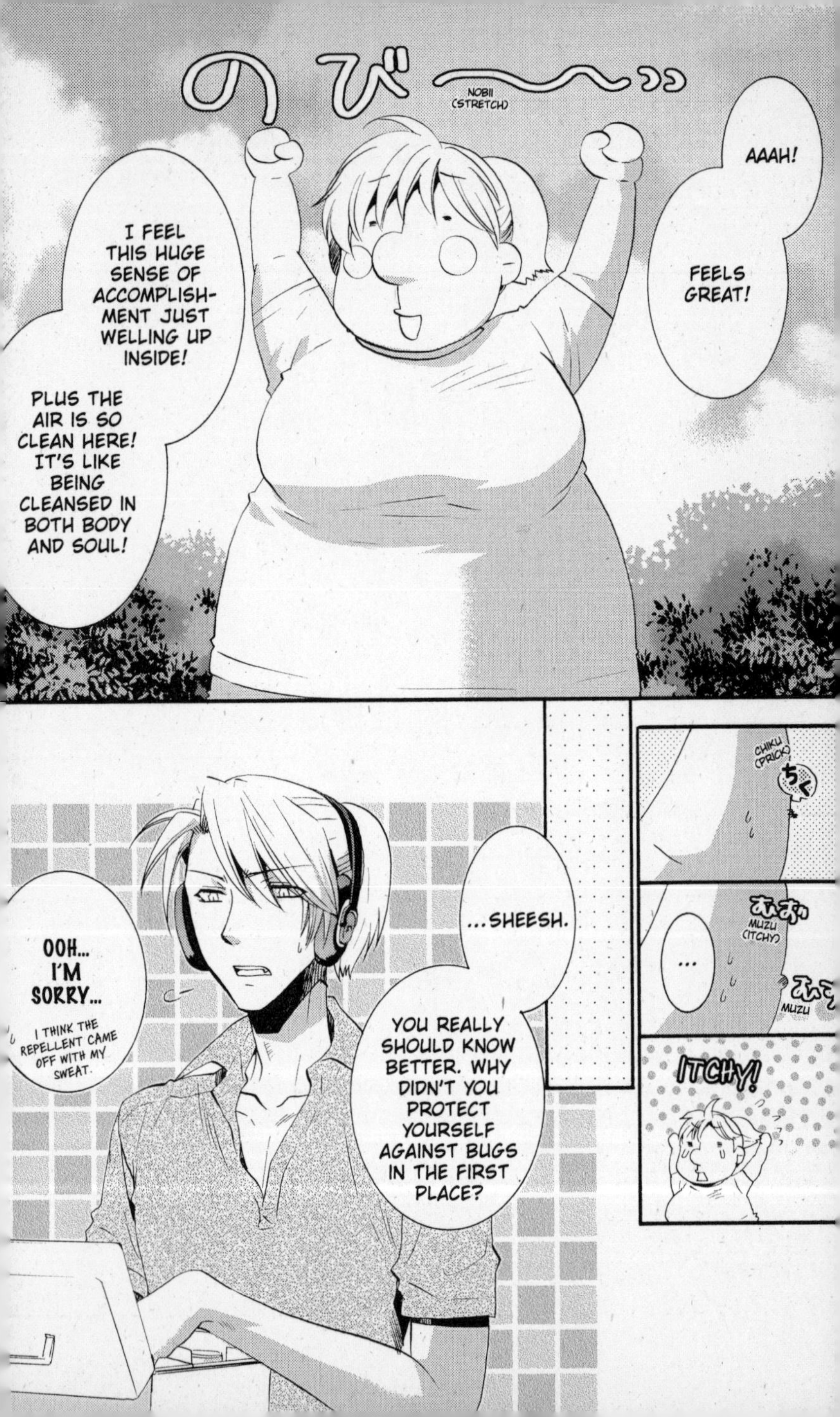
のび～っっ
NOBII (STRETCH)
AAAH!
FEELS GREAT!
I FEEL THIS HUGE SENSE OF ACCOMPLISH-MENT JUST WELLING UP INSIDE!
PLUS THE AIR IS SO CLEAN HERE! IT'S LIKE BEING CLEANSED IN BOTH BODY AND SOUL!
ちく
CHIKU (PRICK)
むずっ
MUZU (ITCHY)
...
むず
MUZU
ITCHY!
...SHEESH.
YOU REALLY SHOULD KNOW BETTER. WHY DIDN'T YOU PROTECT YOURSELF AGAINST BUGS IN THE FIRST PLACE?
OOH... I'M SORRY...
I THINK THE REPELLENT CAME OFF WITH MY SWEAT.

...

THANK YOU.

?

UM... SEN-SEI?

HERE...

BOTTLE: BUG REPELLENT.

N-NOOO!!

NO, THANK YOU!

LIKE, DAB-DAB?

WHAT? YOU WANT ME TO PUT IT ON?

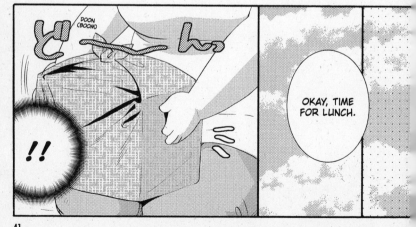

DOON (BOOM)

!!

OKAY, TIME FOR LUNCH.

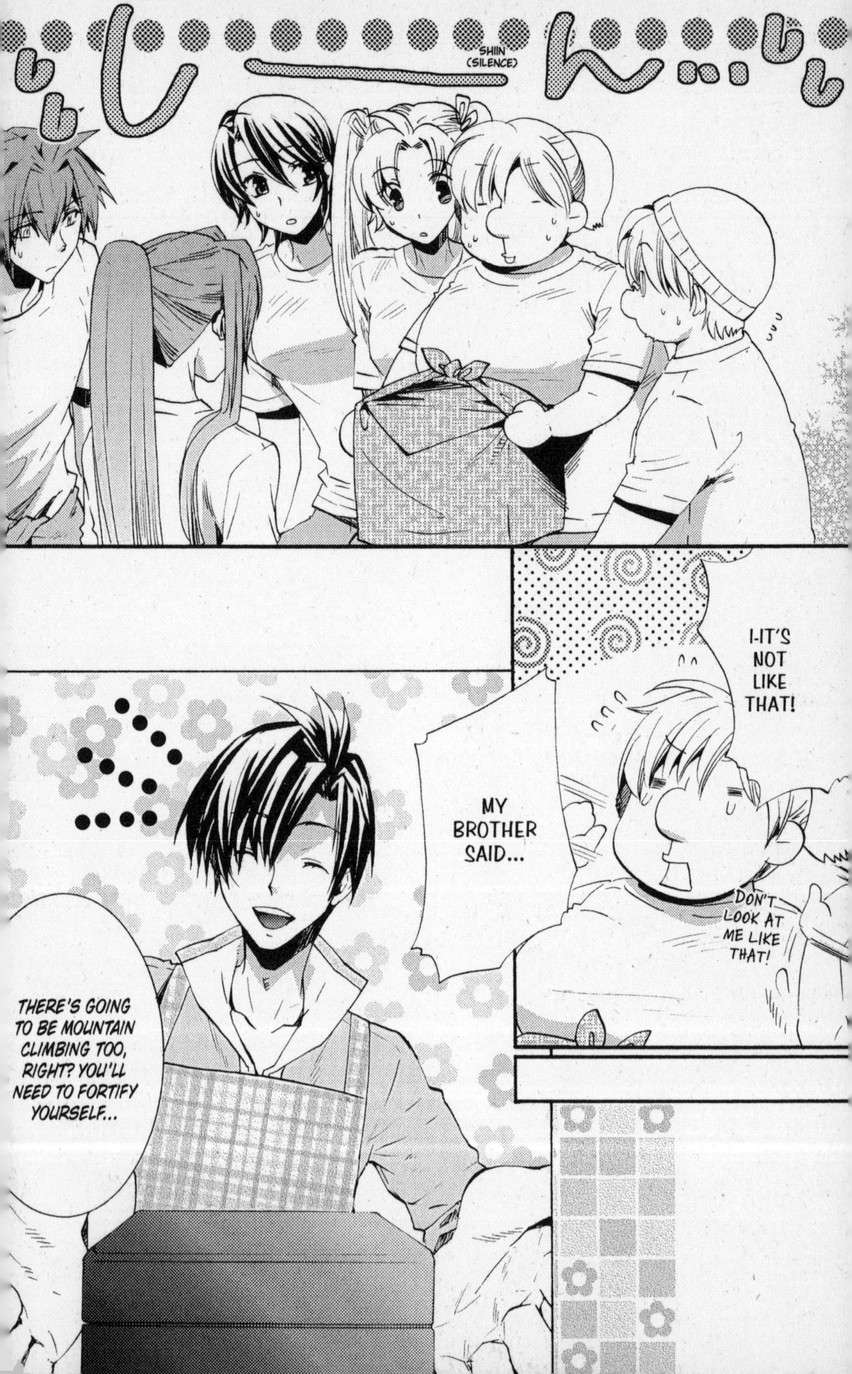
SHIIN (SILENCE)
I-IT'S NOT LIKE THAT!
DON'T LOOK AT ME LIKE THAT!
MY BROTHER SAID...
THERE'S GOING TO BE MOUNTAIN CLIMBING TOO, RIGHT? YOU'LL NEED TO FORTIFY YOURSELF...

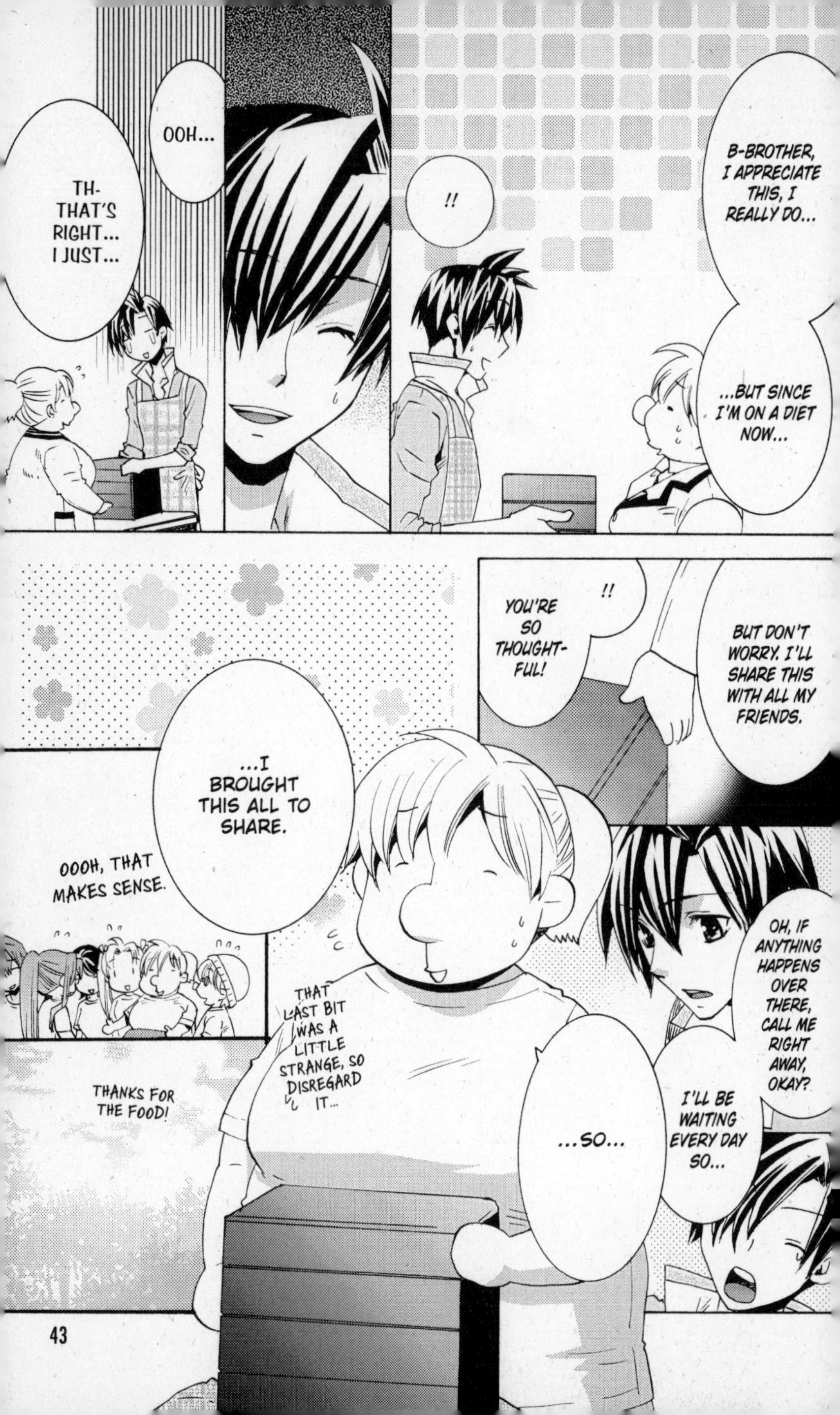
B-BROTHER, I APPRECIATE THIS, I REALLY DO...
...BUT SINCE I'M ON A DIET NOW...
!!
OOH...
TH- THAT'S RIGHT... I JUST...
BUT DON'T WORRY. I'LL SHARE THIS WITH ALL MY FRIENDS.
!!
YOU'RE SO THOUGHT-FUL!
OH, IF ANYTHING HAPPENS OVER THERE, CALL ME RIGHT AWAY, OKAY?
I'LL BE WAITING EVERY DAY SO...
...SO...
...I BROUGHT THIS ALL TO SHARE.
OOOH, THAT MAKES SENSE.
THAT LAST BIT WAS A LITTLE STRANGE, SO DISREGARD IT...
THANKS FOR THE FOOD!

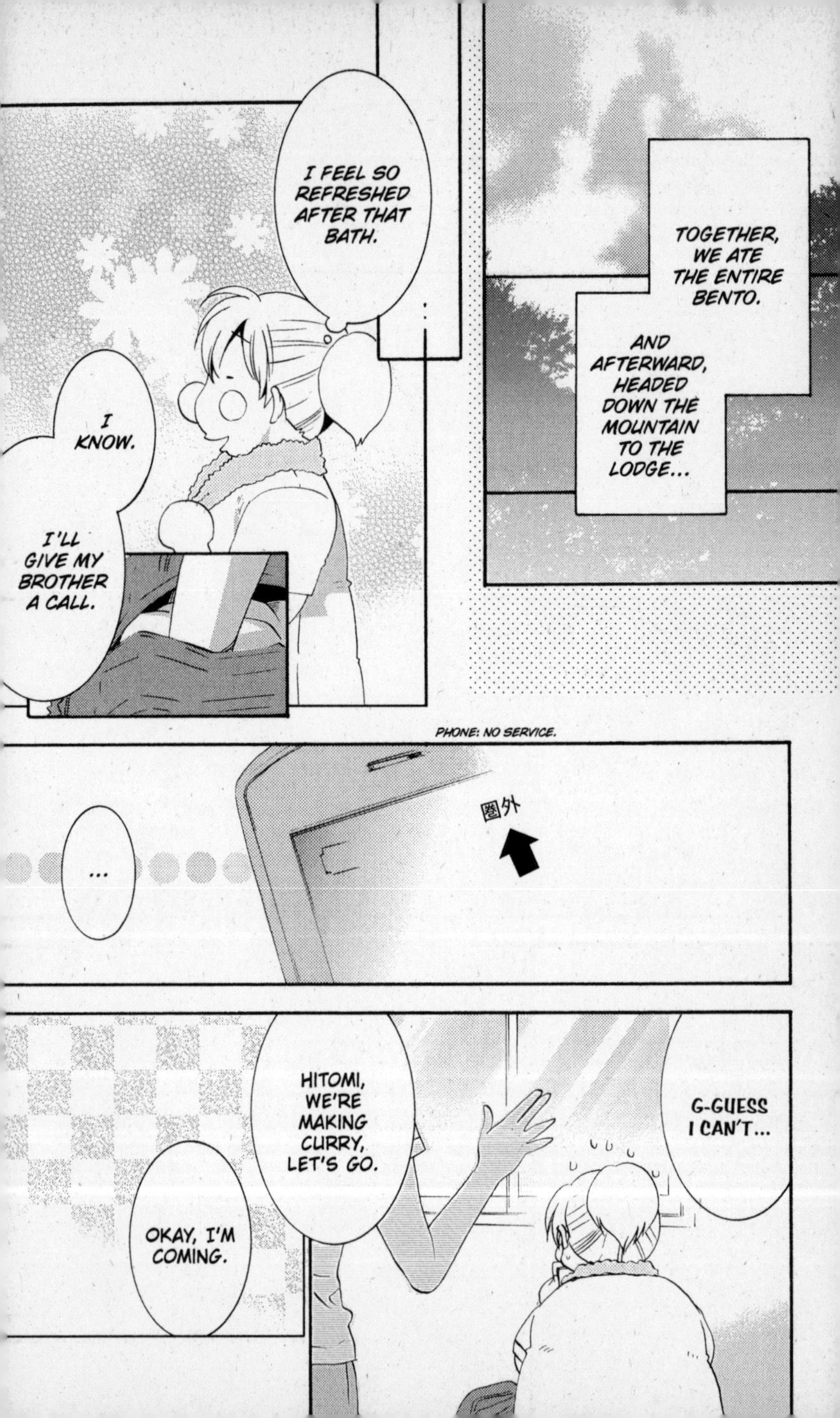
TOGETHER, WE ATE THE ENTIRE BENTO.
AND AFTERWARD, HEADED DOWN THE MOUNTAIN TO THE LODGE...
I FEEL SO REFRESHED AFTER THAT BATH.
I KNOW.
I'LL GIVE MY BROTHER A CALL.
PHONE: NO SERVICE.
圏外
...
G-GUESS I CAN'T...
HITOMI, WE'RE MAKING CURRY, LET'S GO.
OKAY, I'M COMING.

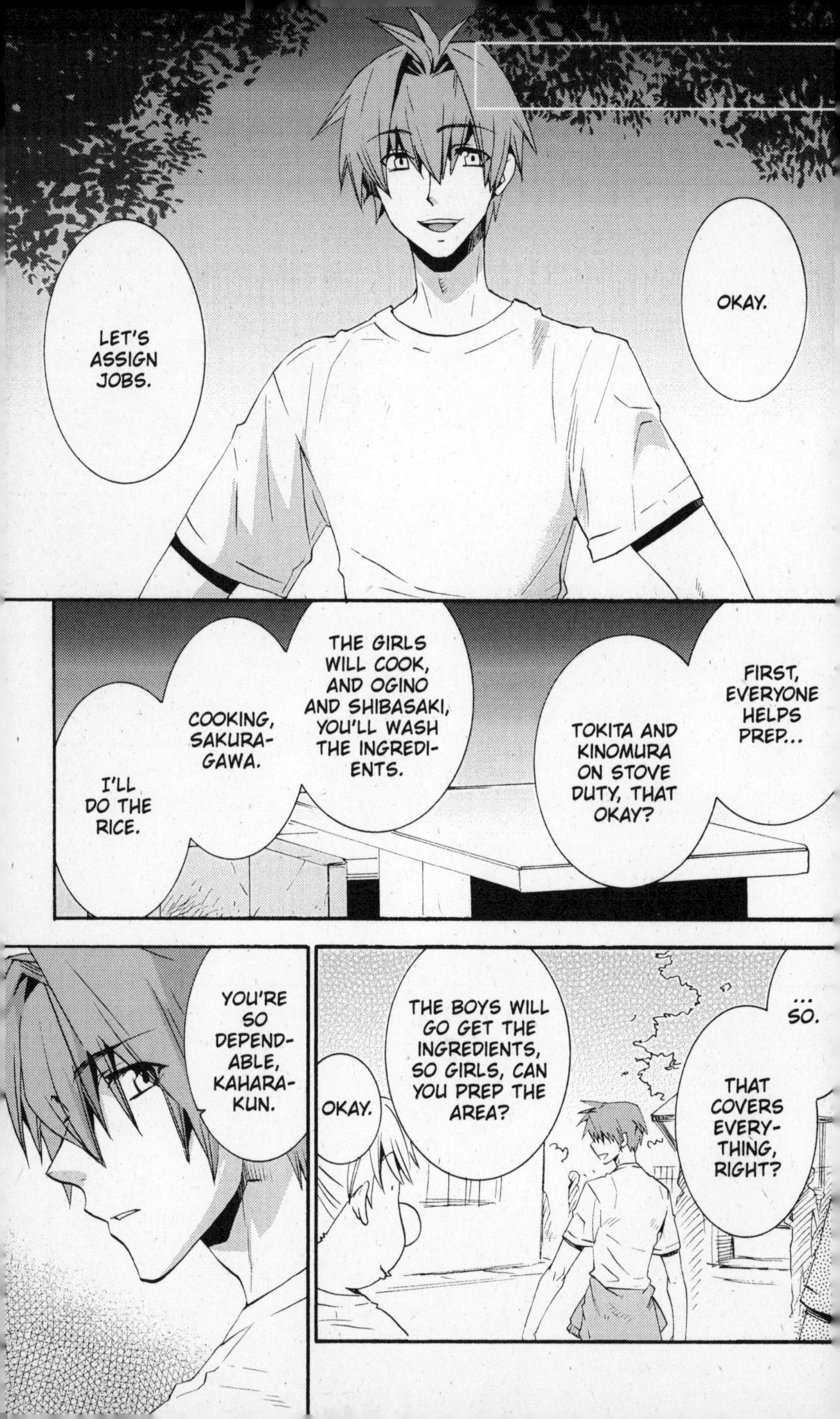
OKAY.
LET'S ASSIGN JOBS.
FIRST, EVERYONE HELPS PREP...
TOKITA AND KINOMURA ON STOVE DUTY, THAT OKAY?
THE GIRLS WILL COOK, AND OGINO AND SHIBASAKI, YOU'LL WASH THE INGREDI-ENTS.
COOKING, SAKURA-GAWA.
I'LL DO THE RICE.
...SO.
THAT COVERS EVERY-THING, RIGHT?
THE BOYS WILL GO GET THE INGREDIENTS, SO GIRLS, CAN YOU PREP THE AREA?
OKAY.
YOU'RE SO DEPEND-ABLE, KAHARA-KUN.

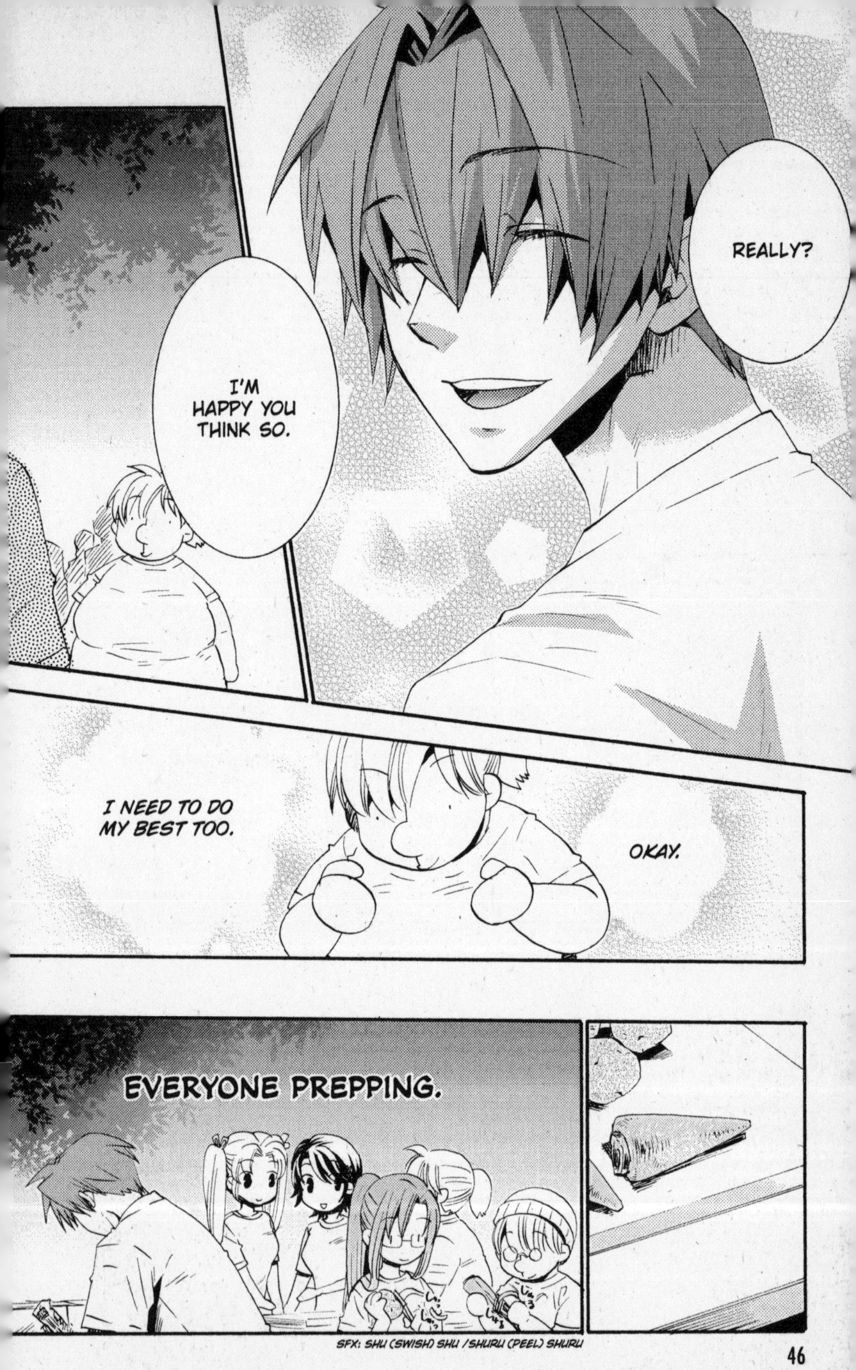
REALLY?
I'M HAPPY YOU THINK SO.
OKAY.
I NEED TO DO MY BEST TOO.
EVERYONE PREPPING.
SFX: SHU (SWISH) SHU / SHURU (PEEL) SHURU

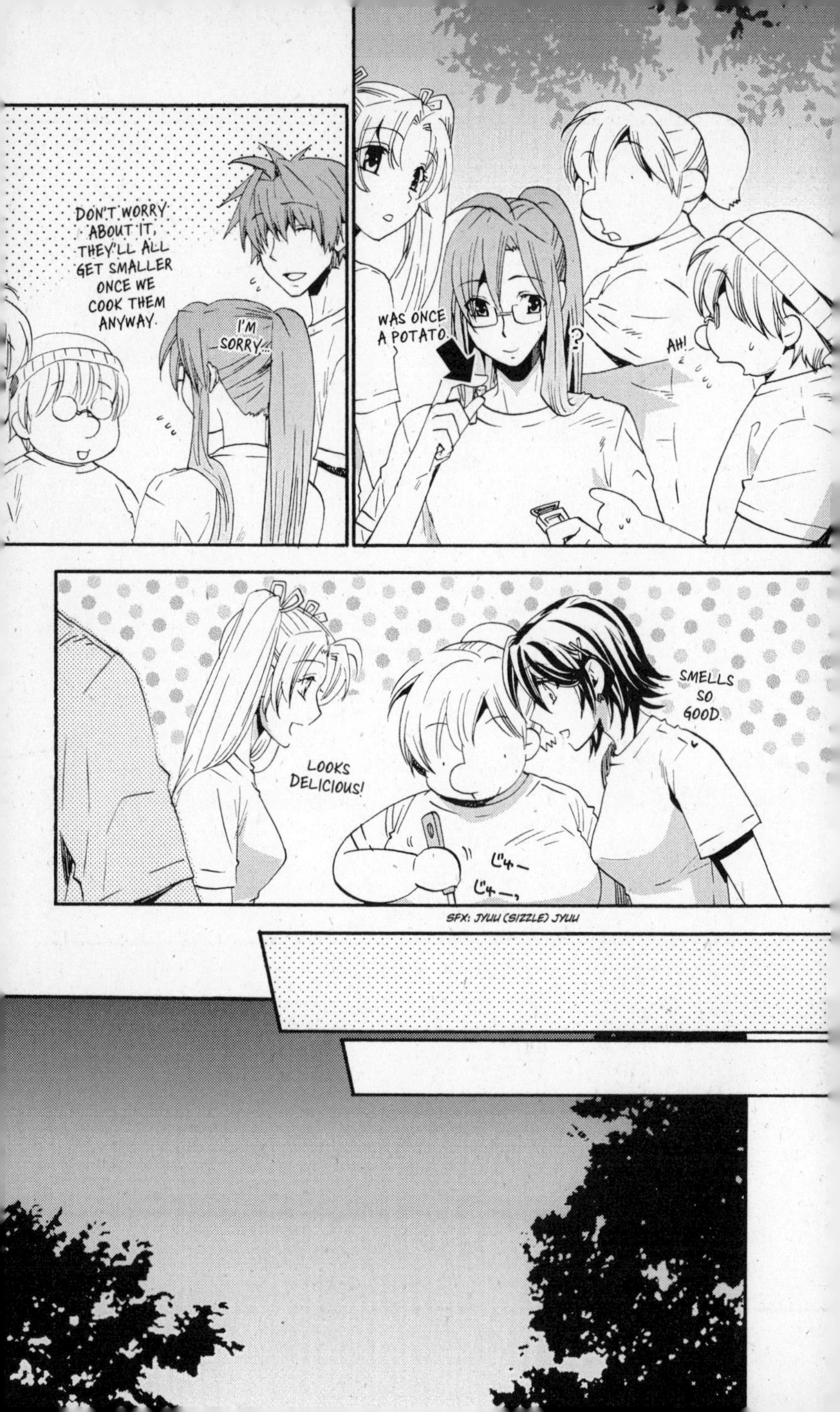
WAS ONCE A POTATO.
?
AH!
I'M SORRY...
DON'T WORRY ABOUT IT, THEY'LL ALL GET SMALLER ONCE WE COOK THEM ANYWAY.
SMELLS SO GOOD.
LOOKS DELICIOUS!
じゅー
じゅー
SFX: JYUU (SIZZLE) JYUU

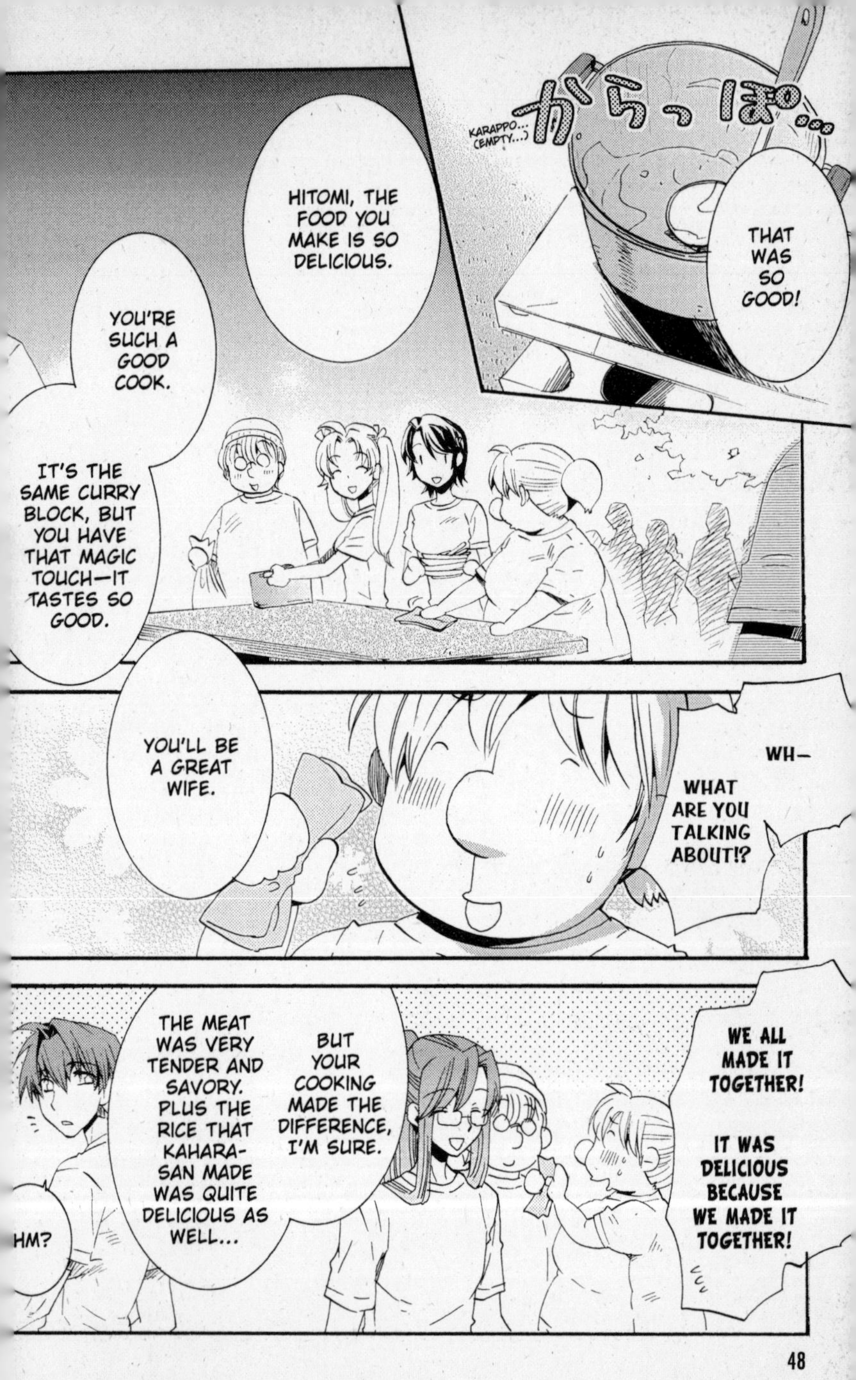
からっぽ…
KARAPPO... (EMPTY...)
THAT WAS SO GOOD!
HITOMI, THE FOOD YOU MAKE IS SO DELICIOUS.
YOU'RE SUCH A GOOD COOK.
IT'S THE SAME CURRY BLOCK, BUT YOU HAVE THAT MAGIC TOUCH—IT TASTES SO GOOD.
YOU'LL BE A GREAT WIFE.
WH— WHAT ARE YOU TALKING ABOUT!?
WE ALL MADE IT TOGETHER!
IT WAS DELICIOUS BECAUSE WE MADE IT TOGETHER!
BUT YOUR COOKING MADE THE DIFFERENCE, I'M SURE.
THE MEAT WAS VERY TENDER AND SAVORY. PLUS THE RICE THAT KAHARA-SAN MADE WAS QUITE DELICIOUS AS WELL...
HM?

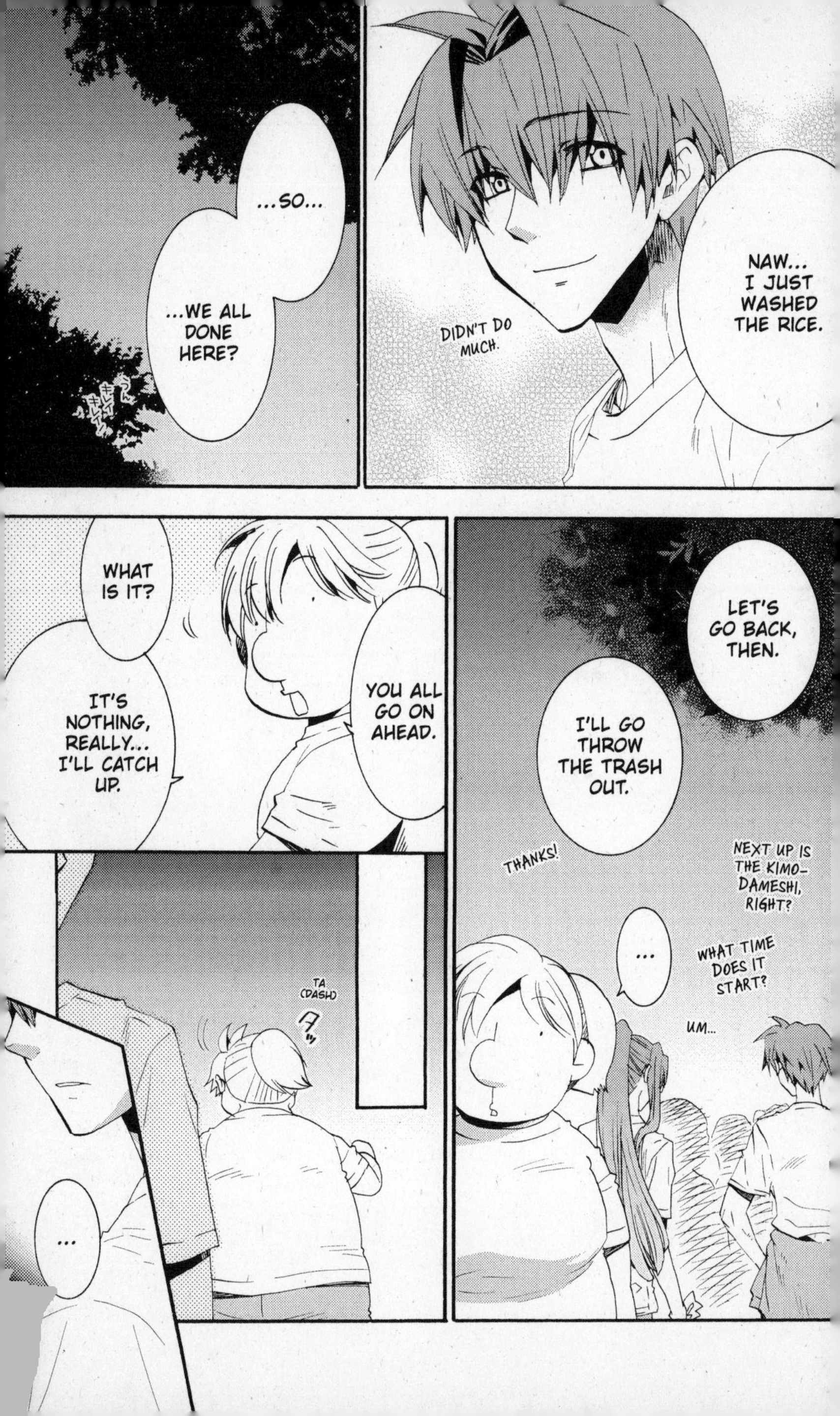
NAW... I JUST WASHED THE RICE.
DIDN'T DO MUCH.
...SO...
...WE ALL DONE HERE?
LET'S GO BACK, THEN.
I'LL GO THROW THE TRASH OUT.
NEXT UP IS THE KIMO-DAMESHI, RIGHT?
THANKS!
...
WHAT TIME DOES IT START?
UM...
YOU ALL GO ON AHEAD.
WHAT IS IT?
IT'S NOTHING, REALLY... I'LL CATCH UP.
TA (DASH)
...

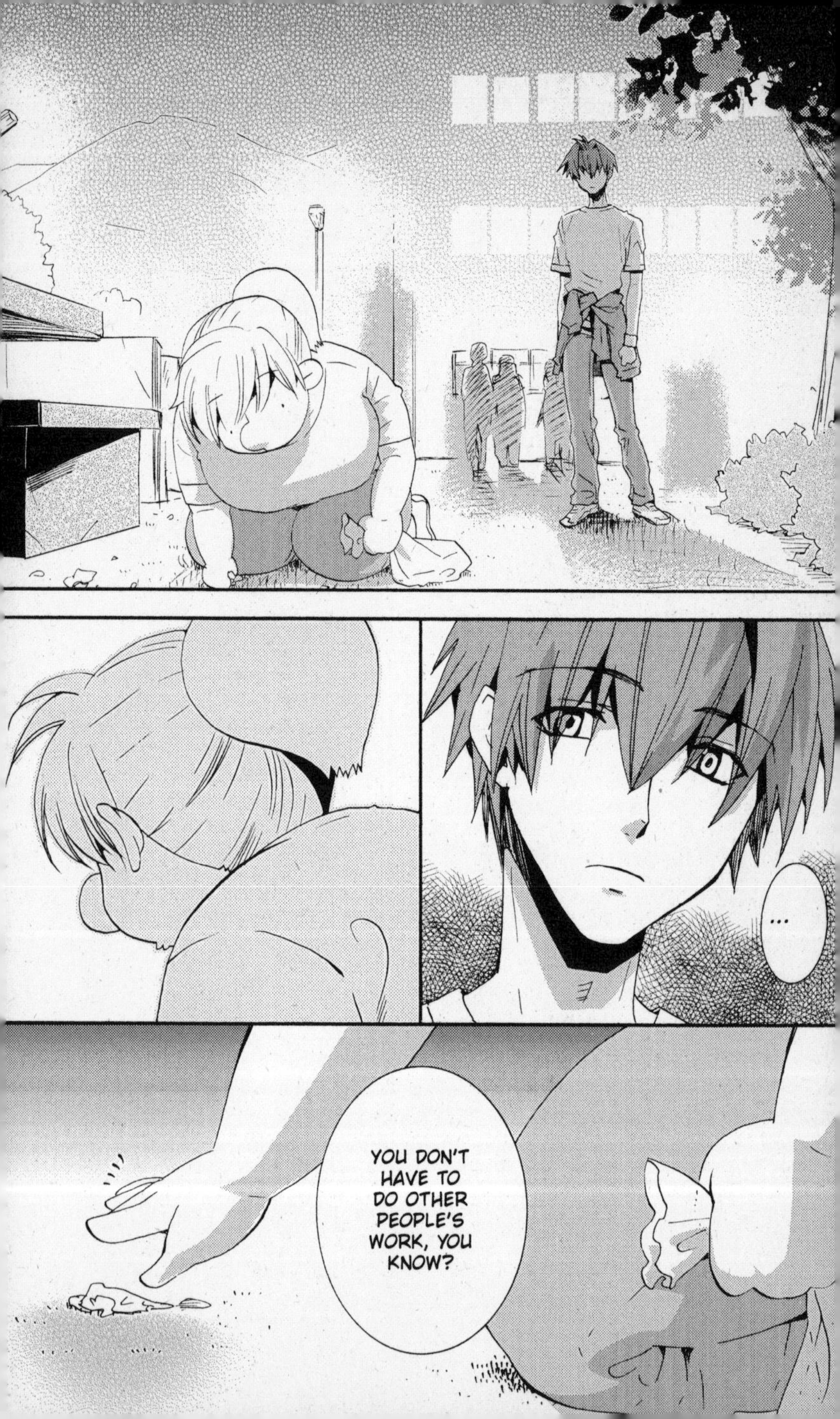
...
YOU DON'T HAVE TO DO OTHER PEOPLE'S WORK, YOU KNOW?

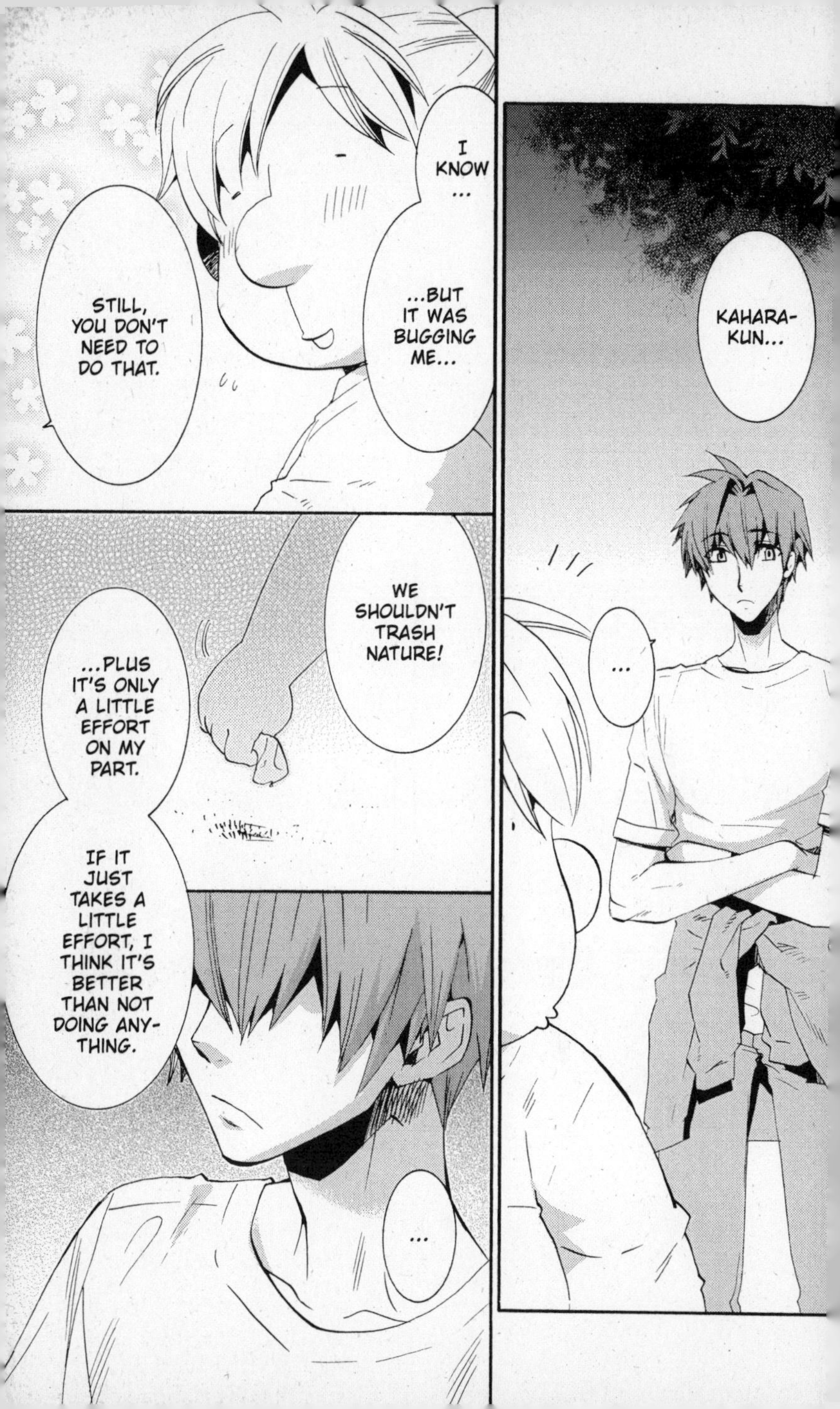
KAHARA-KUN...
...
I KNOW...
...BUT IT WAS BUGGING ME...
STILL, YOU DON'T NEED TO DO THAT.
WE SHOULDN'T TRASH NATURE!
...PLUS IT'S ONLY A LITTLE EFFORT ON MY PART.
IF IT JUST TAKES A LITTLE EFFORT, I THINK IT'S BETTER THAN NOT DOING ANY-THING.
...

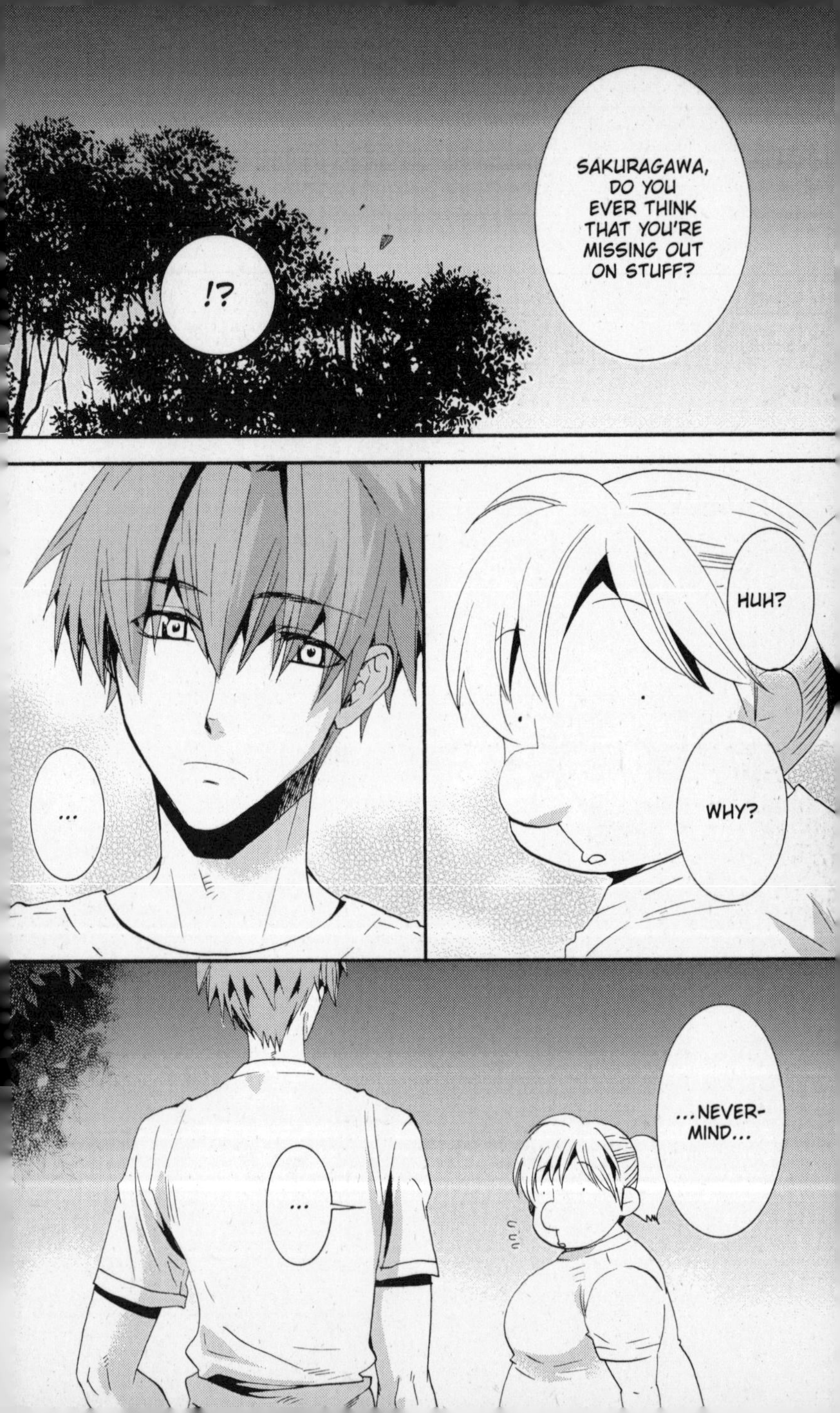
SAKURAGAWA, DO YOU EVER THINK THAT YOU'RE MISSING OUT ON STUFF?
!?
HUH?
WHY?
...
...NEVER-MIND...
...

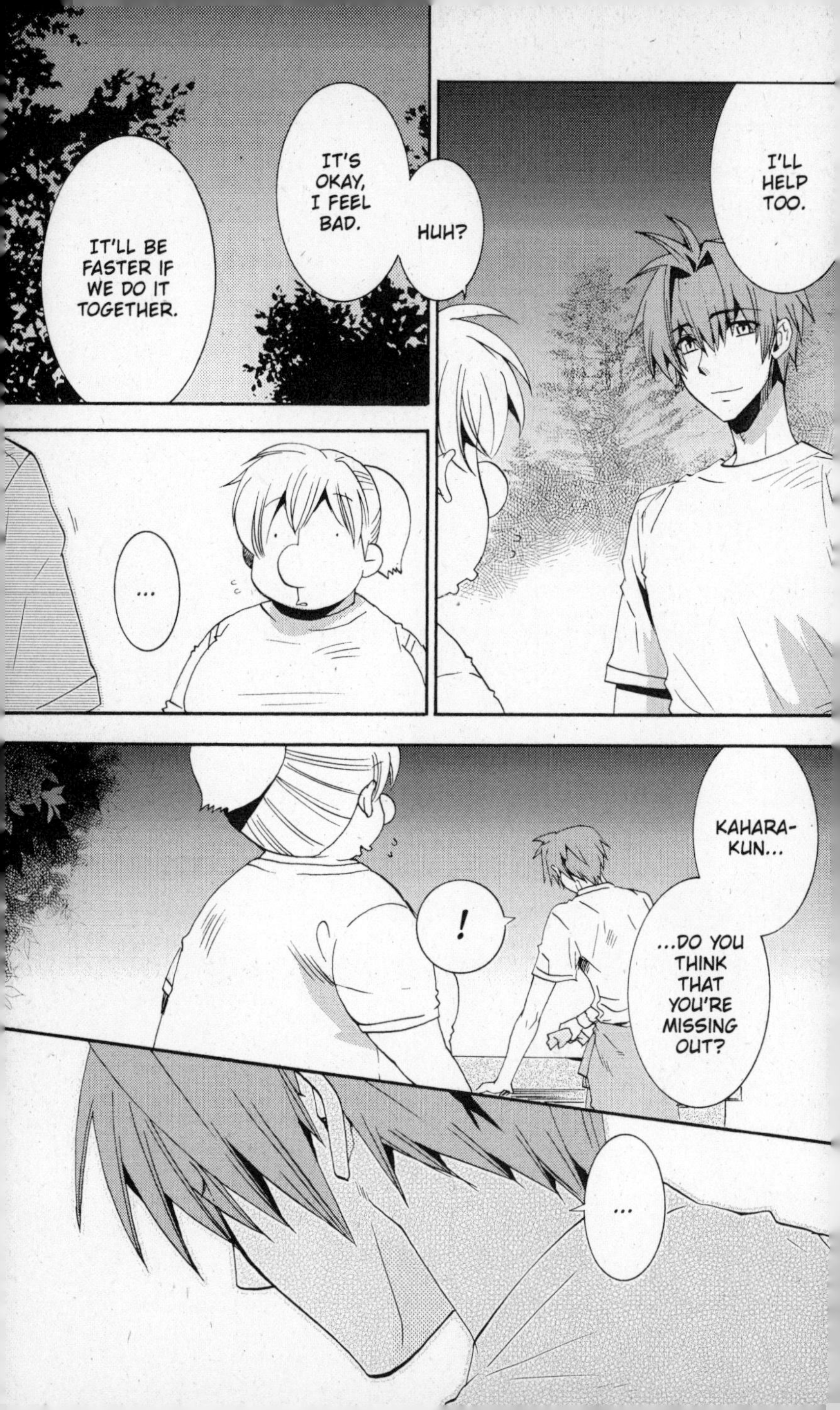
I'LL HELP TOO.
HUH?
IT'S OKAY, I FEEL BAD.
IT'LL BE FASTER IF WE DO IT TOGETHER.
...
KAHARA-KUN...
...DO YOU THINK THAT YOU'RE MISSING OUT?
!
...

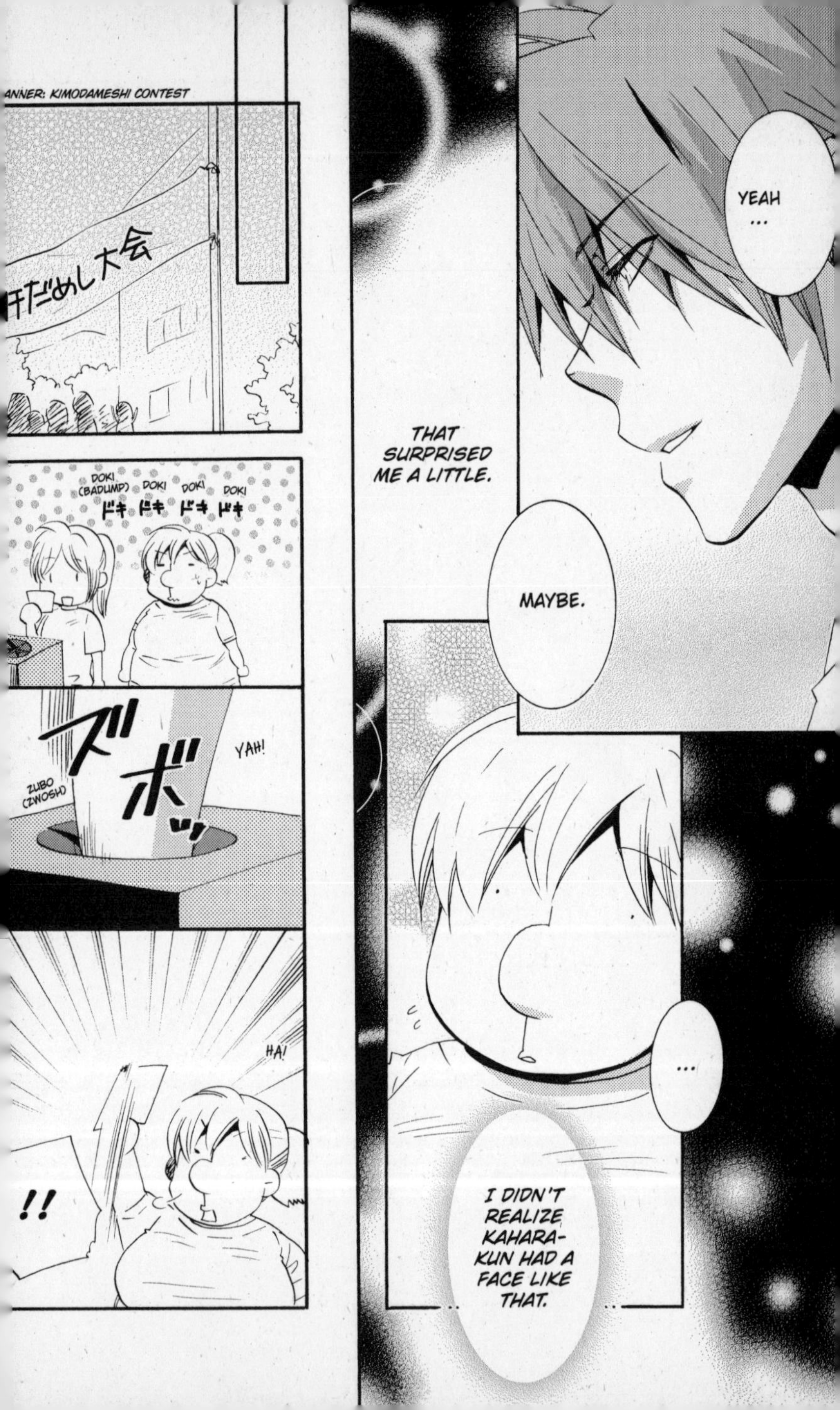
YEAH
...
THAT SURPRISED ME A LITTLE.
MAYBE.
...
I DIDN'T REALIZE KAHARA-KUN HAD A FACE LIKE THAT.
ANNER: KIMODAMESHI CONTEST
だめし大会
DOKI (BADUMP) DOKI DOKI DOKI
ドキ ドキ ドキ ドキ
ズボッ
ZUBO (ZWOSH)
YAH!
HA!
!!

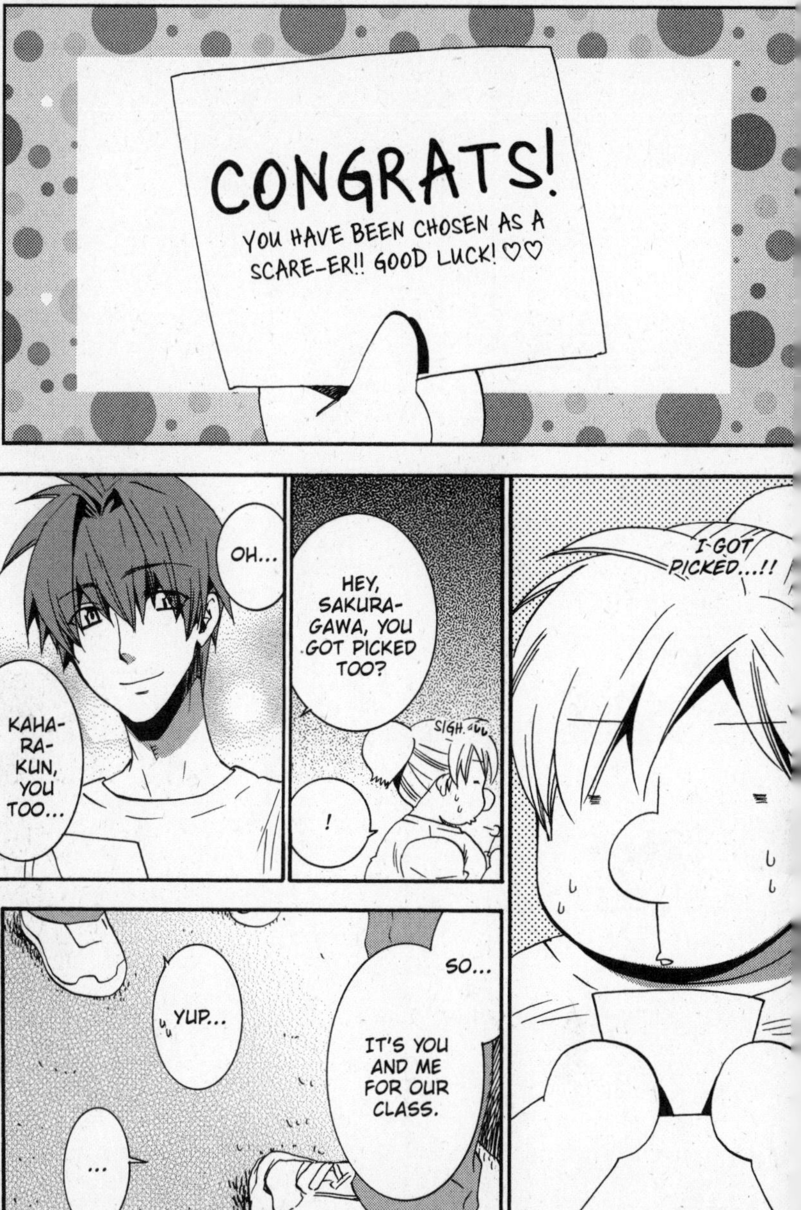
CONGRATS!
YOU HAVE BEEN CHOSEN AS A SCARE-ER!! GOOD LUCK! ♡♡
I GOT PICKED...!!
HEY, SAKURA-GAWA, YOU GOT PICKED TOO?
SIGH.
!
OH...
KAHA-RA-KUN, YOU TOO...
SO...
IT'S YOU AND ME FOR OUR CLASS.
YUP...
...

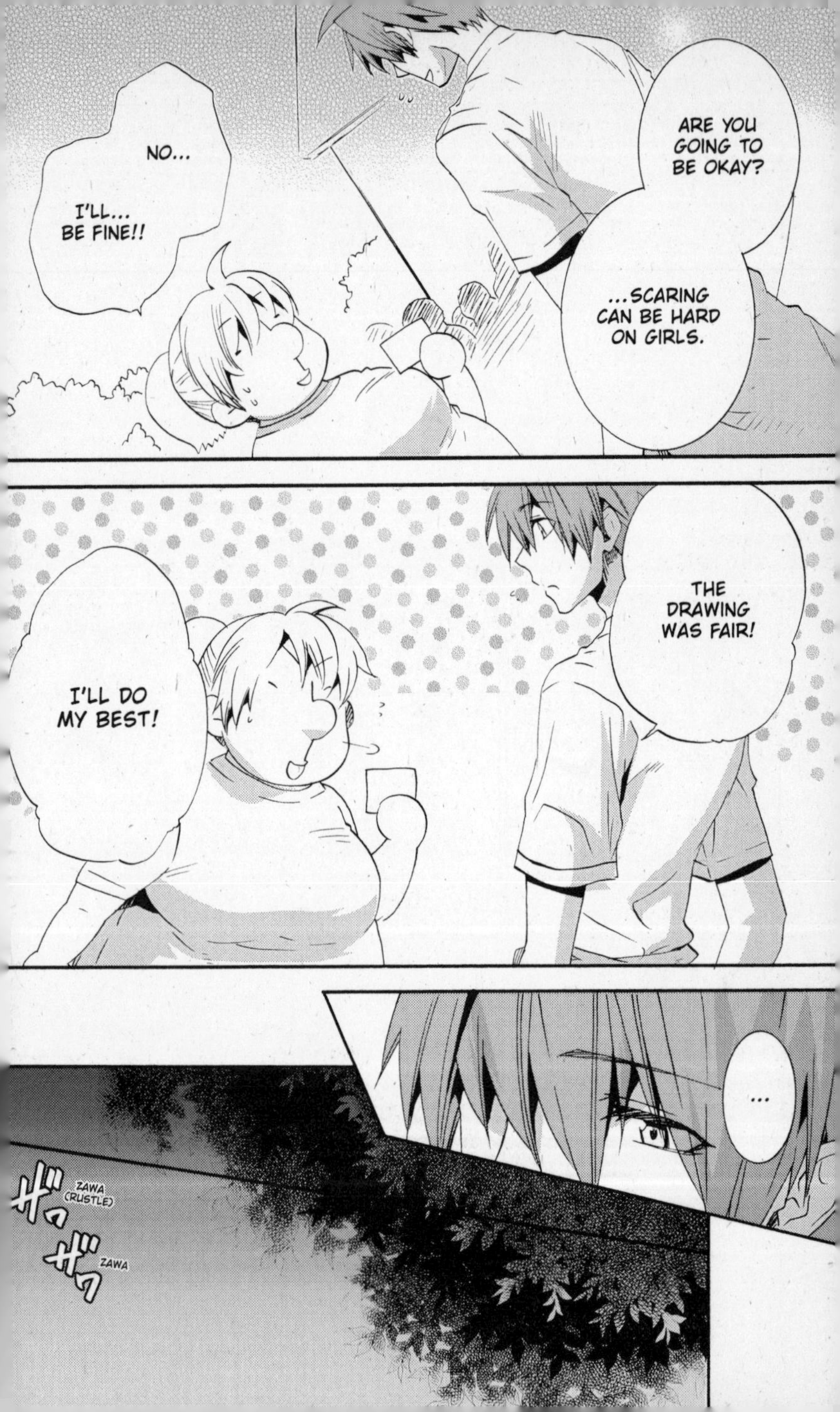
ARE YOU GOING TO BE OKAY?
...SCARING CAN BE HARD ON GIRLS.
NO...
I'LL... BE FINE!!
THE DRAWING WAS FAIR!
I'LL DO MY BEST!
...
ZAWA (RUSTLE)
ZAWA

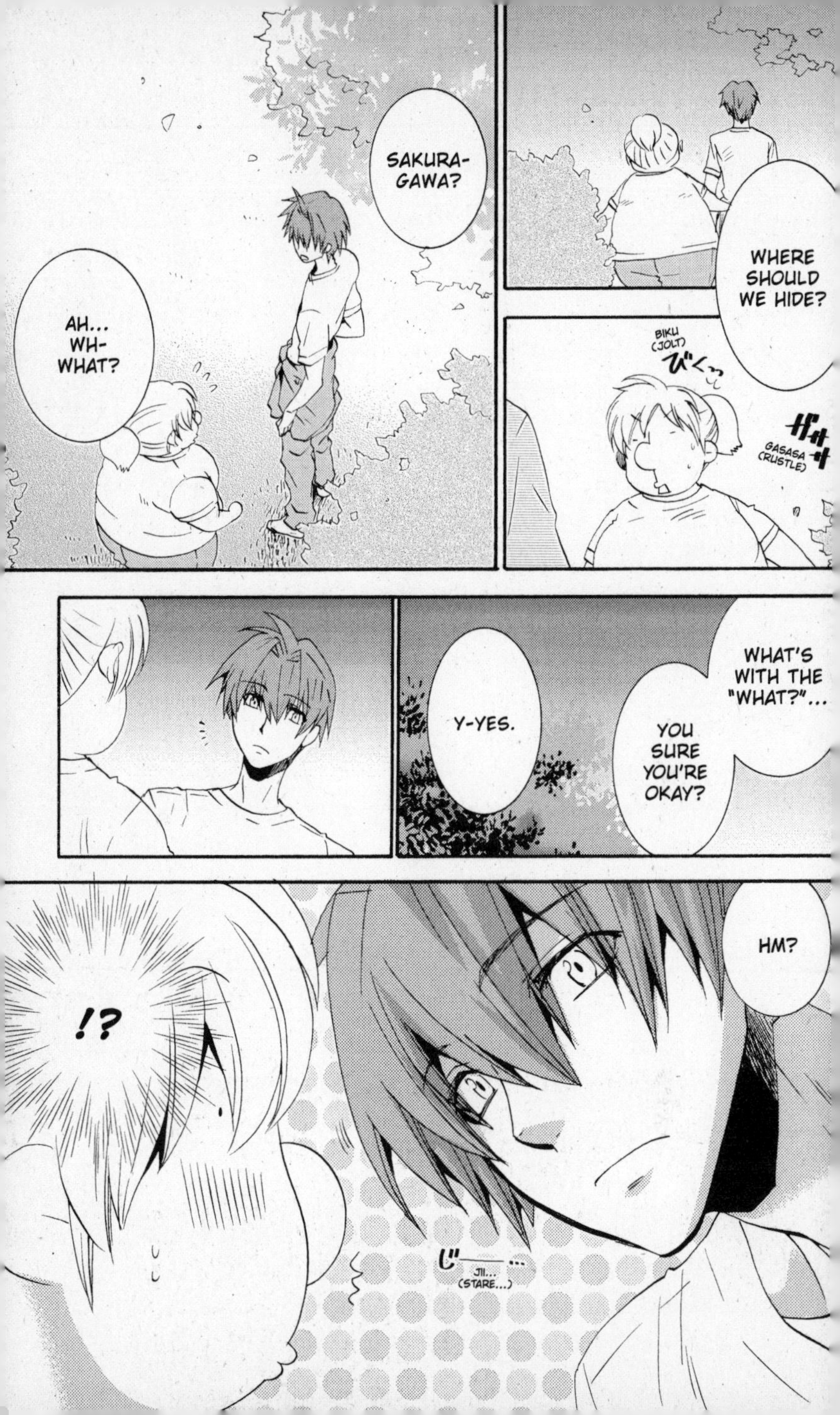
WHERE SHOULD WE HIDE?
BIKU (JOLT)
GASASA (RUSTLE)
SAKURA-GAWA?
AH... WH- WHAT?
WHAT'S WITH THE "WHAT?"...
YOU SURE YOU'RE OKAY?
Y-YES.
HM?
!?
JII... (STARE...)

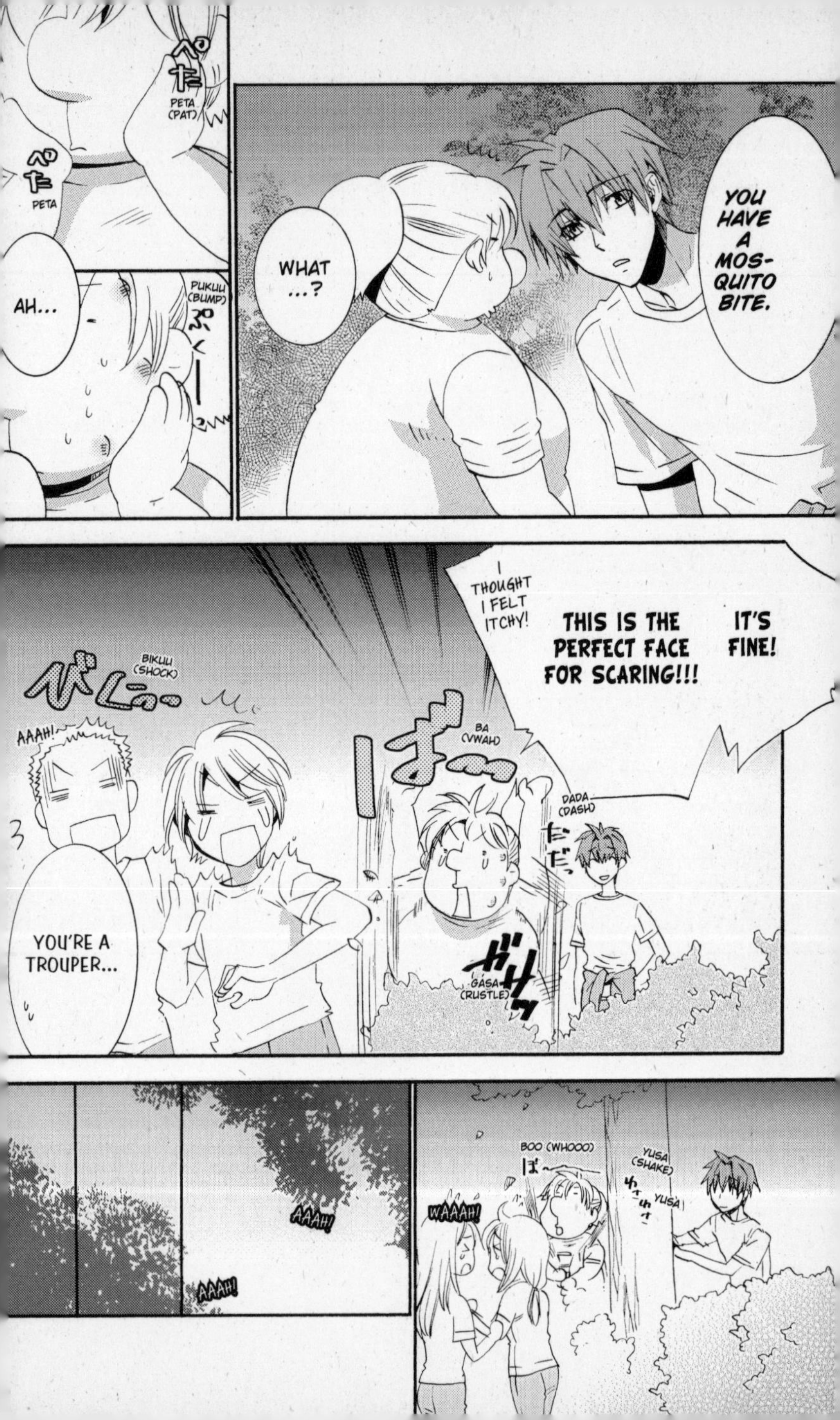

YOU HAVE A MOS-QUITO BITE.
WHAT ...?
PETA (PAT)
PETA
PUKUU (BUMP)
AH...
IT'S FINE!
THIS IS THE PERFECT FACE FOR SCARING!!!
I THOUGHT I FELT ITCHY!
DADA (DASH)
BA (VWAH)
BIKUU (SHOCK)
AAAH!
GASA (RUSTLE)
YOU'RE A TROUPER...
YUSA (SHAKE)
YUSA
BOO (WHOOO)
WAAAH!
AAAH!
AAAH!

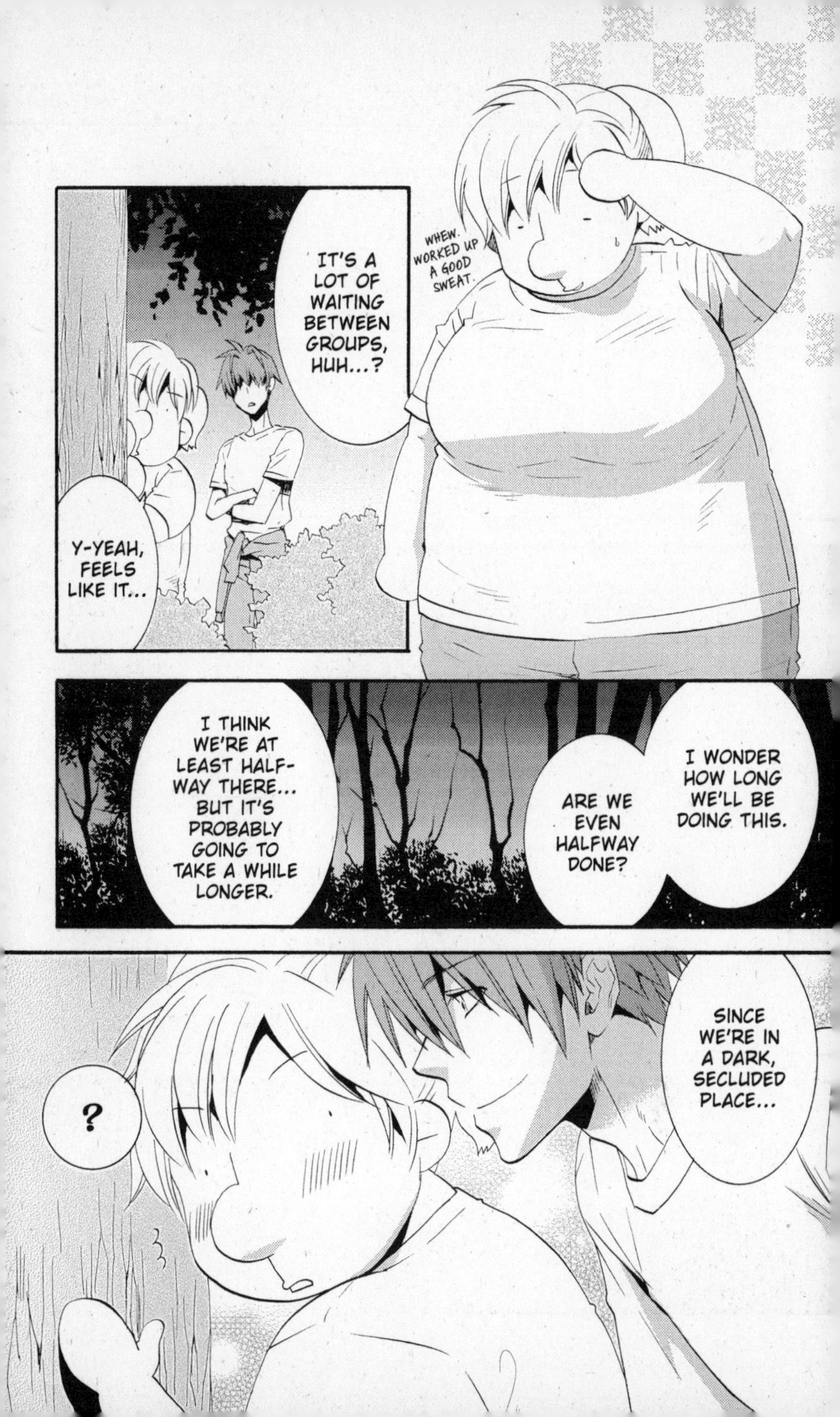
WHEW. WORKED UP A GOOD SWEAT.
IT'S A LOT OF WAITING BETWEEN GROUPS, HUH...?
Y-YEAH, FEELS LIKE IT...
I WONDER HOW LONG WE'LL BE DOING THIS.
ARE WE EVEN HALFWAY DONE?
I THINK WE'RE AT LEAST HALF-WAY THERE... BUT IT'S PROBABLY GOING TO TAKE A WHILE LONGER.
SINCE WE'RE IN A DARK, SECLUDED PLACE...
?

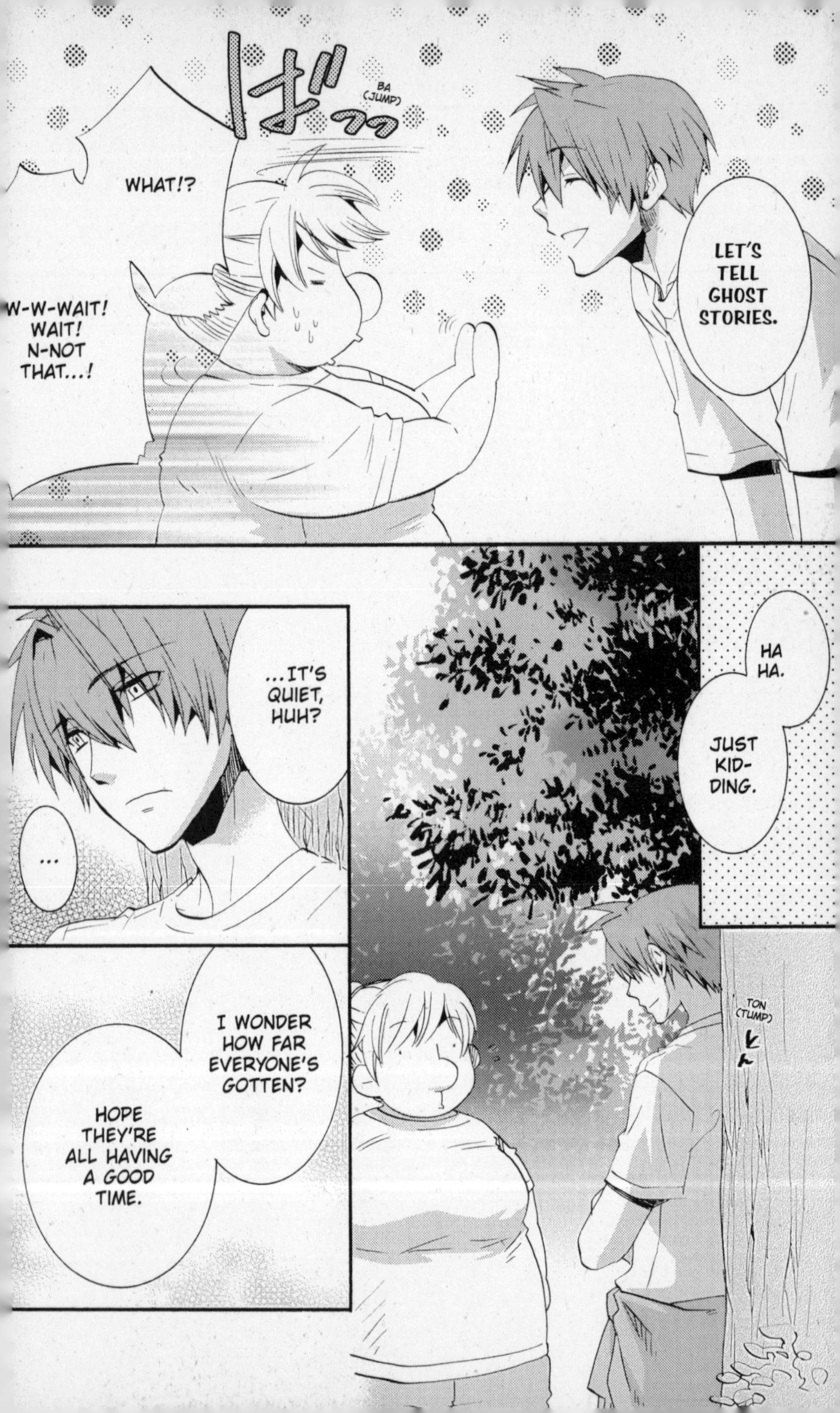
LET'S TELL GHOST STORIES.
ばっ
BA (JUMP)
WHAT!?
W-W-WAIT! WAIT! N-NOT THAT...!
HA HA.
JUST KID-DING.
とん
TON (TUMP)
...IT'S QUIET, HUH?
...
I WONDER HOW FAR EVERYONE'S GOTTEN?
HOPE THEY'RE ALL HAVING A GOOD TIME.

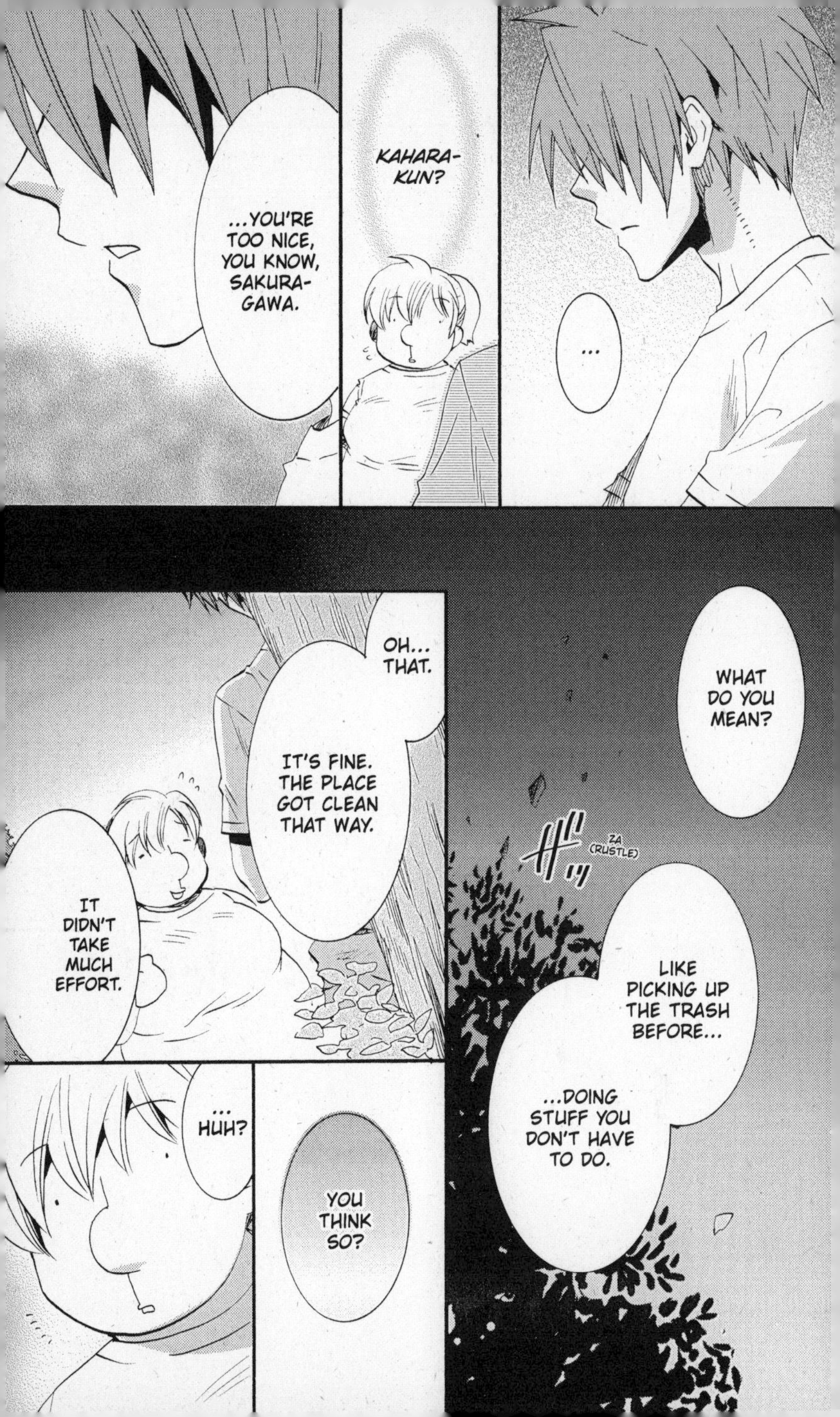
...
KAHARA-KUN?
...YOU'RE TOO NICE, YOU KNOW, SAKURA-GAWA.
WHAT DO YOU MEAN?
ZA (RUSTLE)
LIKE PICKING UP THE TRASH BEFORE...
...DOING STUFF YOU DON'T HAVE TO DO.
OH... THAT.
IT'S FINE. THE PLACE GOT CLEAN THAT WAY.
IT DIDN'T TAKE MUCH EFFORT.
YOU THINK SO?
... HUH?

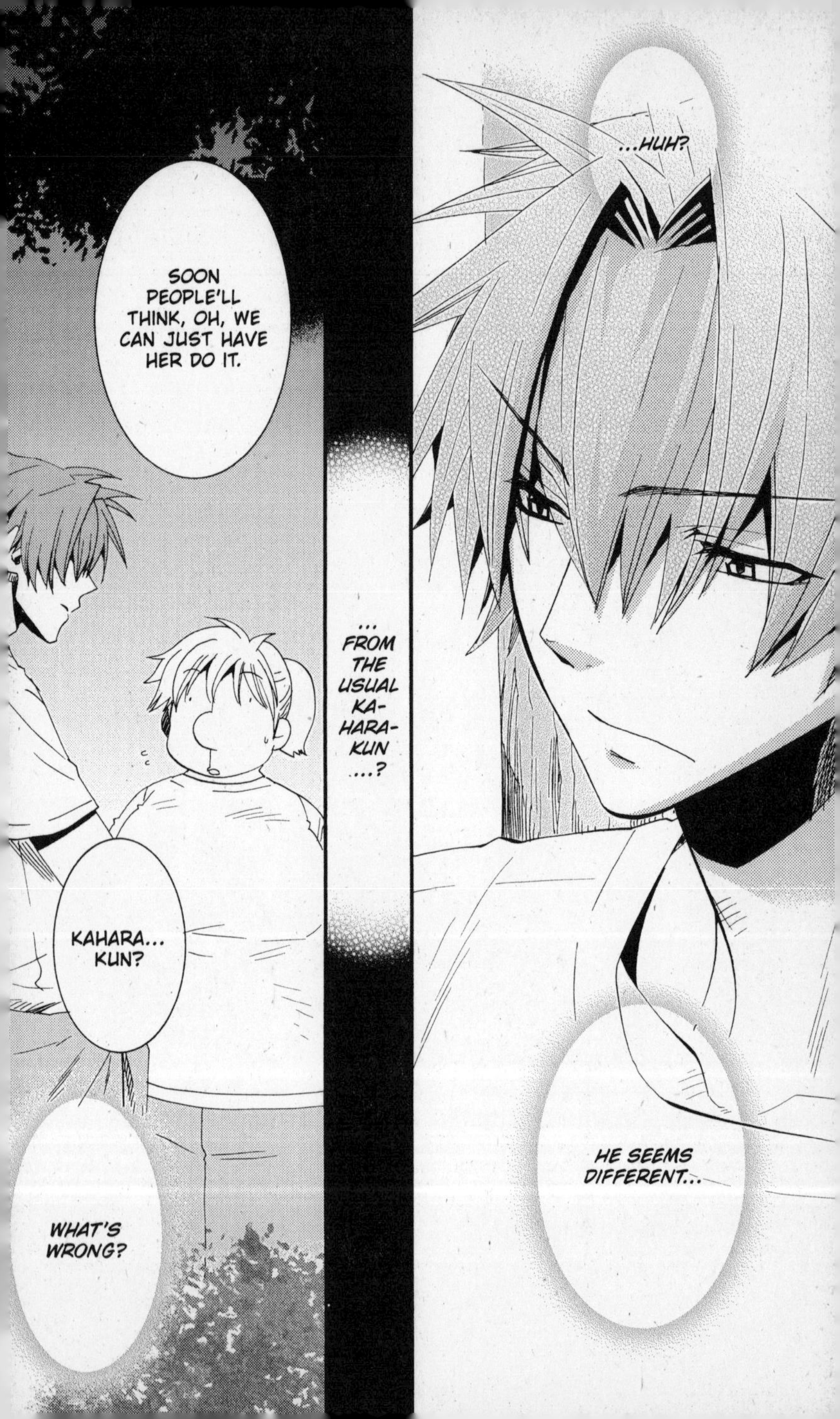
...HUH?
HE SEEMS DIFFERENT...
...FROM THE USUAL KA-HARA-KUN ....?
SOON PEOPLE'LL THINK, OH, WE CAN JUST HAVE HER DO IT.
KAHARA... KUN?
WHAT'S WRONG?

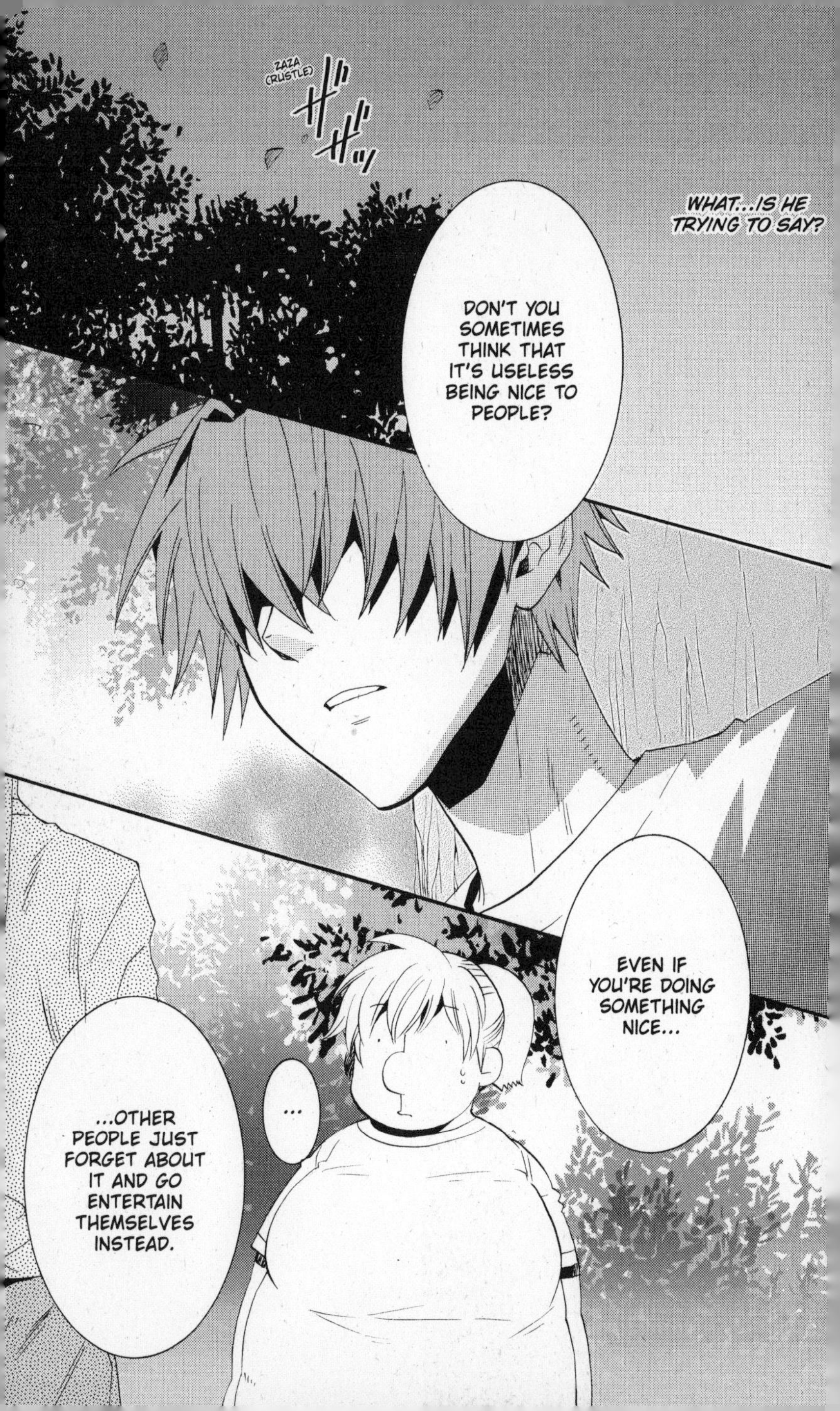
ZAZA (RUSTLE)
WHAT...IS HE TRYING TO SAY?
DON'T YOU SOMETIMES THINK THAT IT'S USELESS BEING NICE TO PEOPLE?
EVEN IF YOU'RE DOING SOMETHING NICE...
...
...OTHER PEOPLE JUST FORGET ABOUT IT AND GO ENTERTAIN THEMSELVES INSTEAD.

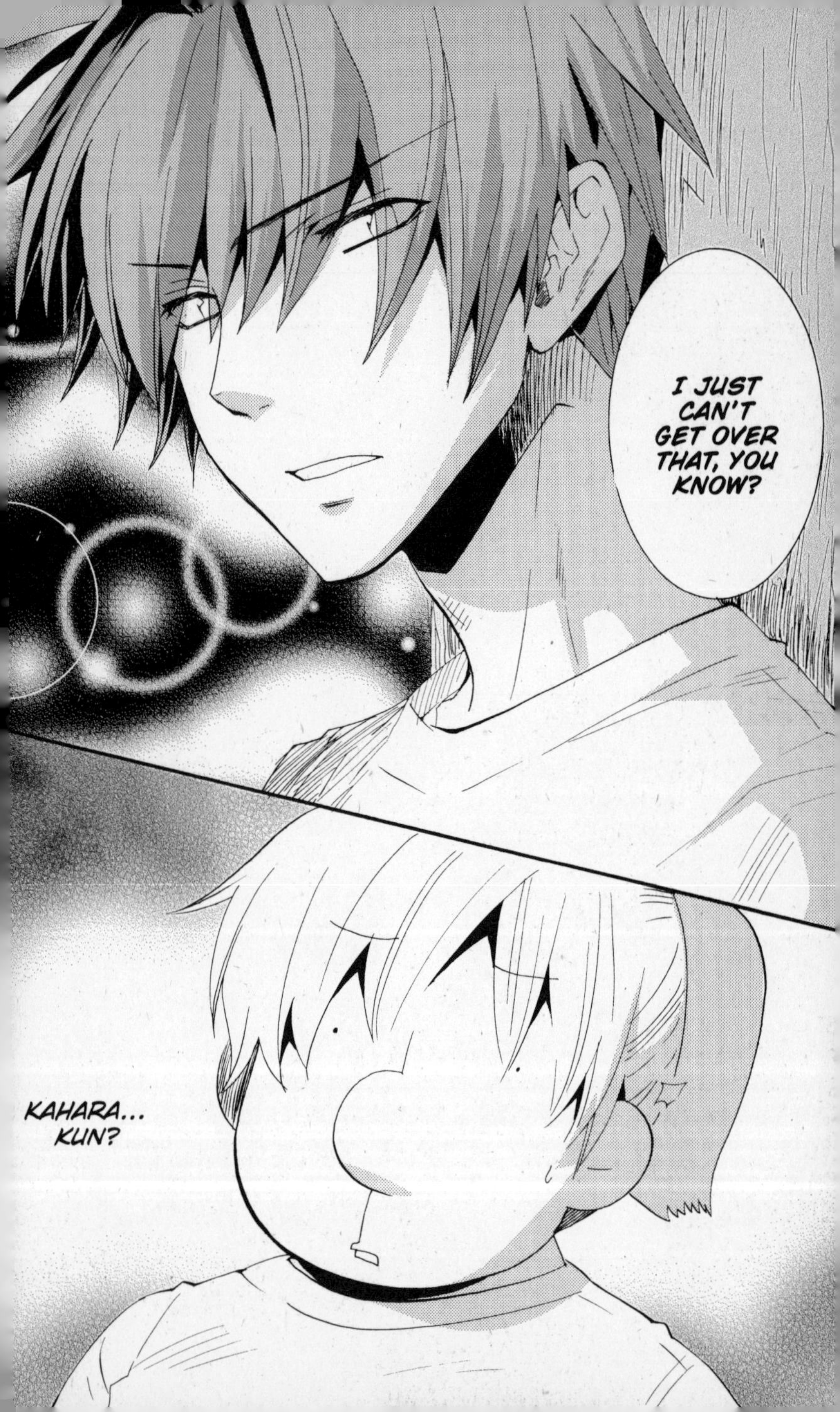
I JUST CAN'T GET OVER THAT, YOU KNOW?
KAHARA... KUN?

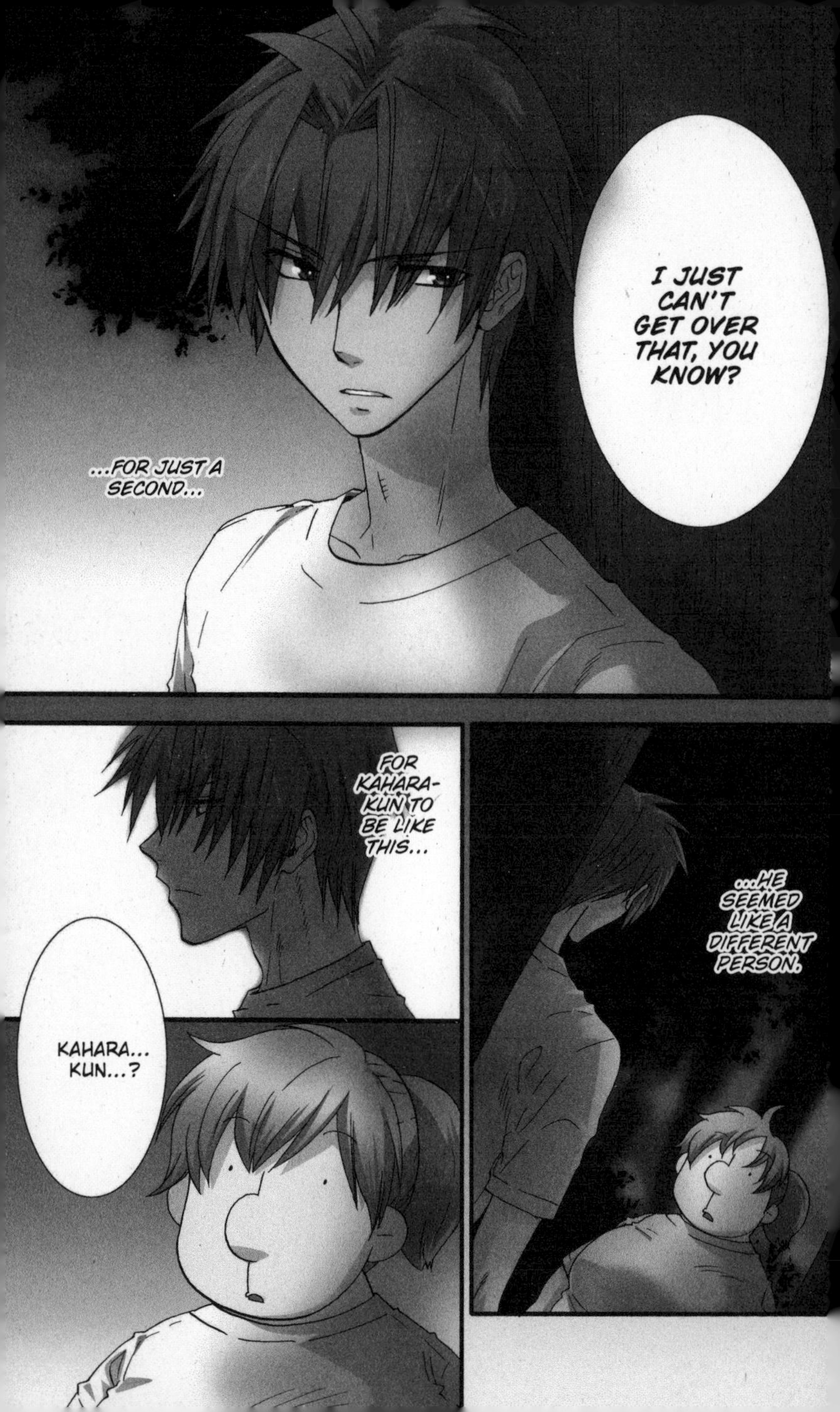
I JUST CAN'T GET OVER THAT, YOU KNOW?
...FOR JUST A SECOND...
...HE SEEMED LIKE A DIFFERENT PERSON.
FOR KAHARA-KUN TO BE LIKE THIS...
KAHARA... KUN...?

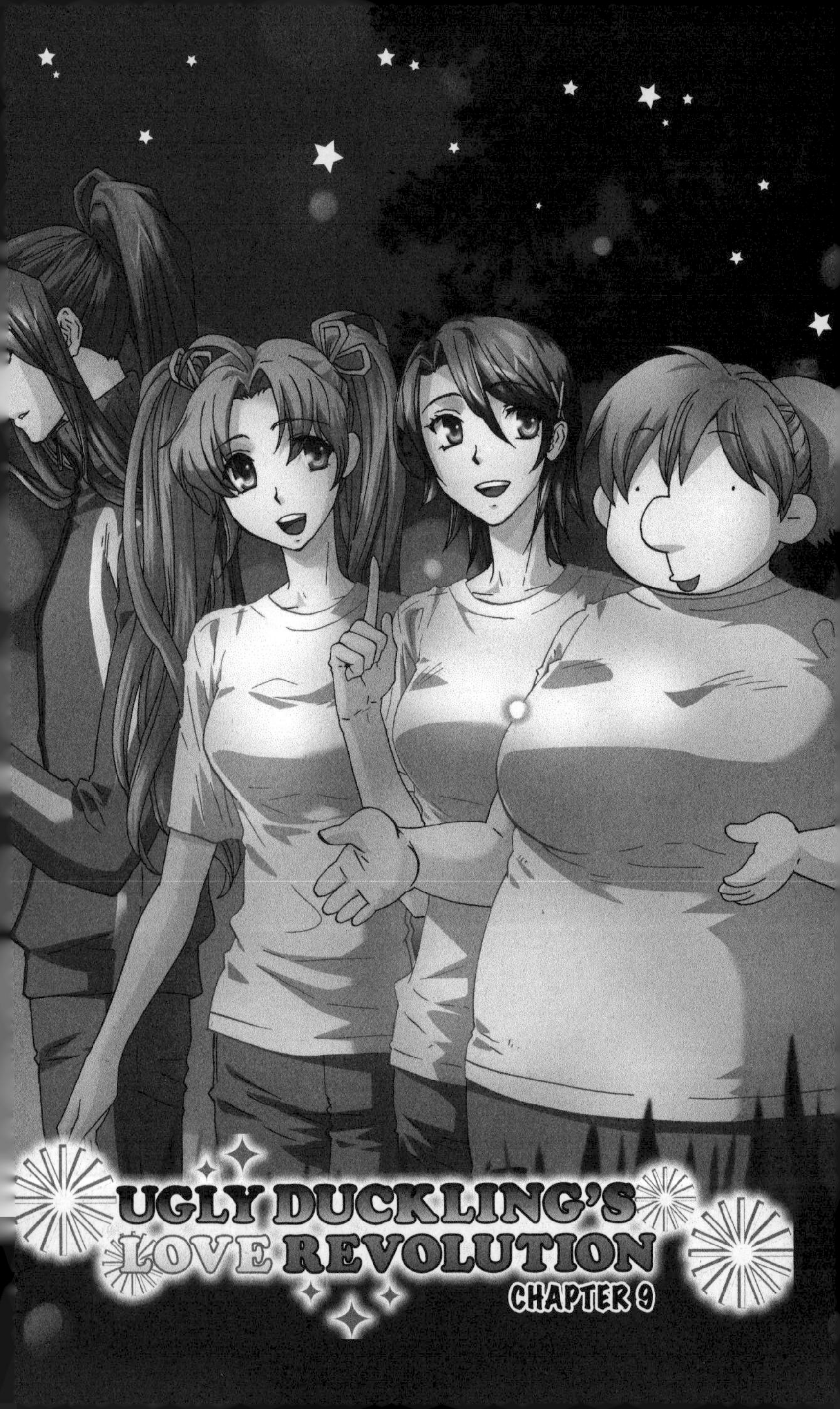
UGLY DUCKLING'S
LOVE REVOLUTION
CHAPTER 9

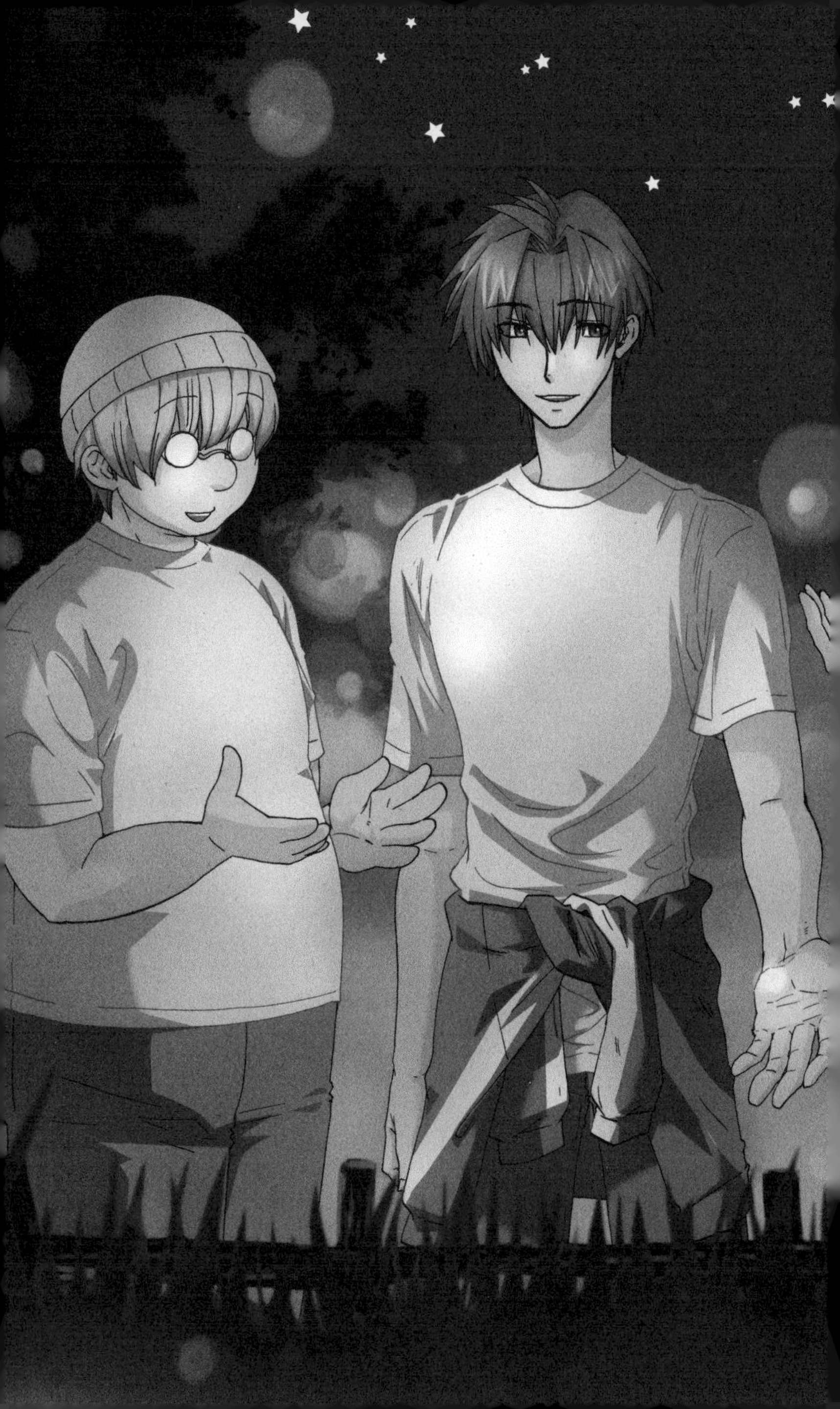

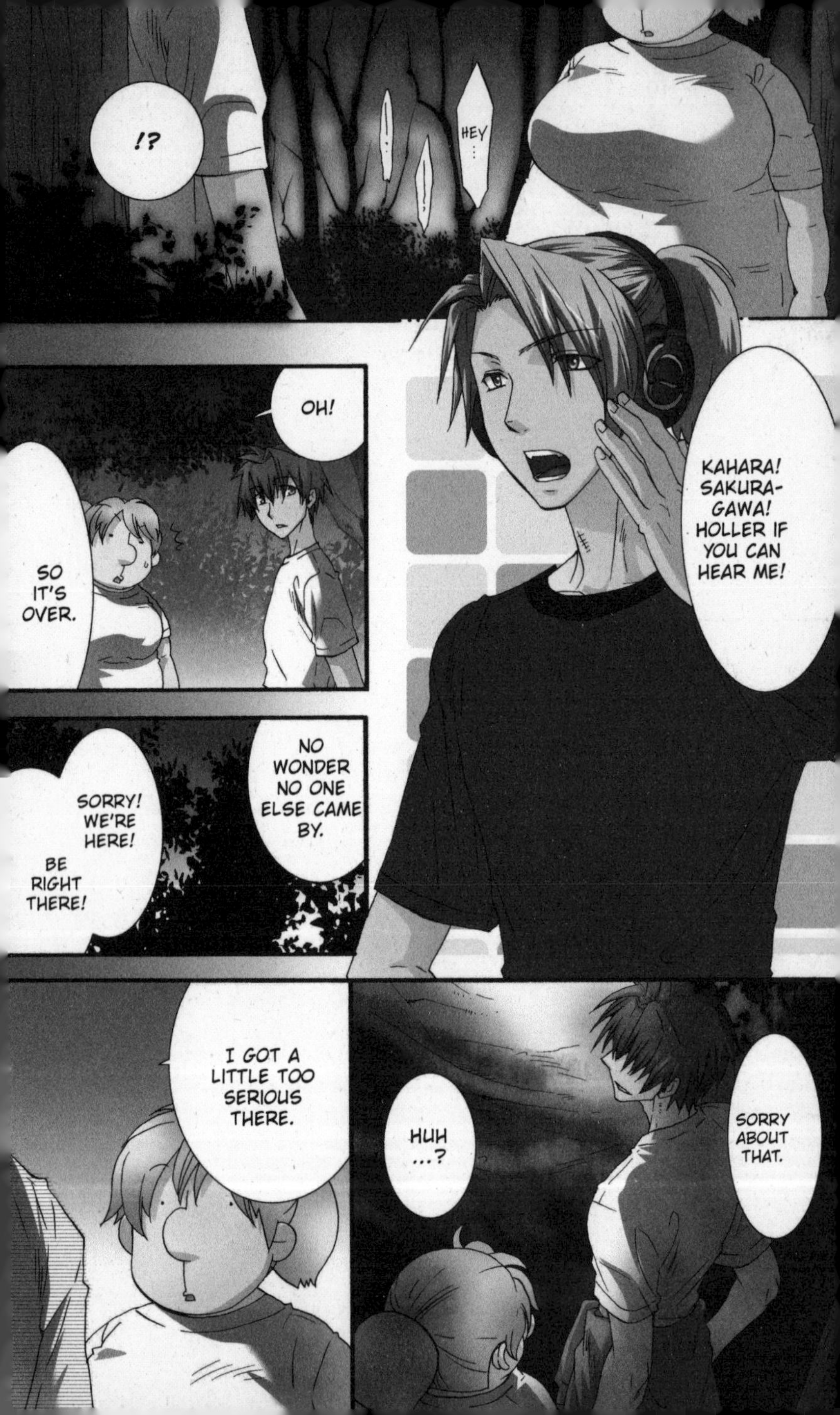
HEY...
!
!
!?
KAHARA! SAKURA-GAWA! HOLLER IF YOU CAN HEAR ME!
OH!
SO IT'S OVER.
NO WONDER NO ONE ELSE CAME BY.
SORRY! WE'RE HERE!
BE RIGHT THERE!
SORRY ABOUT THAT.
HUH ...?
I GOT A LITTLE TOO SERIOUS THERE.

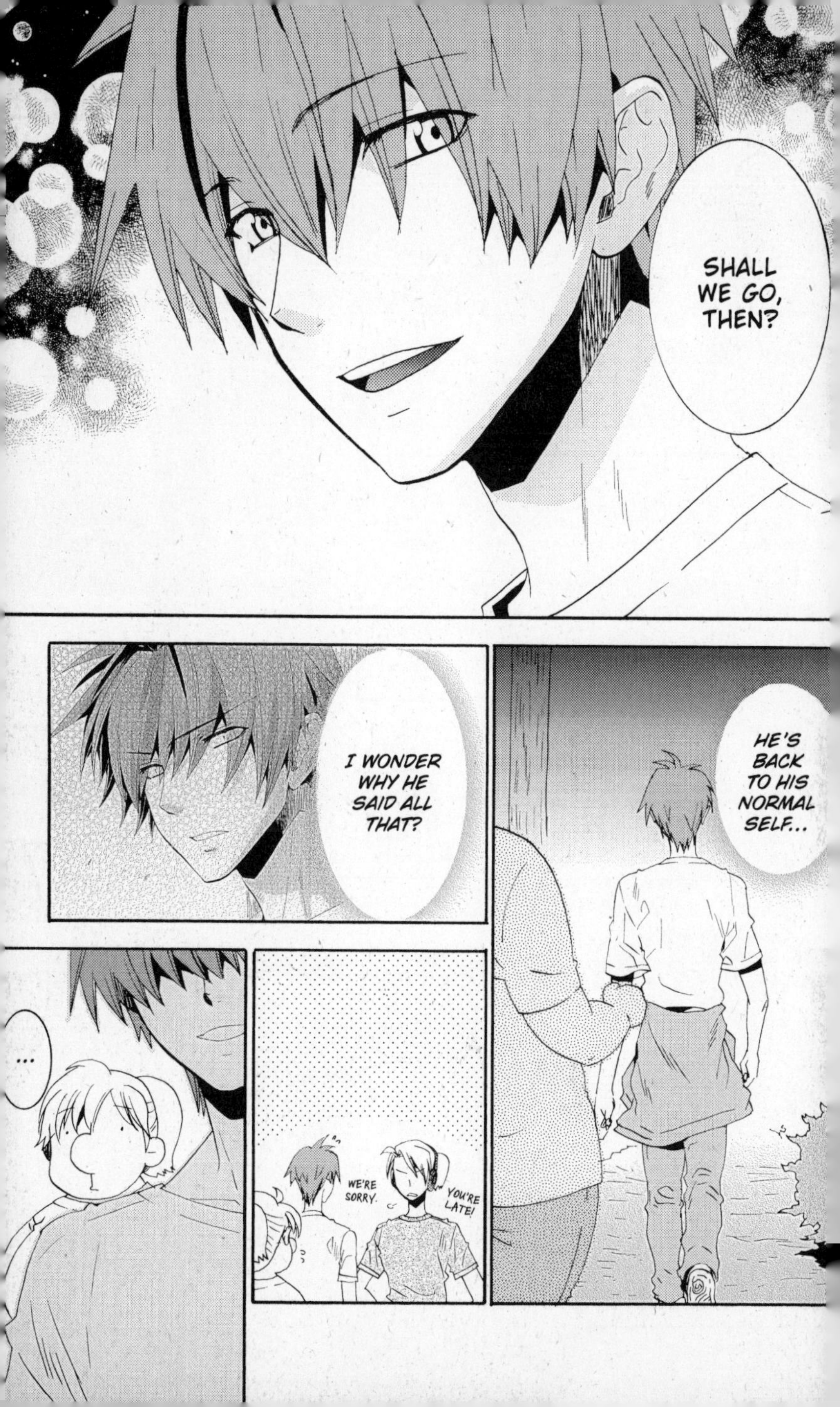
SHALL WE GO, THEN?
HE'S BACK TO HIS NORMAL SELF...
I WONDER WHY HE SAID ALL THAT?
YOU'RE LATE!
WE'RE SORRY.
...

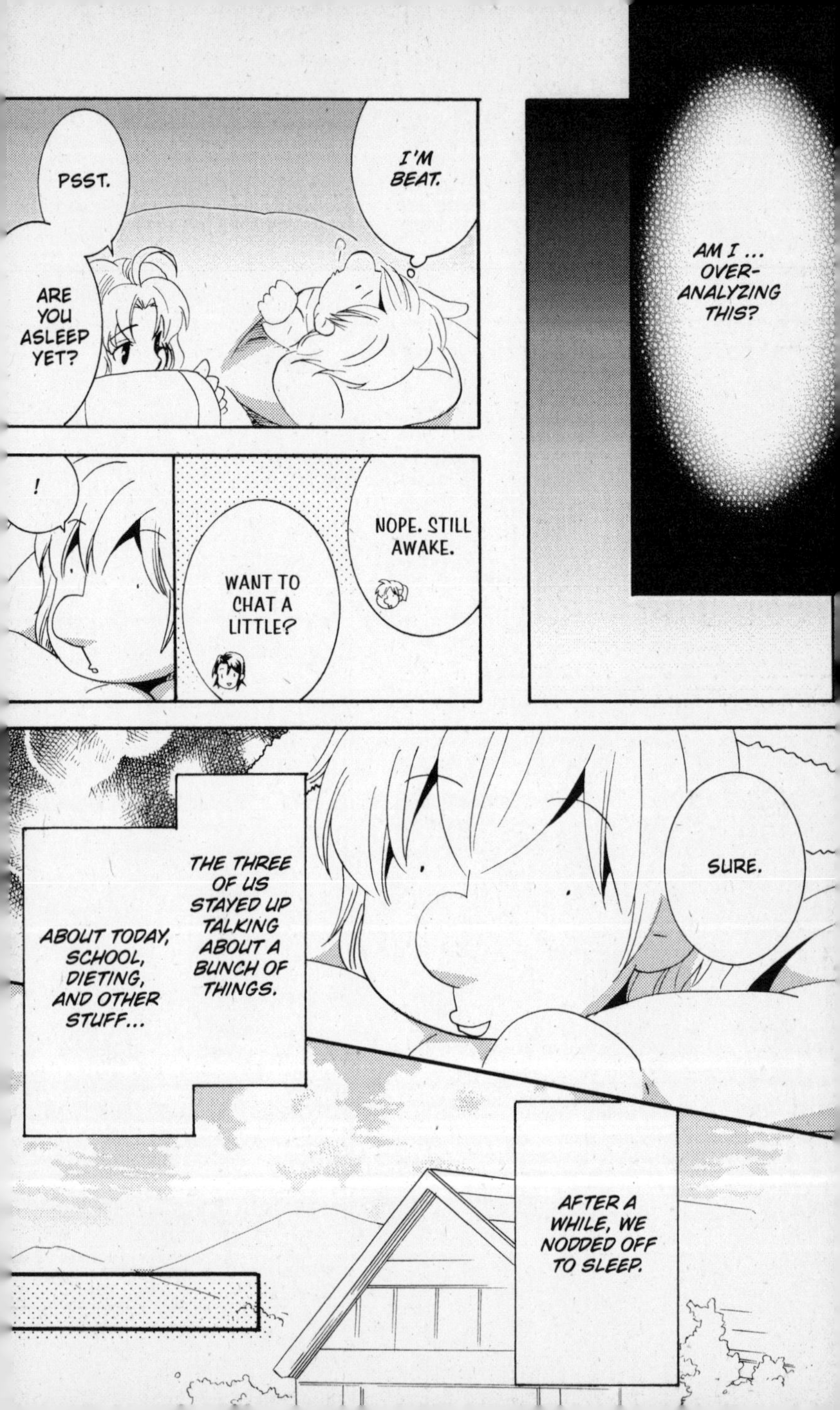
AM I ... OVER-ANALYZING THIS?
I'M BEAT.
PSST.
ARE YOU ASLEEP YET?
NOPE. STILL AWAKE.
WANT TO CHAT A LITTLE?
!
SURE.
THE THREE OF US STAYED UP TALKING ABOUT A BUNCH OF THINGS.
ABOUT TODAY, SCHOOL, DIETING, AND OTHER STUFF...
AFTER A WHILE, WE NODDED OFF TO SLEEP.

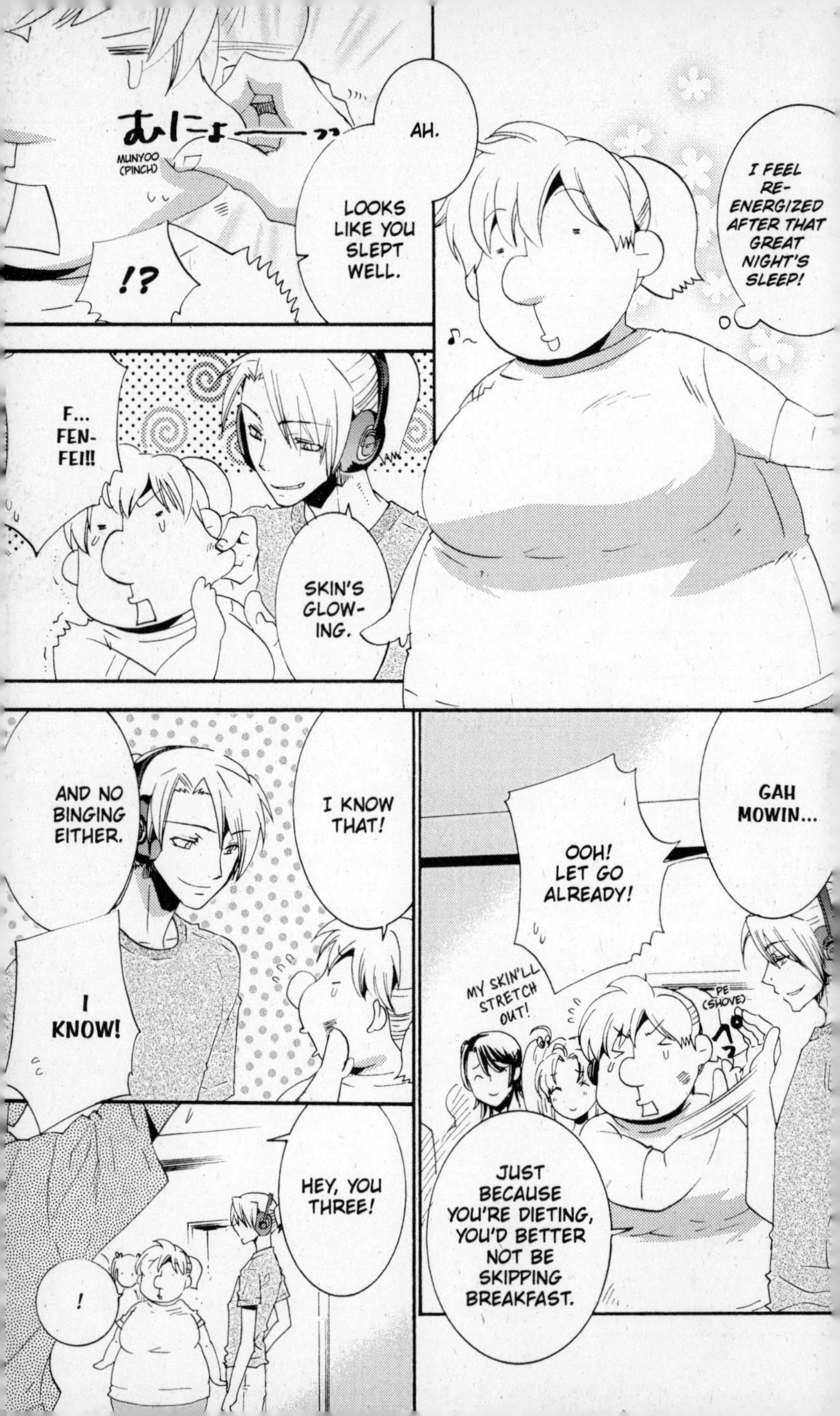
I FEEL RE-ENERGIZED AFTER THAT GREAT NIGHT'S SLEEP!
AH.
LOOKS LIKE YOU SLEPT WELL.
むにょーっ
MUNYOO (PINCH)
!?
F... FEN-FEI!!
SKIN'S GLOW-ING.
GAH MOWIN...
OOH! LET GO ALREADY!
PE (SHOVE)
MY SKIN'LL STRETCH OUT!
JUST BECAUSE YOU'RE DIETING, YOU'D BETTER NOT BE SKIPPING BREAKFAST.
AND NO BINGING EITHER.
I KNOW THAT!
I KNOW!
HEY, YOU THREE!
!

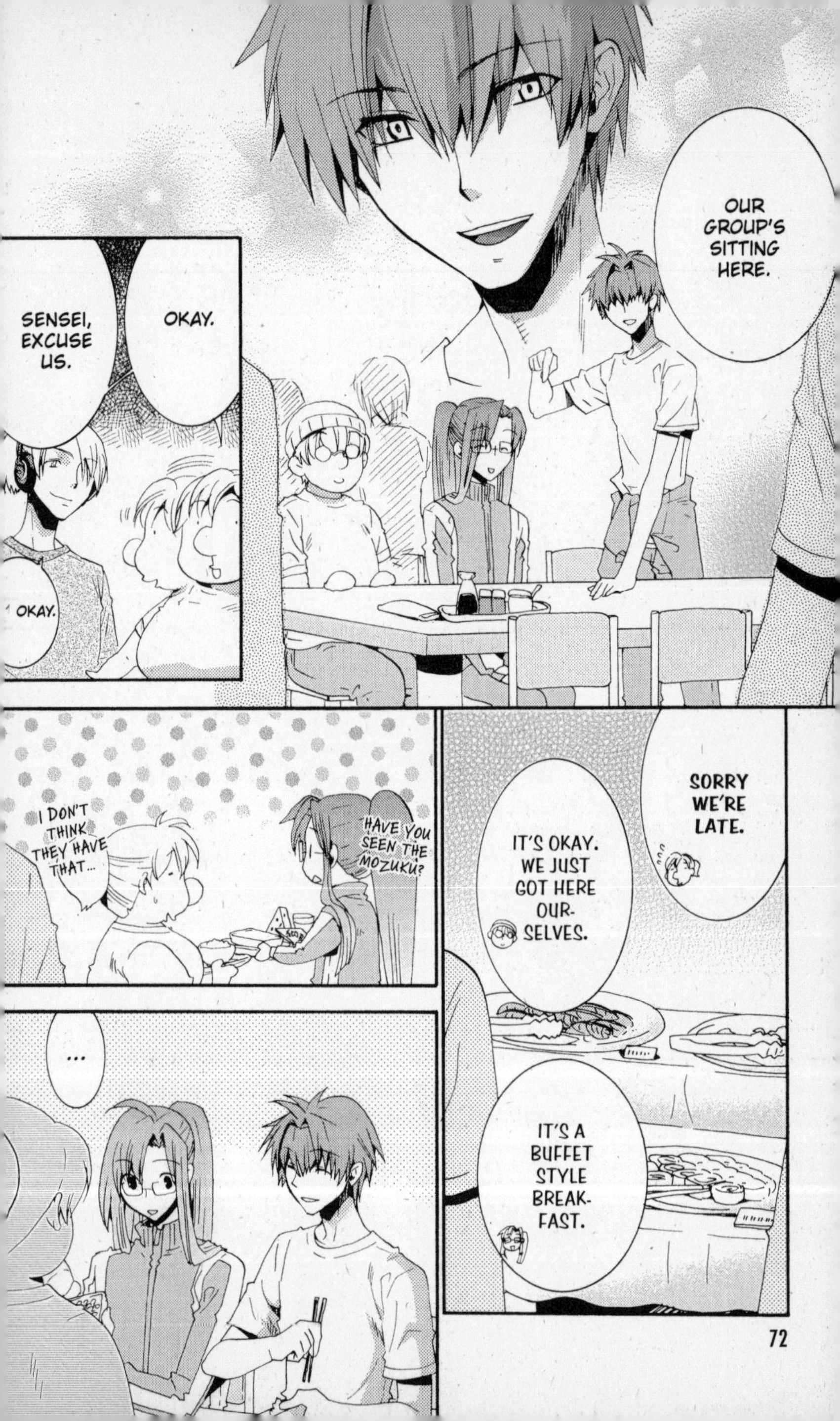
OUR GROUP'S SITTING HERE.
OKAY.
SENSEI, EXCUSE US.
OKAY.
SORRY WE'RE LATE.
IT'S OKAY. WE JUST GOT HERE OUR-SELVES.
IT'S A BUFFET STYLE BREAK-FAST.
HAVE YOU SEEN THE MOZUKU?
I DON'T THINK THEY HAVE THAT...
...

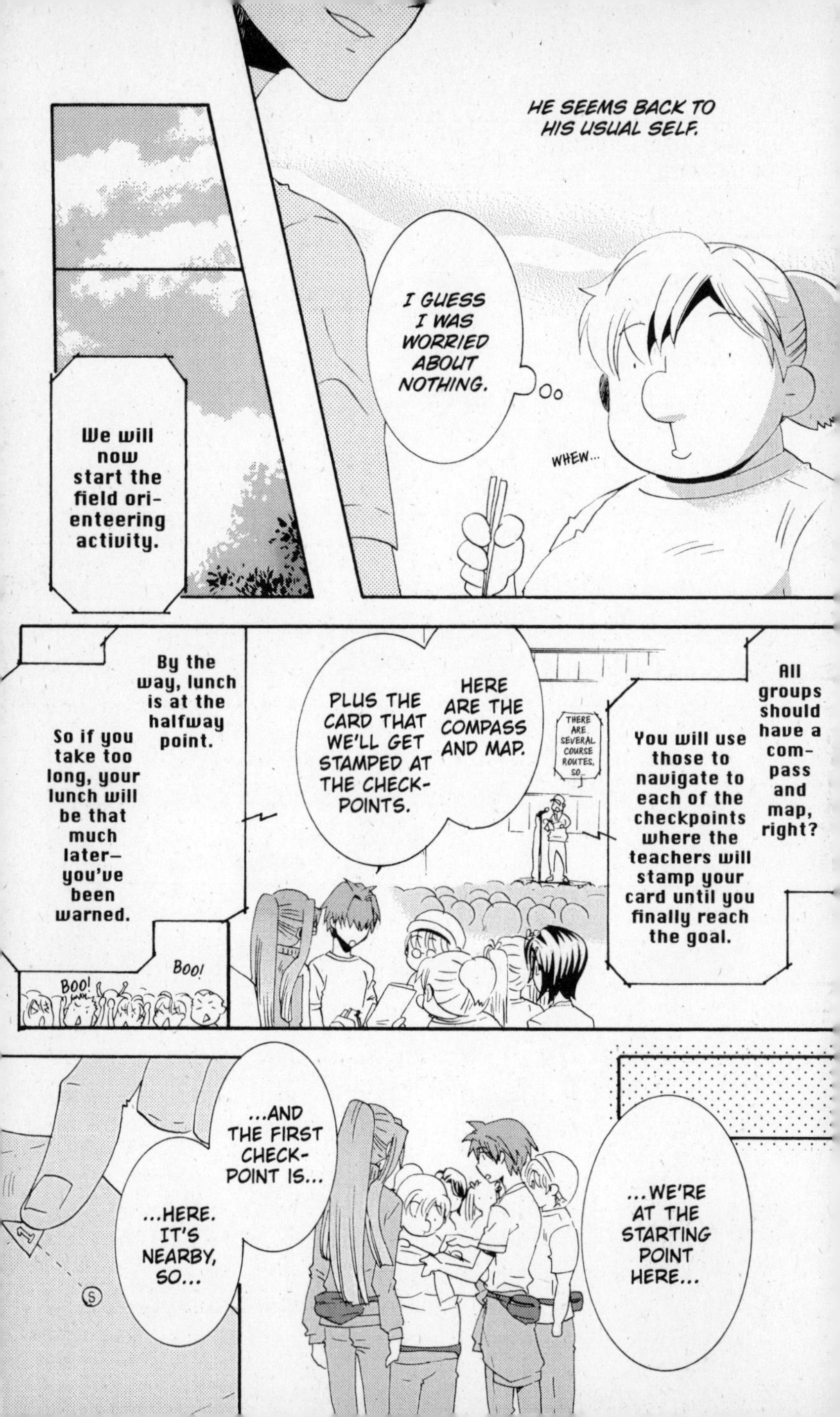
HE SEEMS BACK TO HIS USUAL SELF.
I GUESS I WAS WORRIED ABOUT NOTHING.
WHEW...
We will now start the field ori-enteering activity.
All groups should have a com-pass and map, right?
You will use those to navigate to each of the checkpoints where the teachers will stamp your card until you finally reach the goal.
THERE ARE SEVERAL COURSE ROUTES, SO...
HERE ARE THE COMPASS AND MAP.
PLUS THE CARD THAT WE'LL GET STAMPED AT THE CHECK-POINTS.
By the way, lunch is at the halfway point.
So if you take too long, your lunch will be that much later—you've been warned.
BOO!
BOO!
...WE'RE AT THE STARTING POINT HERE...
...AND THE FIRST CHECK-POINT IS...
...HERE. IT'S NEARBY, SO...

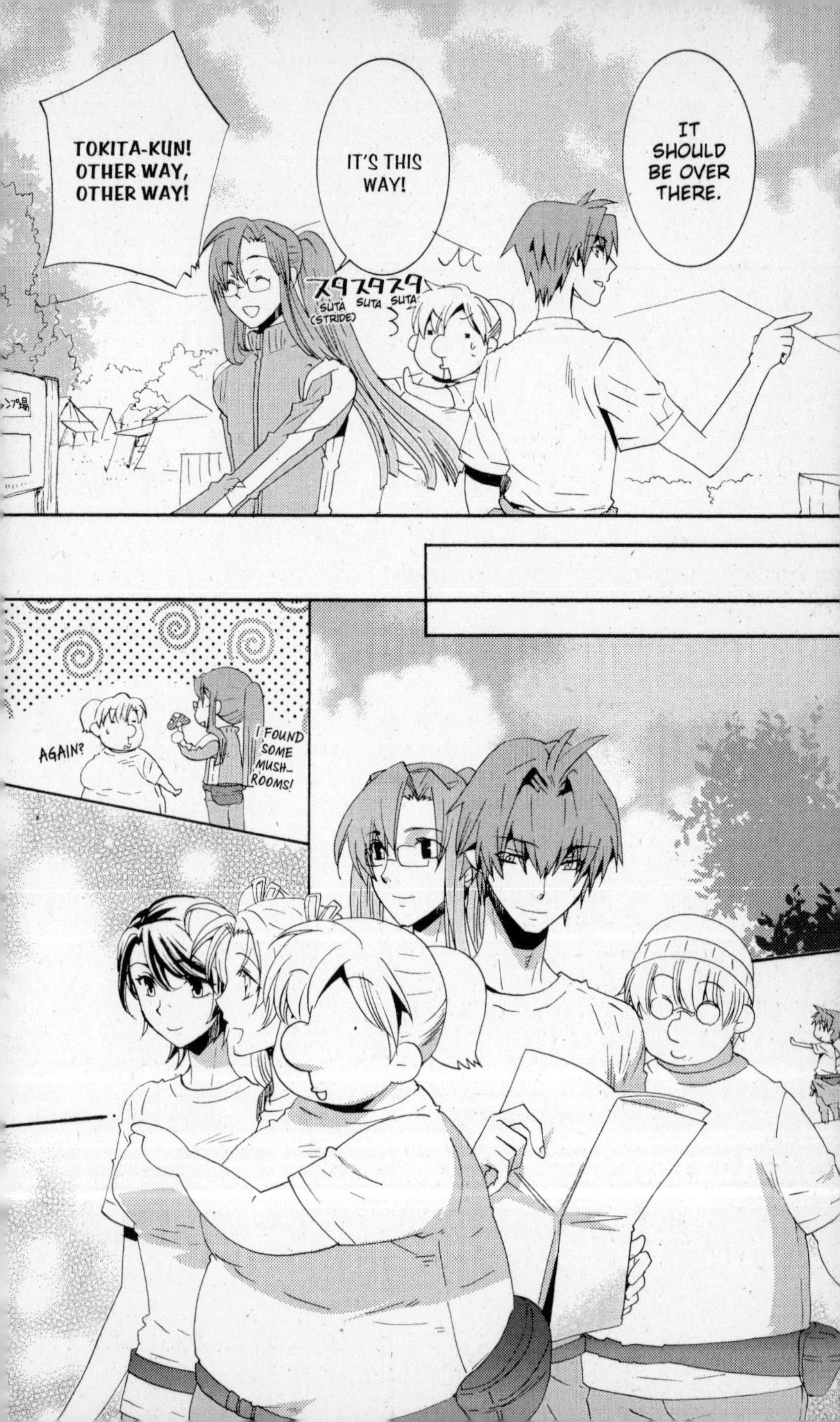
IT SHOULD BE OVER THERE.
IT'S THIS WAY!
スタスタスタ
SUTA SUTA SUTA (STRIDE)
TOKITA-KUN! OTHER WAY, OTHER WAY!
I FOUND SOME MUSH-ROOMS!
AGAIN?

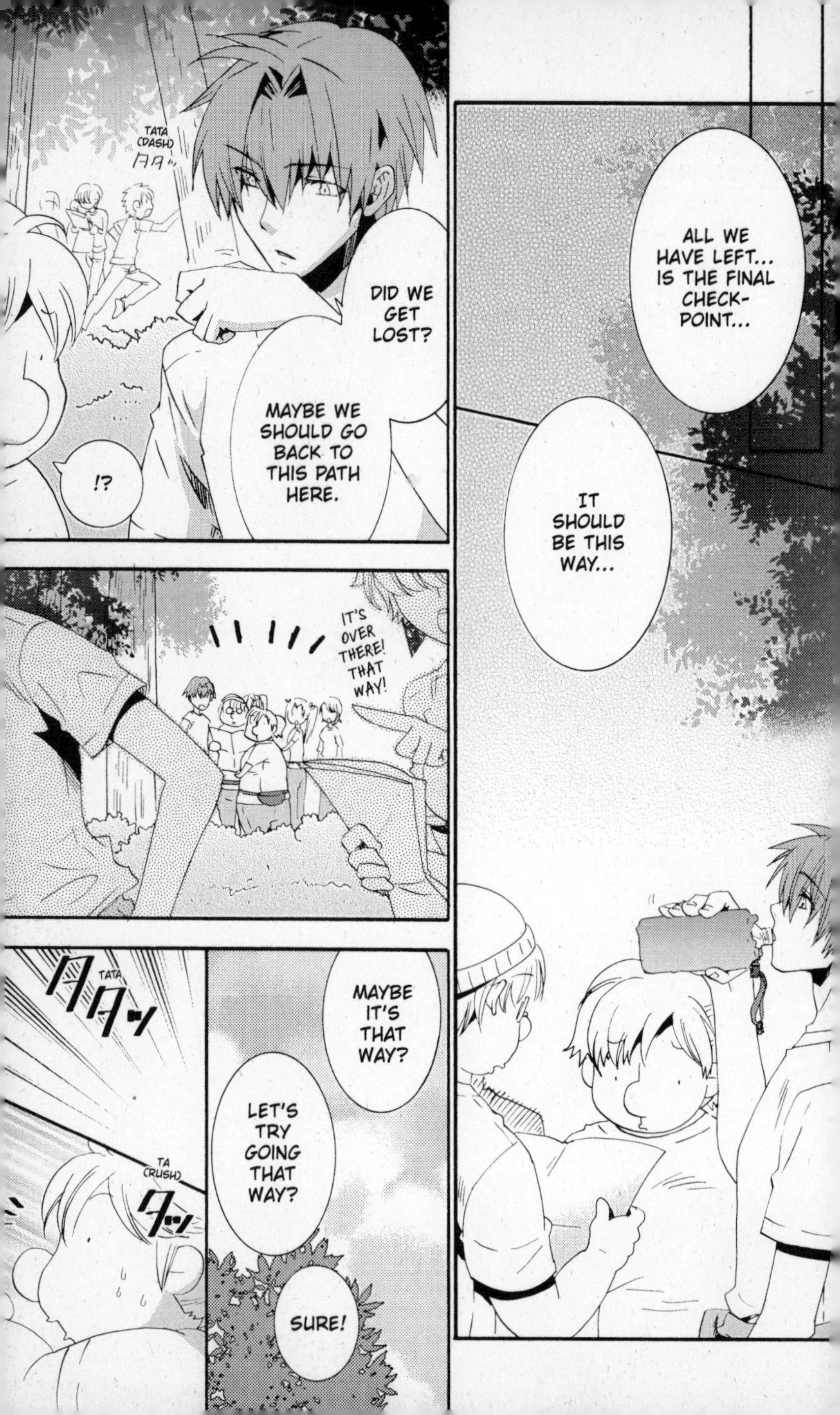
ALL WE HAVE LEFT... IS THE FINAL CHECK-POINT...
IT SHOULD BE THIS WAY...
DID WE GET LOST?
TATA (DASH)
MAYBE WE SHOULD GO BACK TO THIS PATH HERE.
!?
IT'S OVER THERE! THAT WAY!
MAYBE IT'S THAT WAY?
LET'S TRY GOING THAT WAY?
SURE!
TATA
TA (RUSH)

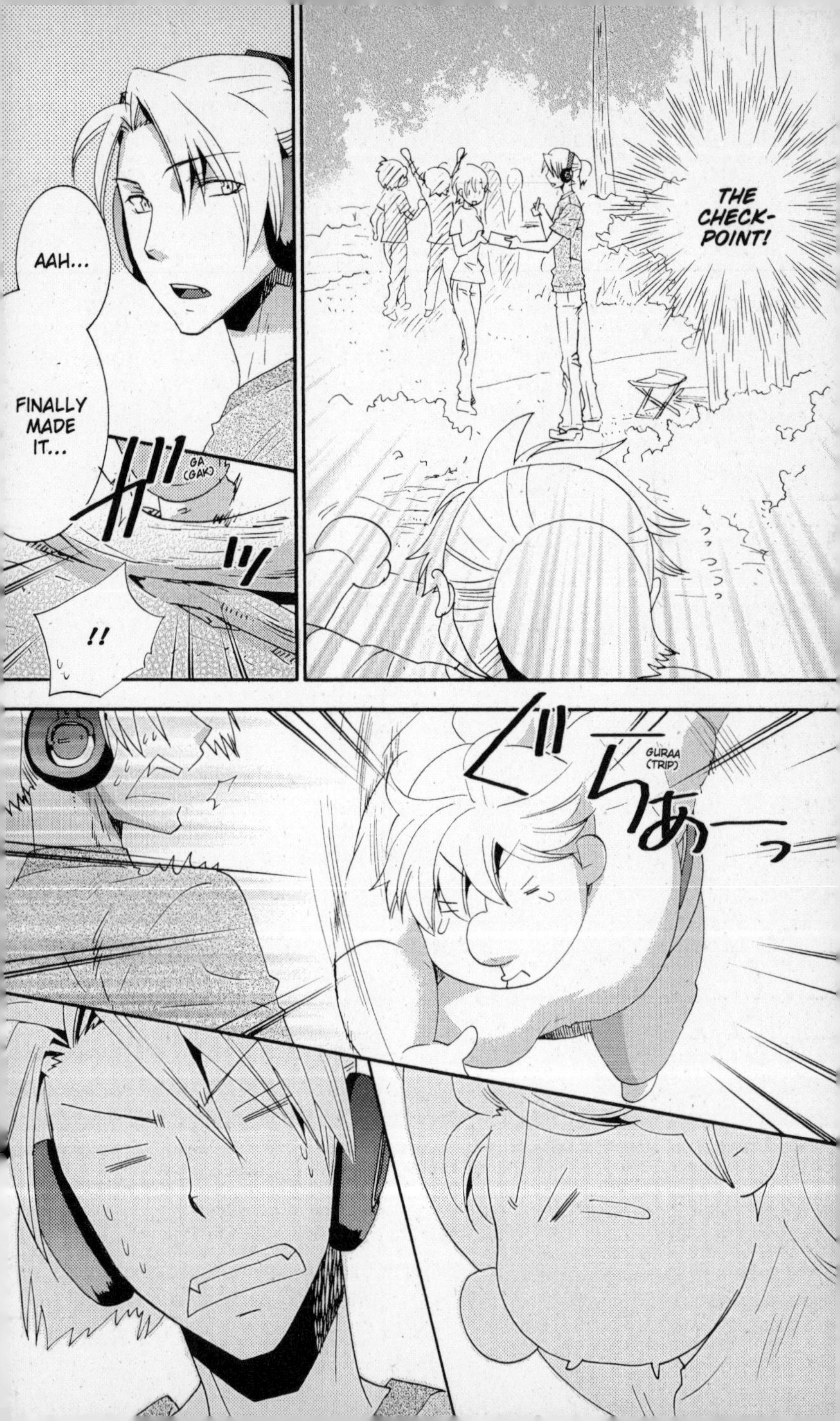
THE CHECK-POINT!
AAH...
FINALLY MADE IT...
ガッ
GA (GAK)
!!
ぐらあーっ
GURAA (TRIP)

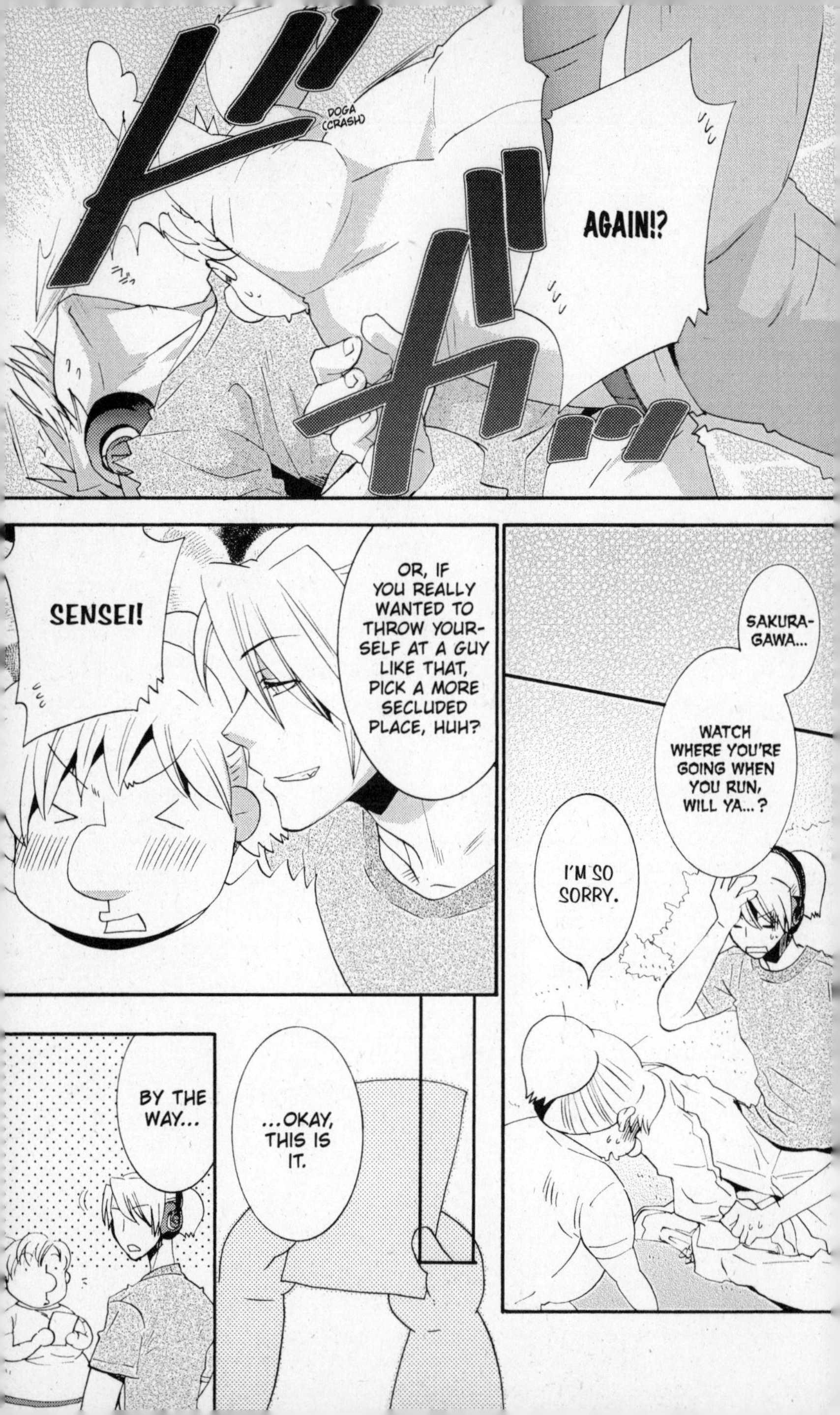
DOGA (CRASH)
AGAIN!?
SAKURA-GAWA...
WATCH WHERE YOU'RE GOING WHEN YOU RUN, WILL YA...?
I'M SO SORRY.
OR, IF YOU REALLY WANTED TO THROW YOUR-SELF AT A GUY LIKE THAT, PICK A MORE SECLUDED PLACE, HUH?
SENSEI!
...OKAY, THIS IS IT.
BY THE WAY...

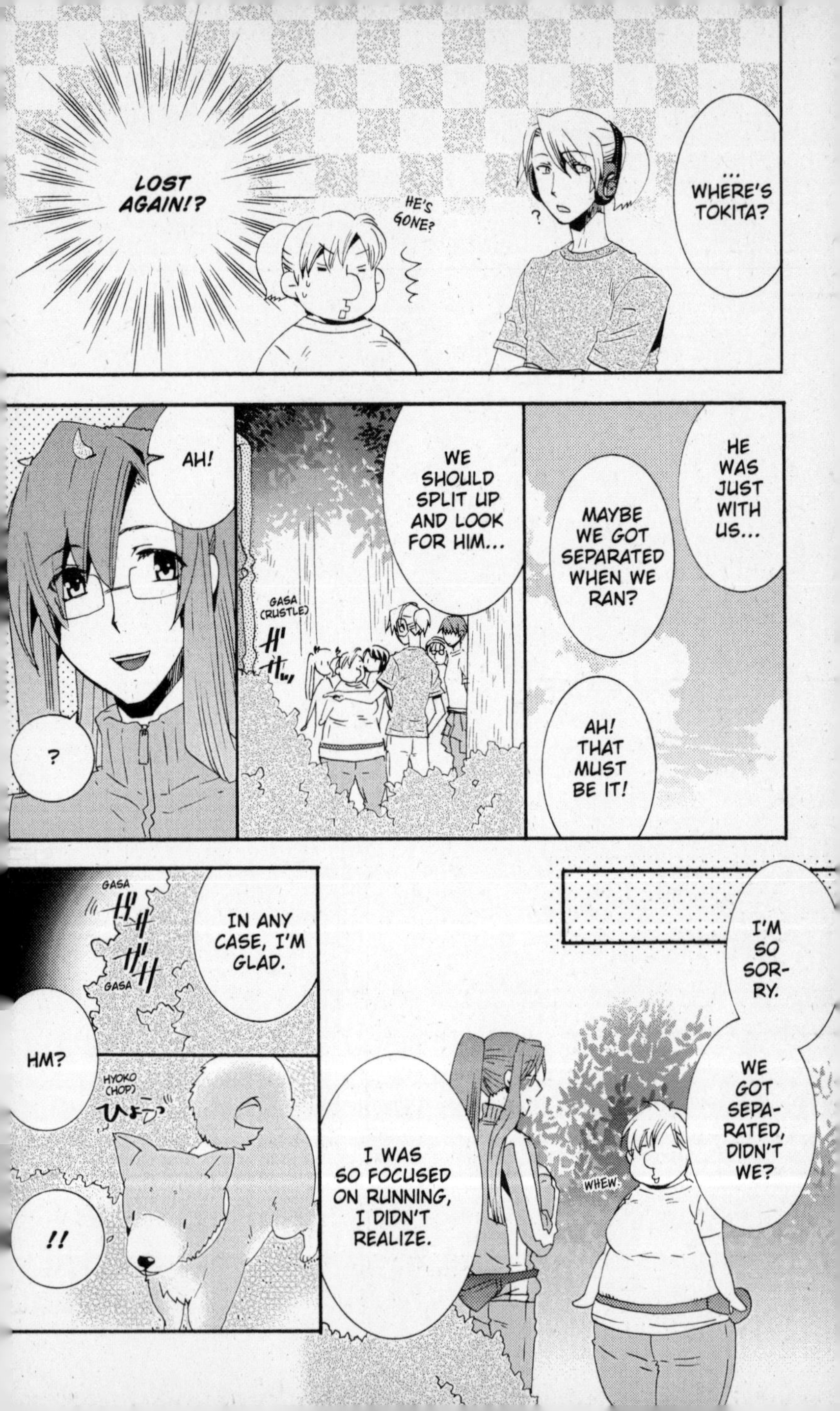

... WHERE'S TOKITA?
HE'S GONE?
LOST AGAIN!?
HE WAS JUST WITH US...
MAYBE WE GOT SEPARATED WHEN WE RAN?
AH! THAT MUST BE IT!
WE SHOULD SPLIT UP AND LOOK FOR HIM...
GASA (RUSTLE)
AH!
?
I'M SO SORRY.
WE GOT SEPA-RATED, DIDN'T WE?
WHEW.
I WAS SO FOCUSED ON RUNNING, I DIDN'T REALIZE.
IN ANY CASE, I'M GLAD.
GASA
GASA
HM?
HYOKO (HOP)
!!

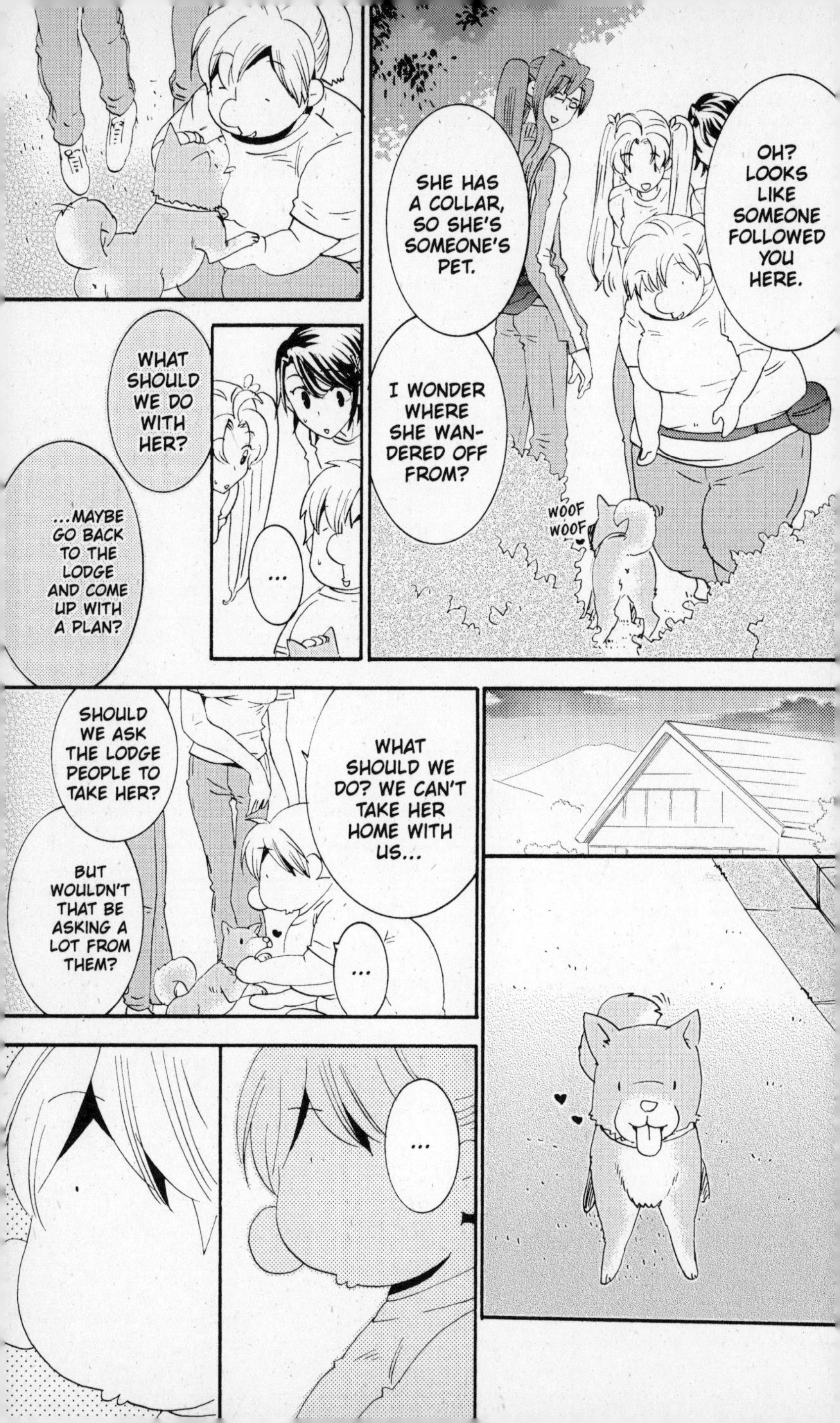
OH? LOOKS LIKE SOMEONE FOLLOWED YOU HERE.
SHE HAS A COLLAR, SO SHE'S SOMEONE'S PET.
I WONDER WHERE SHE WAN-DERED OFF FROM?
WOOF WOOF
...
WHAT SHOULD WE DO WITH HER?
...MAYBE GO BACK TO THE LODGE AND COME UP WITH A PLAN?
WHAT SHOULD WE DO? WE CAN'T TAKE HER HOME WITH US...
SHOULD WE ASK THE LODGE PEOPLE TO TAKE HER?
BUT WOULDN'T THAT BE ASKING A LOT FROM THEM?
...
...

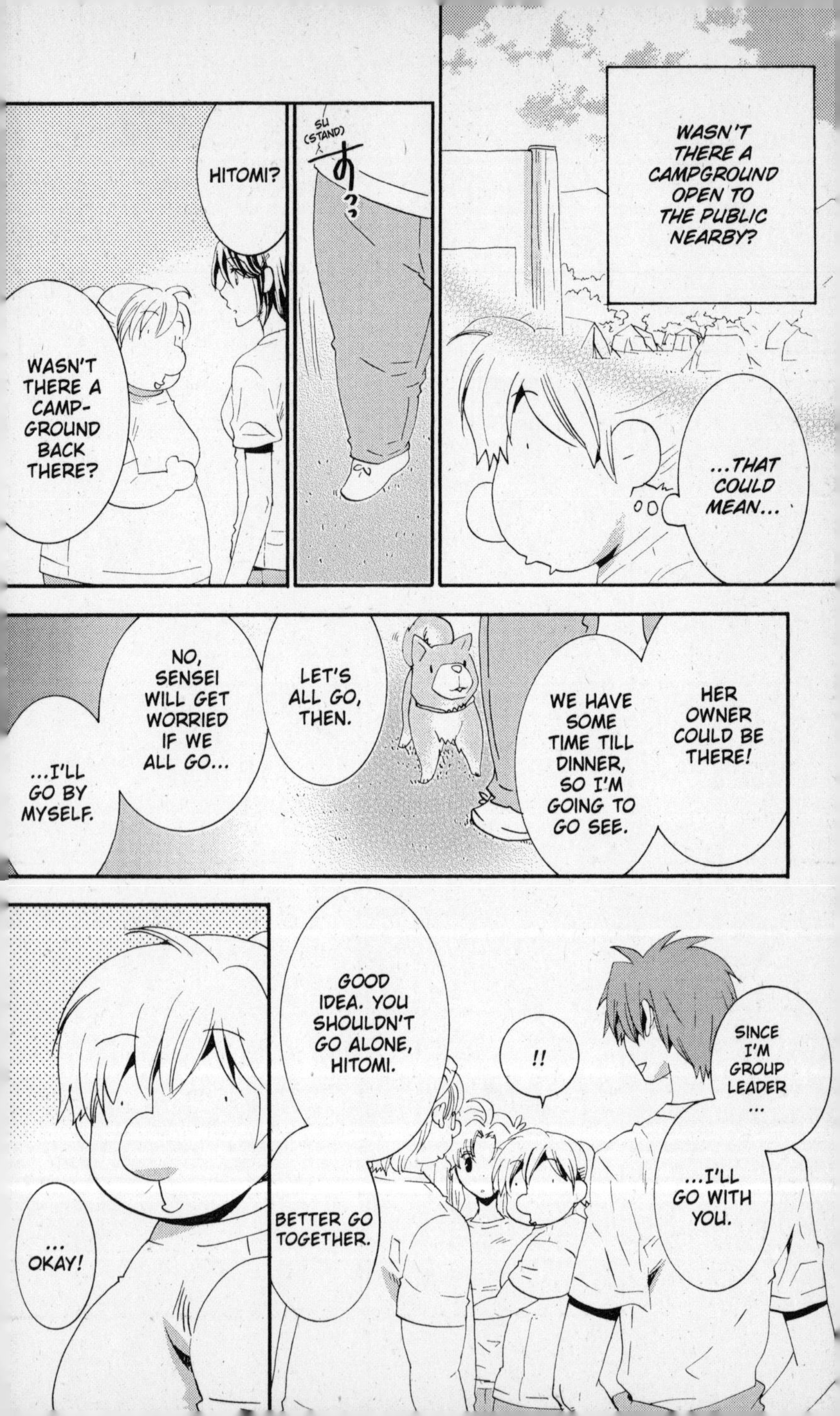
WASN'T THERE A CAMPGROUND OPEN TO THE PUBLIC NEARBY?
...THAT COULD MEAN...
SU (STAND)
す
HITOMI?
WASN'T THERE A CAMP-GROUND BACK THERE?
HER OWNER COULD BE THERE!
WE HAVE SOME TIME TILL DINNER, SO I'M GOING TO GO SEE.
LET'S ALL GO, THEN.
NO, SENSEI WILL GET WORRIED IF WE ALL GO...
...I'LL GO BY MYSELF.
SINCE I'M GROUP LEADER ...
...I'LL GO WITH YOU.
!!
GOOD IDEA. YOU SHOULDN'T GO ALONE, HITOMI.
BETTER GO TOGETHER.
... OKAY!

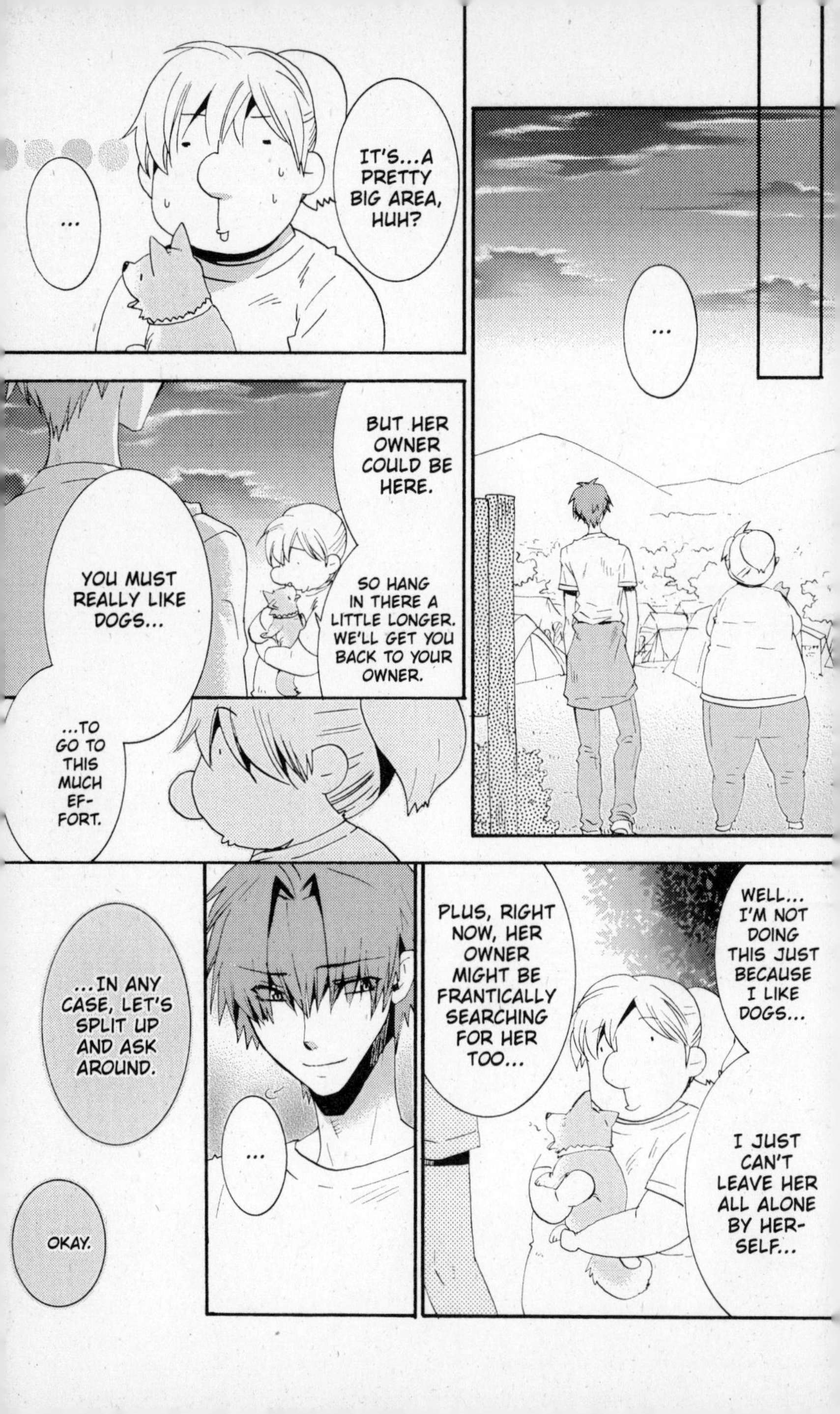
...
IT'S...A PRETTY BIG AREA, HUH?
...
BUT HER OWNER COULD BE HERE.
SO HANG IN THERE A LITTLE LONGER. WE'LL GET YOU BACK TO YOUR OWNER.
YOU MUST REALLY LIKE DOGS...
...TO GO TO THIS MUCH EF-FORT.
WELL... I'M NOT DOING THIS JUST BECAUSE I LIKE DOGS...
I JUST CAN'T LEAVE HER ALL ALONE BY HER-SELF...
PLUS, RIGHT NOW, HER OWNER MIGHT BE FRANTICALLY SEARCHING FOR HER TOO...
...
...IN ANY CASE, LET'S SPLIT UP AND ASK AROUND.
OKAY.

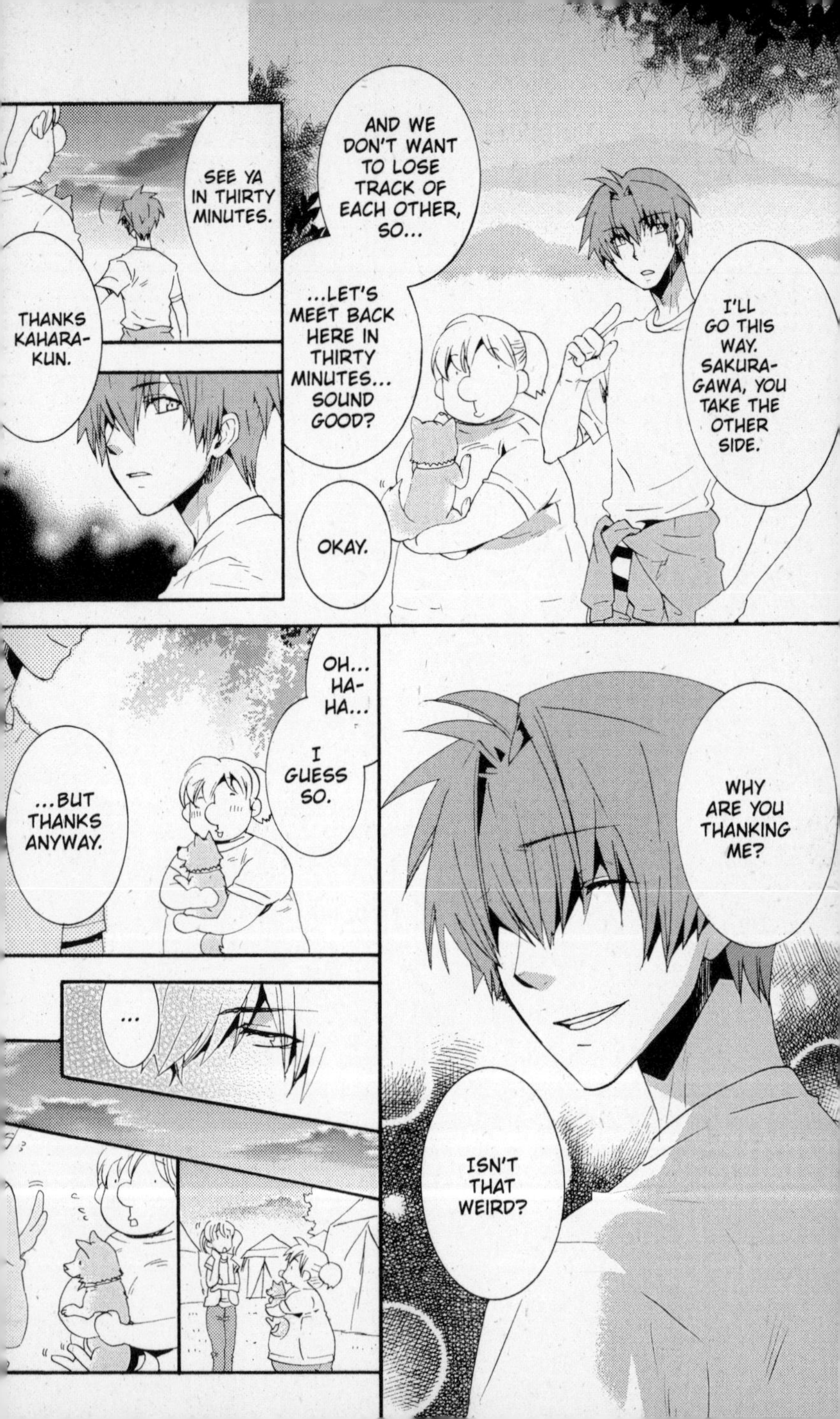
I'LL GO THIS WAY. SAKURA-GAWA, YOU TAKE THE OTHER SIDE.
AND WE DON'T WANT TO LOSE TRACK OF EACH OTHER, SO...
...LET'S MEET BACK HERE IN THIRTY MINUTES... SOUND GOOD?
OKAY.
SEE YA IN THIRTY MINUTES.
THANKS KAHARA-KUN.
WHY ARE YOU THANKING ME?
ISN'T THAT WEIRD?
OH... HA-HA...
I GUESS SO.
...BUT THANKS ANYWAY.
...

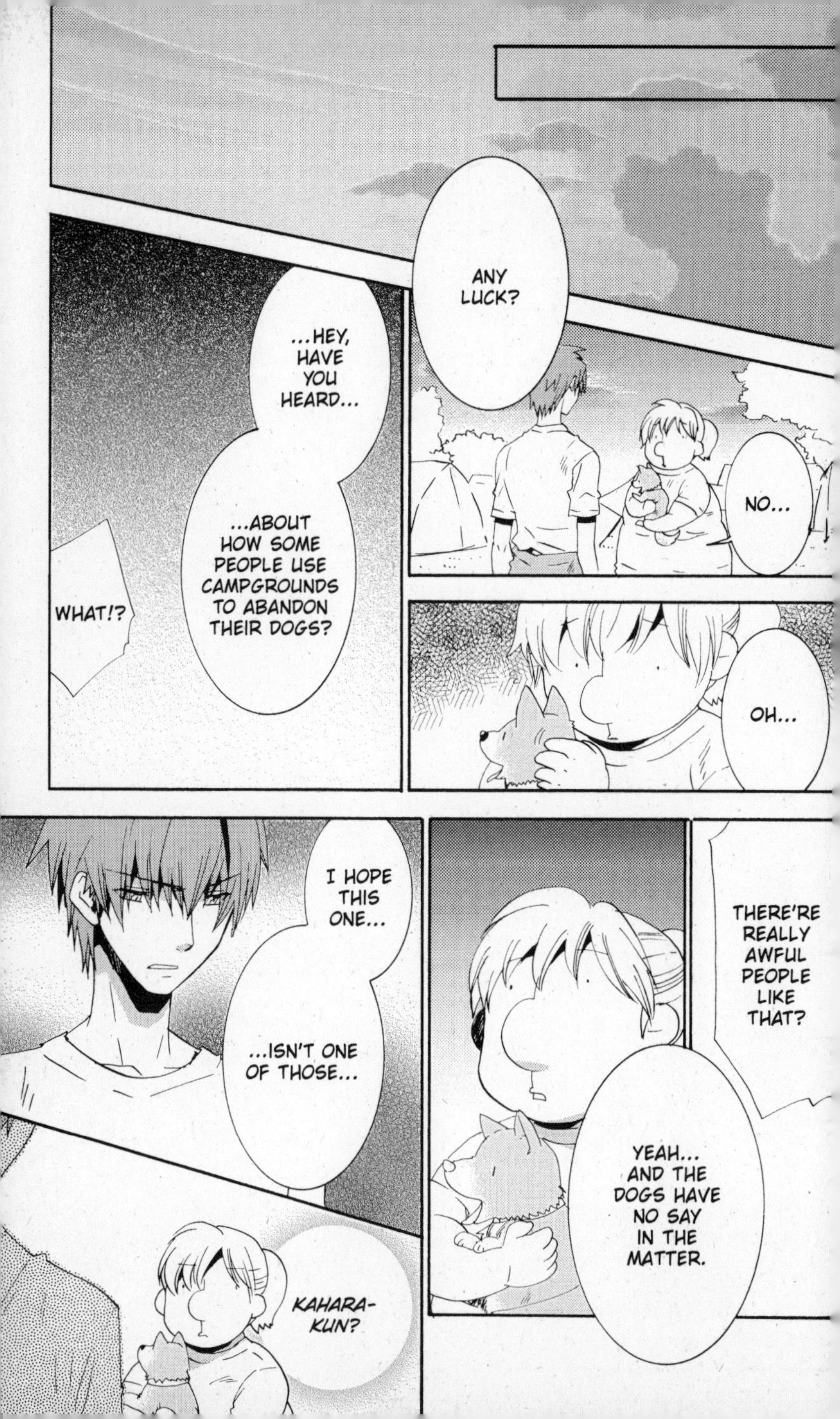
ANY LUCK?
NO...
OH...
...HEY, HAVE YOU HEARD...
...ABOUT HOW SOME PEOPLE USE CAMPGROUNDS TO ABANDON THEIR DOGS?
WHAT!?
THERE'RE REALLY AWFUL PEOPLE LIKE THAT?
YEAH... AND THE DOGS HAVE NO SAY IN THE MATTER.
I HOPE THIS ONE...
...ISN'T ONE OF THOSE...
KAHARA-KUN?

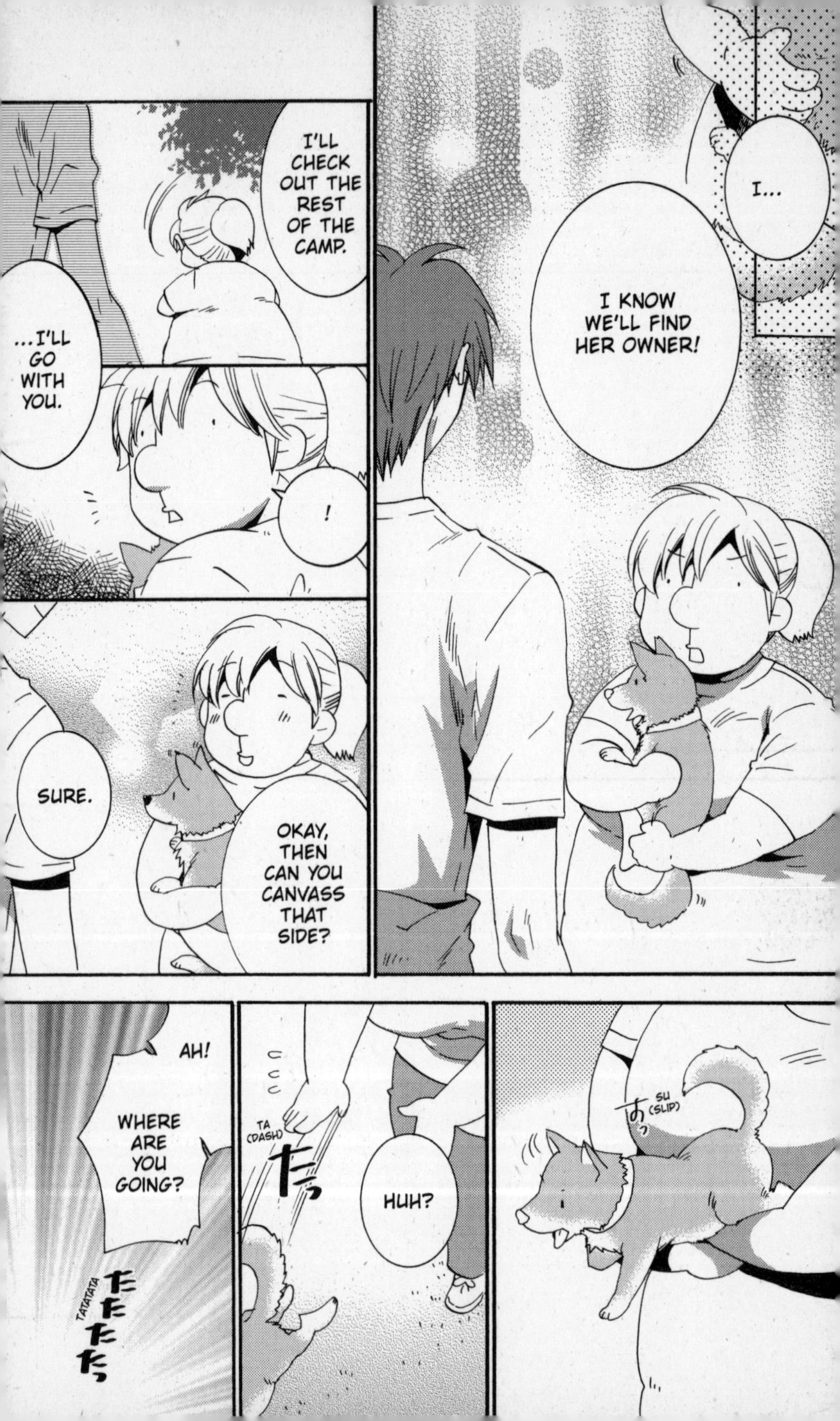
I...
I KNOW WE'LL FIND HER OWNER!
I'LL CHECK OUT THE REST OF THE CAMP.
...I'LL GO WITH YOU.
!
OKAY, THEN CAN YOU CANVASS THAT SIDE?
SURE.
すっ
SU (SLIP)
TA (DASH)
ダッ
HUH?
AH!
WHERE ARE YOU GOING?
TATATATA
たたたたっ

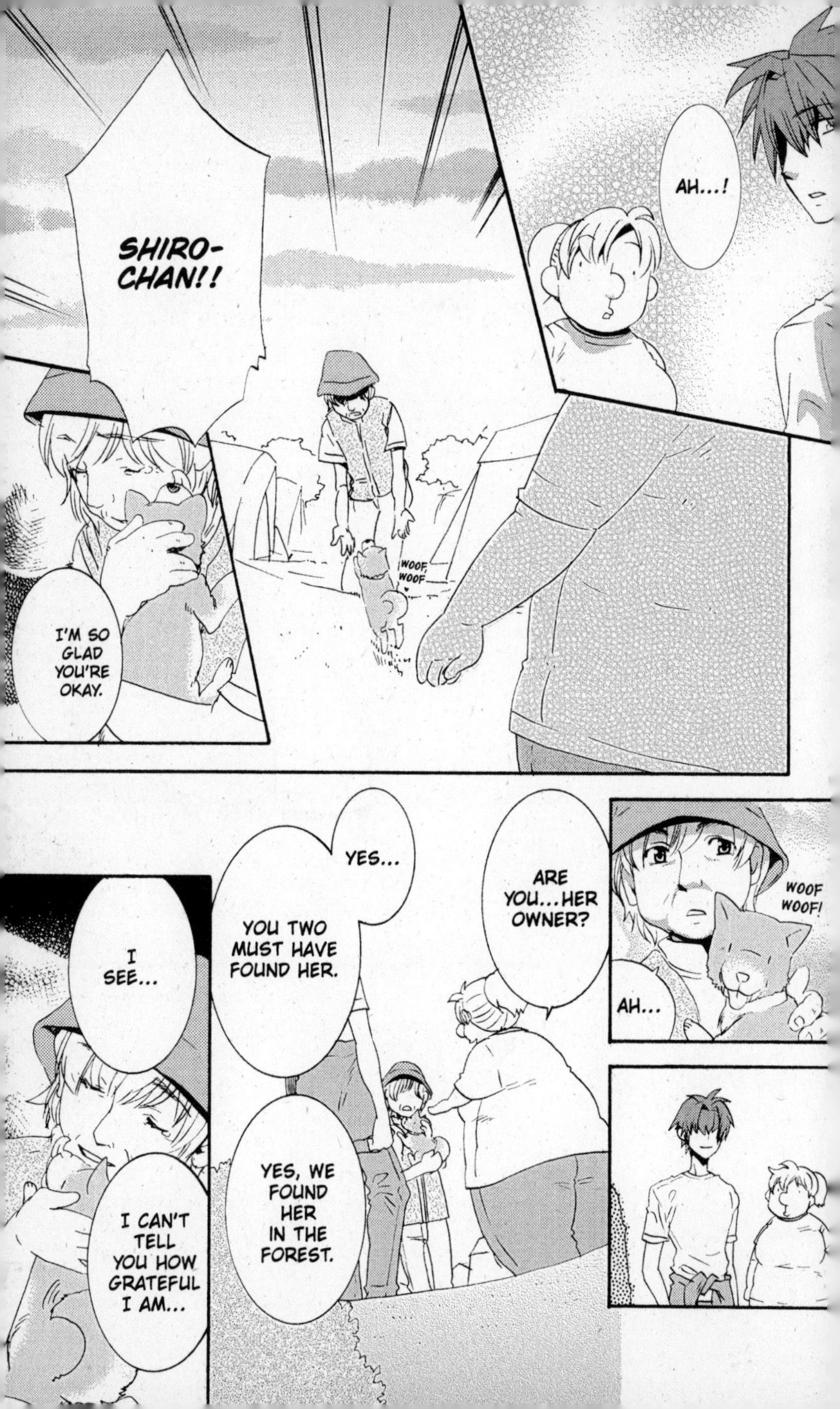
AH...!
SHIRO-CHAN!!
WOOF, WOOF
I'M SO GLAD YOU'RE OKAY.
WOOF WOOF!
AH...
ARE YOU...HER OWNER?
YES... YOU TWO MUST HAVE FOUND HER.
YES, WE FOUND HER IN THE FOREST.
I SEE...
I CAN'T TELL YOU HOW GRATEFUL I AM...

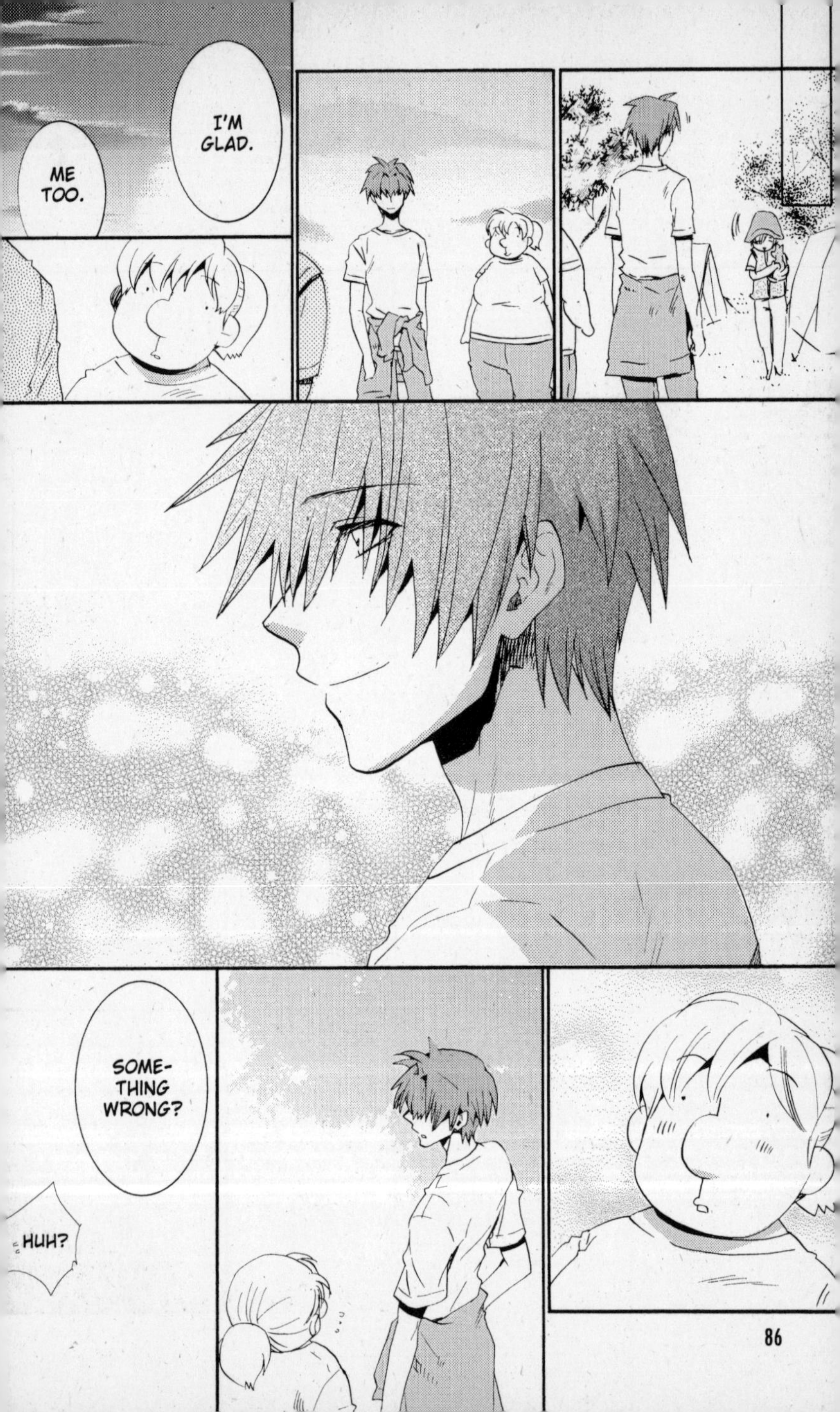
I'M GLAD.
ME TOO.
SOME-THING WRONG?
HUH?

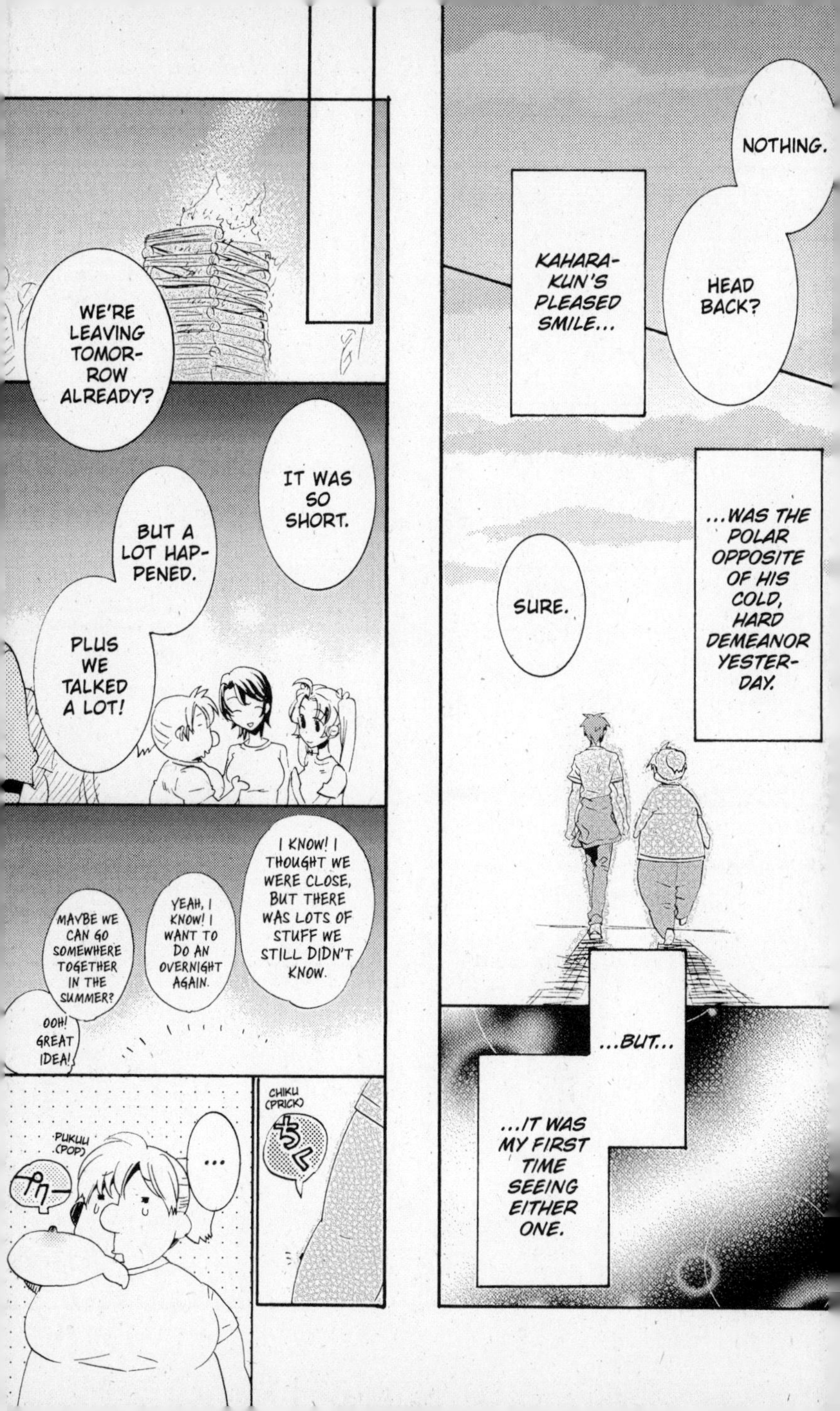
NOTHING.
HEAD BACK?
KAHARA-KUN'S PLEASED SMILE...
...WAS THE POLAR OPPOSITE OF HIS COLD, HARD DEMEANOR YESTERDAY.
SURE.
...BUT...
...IT WAS MY FIRST TIME SEEING EITHER ONE.
WE'RE LEAVING TOMORROW ALREADY?
IT WAS SO SHORT.
BUT A LOT HAPPENED.
PLUS WE TALKED A LOT!
I KNOW! I THOUGHT WE WERE CLOSE, BUT THERE WAS LOTS OF STUFF WE STILL DIDN'T KNOW.
YEAH, I KNOW! I WANT TO DO AN OVERNIGHT AGAIN.
MAYBE WE CAN GO SOMEWHERE TOGETHER IN THE SUMMER?
OOH! GREAT IDEA!
CHIKU (PRICK)
ちく
...
PUKUU (POP)
ぷくー

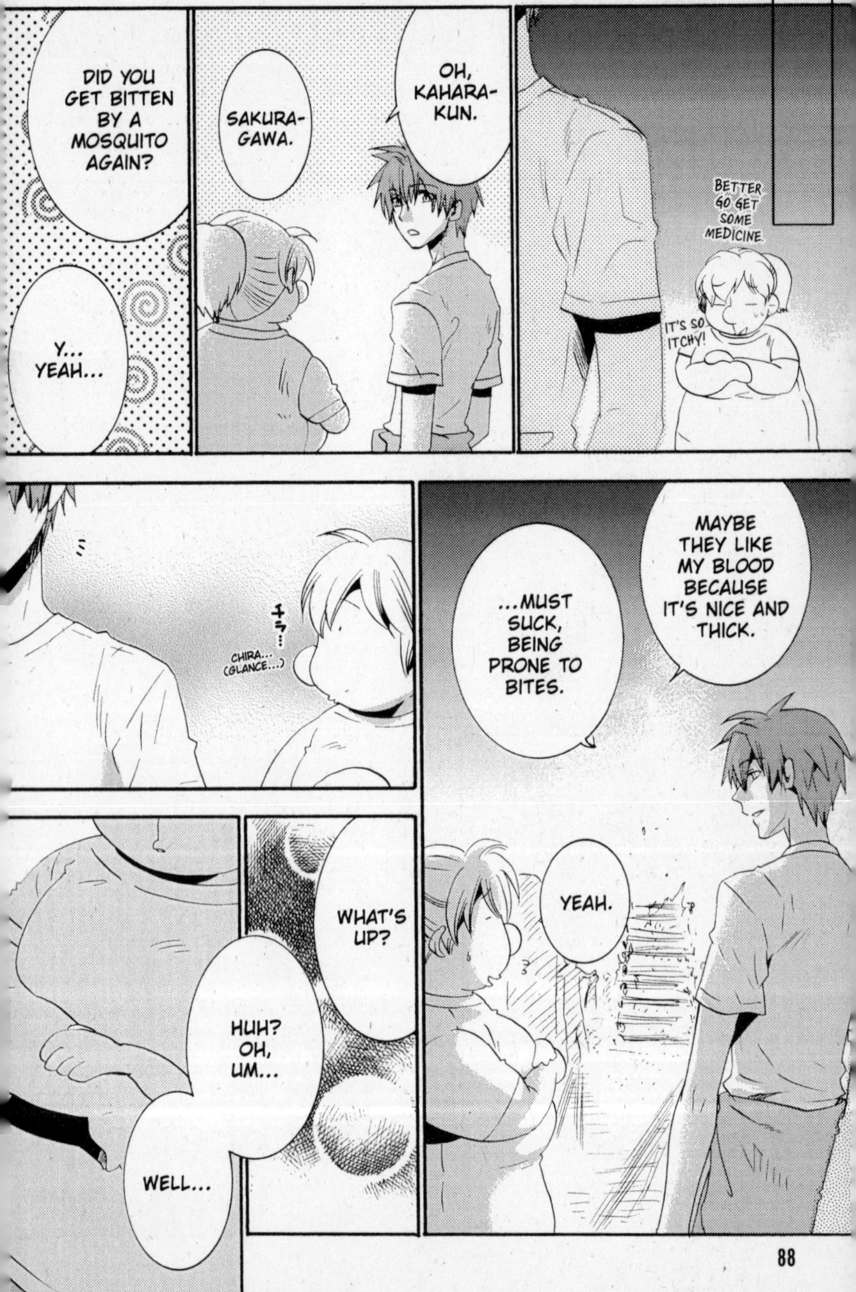
BETTER GO GET SOME MEDICINE.
IT'S SO ITCHY!
OH, KAHARA-KUN.
SAKURA-GAWA.
DID YOU GET BITTEN BY A MOSQUITO AGAIN?
Y... YEAH...
MAYBE THEY LIKE MY BLOOD BECAUSE IT'S NICE AND THICK.
...MUST SUCK, BEING PRONE TO BITES.
YEAH.
CHIRA... (GLANCE...)
WHAT'S UP?
HUH? OH, UM...
WELL...

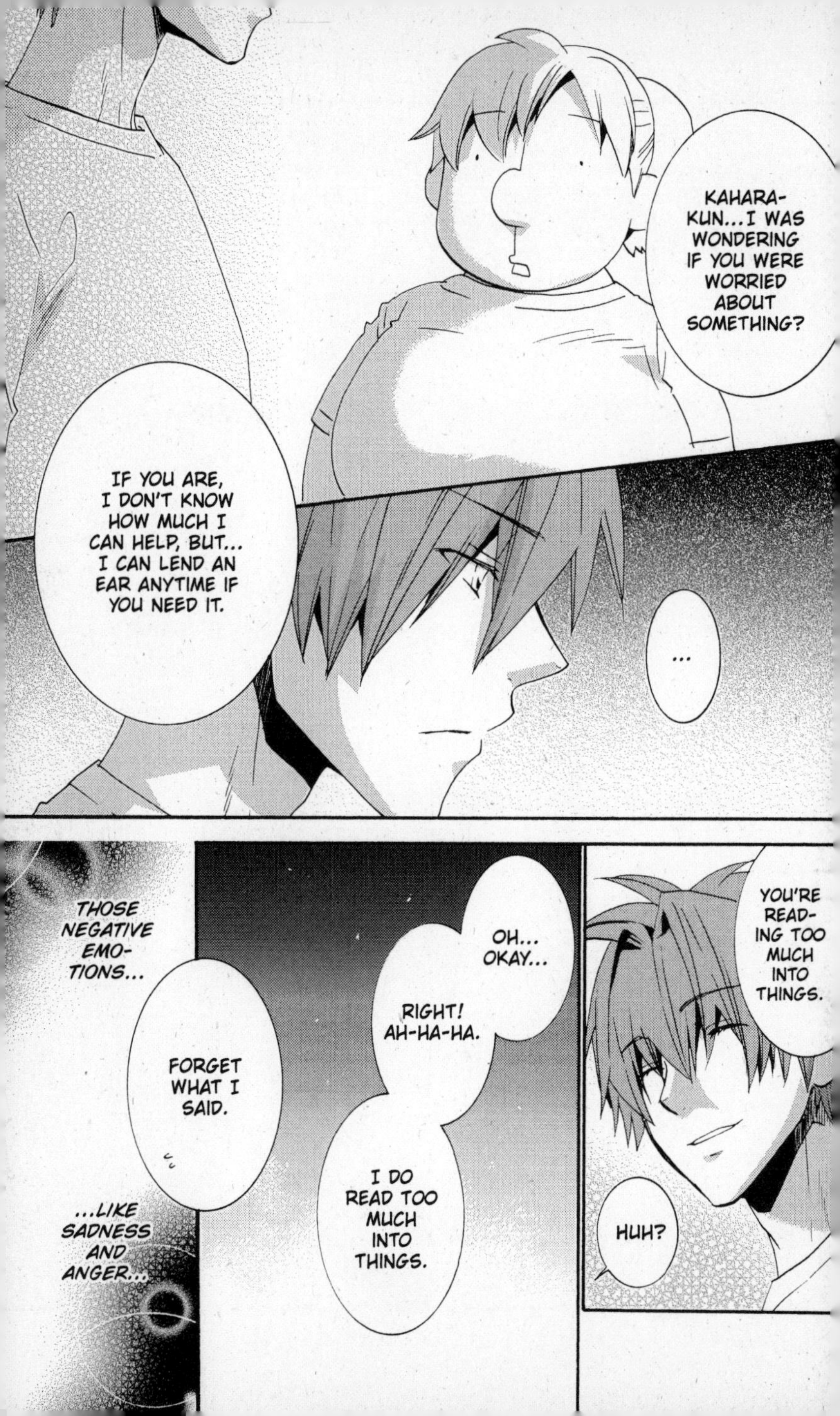
KAHARA-KUN... I WAS WONDERING IF YOU WERE WORRIED ABOUT SOMETHING?
IF YOU ARE, I DON'T KNOW HOW MUCH I CAN HELP, BUT... I CAN LEND AN EAR ANYTIME IF YOU NEED IT.
...
YOU'RE READING TOO MUCH INTO THINGS.
HUH?
OH... OKAY...
RIGHT! AH-HA-HA.
I DO READ TOO MUCH INTO THINGS.
FORGET WHAT I SAID.
THOSE NEGATIVE EMOTIONS...
...LIKE SADNESS AND ANGER...

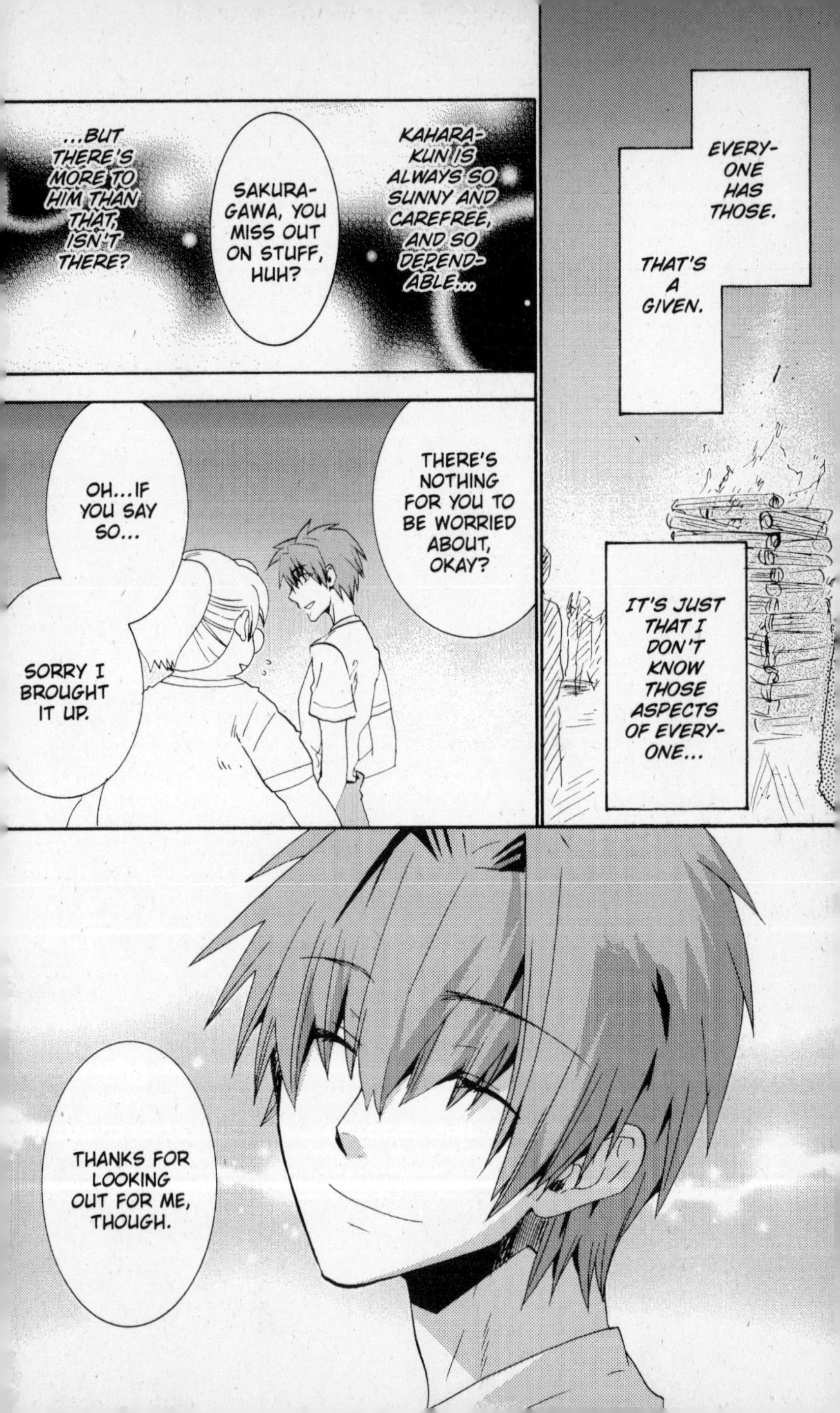
EVERY-ONE HAS THOSE.
THAT'S A GIVEN.
IT'S JUST THAT I DON'T KNOW THOSE ASPECTS OF EVERY-ONE...
KAHARA-KUN IS ALWAYS SO SUNNY AND CAREFREE, AND SO DEPEND-ABLE...
SAKURA-GAWA, YOU MISS OUT ON STUFF, HUH?
...BUT THERE'S MORE TO HIM THAN THAT, ISN'T THERE?
THERE'S NOTHING FOR YOU TO BE WORRIED ABOUT, OKAY?
OH...IF YOU SAY SO...
SORRY I BROUGHT IT UP.
THANKS FOR LOOKING OUT FOR ME, THOUGH.

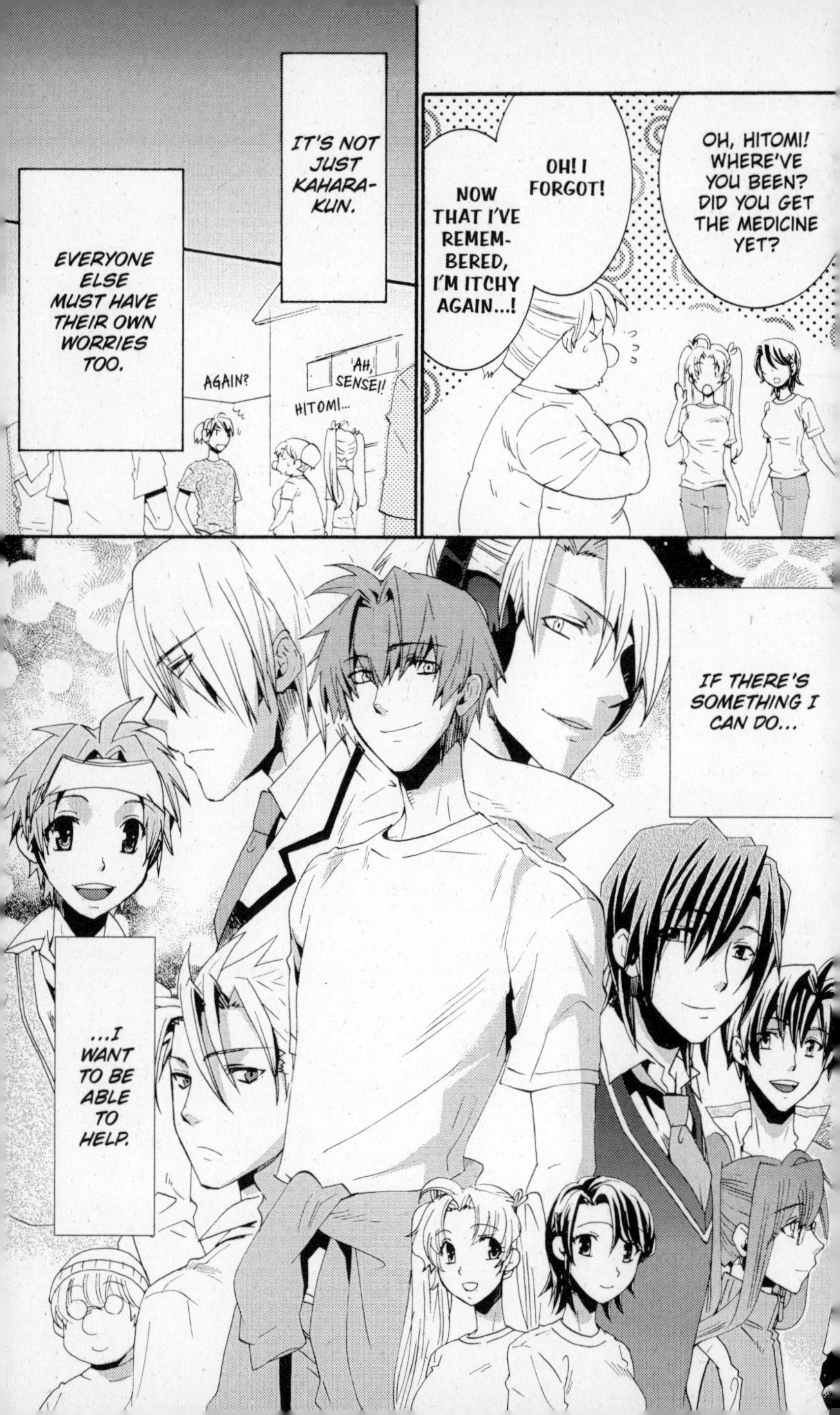
OH, HITOMI! WHERE'VE YOU BEEN? DID YOU GET THE MEDICINE YET?
OH! I FORGOT!
NOW THAT I'VE REMEMBERED, I'M ITCHY AGAIN...!
IT'S NOT JUST KAHARA-KUN.
EVERYONE ELSE MUST HAVE THEIR OWN WORRIES TOO.
AH, SENSEI!
HITOMI...
AGAIN?
IF THERE'S SOMETHING I CAN DO...
...I WANT TO BE ABLE TO HELP.

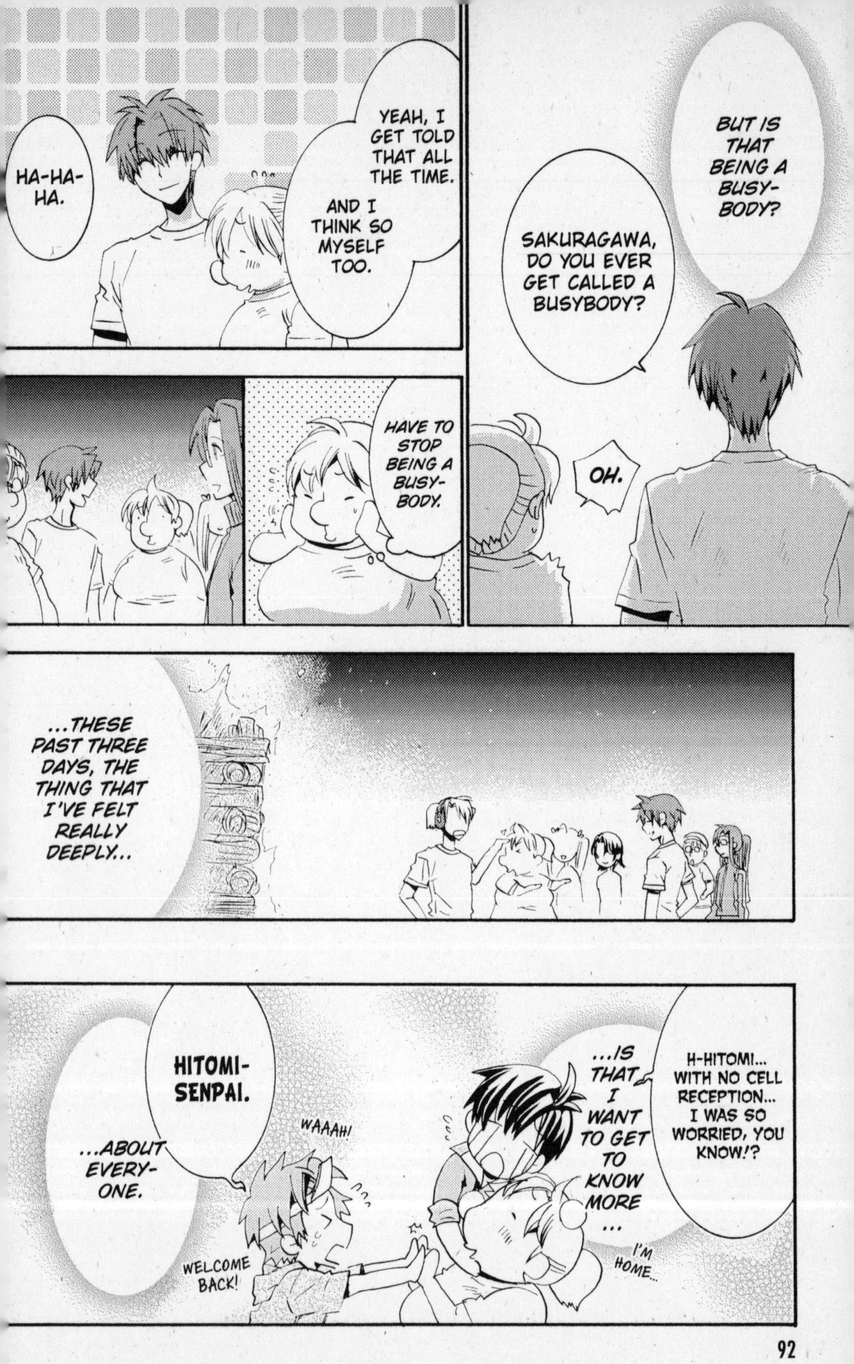
BUT IS THAT BEING A BUSY-BODY?
SAKURAGAWA, DO YOU EVER GET CALLED A BUSYBODY?
OH.
YEAH, I GET TOLD THAT ALL THE TIME.
AND I THINK SO MYSELF TOO.
HA-HA-HA.
HAVE TO STOP BEING A BUSY-BODY.
...THESE PAST THREE DAYS, THE THING THAT I'VE FELT REALLY DEEPLY...
H-HITOMI... WITH NO CELL RECEPTION... I WAS SO WORRIED, YOU KNOW!?
...IS THAT I WANT TO GET TO KNOW MORE...
I'M HOME...
WAAAH!
HITOMI-SENPAI.
WELCOME BACK!
...ABOUT EVERY-ONE.

LOVEREVO!!

UGLY DUCKLING'S LOVE REVOLUTION

OUR HEROINE IS A 220-POUND HIGH SCHOOL SOPHOMORE. ONE DAY, A GROUP OF THE MOST GORGEOUS GUYS...LIKE THE SCHOOL'S #1 COOL GUY AND THE DOC WITH A REPUTATION AS LADIES' MAN... MOVES INTO HER FATHER'S APARTMENT COMPLEX!! WHAT NOW...!?

STORY CHARACTERS

HITOMI SAKURAGAWA

FAMOUS FOR HER BEAUTY WHEN SHE WAS LITTLE, SHE FELL PREY TO THE SEDUCTION OF SWEETS. BEFORE SHE REALIZED IT, SHE HAD SWELLED TO 220 LBS. OPTIMISTIC AND BRIGHT. A HIGH SCHOOL SOPHOMORE WORKING HARD ON HER DIET.

HITOMI'S BROTHER

HITOMI'S OLDER BROTHER. THINKS HIS SISTER IS THE CUTEST PERSON IN THE WORLD. AVIDLY CHEERS HER ON WITH HER DIET. WORKING AS THE APARTMENT MANAGER FOR WHERE THE OTHER STORY CHARACTERS LIVE.

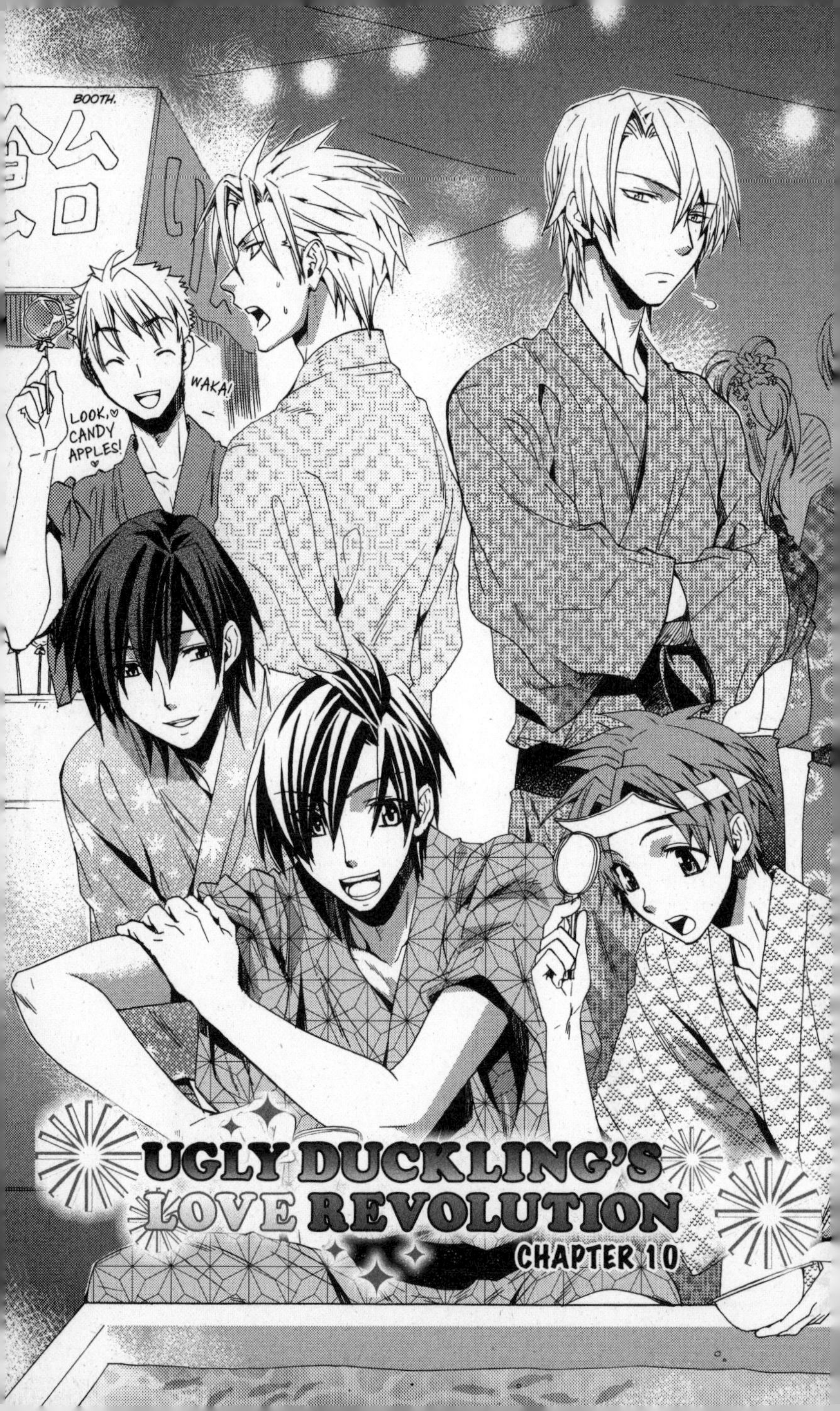
BOOTH.
WAKA!
LOOK, CANDY APPLES!
UGLY DUCKLING'S LOVE REVOLUTION
CHAPTER 10

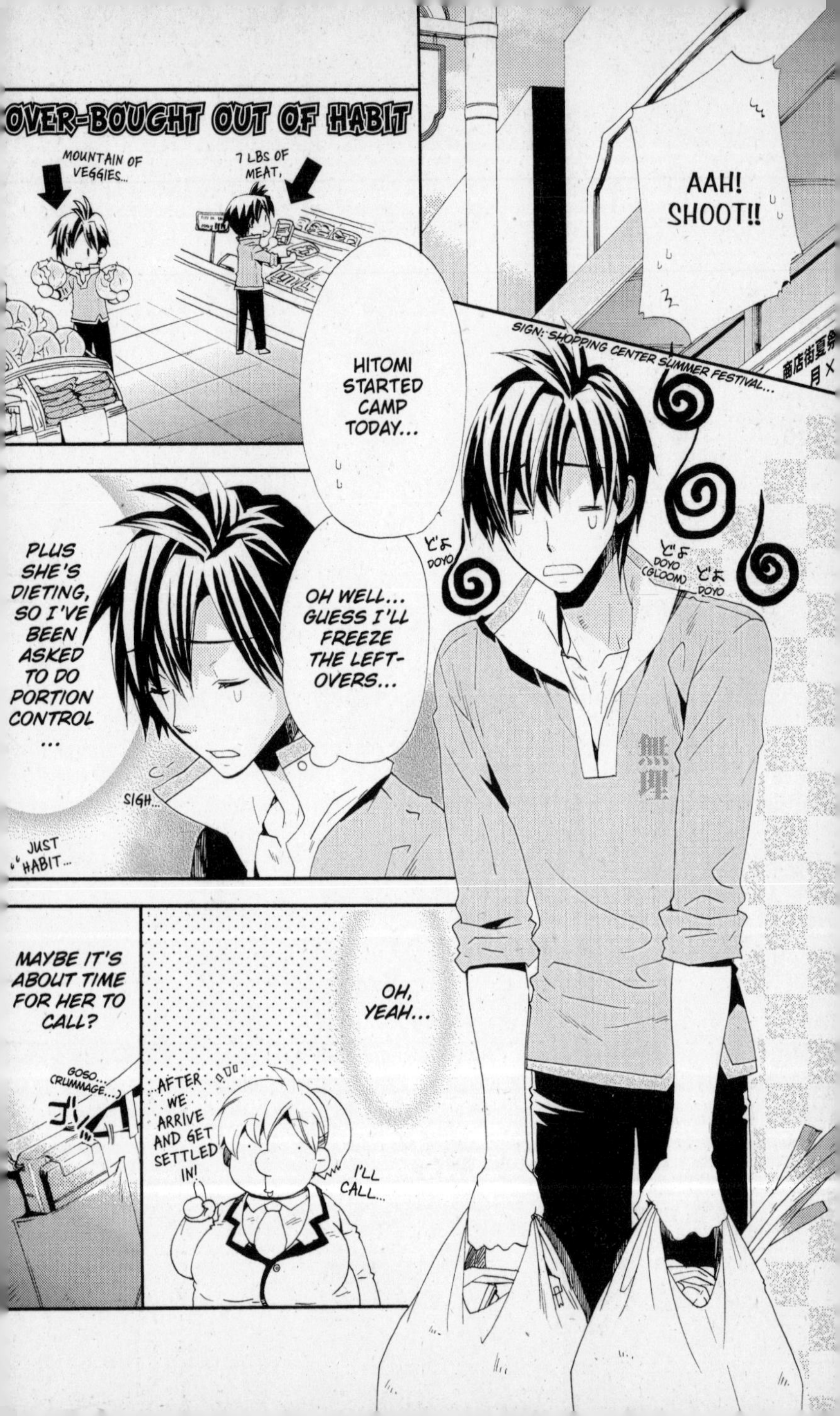
AAH! SHOOT!!
SIGN: SHOPPING CENTER SUMMER FESTIVAL...
商店街夏祭
月 ×
HITOMI STARTED CAMP TODAY...
OH WELL... GUESS I'LL FREEZE THE LEFT-OVERS...
どよ DOYO
どよ DOYO (GLOOM)
どよ DOYO
無理
OVER-BOUGHT OUT OF HABIT
7 LBS OF MEAT,
MOUNTAIN OF VEGGIES...
PLUS SHE'S DIETING, SO I'VE BEEN ASKED TO DO PORTION CONTROL ...
SIGH...
JUST HABIT...
OH, YEAH...
MAYBE IT'S ABOUT TIME FOR HER TO CALL?
...AFTER WE ARRIVE AND GET SETTLED IN!
I'LL CALL...
GOSO... (RUMMAGE...)

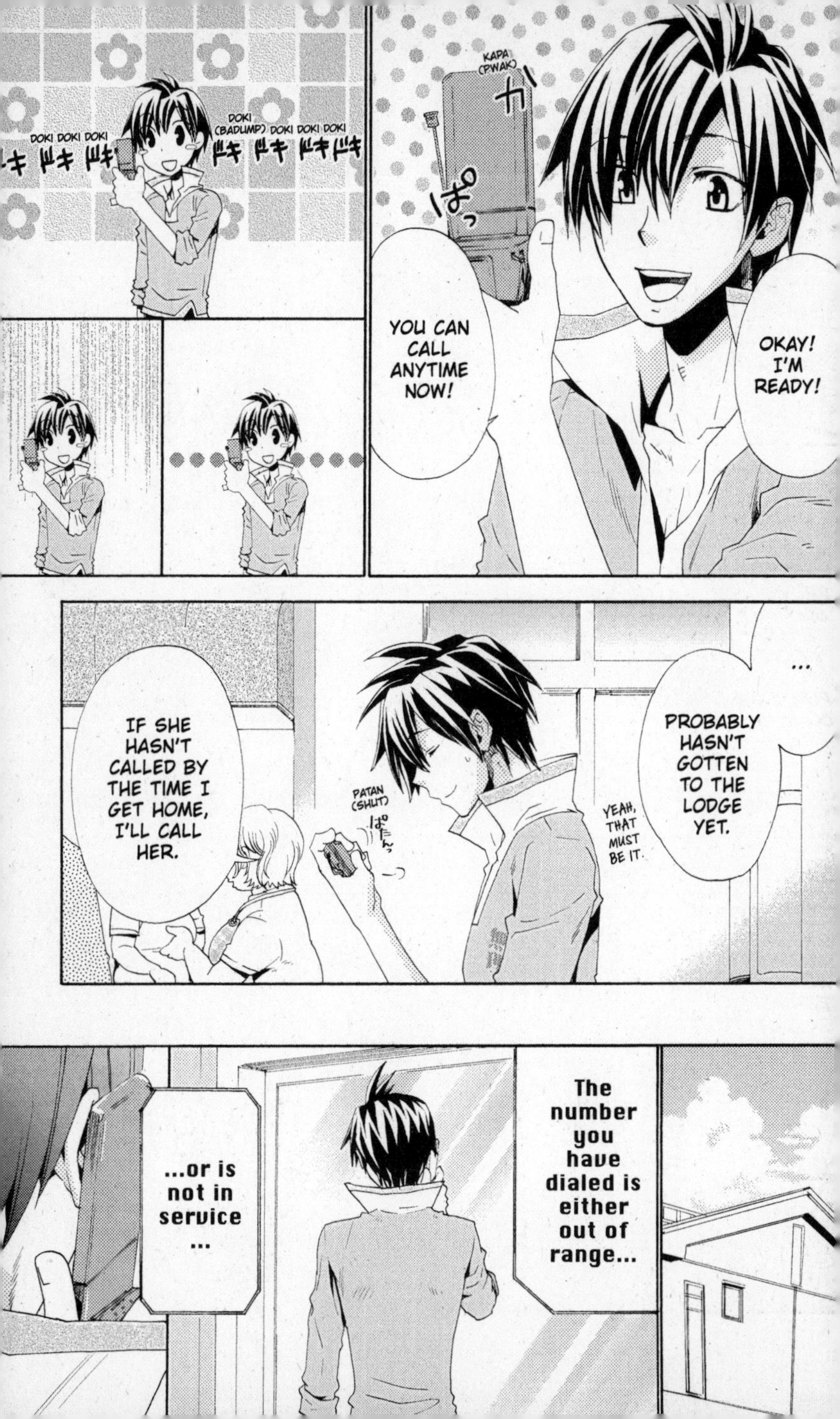
KAPA (PWAK)
OKAY! I'M READY!
YOU CAN CALL ANYTIME NOW!
DOKI (BADUMP) DOKI DOKI DOKI
DOKI DOKI DOKI
...
PROBABLY HASN'T GOTTEN TO THE LODGE YET.
YEAH, THAT MUST BE IT.
PATAN (SHUT)
IF SHE HASN'T CALLED BY THE TIME I GET HOME, I'LL CALL HER.
The number you have dialed is either out of range...
...or is not in service ...

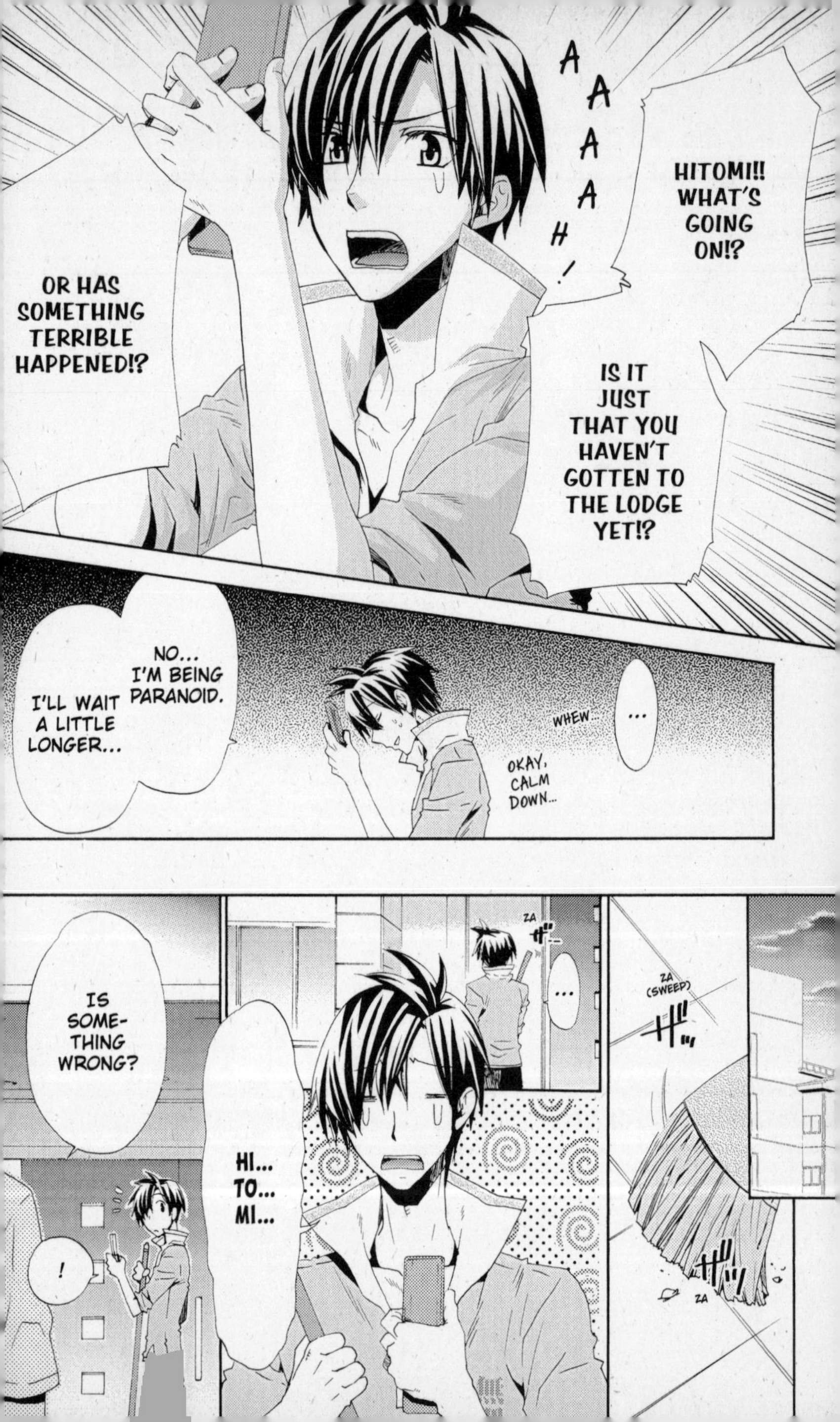
AAAAH!
HITOMI!! WHAT'S GOING ON!?
IS IT JUST THAT YOU HAVEN'T GOTTEN TO THE LODGE YET!?
OR HAS SOMETHING TERRIBLE HAPPENED!?
...
WHEW...
OKAY, CALM DOWN...
NO... I'M BEING PARANOID.
I'LL WAIT A LITTLE LONGER...
ZA (SWEEP)
ZA
ZA
...
HI... TO... MI...
IS SOMETHING WRONG?
!

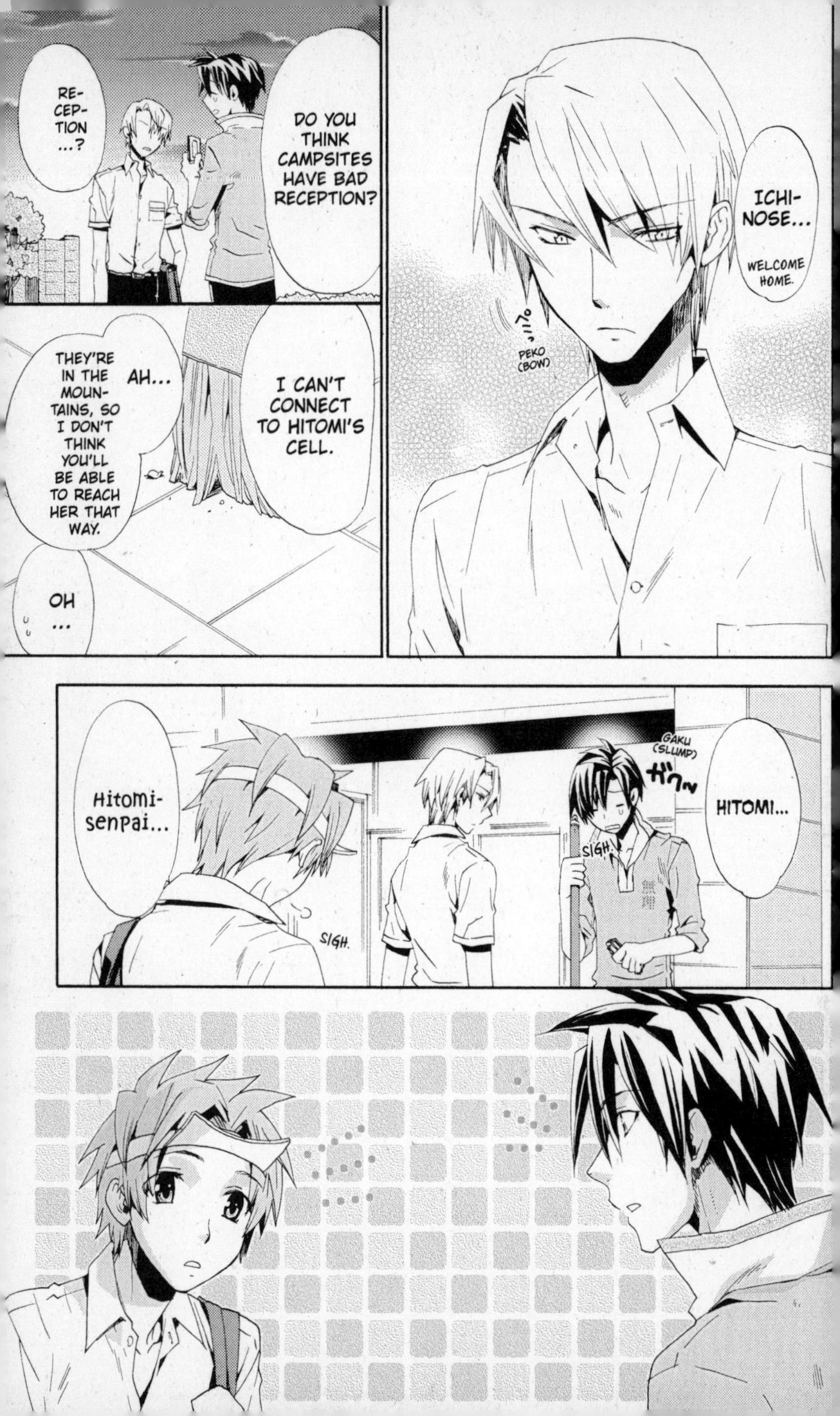
ICHI-NOSE...
WELCOME HOME.
PEKO (BOW)
DO YOU THINK CAMPSITES HAVE BAD RECEPTION?
RE-CEP-TION ...?
I CAN'T CONNECT TO HITOMI'S CELL.
AH...
THEY'RE IN THE MOUN-TAINS, SO I DON'T THINK YOU'LL BE ABLE TO REACH HER THAT WAY.
OH ...
HITOMI...
GAKU (SLUMP)
SIGH.
Hitomi-senpai...
SIGH.

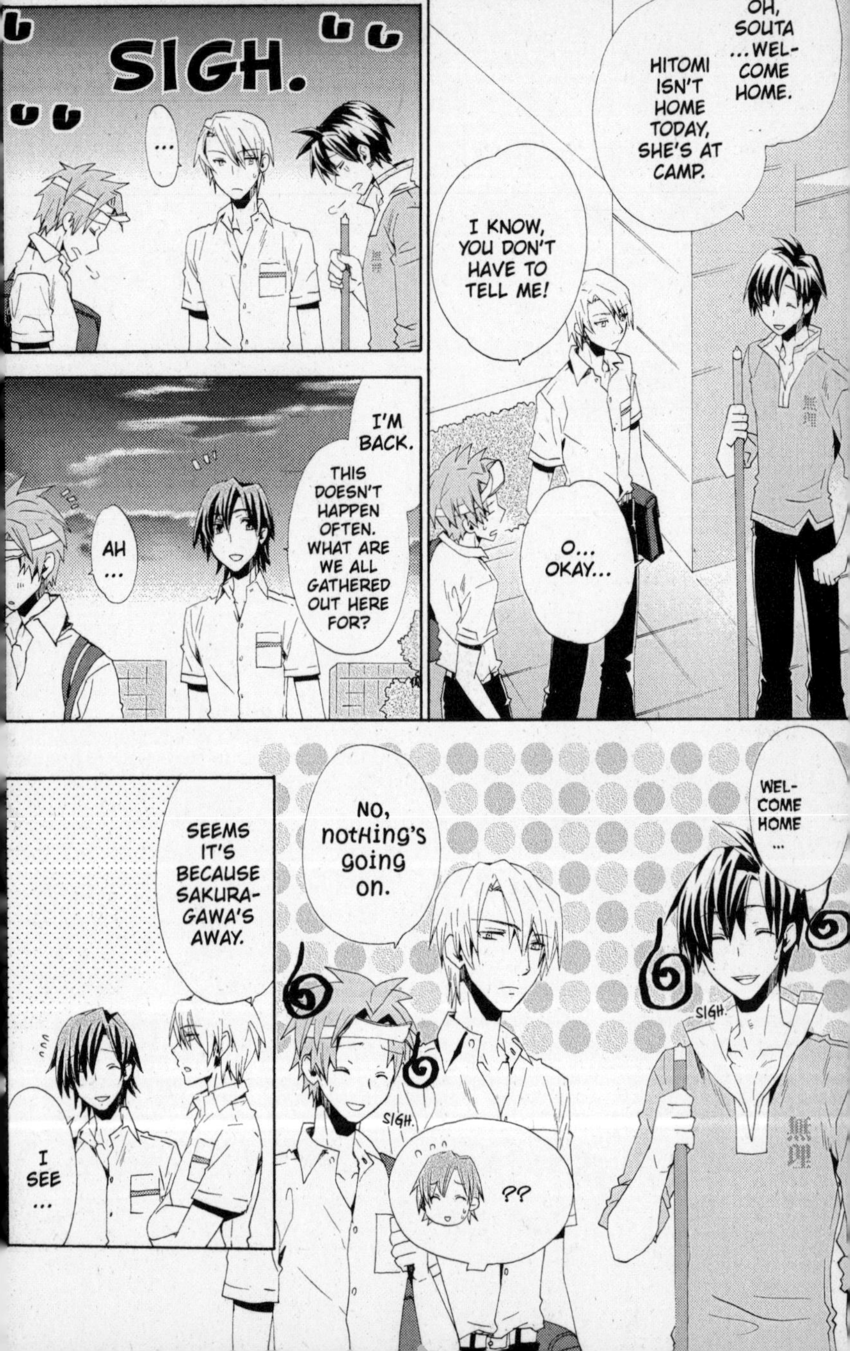

OH, SOUTA ...WELCOME HOME.
HITOMI ISN'T HOME TODAY, SHE'S AT CAMP.
I KNOW, YOU DON'T HAVE TO TELL ME!
O... OKAY...
SIGH.
...
I'M BACK.
THIS DOESN'T HAPPEN OFTEN. WHAT ARE WE ALL GATHERED OUT HERE FOR?
AH ...
WELCOME HOME ...
SIGH.
NO, nothing's going on.
SIGH.
??
SEEMS IT'S BECAUSE SAKURAGAWA'S AWAY.
I SEE ...

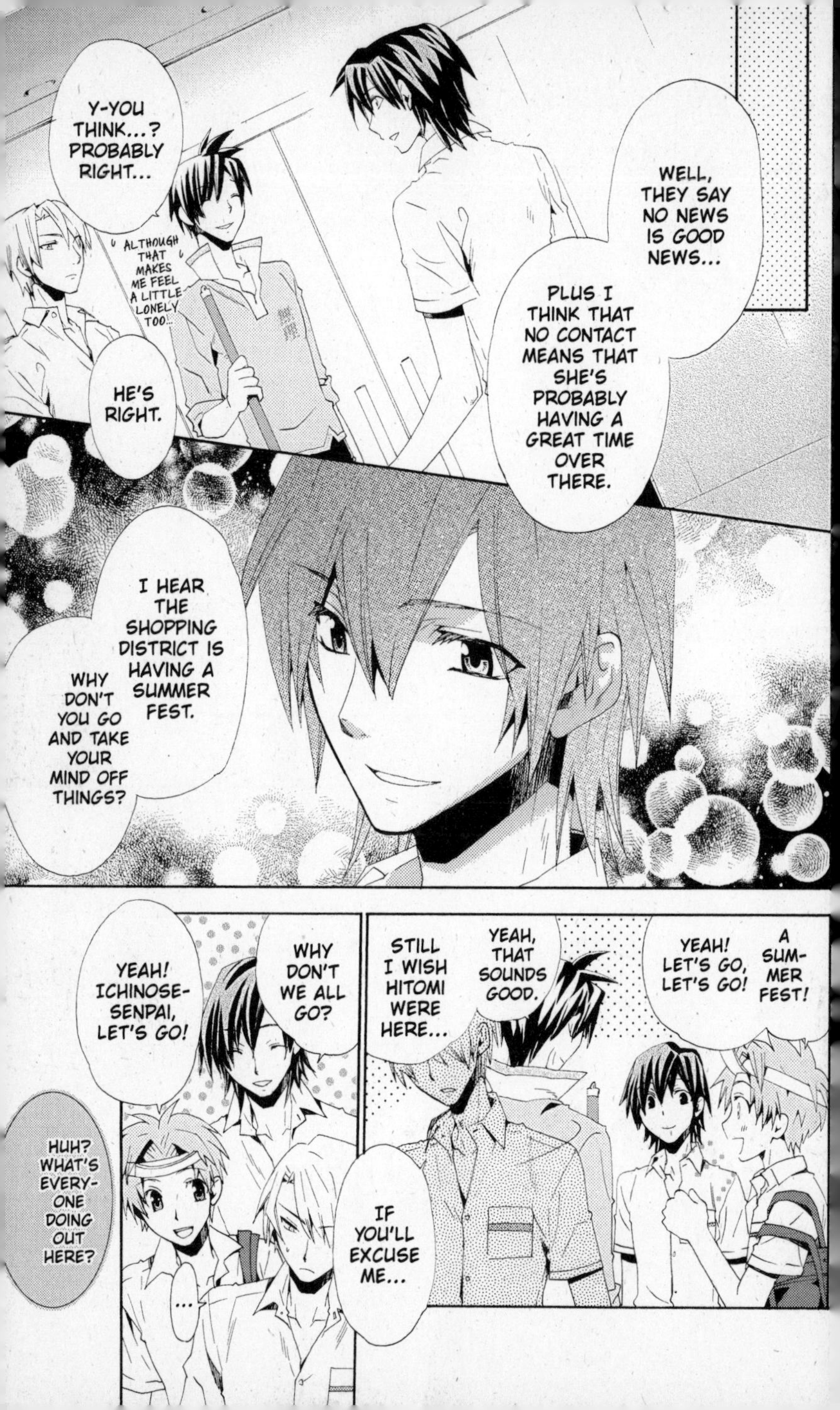
WELL, THEY SAY NO NEWS IS GOOD NEWS...
PLUS I THINK THAT NO CONTACT MEANS THAT SHE'S PROBABLY HAVING A GREAT TIME OVER THERE.
Y-YOU THINK...? PROBABLY RIGHT...
ALTHOUGH THAT MAKES ME FEEL A LITTLE LONELY TOO...
HE'S RIGHT.
I HEAR THE SHOPPING DISTRICT IS HAVING A SUMMER FEST.
WHY DON'T YOU GO AND TAKE YOUR MIND OFF THINGS?
A SUMMER FEST!
YEAH! LET'S GO, LET'S GO!
YEAH, THAT SOUNDS GOOD.
STILL I WISH HITOMI WERE HERE...
WHY DON'T WE ALL GO?
YEAH! ICHINOSE-SENPAI, LET'S GO!
HUH? WHAT'S EVERYONE DOING OUT HERE?
...
IF YOU'LL EXCUSE ME...

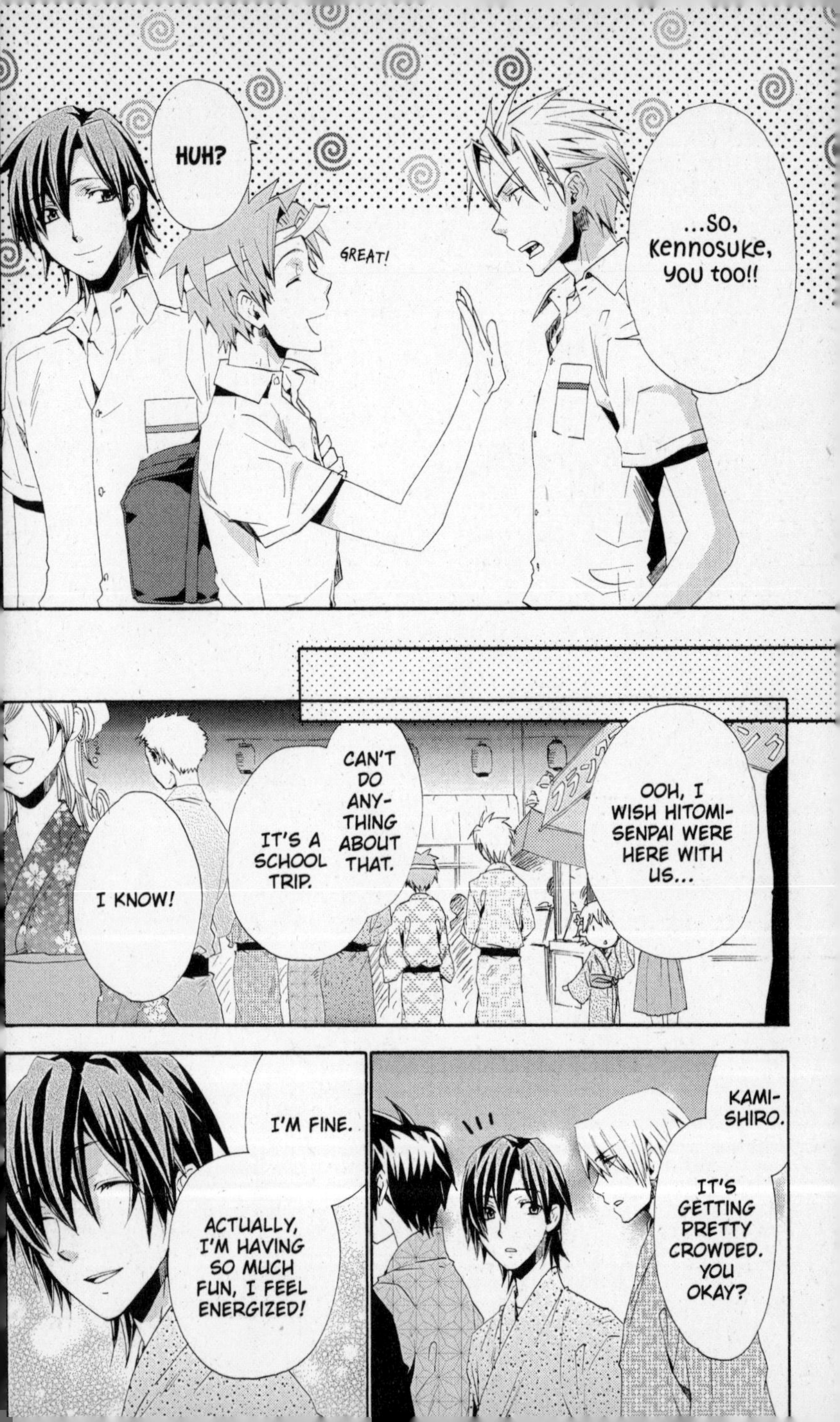
...So, Kennosuke, you too!!
GREAT!
HUH?
OOH, I WISH HITOMI-SENPAI WERE HERE WITH US...
CAN'T DO ANY-THING ABOUT THAT.
IT'S A SCHOOL TRIP.
I KNOW!
KAMI-SHIRO.
IT'S GETTING PRETTY CROWDED. YOU OKAY?
I'M FINE.
ACTUALLY, I'M HAVING SO MUCH FUN, I FEEL ENERGIZED!

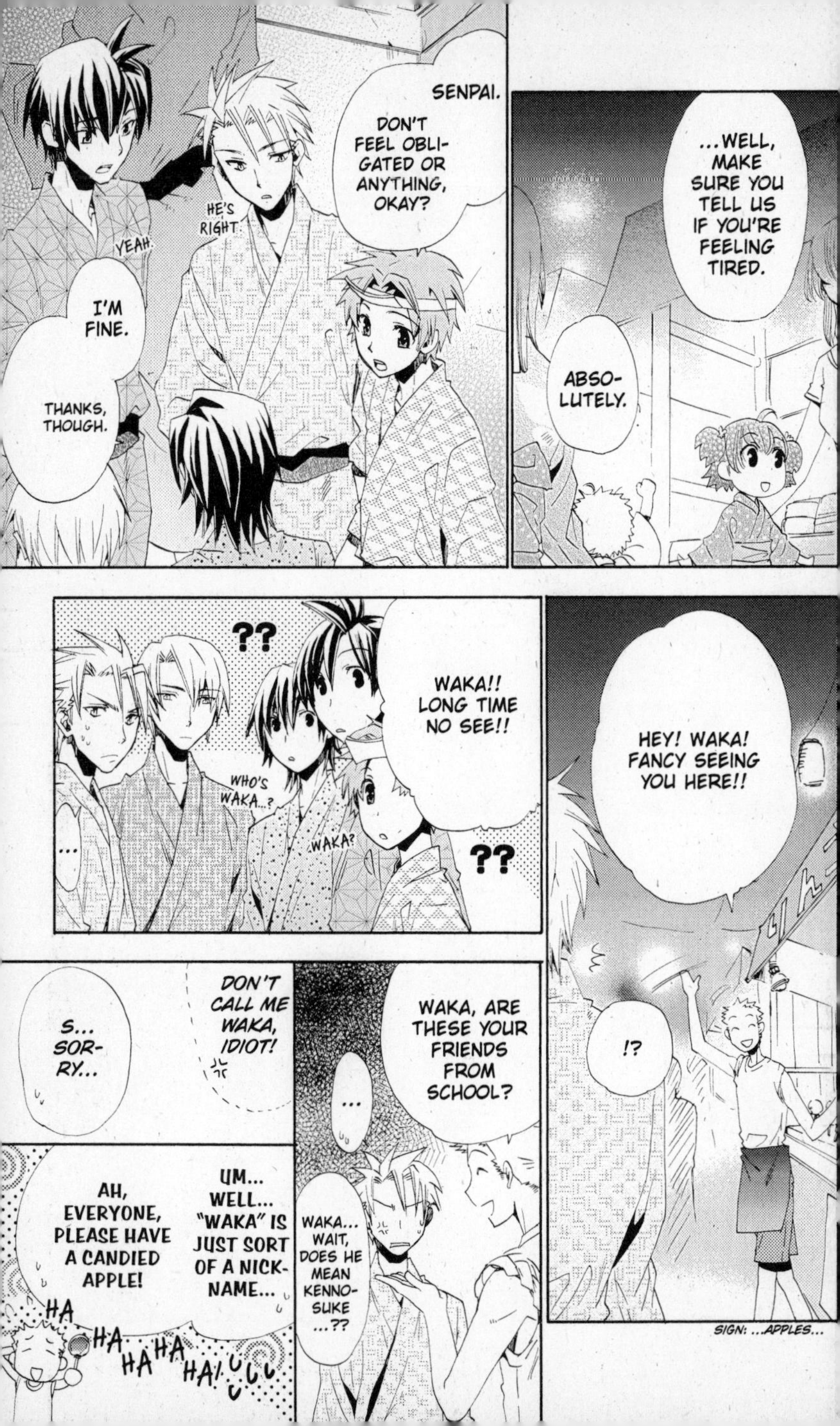
...WELL, MAKE SURE YOU TELL US IF YOU'RE FEELING TIRED.
ABSOLUTELY.
SENPAI.
DON'T FEEL OBLIGATED OR ANYTHING, OKAY?
HE'S RIGHT
YEAH.
I'M FINE.
THANKS, THOUGH.
HEY! WAKA! FANCY SEEING YOU HERE!!
!?
SIGN: ...APPLES...
WAKA!! LONG TIME NO SEE!!
??
??
WHO'S WAKA...?
WAKA?
...
WAKA, ARE THESE YOUR FRIENDS FROM SCHOOL?
...
DON'T CALL ME WAKA, IDIOT!
S... SORRY...
WAKA... WAIT, DOES HE MEAN KENNOSUKE...??
UM... WELL... "WAKA" IS JUST SORT OF A NICKNAME...
AH, EVERYONE, PLEASE HAVE A CANDIED APPLE!
HA HA HA HA HA!

FIVE GUYS EATING CANDIED APPLES.

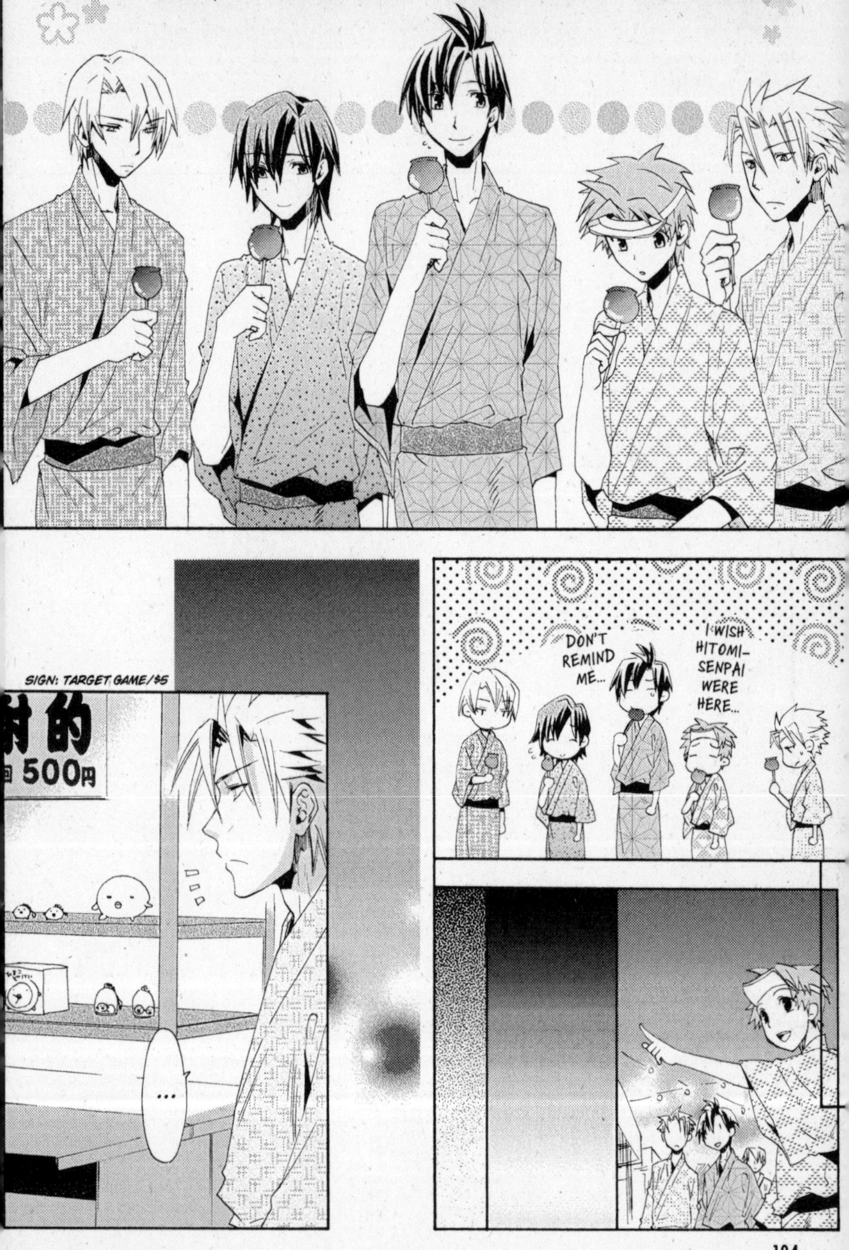
I WISH HITOMI-SENPAI WERE HERE...
DON'T REMIND ME...
SIGN: TARGET GAME/$5
500円
...

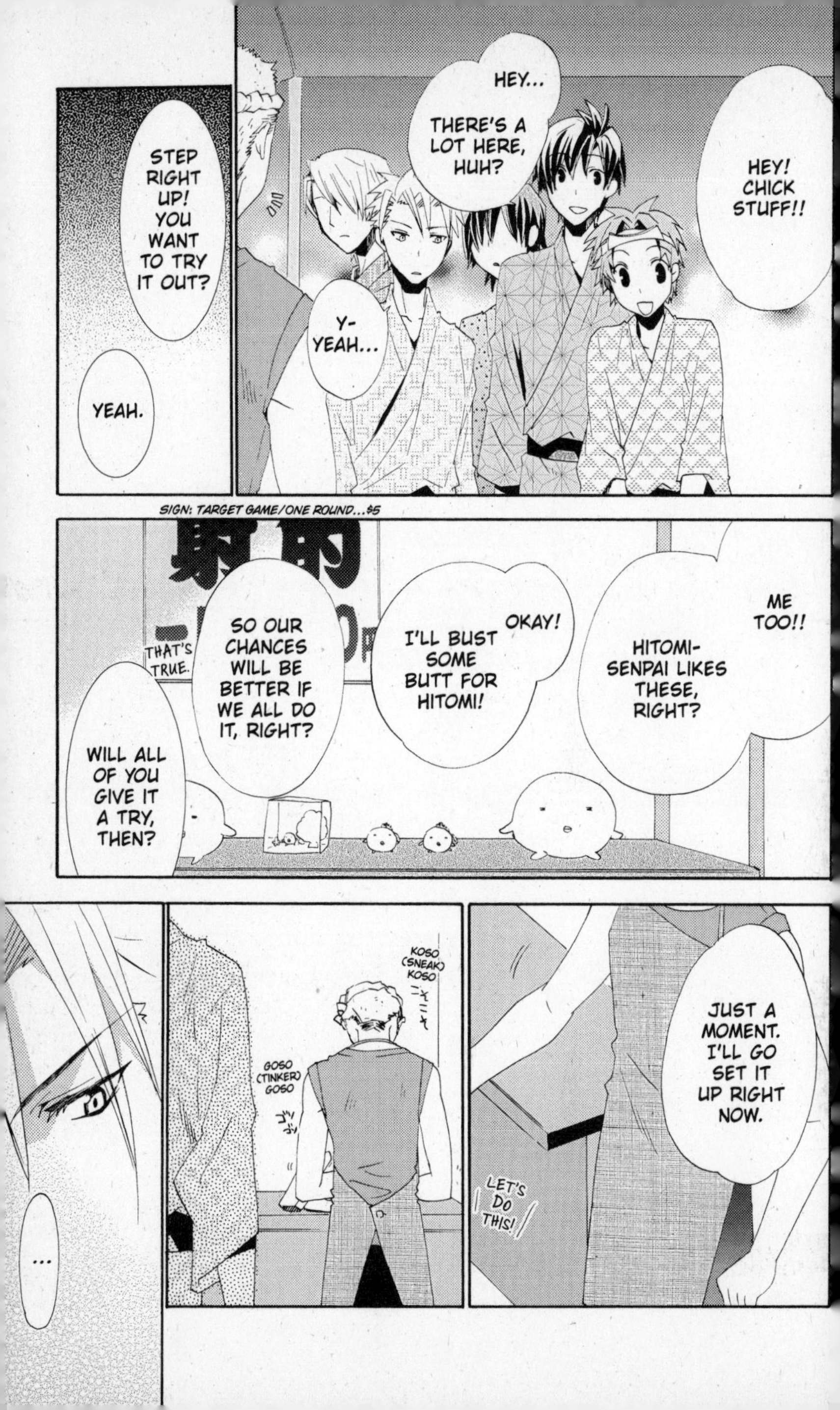
HEY! CHICK STUFF!!
HEY... THERE'S A LOT HERE, HUH?
Y-YEAH...
STEP RIGHT UP! YOU WANT TO TRY IT OUT?
YEAH.
SIGN: TARGET GAME/ONE ROUND...$5
ME TOO!!
HITOMI-SENPAI LIKES THESE, RIGHT?
OKAY! I'LL BUST SOME BUTT FOR HITOMI!
SO OUR CHANCES WILL BE BETTER IF WE ALL DO IT, RIGHT?
THAT'S TRUE.
WILL ALL OF YOU GIVE IT A TRY, THEN?
JUST A MOMENT. I'LL GO SET IT UP RIGHT NOW.
LET'S DO THIS!
KOSO (SNEAK) KOSO
GOSO (TINKER) GOSO
...

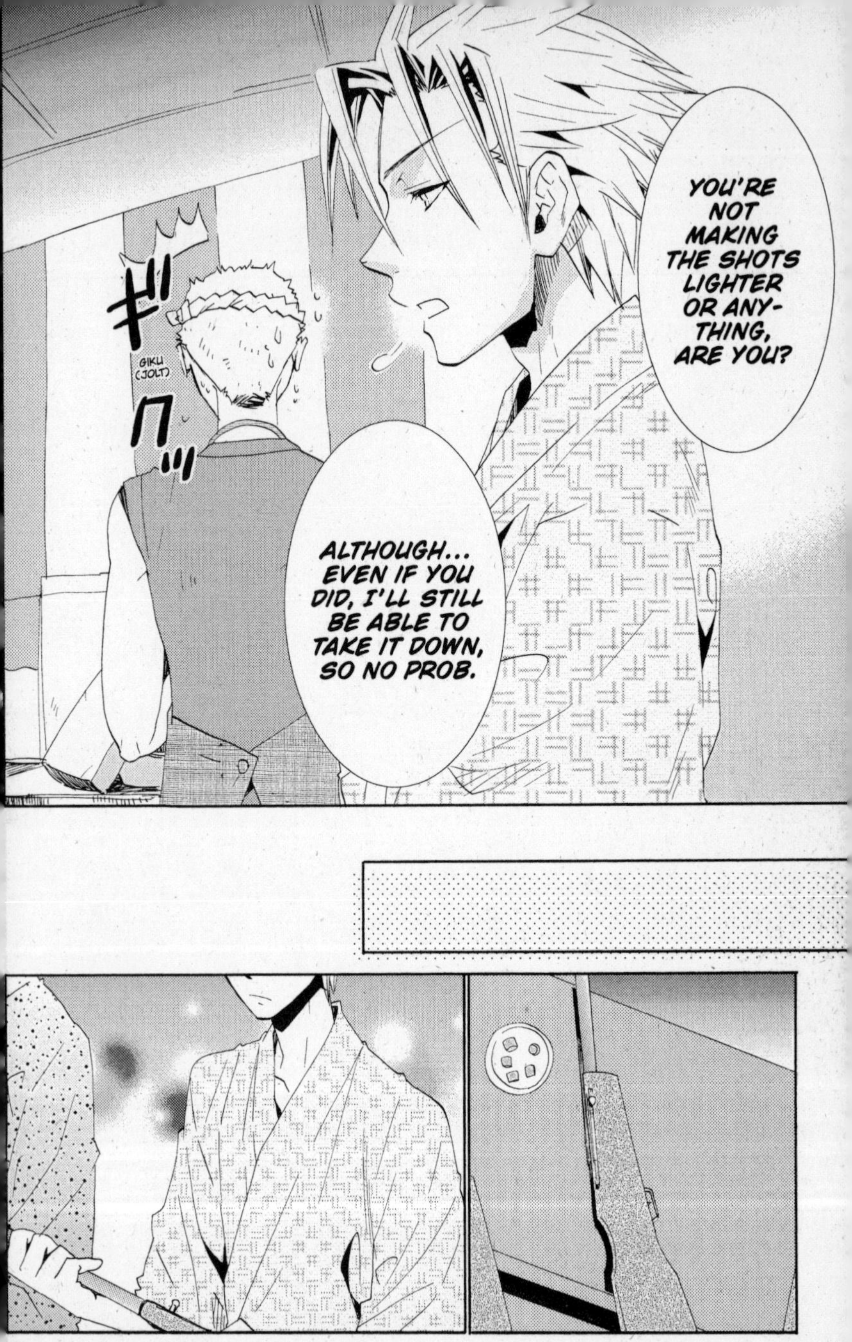
YOU'RE NOT MAKING THE SHOTS LIGHTER OR ANY-THING, ARE YOU?
ギクッ
GIKU (JOLT)
ALTHOUGH... EVEN IF YOU DID, I'LL STILL BE ABLE TO TAKE IT DOWN, SO NO PROB.

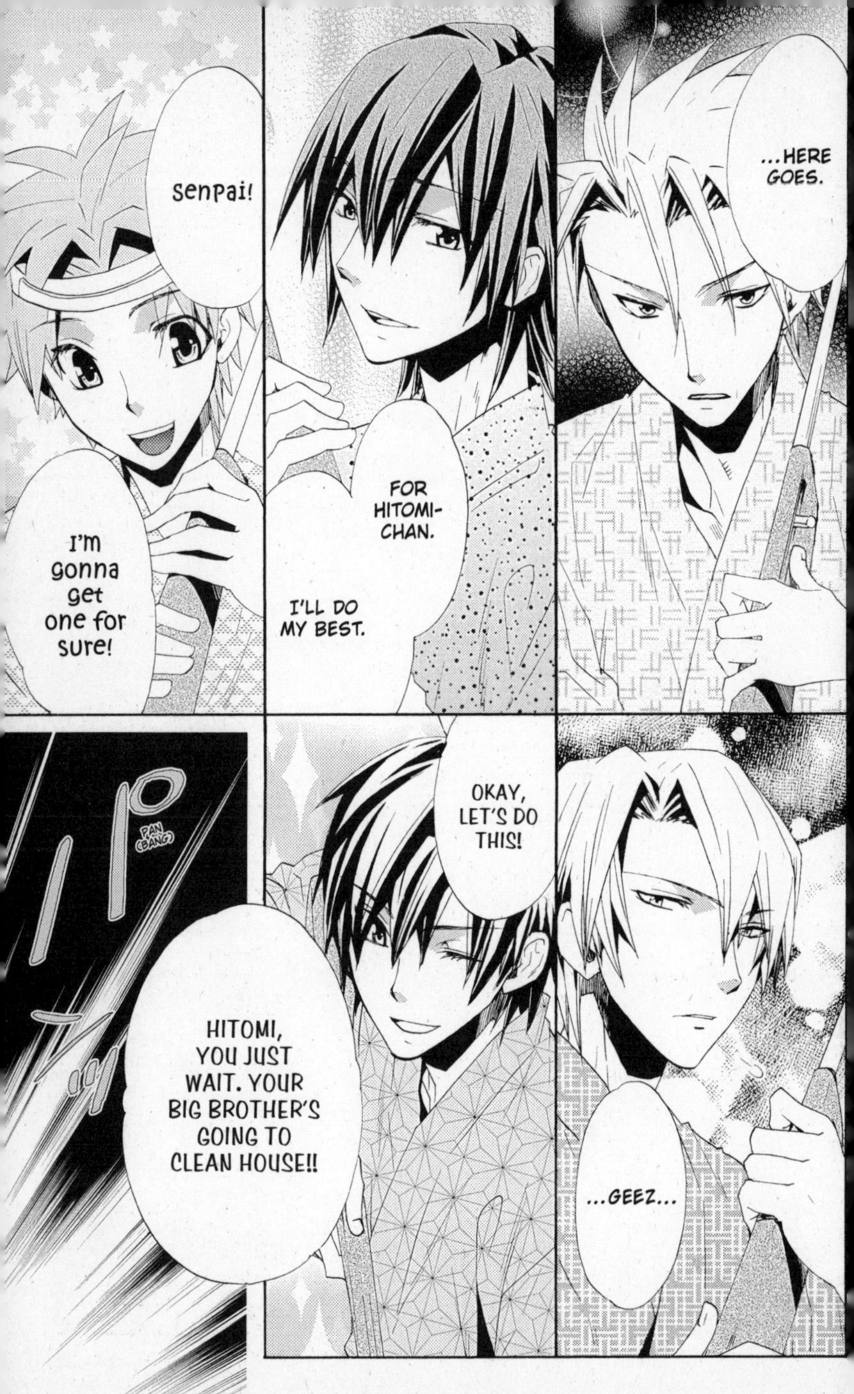
...HERE GOES.
FOR HITOMI-CHAN.
I'LL DO MY BEST.
Senpai!
I'm gonna get one for sure!
...GEEZ...
OKAY, LET'S DO THIS!
HITOMI, YOU JUST WAIT. YOUR BIG BROTHER'S GOING TO CLEAN HOUSE!!
PAN (BANG)

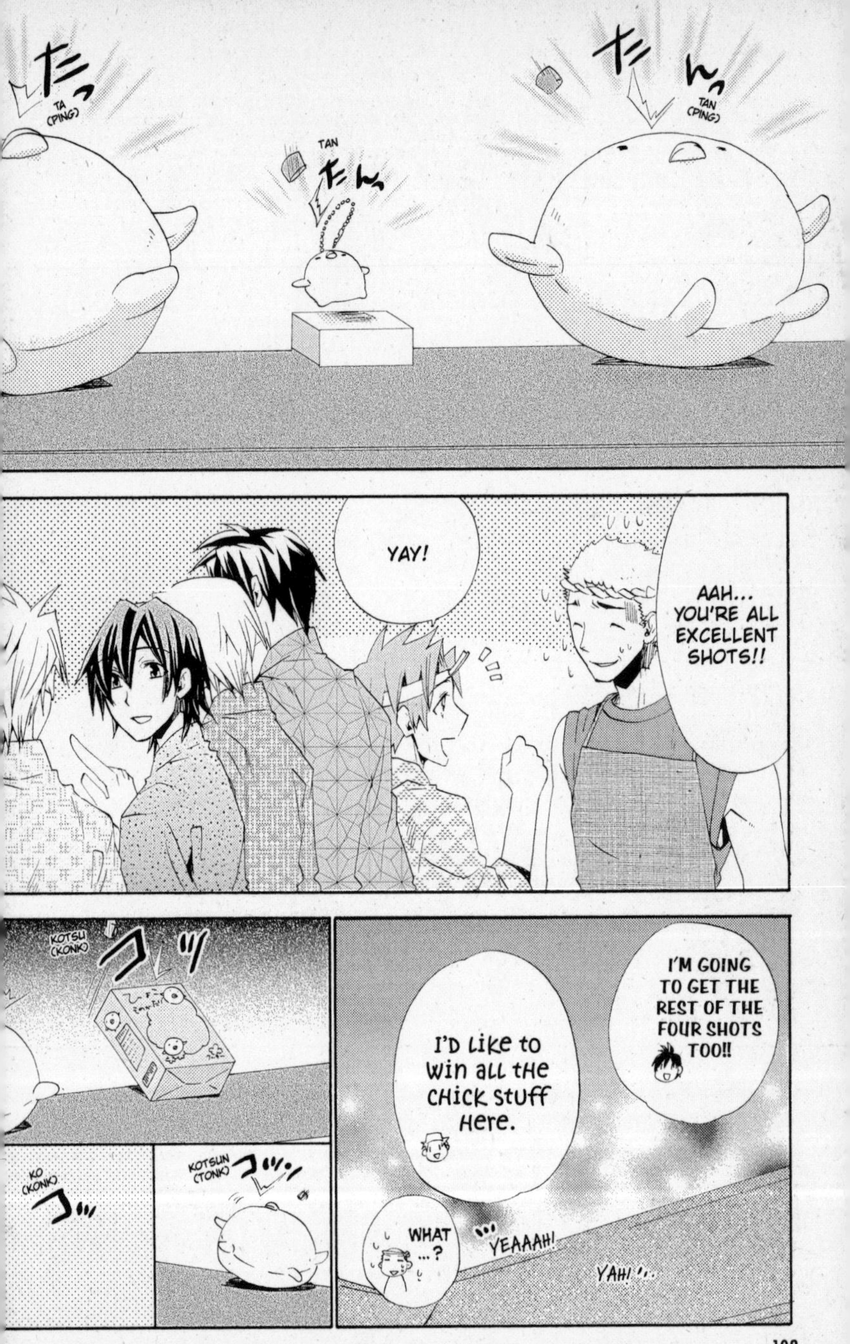
たんっ
TAN (PING)
TAN
たん
たっ
TA (PING)
AAH... YOU'RE ALL EXCELLENT SHOTS!!
YAY!
I'M GOING TO GET THE REST OF THE FOUR SHOTS TOO!!
I'D LIKE TO WIN ALL THE CHICK STUFF HERE.
YEAAAH!
YAH!
WHAT ...?
KOTSU (KONK)
コッ
KOTSUN (TONK)
コツンッ
KO (KONK)
コッ

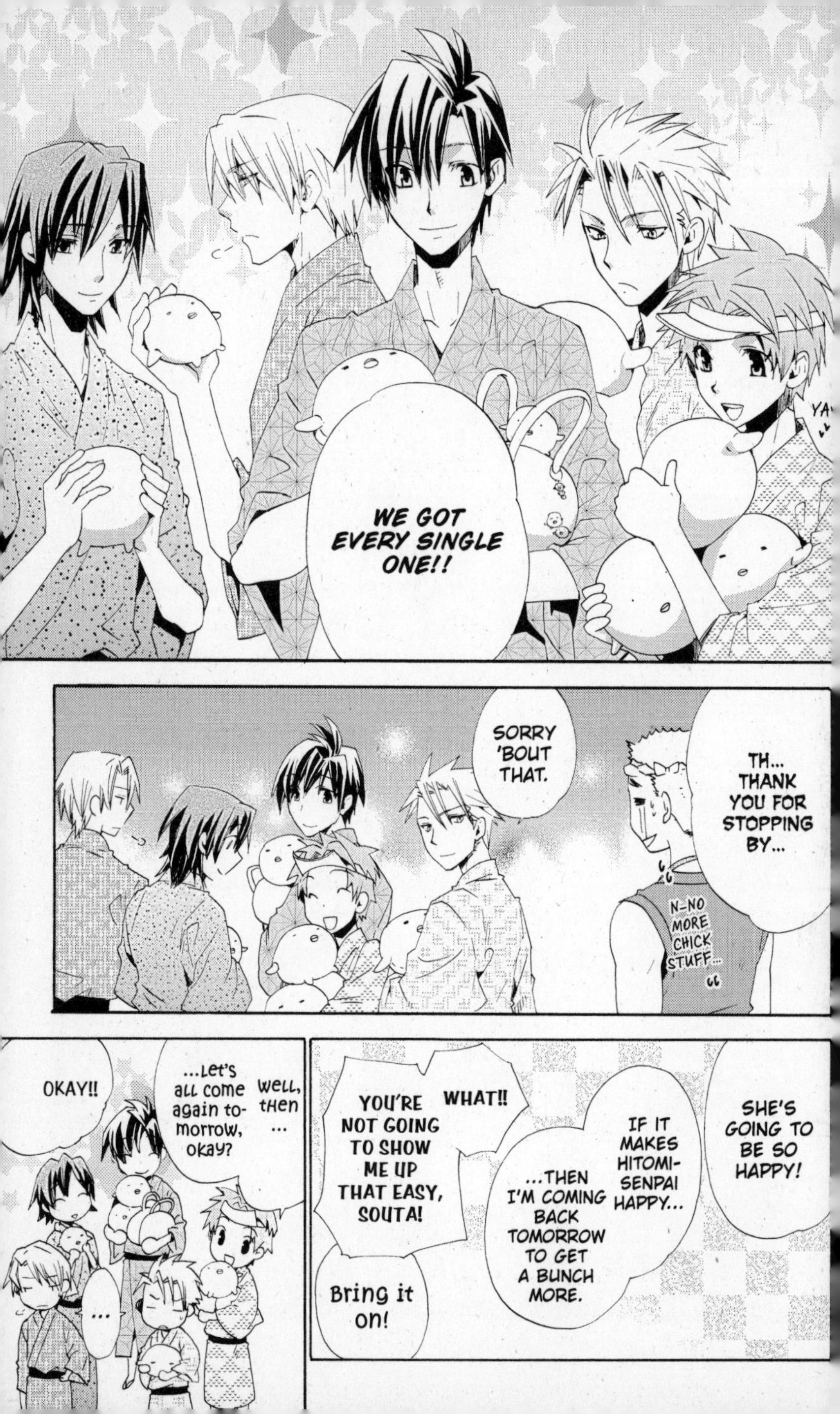
YA
WE GOT EVERY SINGLE ONE!!
TH... THANK YOU FOR STOPPING BY...
N-NO MORE CHICK STUFF...
SORRY 'BOUT THAT.
SHE'S GOING TO BE SO HAPPY!
IF IT MAKES HITOMI-SENPAI HAPPY...
...THEN I'M COMING BACK TOMORROW TO GET A BUNCH MORE.
WHAT!!
YOU'RE NOT GOING TO SHOW ME UP THAT EASY, SOUTA!
Bring it on!
Well, then ...
...Let's all come again to-morrow, okay?
OKAY!!
...

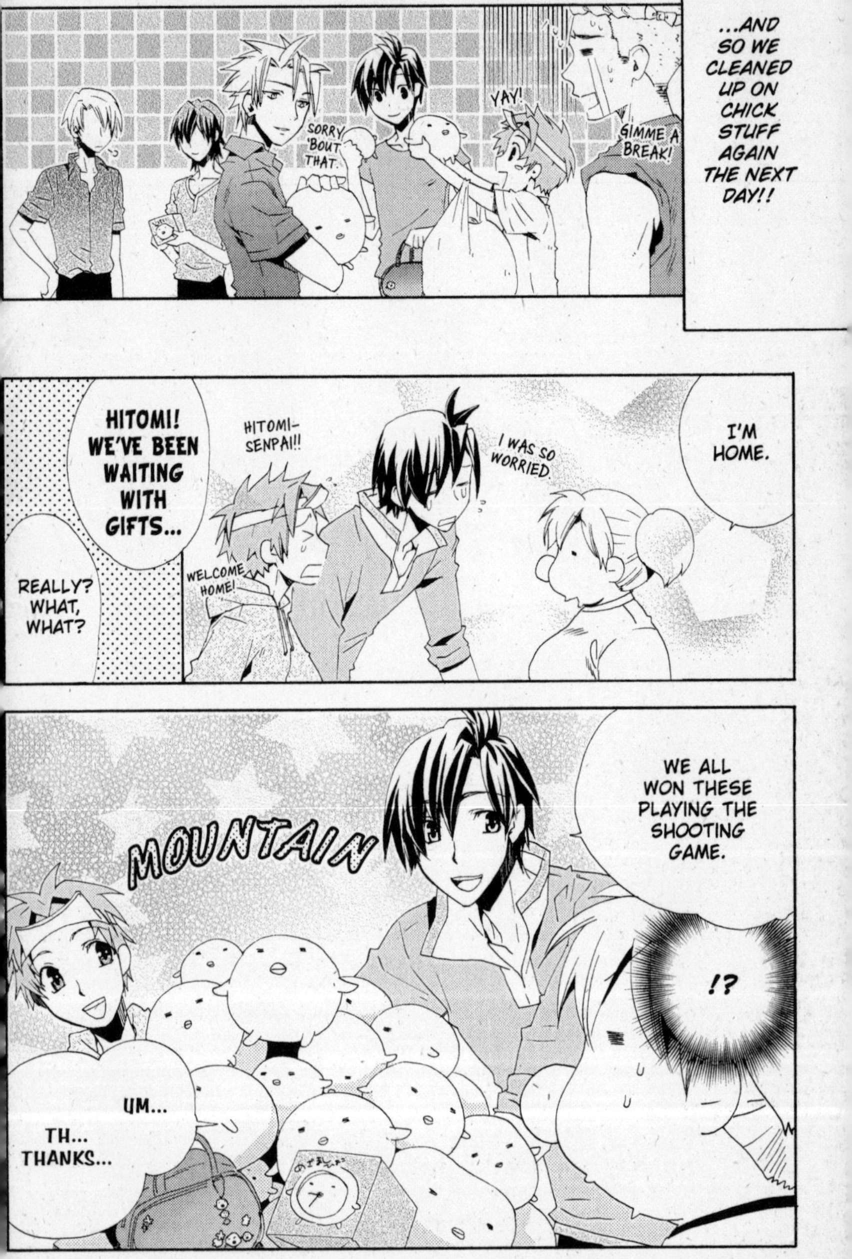
...AND SO WE CLEANED UP ON CHICK STUFF AGAIN THE NEXT DAY!!
GIMME A BREAK!
YAY!
SORRY 'BOUT THAT.
I'M HOME.
I WAS SO WORRIED.
HITOMI-SENPAI!!
WELCOME HOME!
HITOMI! WE'VE BEEN WAITING WITH GIFTS...
REALLY? WHAT, WHAT?
WE ALL WON THESE PLAYING THE SHOOTING GAME.
!?
MOUNTAIN
UM...
TH... THANKS...

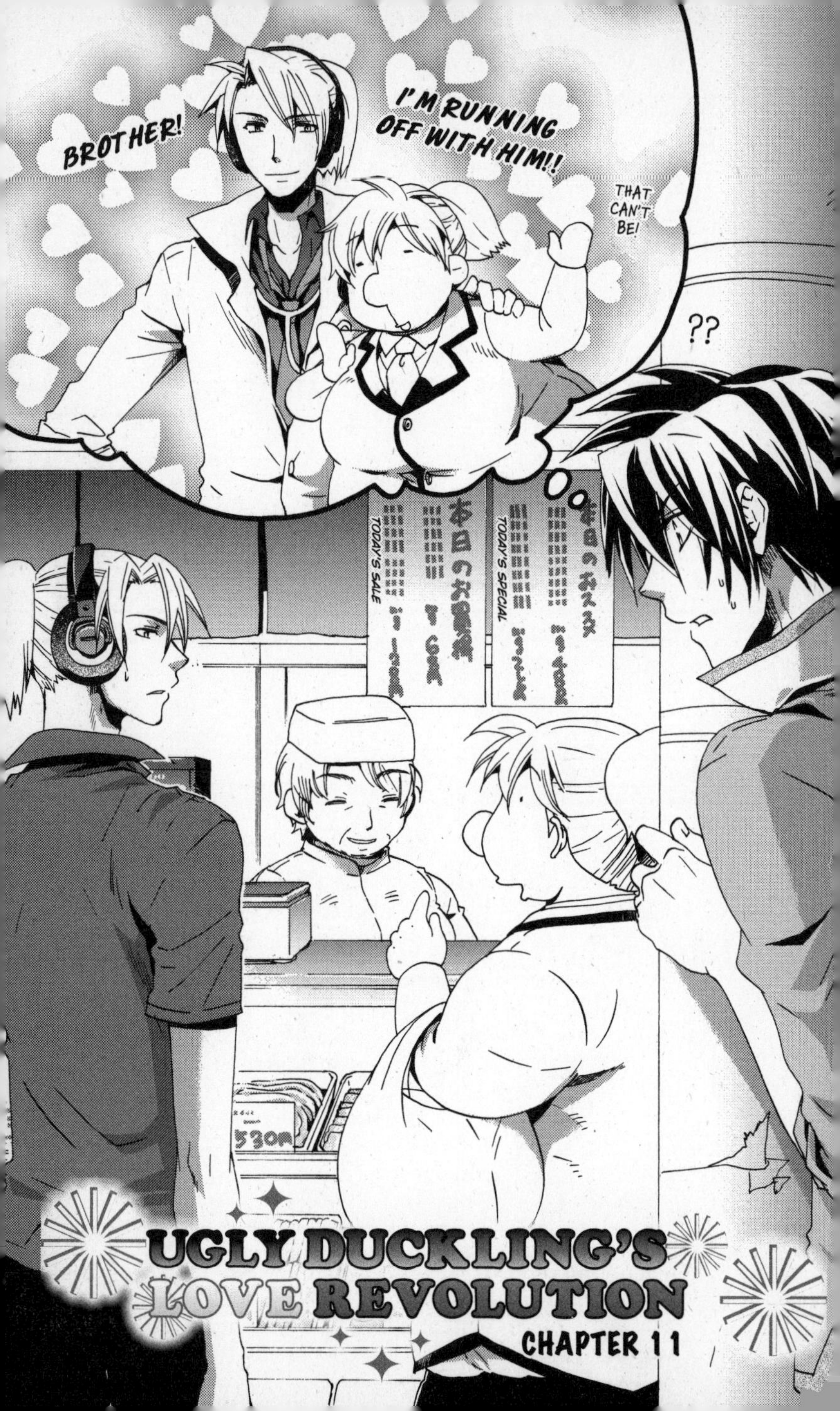

BROTHER!
I'M RUNNING OFF WITH HIM!!
THAT CAN'T BE!
??
TODAY'S SPECIAL
TODAY'S SALE
UGLY DUCKLING'S LOVE REVOLUTION
CHAPTER 11

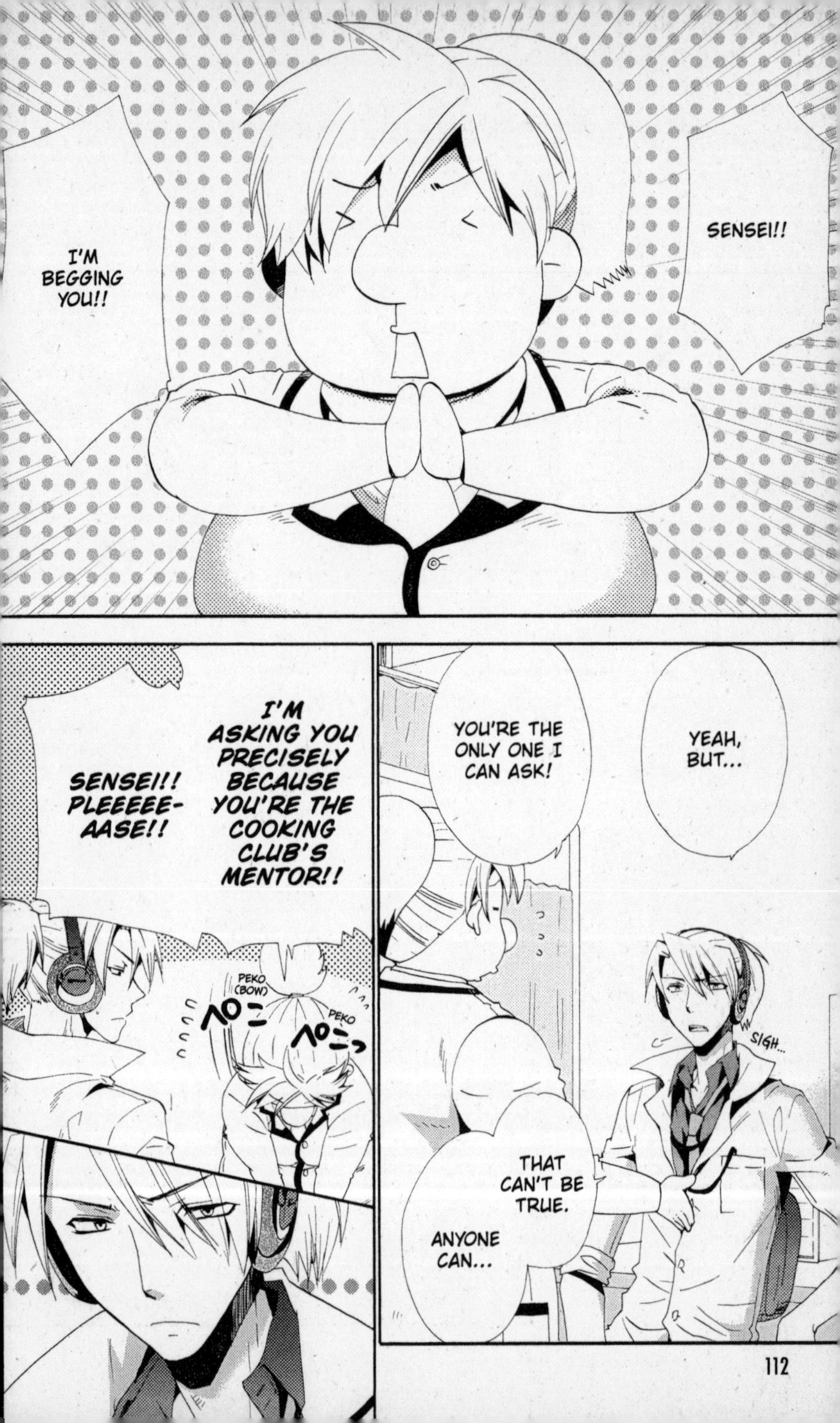
SENSEI!!
I'M BEGGING YOU!!
YEAH, BUT...
YOU'RE THE ONLY ONE I CAN ASK!
SIGH...
THAT CAN'T BE TRUE.
ANYONE CAN...
I'M ASKING YOU PRECISELY BECAUSE YOU'RE THE COOKING CLUB'S MENTOR!!
SENSEI!!! PLEEEEE-AASE!!
PEKO (BOW)
PEKO

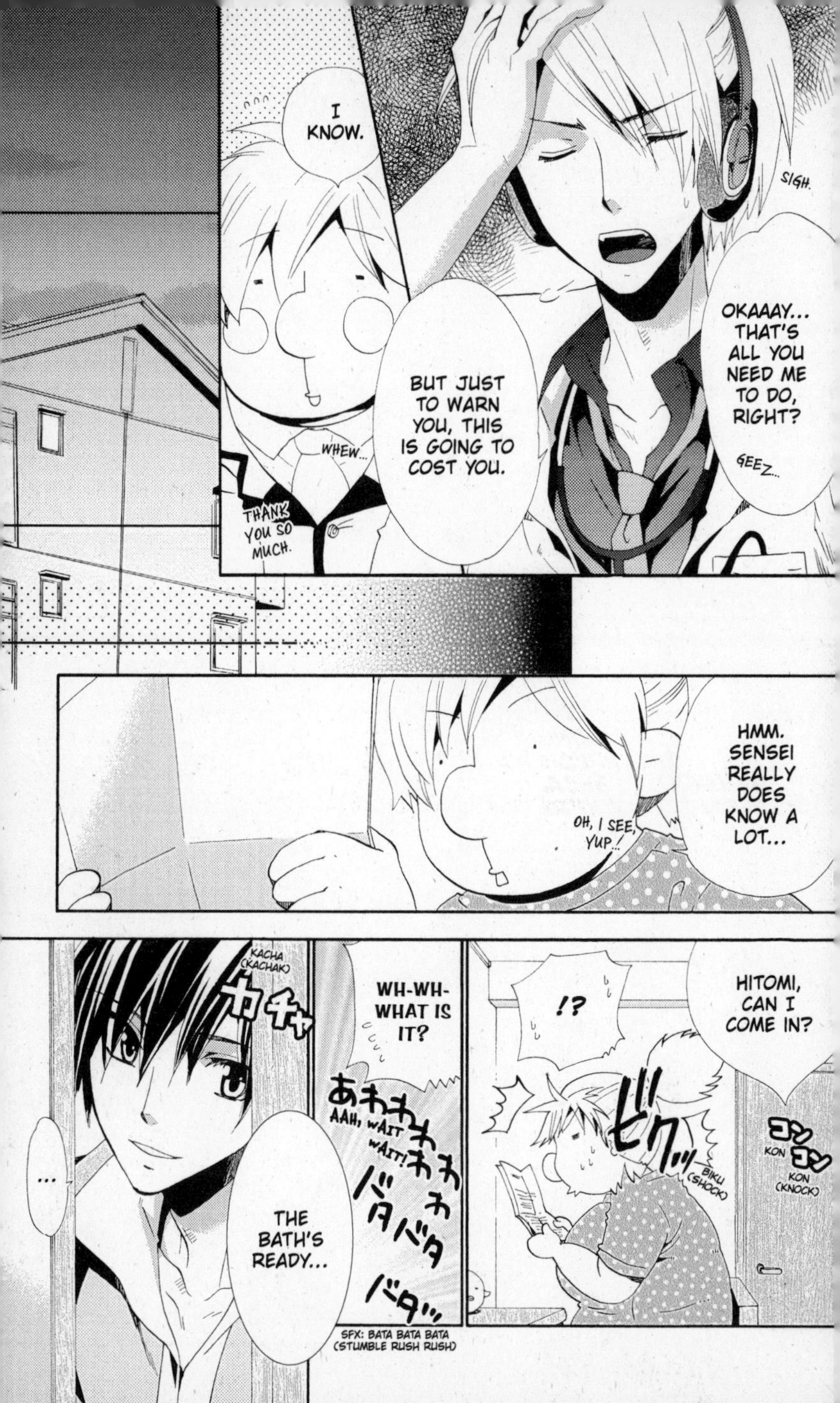
SIGH.
OKAAAY... THAT'S ALL YOU NEED ME TO DO, RIGHT?
GEEZ...
I KNOW.
BUT JUST TO WARN YOU, THIS IS GOING TO COST YOU.
WHEW...
THANK YOU SO MUCH.
HMM. SENSEI REALLY DOES KNOW A LOT...
OH, I SEE, YUP!
HITOMI, CAN I COME IN?
KON KON (KNOCK)
!?
BIKU (SHOCK)
WH-WH-WHAT IS IT?
AAH, WAIT WAIT!
THE BATH'S READY...
SFX: BATA BATA BATA (STUMBLE RUSH RUSH)
KACHA (KACHAK)
...

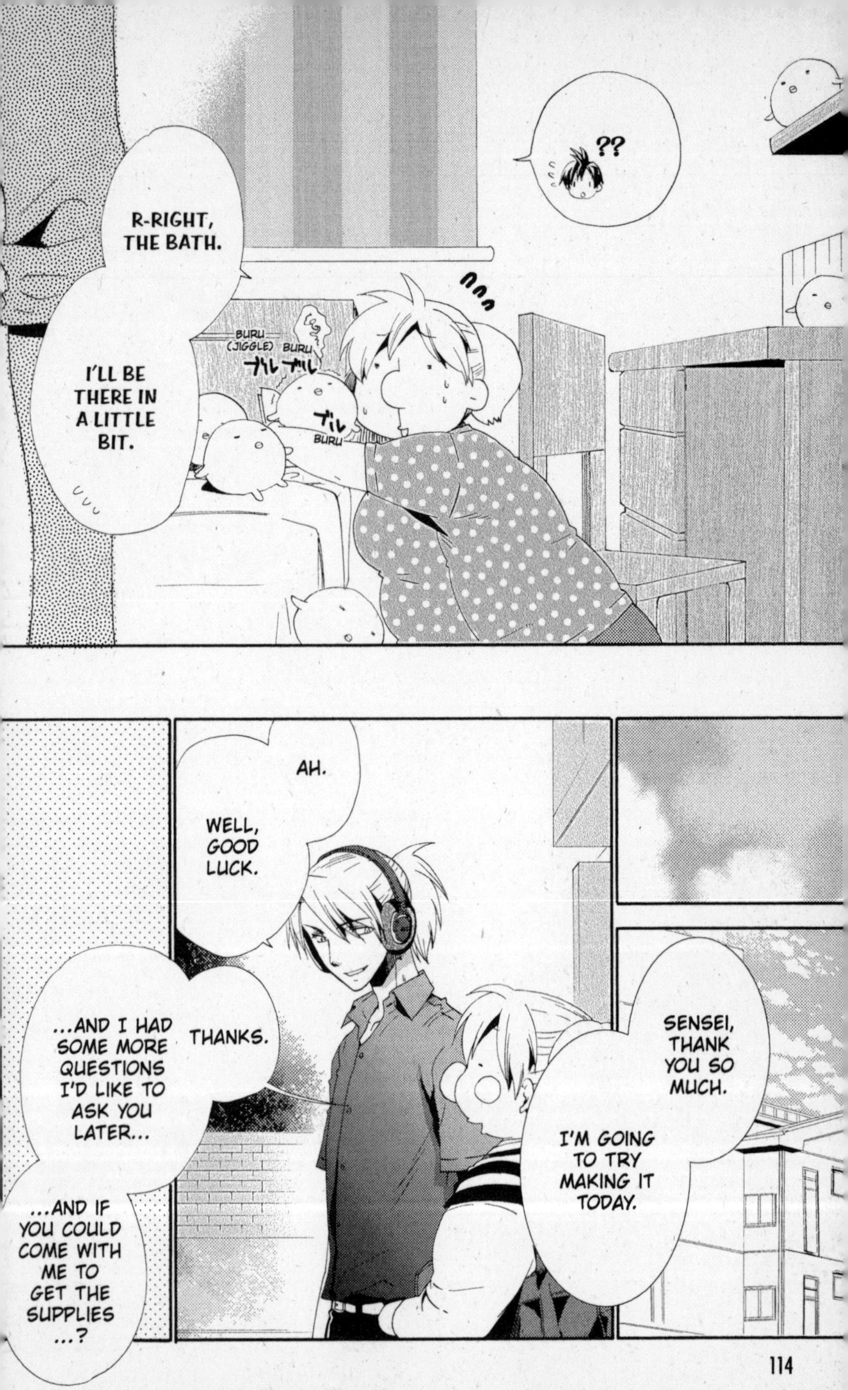
??
R-RIGHT, THE BATH.
I'LL BE THERE IN A LITTLE BIT.
BURU (JIGGLE) BURU
ブルブル
ブル
BURU
SENSEI, THANK YOU SO MUCH.
I'M GOING TO TRY MAKING IT TODAY.
AH.
WELL, GOOD LUCK.
THANKS.
...AND I HAD SOME MORE QUESTIONS I'D LIKE TO ASK YOU LATER...
...AND IF YOU COULD COME WITH ME TO GET THE SUPPLIES ...?

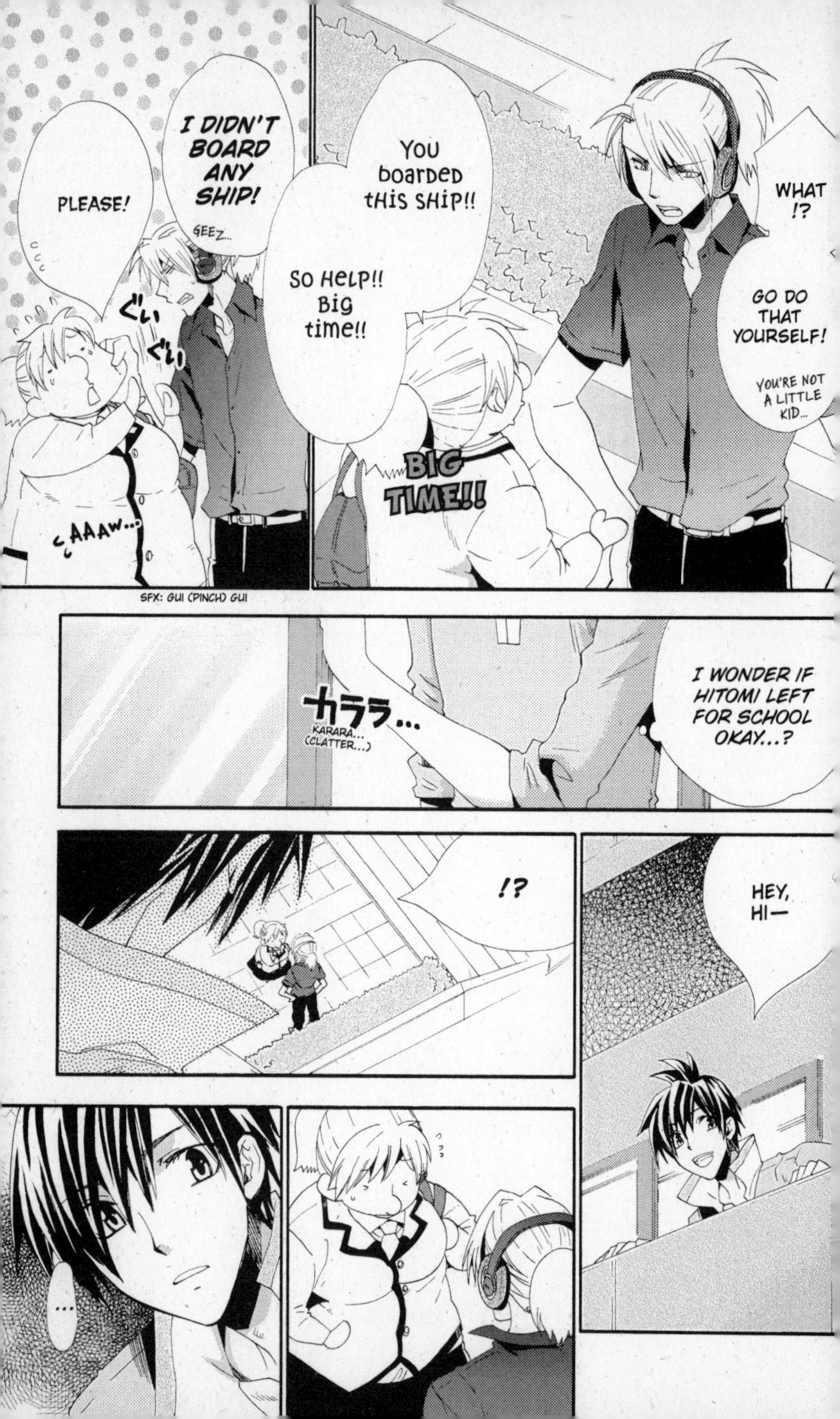
WHAT !?
You boarded tHIS SHIP!!
SO HELP!! Big time!!
GO DO THAT YOURSELF!
YOU'RE NOT A LITTLE KID...
BIG TIME!!
I DIDN'T BOARD ANY SHIP!
GEEZ..
PLEASE!
ぐい ぐい
CAAAW...
SFX: GUI (PINCH) GUI
I WONDER IF HITOMI LEFT FOR SCHOOL OKAY...?
カララ...
KARARA... (CLATTER...)
HEY, HI—
!?
...

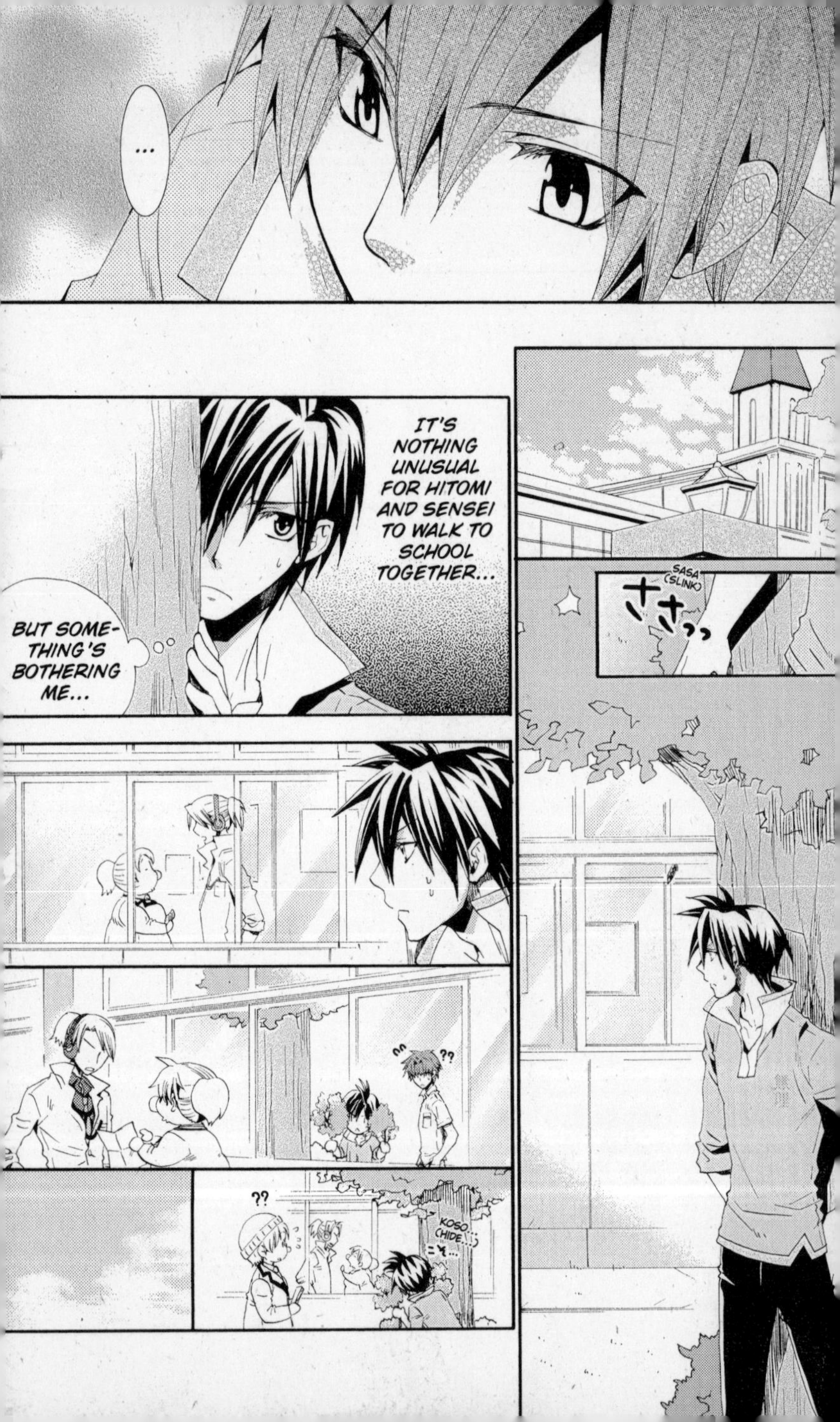
...
SASA (SLINK)
さささっっ
IT'S NOTHING UNUSUAL FOR HITOMI AND SENSEI TO WALK TO SCHOOL TOGETHER...
BUT SOME-THING'S BOTHERING ME...
??
??
??
KOSO (HIDE...)
こそ...

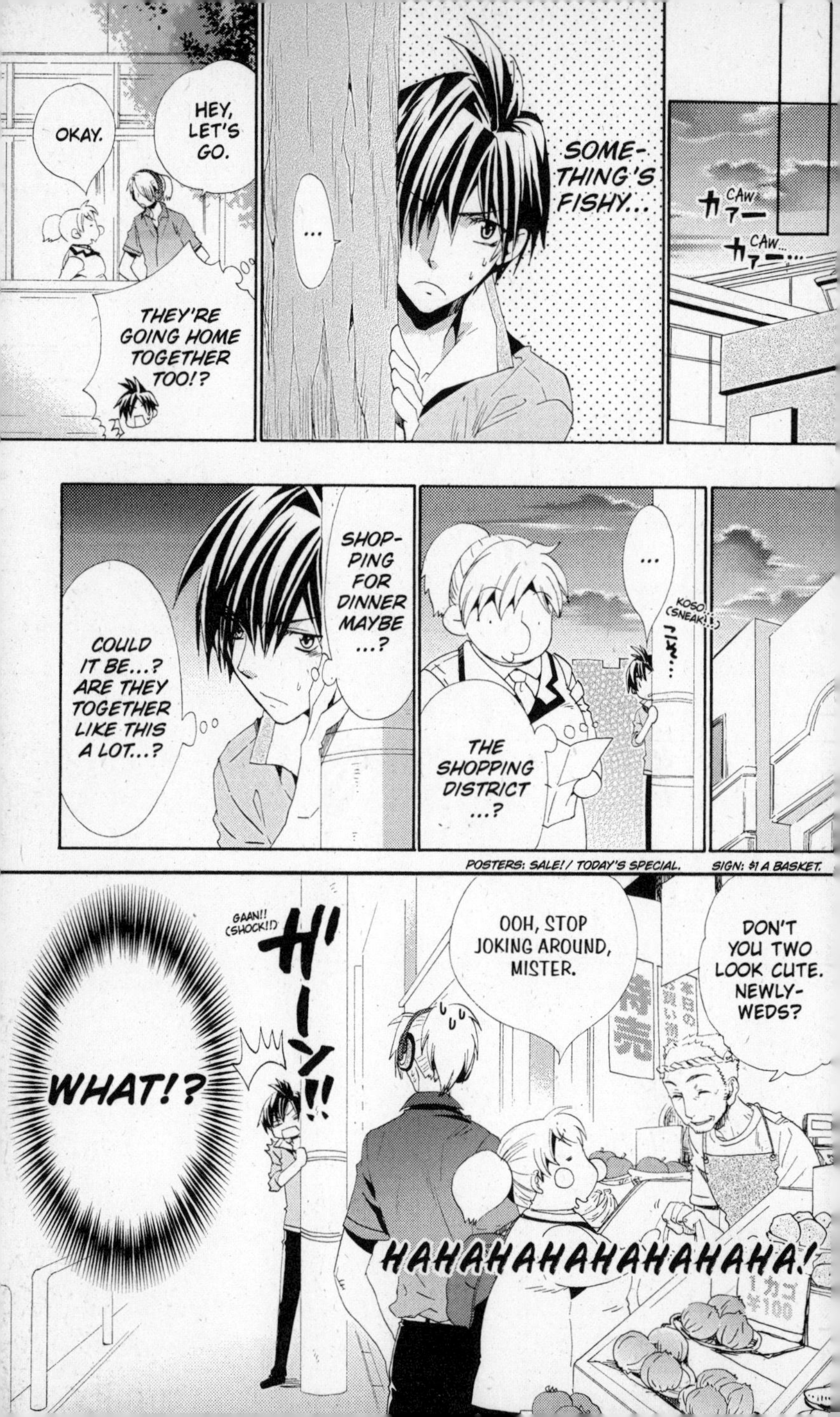

カァー CAW
カァー… CAW...
SOME-THING'S FISHY...
...
HEY, LET'S GO.
OKAY.
THEY'RE GOING HOME TOGETHER TOO!?
...
KOSO (SNEAK!)
こそ…
THE SHOPPING DISTRICT ...?
SHOP-PING FOR DINNER MAYBE ...?
COULD IT BE...? ARE THEY TOGETHER LIKE THIS A LOT...?
POSTERS: SALE! / TODAY'S SPECIAL.
SIGN: $1 A BASKET.
DON'T YOU TWO LOOK CUTE. NEWLY-WEDS?
OOH, STOP JOKING AROUND, MISTER.
HAHAHAHAHAHAHAHAHA!
1カゴ ¥100
GAAN!! (SHOCK!!)
ガーン!!
WHAT!?

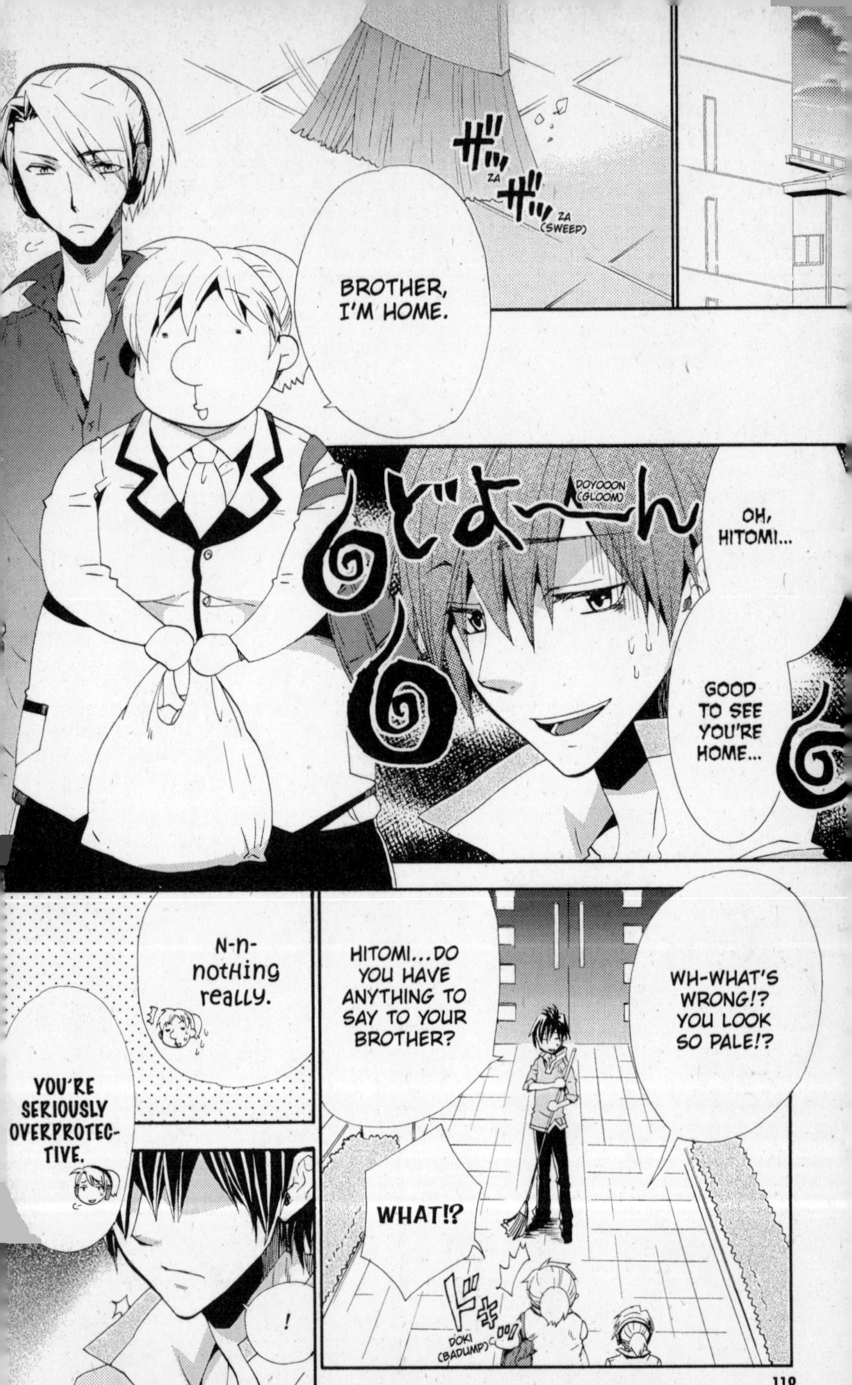
ZA
ZA (SWEEP)
BROTHER, I'M HOME.
DOYOOON (GLOOM)
OH, HITOMI...
GOOD TO SEE YOU'RE HOME...
WH-WHAT'S WRONG!? YOU LOOK SO PALE!?
HITOMI...DO YOU HAVE ANYTHING TO SAY TO YOUR BROTHER?
WHAT!?
DOKI (BADUMP)
N-n-nothing really.
YOU'RE SERIOUSLY OVERPROTEC-TIVE.
!

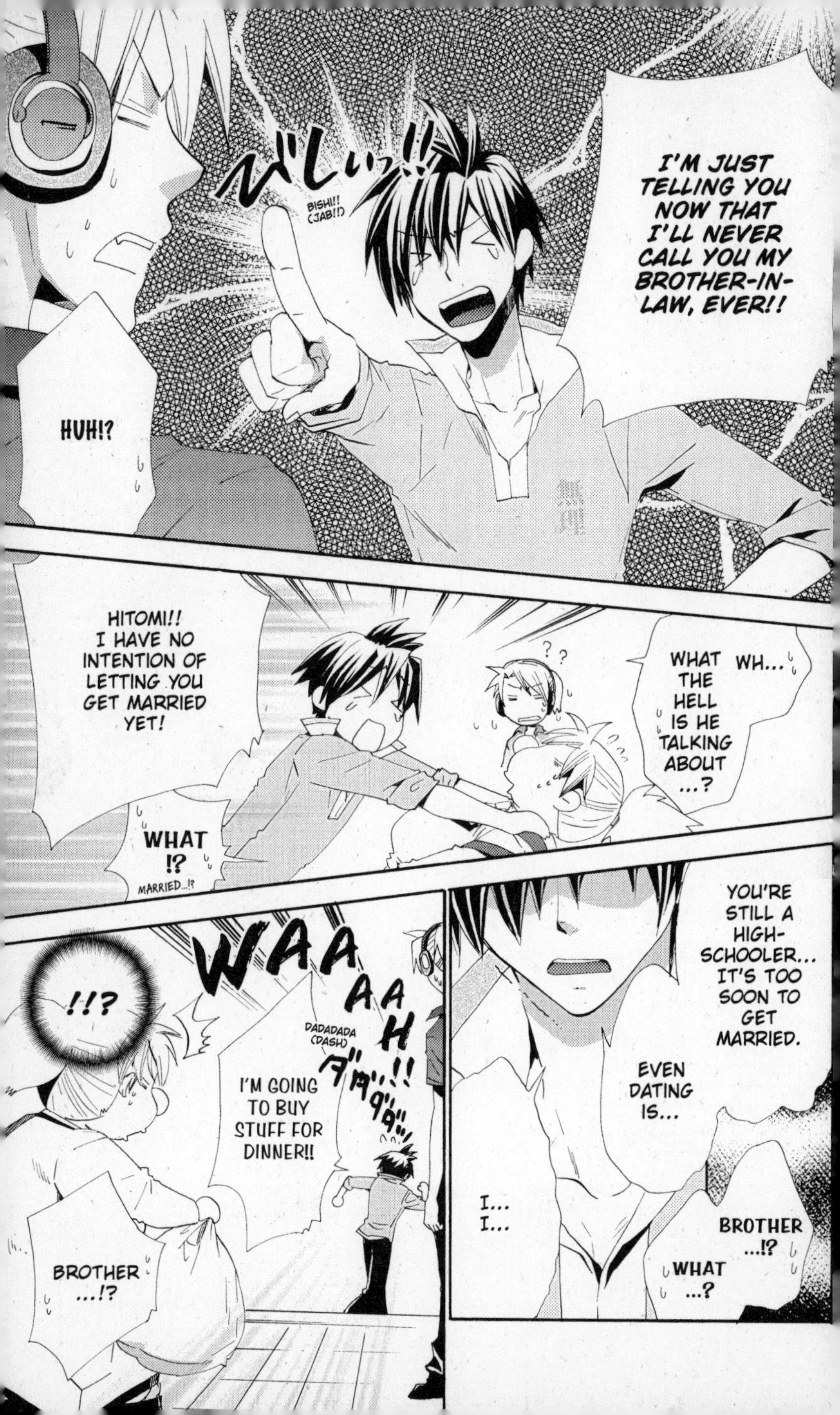
I'M JUST TELLING YOU NOW THAT I'LL NEVER CALL YOU MY BROTHER-IN-LAW, EVER!!
びしっ!!
BISHI!! (JAB!!)
HUH!?
WH...
WHAT THE HELL IS HE TALKING ABOUT ...?
HITOMI!! I HAVE NO INTENTION OF LETTING YOU GET MARRIED YET!
WHAT !?
MARRIED...!?
YOU'RE STILL A HIGH-SCHOOLER... IT'S TOO SOON TO GET MARRIED.
EVEN DATING IS...
I... I...
BROTHER ...!?
WHAT ...?
WAAAAAH!!
DADADADA (DASH)
ダダダダ
I'M GOING TO BUY STUFF FOR DINNER!!
!!?
BROTHER ...!?

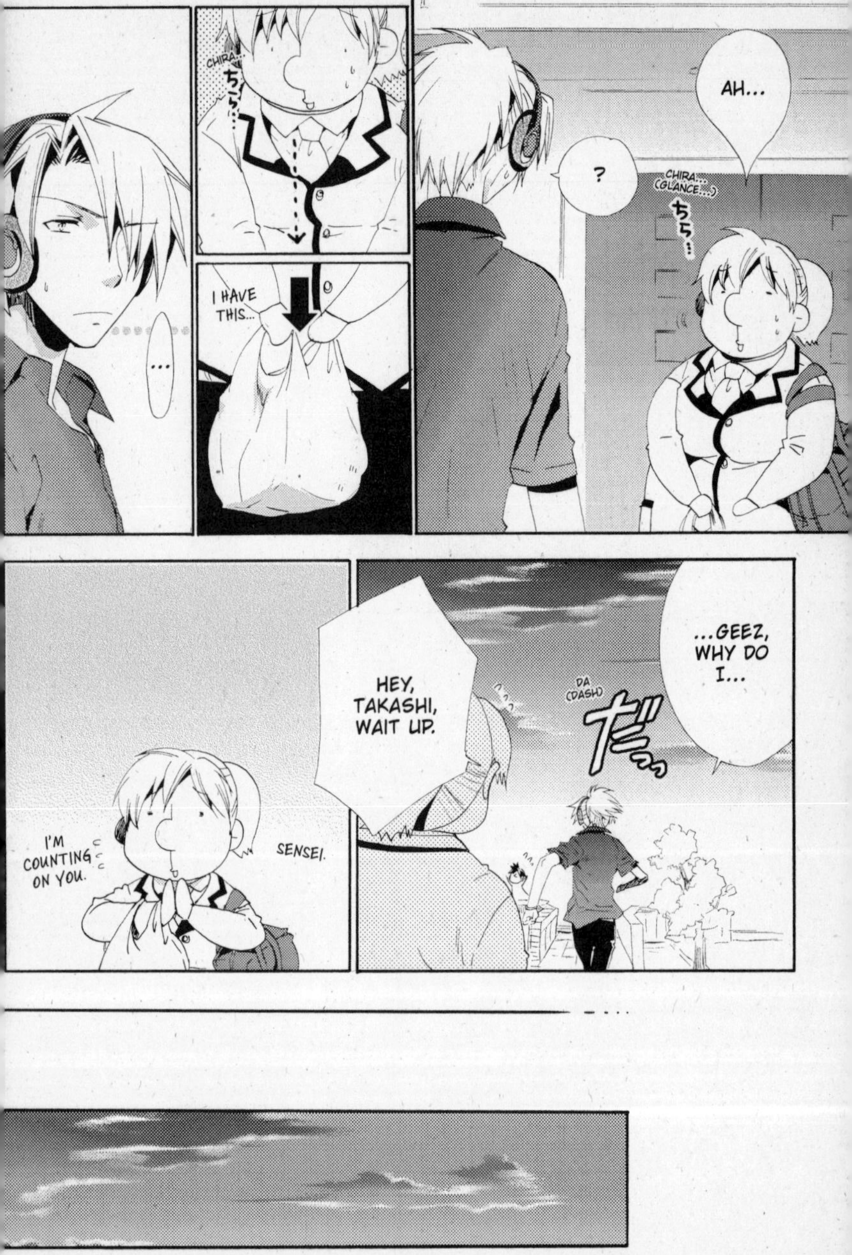
AH...
?
CHIRA... (GLANCE...)
ちら…
CHIRA...
ちら…
I HAVE THIS...
...
...GEEZ, WHY DO I...
DA (DASH)
だっ
HEY, TAKASHI, WAIT UP.
SENSEI.
I'M COUNTING ON YOU.

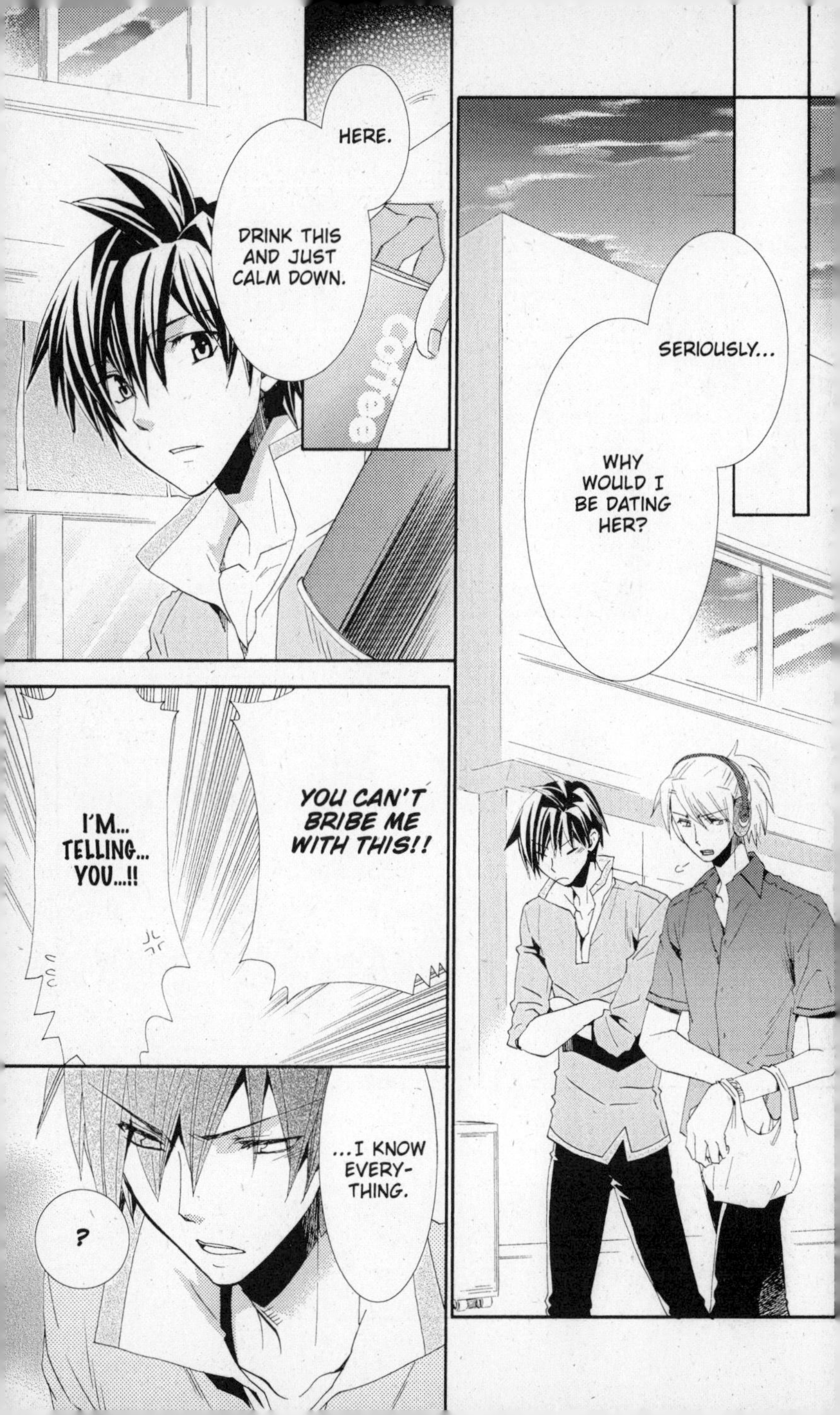
SERIOUSLY...
WHY WOULD I BE DATING HER?
HERE.
DRINK THIS AND JUST CALM DOWN.
Coffee
YOU CAN'T BRIBE ME WITH THIS!!
I'M... TELLING... YOU...!!
...I KNOW EVERY-THING.
?

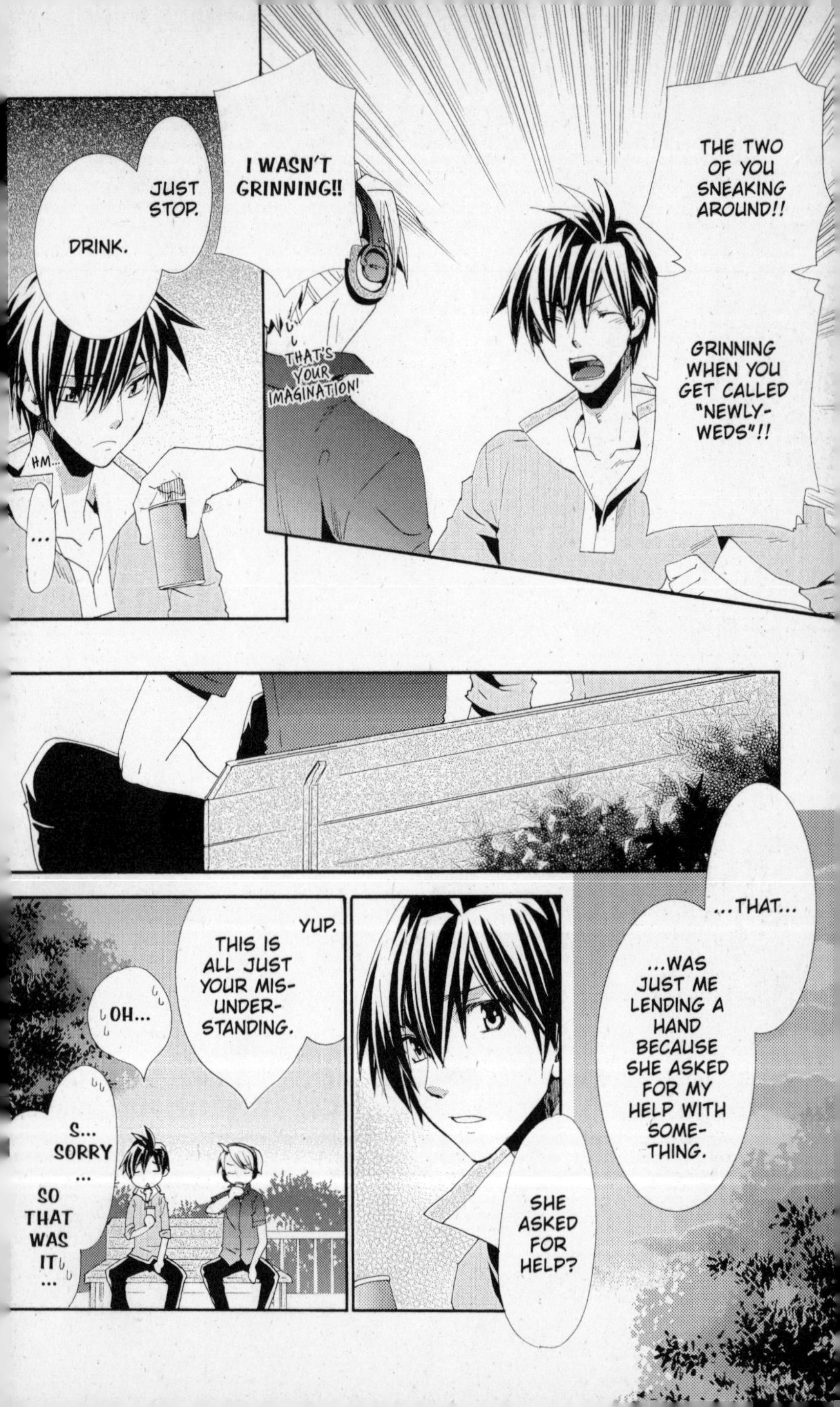
THE TWO OF YOU SNEAKING AROUND!!
GRINNING WHEN YOU GET CALLED "NEWLY-WEDS"!!
I WASN'T GRINNING!!
THAT'S YOUR IMAGINATION!
JUST STOP.
DRINK.
HM...
...
...THAT...
...WAS JUST ME LENDING A HAND BECAUSE SHE ASKED FOR MY HELP WITH SOMETHING.
SHE ASKED FOR HELP?
YUP.
THIS IS ALL JUST YOUR MIS-UNDER-STANDING.
OH...
S... SORRY ...
SO THAT WAS IT ...

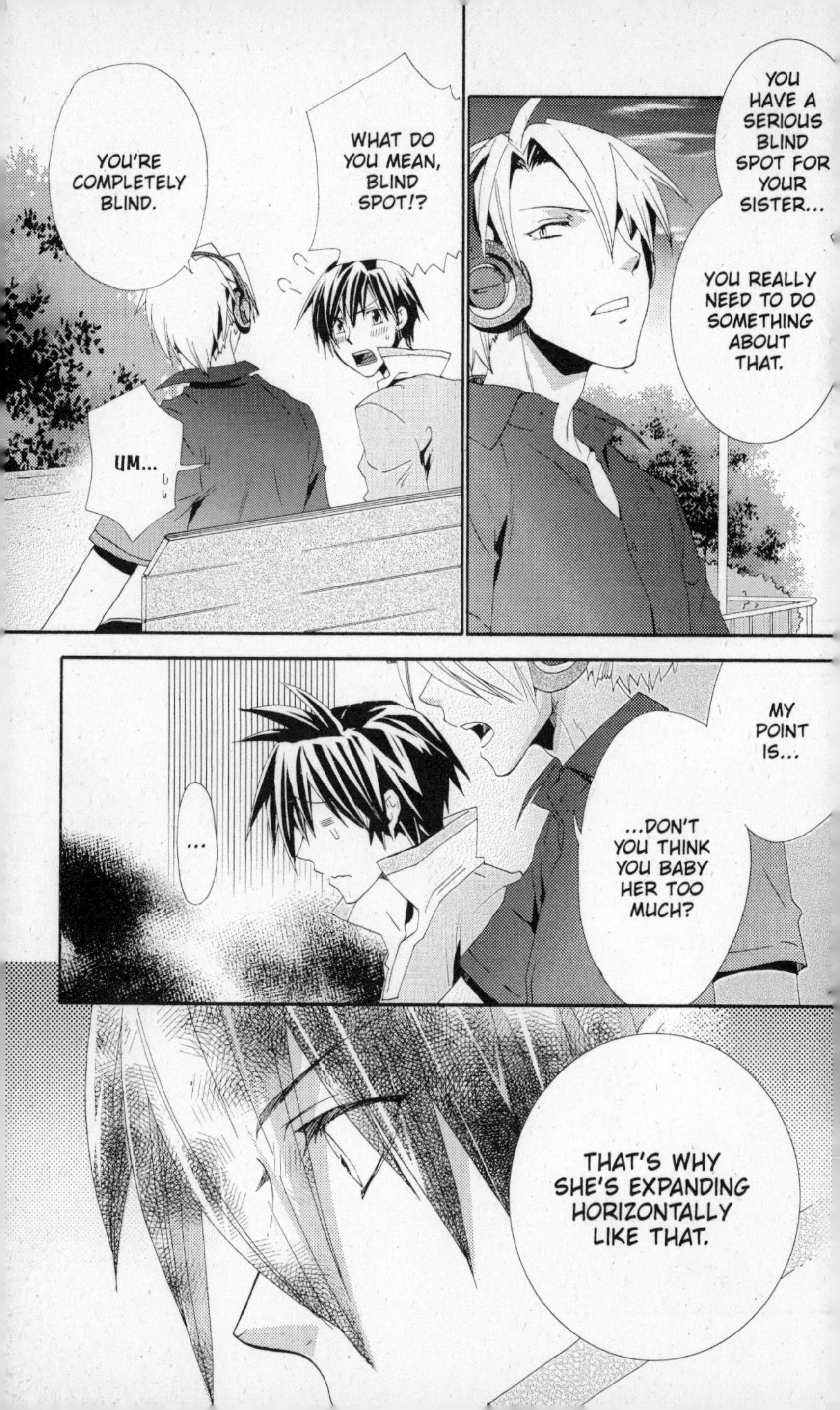
YOU HAVE A SERIOUS BLIND SPOT FOR YOUR SISTER...
YOU REALLY NEED TO DO SOMETHING ABOUT THAT.
WHAT DO YOU MEAN, BLIND SPOT!?
YOU'RE COMPLETELY BLIND.
UM...
MY POINT IS...
...DON'T YOU THINK YOU BABY HER TOO MUCH?
...
THAT'S WHY SHE'S EXPANDING HORIZONTALLY LIKE THAT.

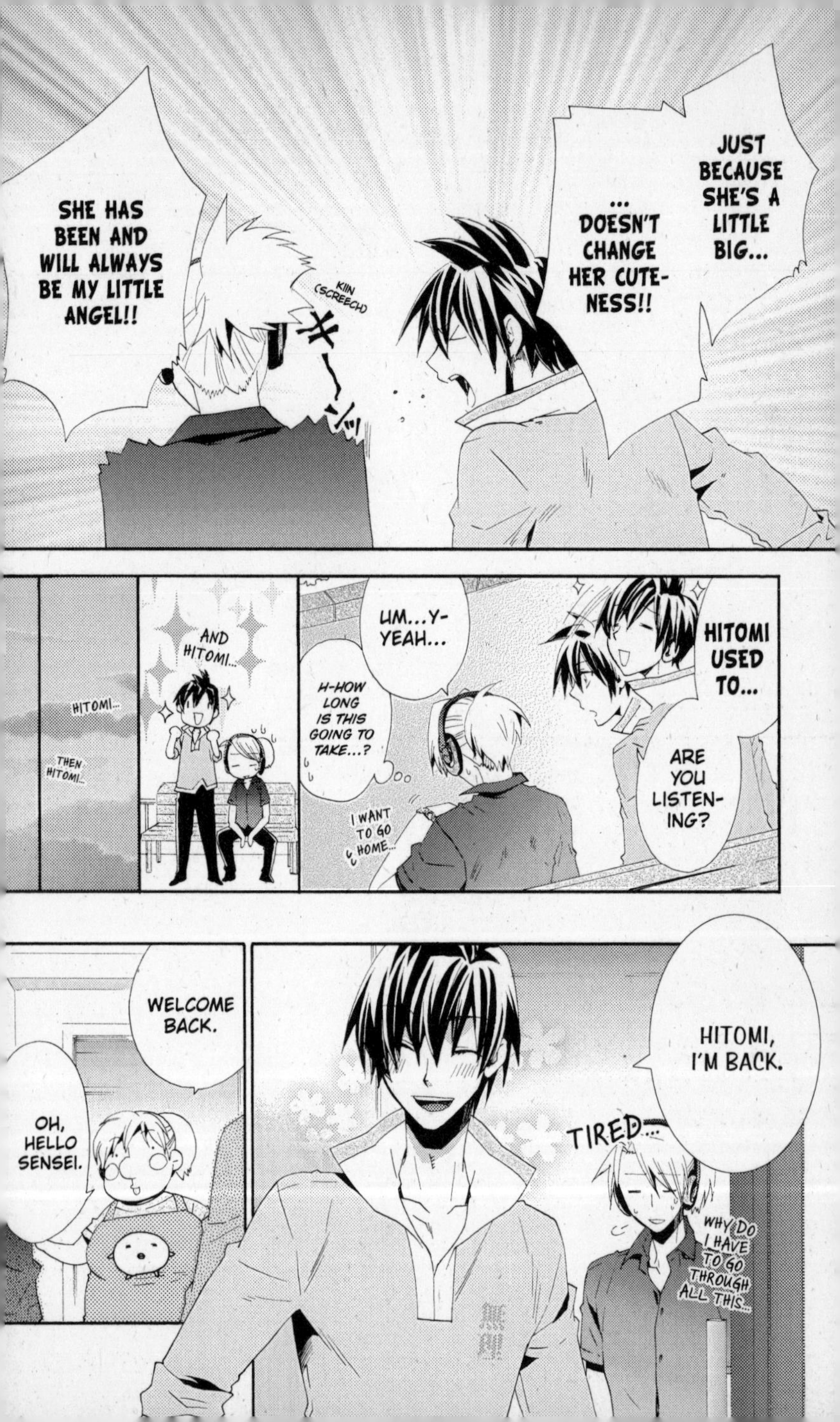
JUST BECAUSE SHE'S A LITTLE BIG...
...DOESN'T CHANGE HER CUTE-NESS!!
KIIN (SCREECH)
SHE HAS BEEN AND WILL ALWAYS BE MY LITTLE ANGEL!!
HITOMI USED TO...
UM...Y-YEAH...
ARE YOU LISTEN-ING?
H-HOW LONG IS THIS GOING TO TAKE...?
I WANT TO GO HOME...
AND HITOMI...
HITOMI...
THEN HITOMI...
HITOMI, I'M BACK.
TIRED...
WHY DO I HAVE TO GO THROUGH ALL THIS...
WELCOME BACK.
OH, HELLO SENSEI.

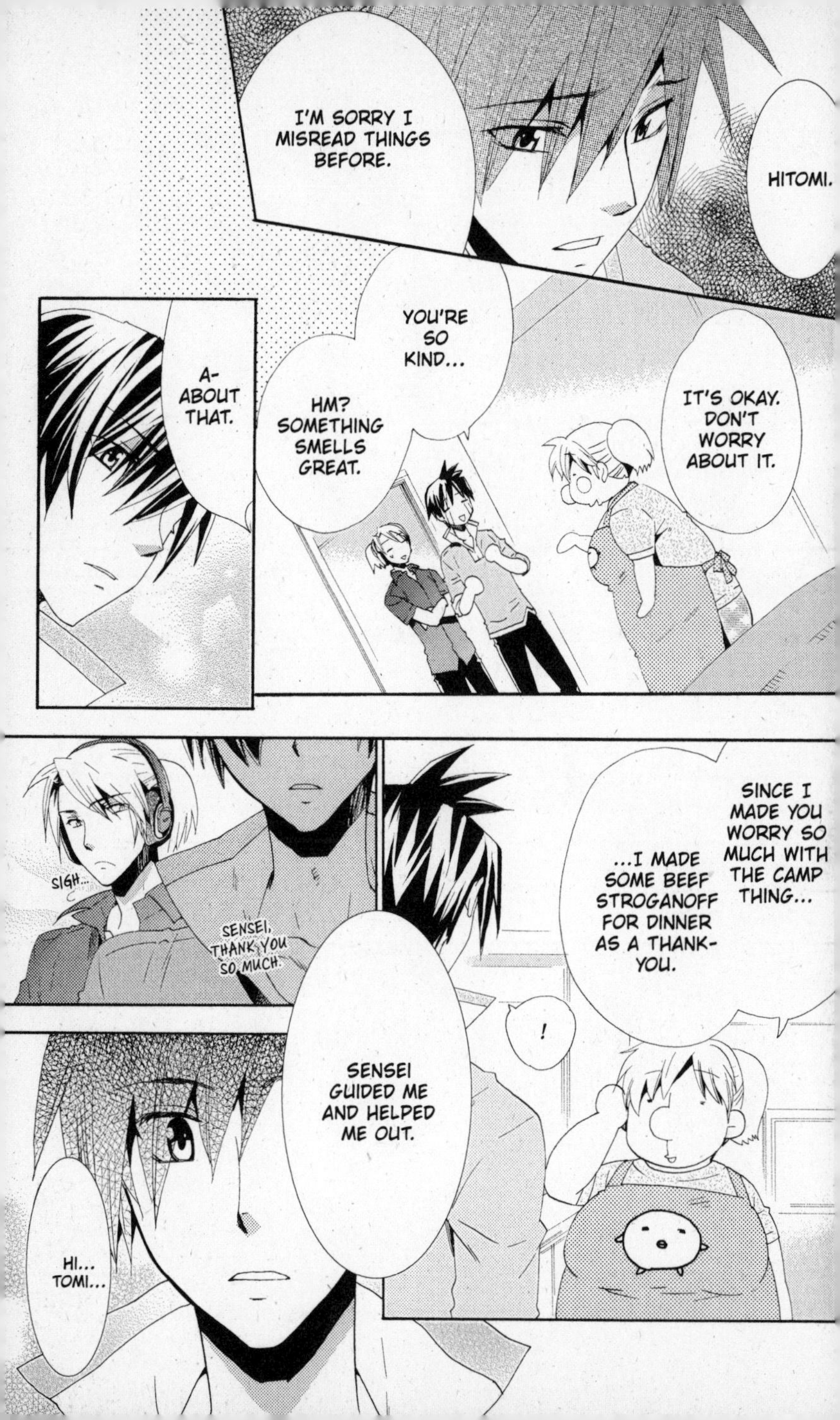
HITOMI.
I'M SORRY I MISREAD THINGS BEFORE.
IT'S OKAY. DON'T WORRY ABOUT IT.
YOU'RE SO KIND...
HM? SOMETHING SMELLS GREAT.
A- ABOUT THAT.
SINCE I MADE YOU WORRY SO MUCH WITH THE CAMP THING...
...I MADE SOME BEEF STROGANOFF FOR DINNER AS A THANK-YOU.
!
SENSEI, THANK YOU SO MUCH.
SIGH...
SENSEI GUIDED ME AND HELPED ME OUT.
HI... TOMI...

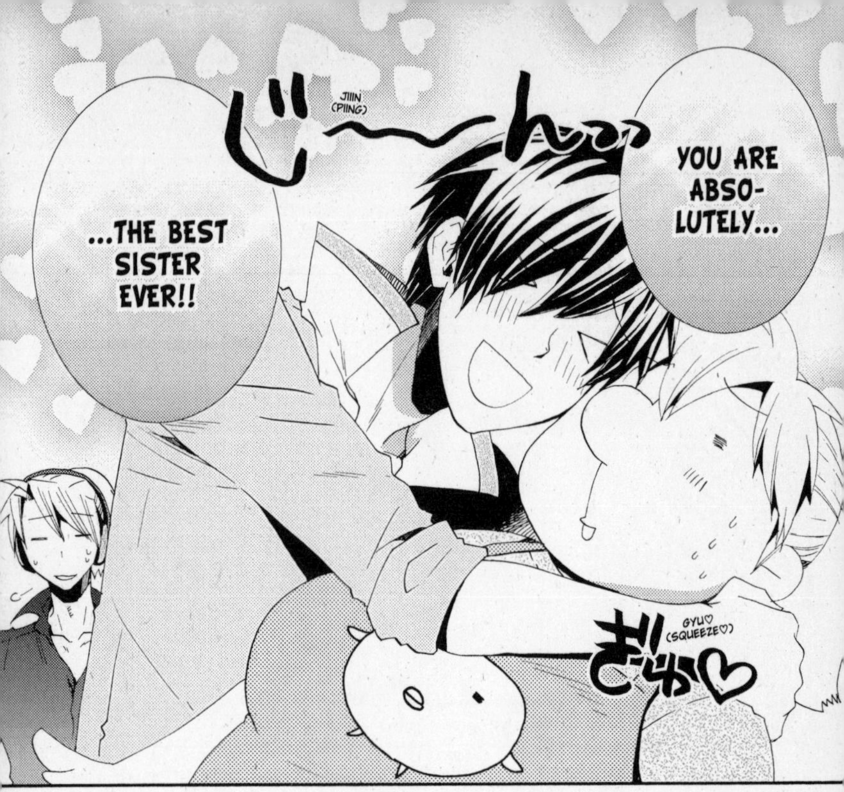
YOU ARE ABSO-LUTELY...
JIIN (PIING)
...THE BEST SISTER EVER!!
GYU♡ (SQUEEZE♡)

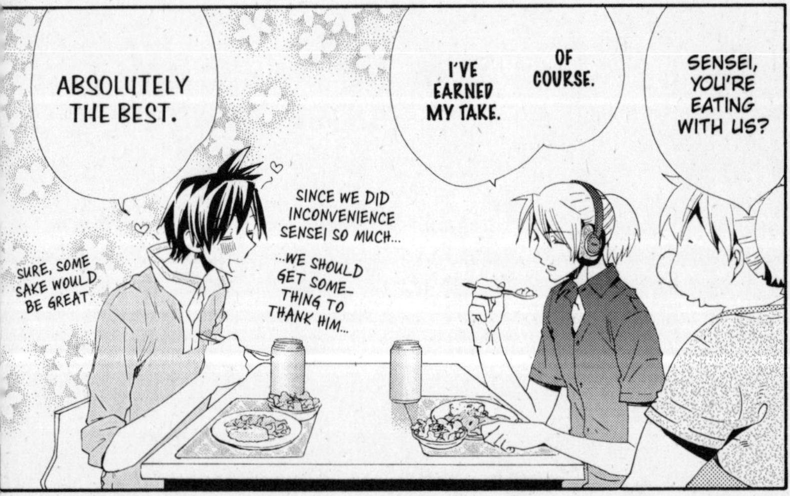
SENSEI, YOU'RE EATING WITH US?
OF COURSE.
I'VE EARNED MY TAKE.
ABSOLUTELY THE BEST.
SINCE WE DID INCONVENIENCE SENSEI SO MUCH...
...WE SHOULD GET SOME-THING TO THANK HIM...
SURE, SOME SAKE WOULD BE GREAT.

LOVEREVO!!

UGLY DUCKLING'S LOVE REVOLUTION

STORY CHARACTERS

REN ICHINOSE

PERFECTION PERSONIFIED, THE NO.1 MOST POPULAR GUY IN SCHOOL. WITH A DETACHED, COOL PERSONALITY, HE'S ALSO VERY BLUNT WITH HIS COMMENTS. JUNIOR.

SOUTA FUKAMI

LOVES SPORTS! LOVES SWEETS! QUITE THE ENERGETIC GUY. FOR SOME REASON, VERY ATTACHED TO HITOMI. IS IN THE SAME EXTRACURRICULAR CLUB AS HITOMI AS WELL. FRESHMAN.

KENNOSUKE TACHIBANA

TOUGH GUY WITH A BRUSQUE PERSONALITY. SINCE HIS FATHER IS A YAKUZA BOSS, IS CALLED "WAKA" AT HOME. HAS THREE SISTERS. A FRESHMAN BASKETBALL STAR.

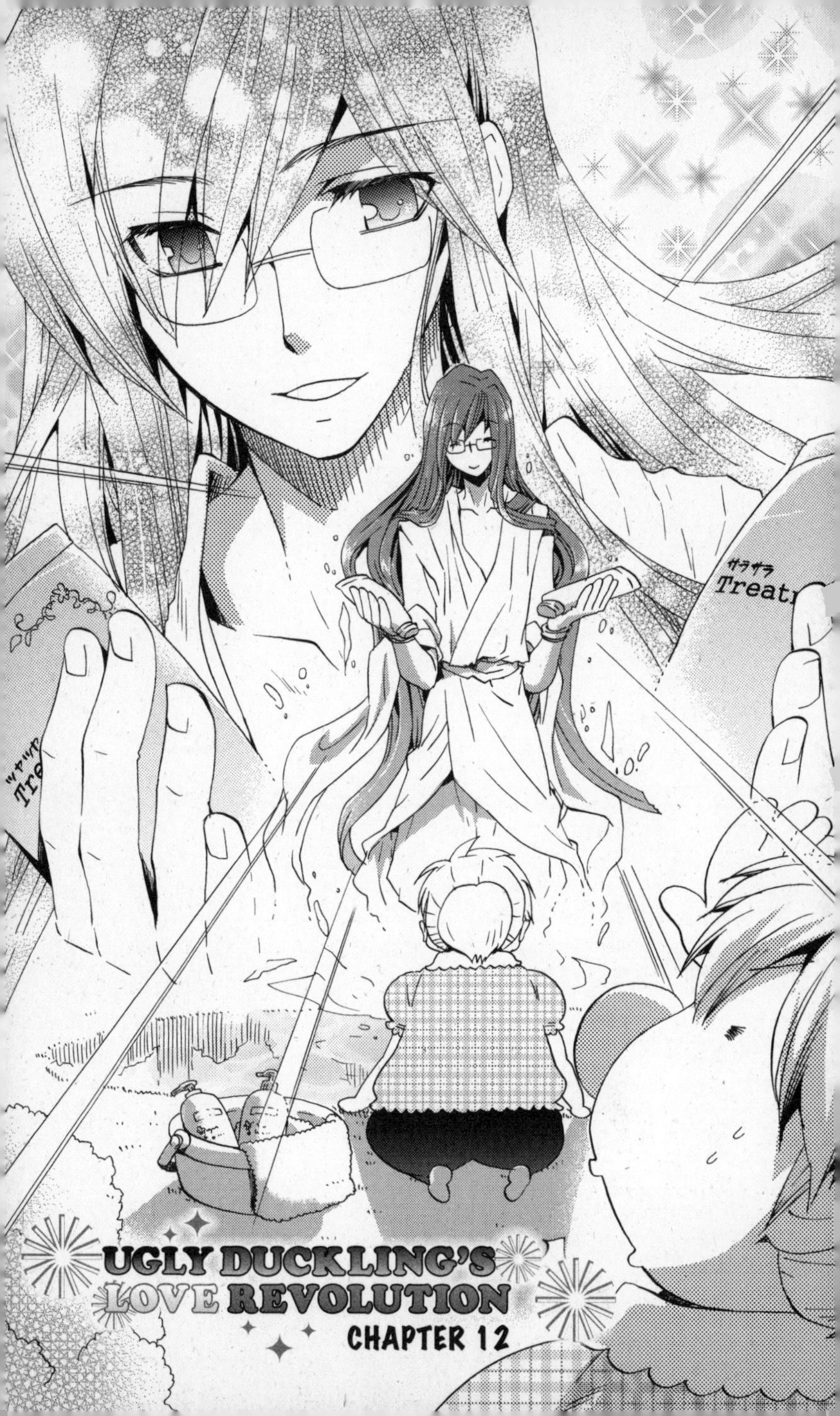
UGLY DUCKLING'S LOVE REVOLUTION
CHAPTER 12

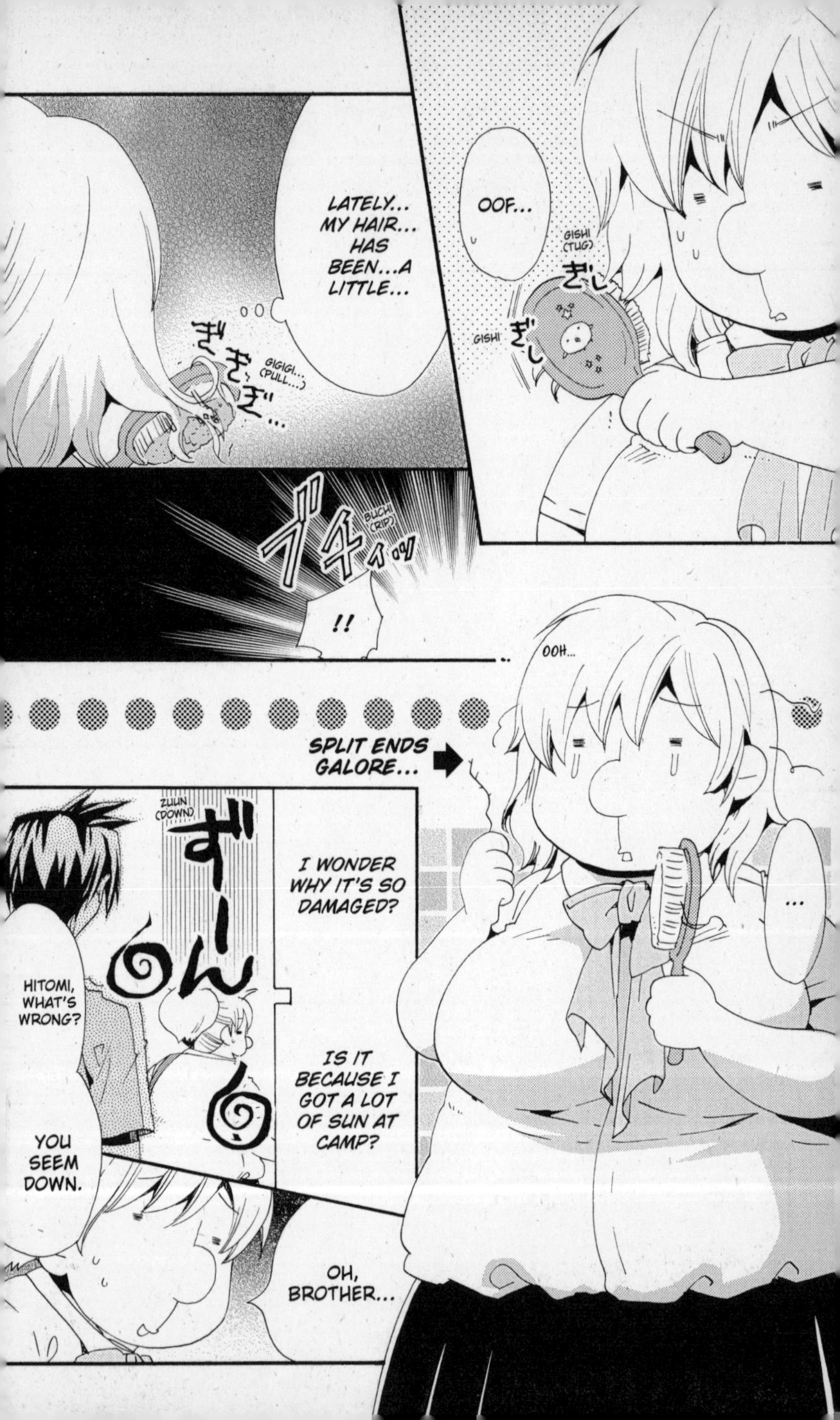
OOF...
GISHI (TUG)
ぎし
GISHI
ぎし
LATELY... MY HAIR... HAS BEEN...A LITTLE...
GIGIGI... (PULL...)
ぎぎぎ...
BUCHI (RIP)
ブチィッ
!!
OOH...
SPLIT ENDS GALORE...
...
I WONDER WHY IT'S SO DAMAGED?
ZUUN (DOWN)
ずーん
IS IT BECAUSE I GOT A LOT OF SUN AT CAMP?
HITOMI, WHAT'S WRONG?
YOU SEEM DOWN.
OH, BROTHER...

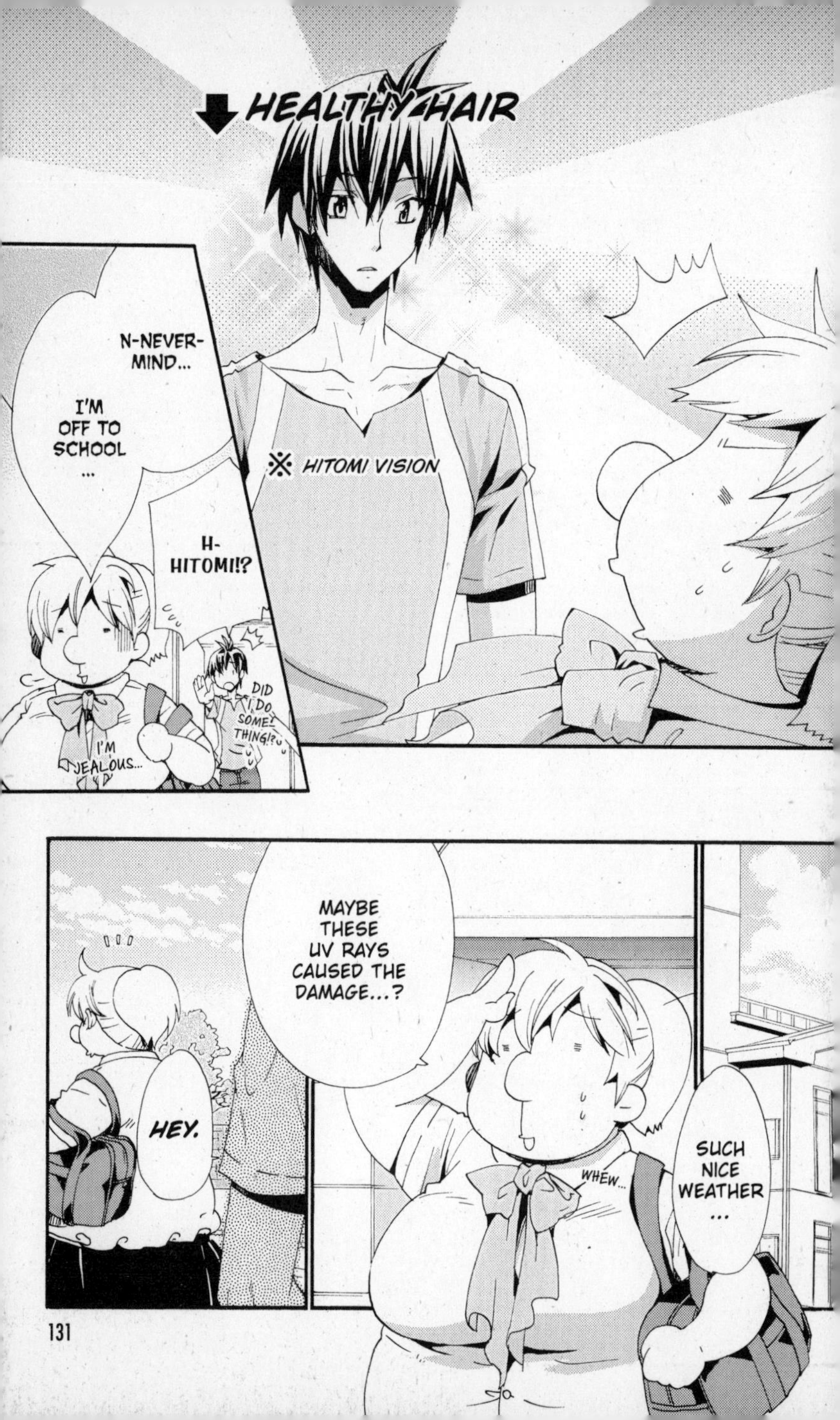
HEALTHY HAIR
※ HITOMI VISION
N-NEVER-MIND...
I'M OFF TO SCHOOL ...
H-HITOMI!?
DID I DO SOME-THING!?
I'M JEALOUS...
SUCH NICE WEATHER ...
WHEW...
MAYBE THESE UV RAYS CAUSED THE DAMAGE...?
HEY.

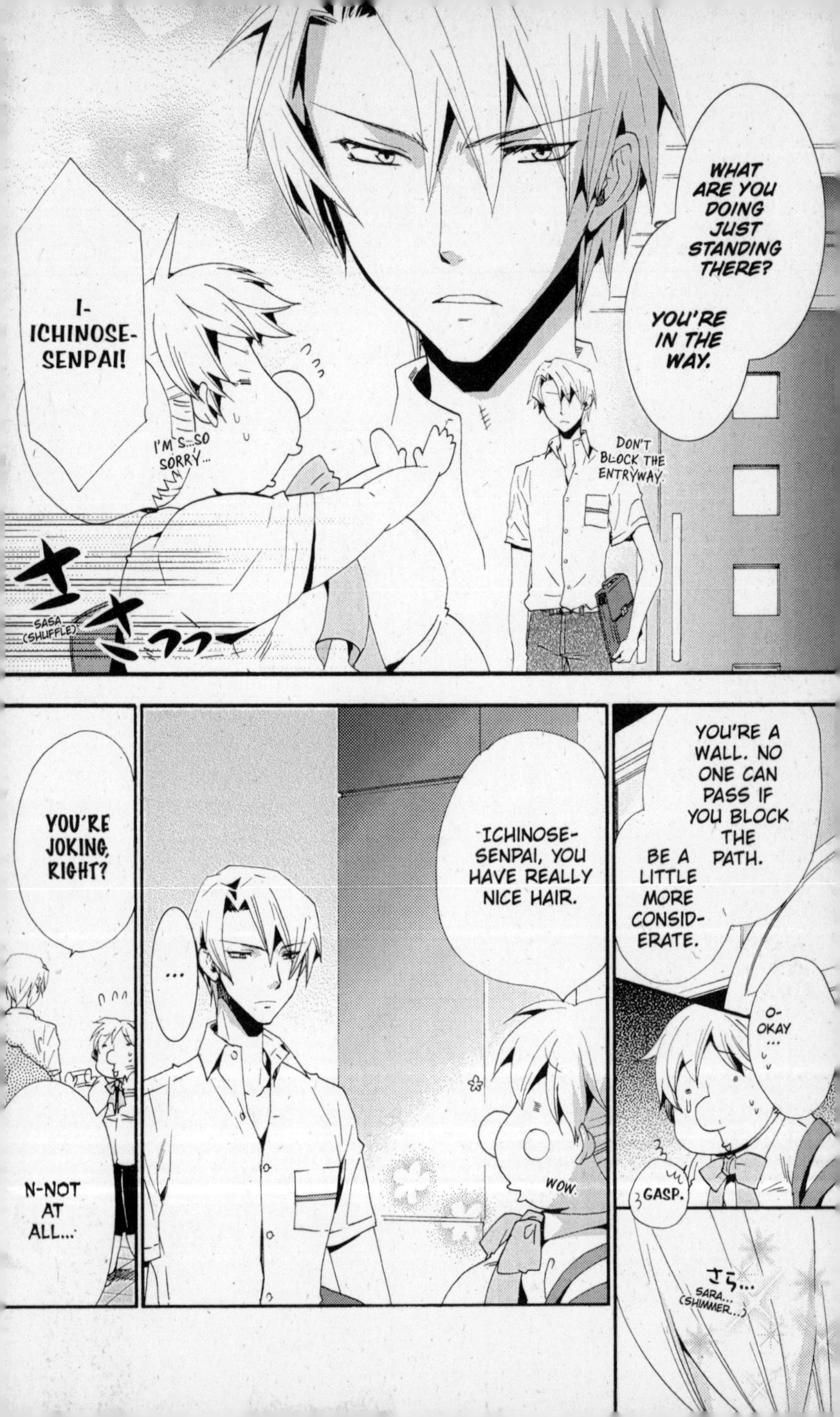
WHAT ARE YOU DOING JUST STANDING THERE?
YOU'RE IN THE WAY.
DON'T BLOCK THE ENTRYWAY.
I-ICHINOSE-SENPAI!
I'M S...SO SORRY...
SASA (SHUFFLE)
YOU'RE A WALL. NO ONE CAN PASS IF YOU BLOCK THE PATH.
BE A LITTLE MORE CONSIDERATE.
O-OKAY...
GASP.
さら...
SARA... (SHIMMER...)
ICHINOSE-SENPAI, YOU HAVE REALLY NICE HAIR.
WOW.
...
YOU'RE JOKING, RIGHT?
N-NOT AT ALL...

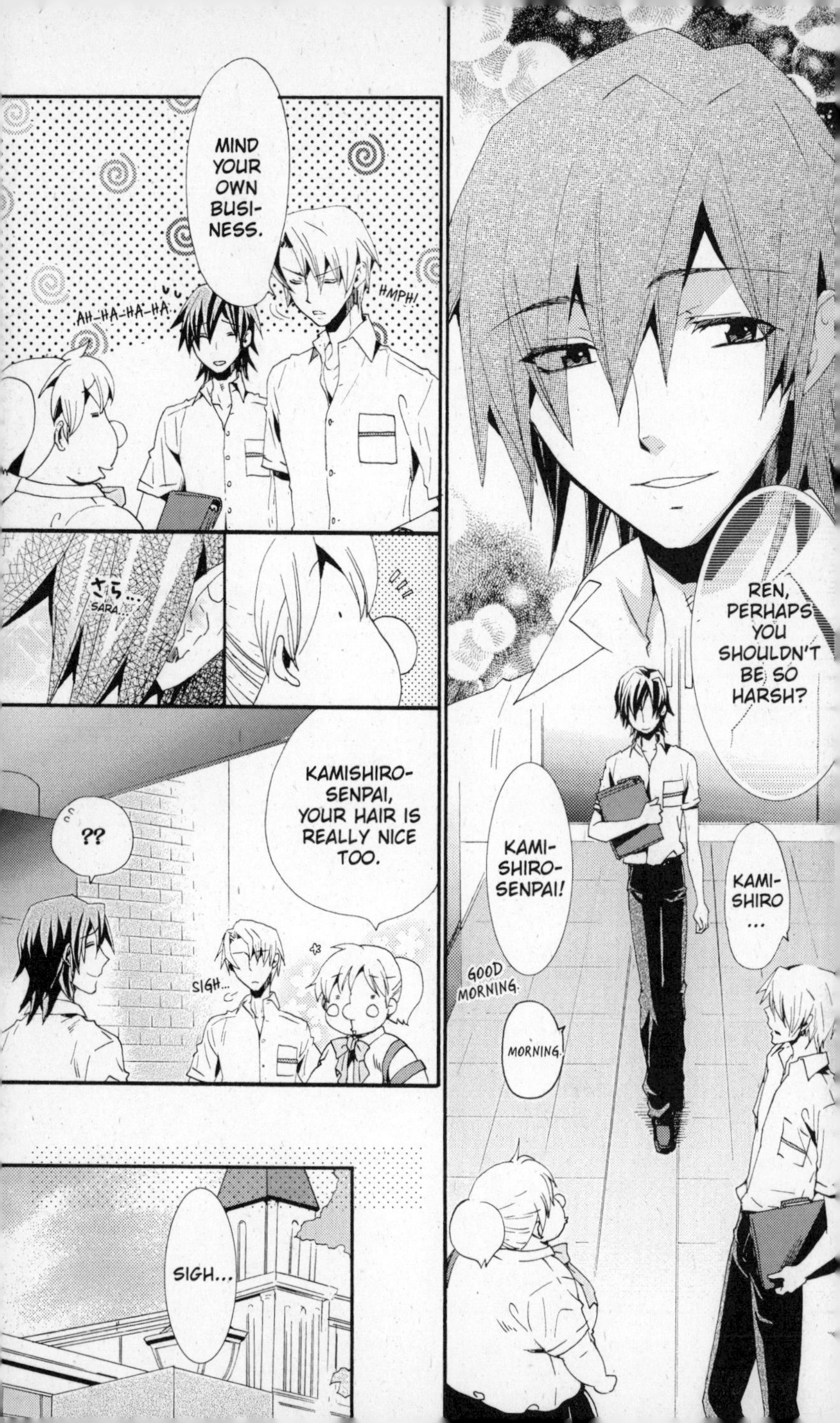
REN, PERHAPS YOU SHOULDN'T BE SO HARSH?
KAMI-SHIRO...
KAMI-SHIRO-SENPAI!
GOOD MORNING.
MORNING.
MIND YOUR OWN BUSI-NESS.
HMPH!
AH-HA-HA-HA
さら…
SARA...
KAMISHIRO-SENPAI, YOUR HAIR IS REALLY NICE TOO.
SIGH...
??
SIGH...

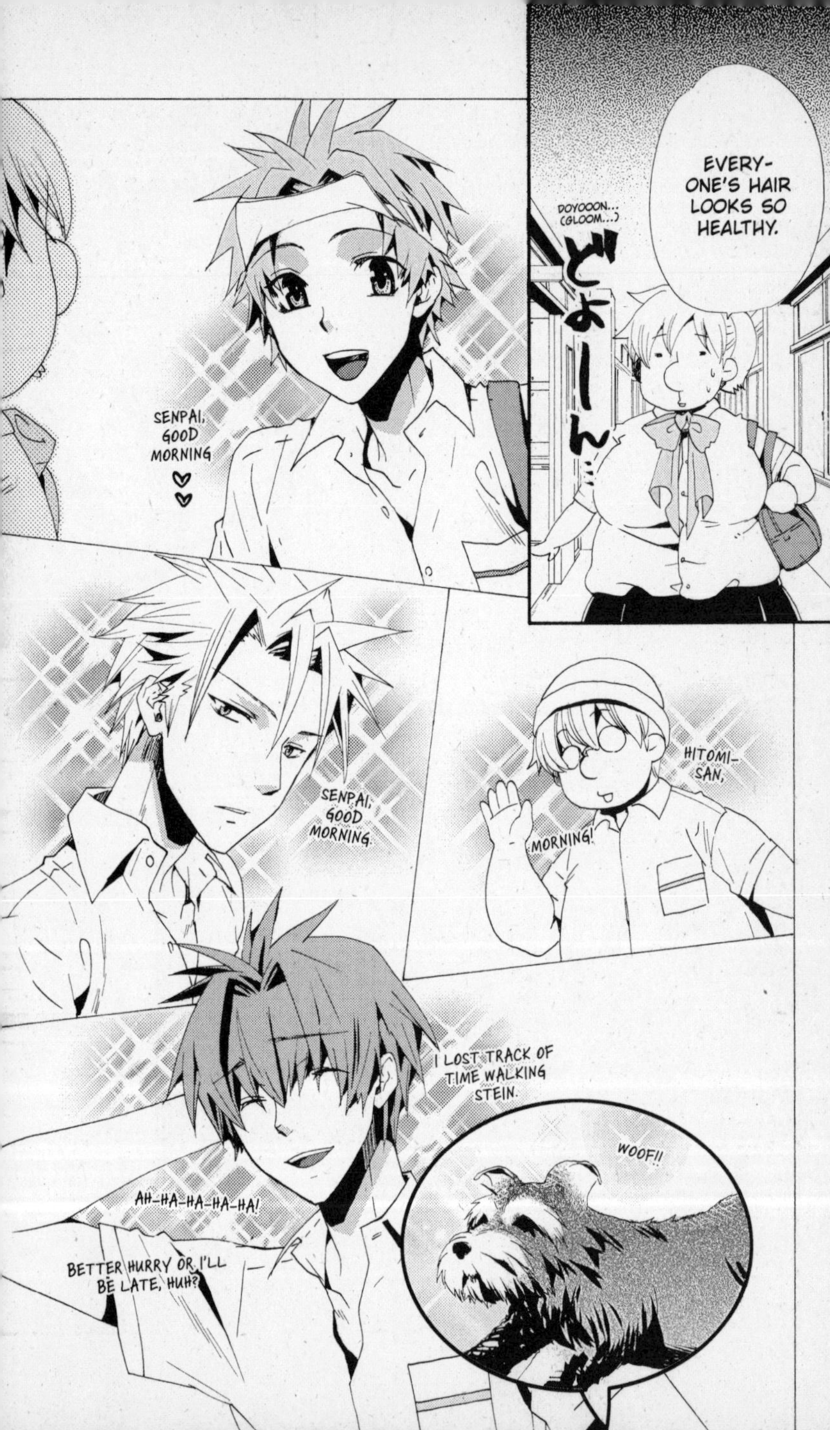
EVERY-ONE'S HAIR LOOKS SO HEALTHY.
DOYOOON... (GLOOM...)
どよーん
SENPAI, GOOD MORNING ♡ ♡
HITOMI-SAN,
MORNING!
SENPAI, GOOD MORNING.
I LOST TRACK OF TIME WALKING STEIN.
WOOF!!
AH-HA-HA-HA-HA!
BETTER HURRY OR I'LL BE LATE, HUH?

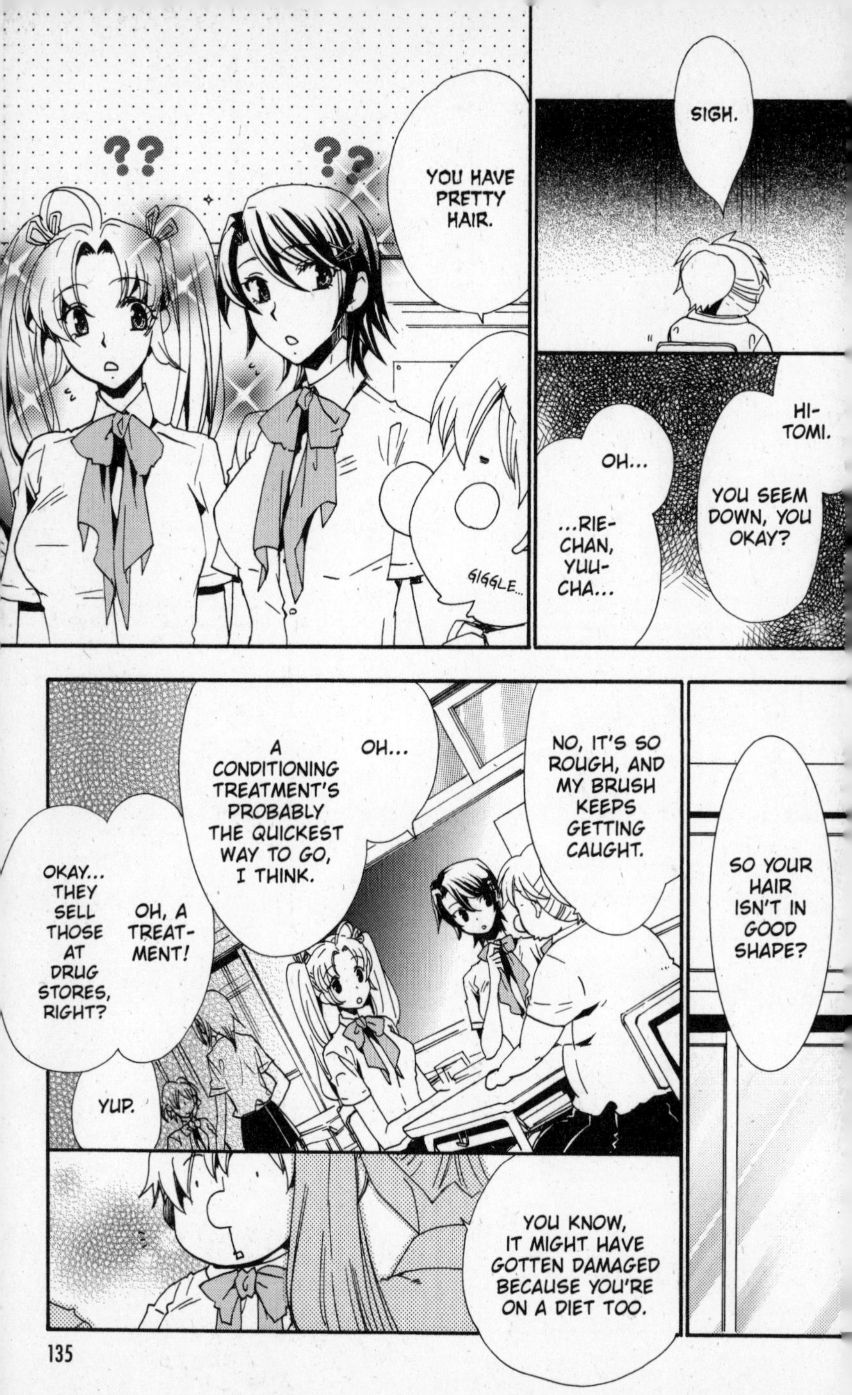
SIGH.
HI-TOMI.
YOU SEEM DOWN, YOU OKAY?
OH...
...RIE-CHAN, YUU-CHA...
YOU HAVE PRETTY HAIR.
GIGGLE...
SO YOUR HAIR ISN'T IN GOOD SHAPE?
NO, IT'S SO ROUGH, AND MY BRUSH KEEPS GETTING CAUGHT.
OH...
A CONDITIONING TREATMENT'S PROBABLY THE QUICKEST WAY TO GO, I THINK.
OH, A TREATMENT!
OKAY... THEY SELL THOSE AT DRUG STORES, RIGHT?
YUP.
YOU KNOW, IT MIGHT HAVE GOTTEN DAMAGED BECAUSE YOU'RE ON A DIET TOO.

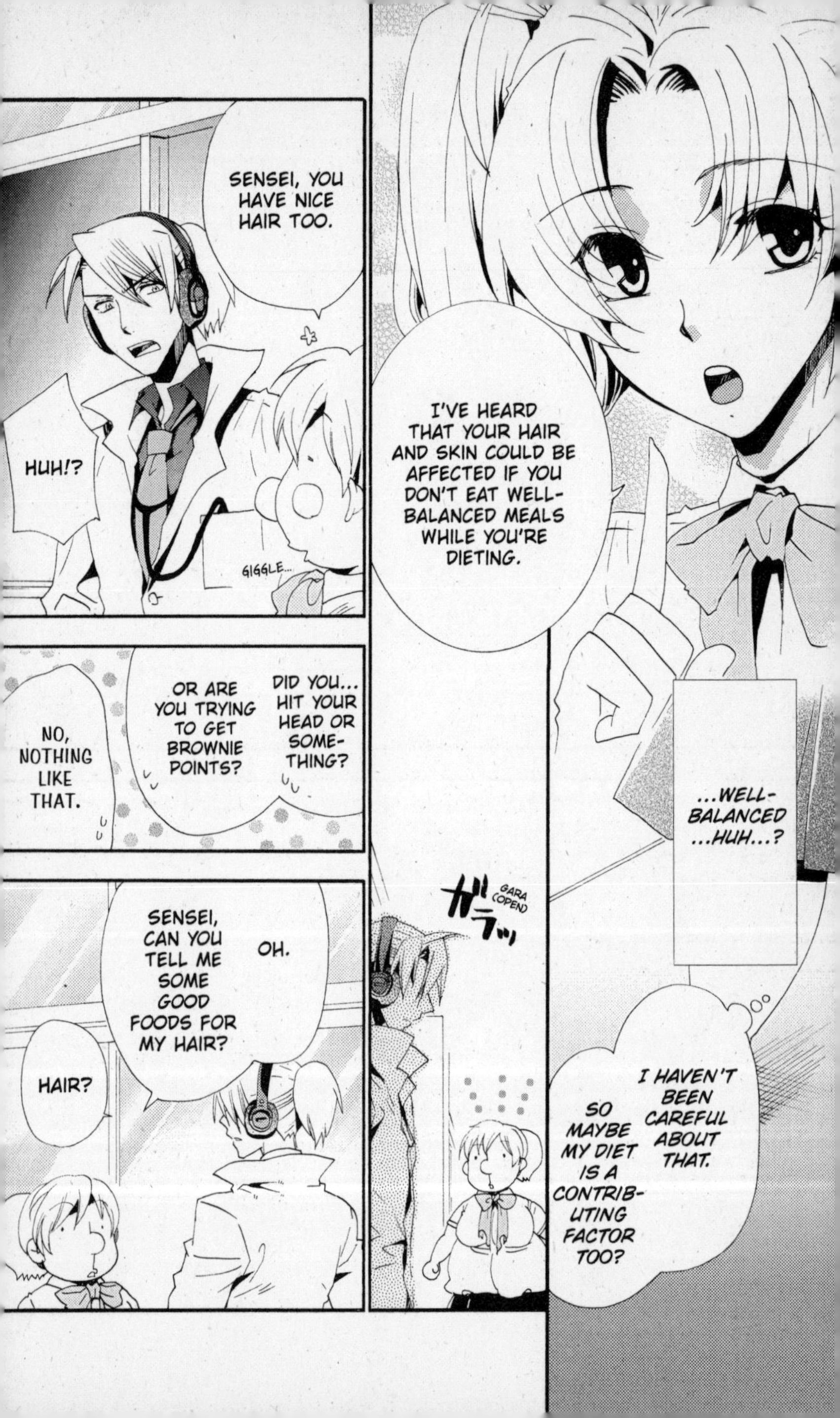
I'VE HEARD THAT YOUR HAIR AND SKIN COULD BE AFFECTED IF YOU DON'T EAT WELL-BALANCED MEALS WHILE YOU'RE DIETING.
...WELL-BALANCED ...HUH...?
I HAVEN'T BEEN CAREFUL ABOUT THAT.
SO MAYBE MY DIET IS A CONTRIB-UTING FACTOR TOO?
GARA (OPEN)
SENSEI, YOU HAVE NICE HAIR TOO.
HUH!?
GIGGLE...
DID YOU... HIT YOUR HEAD OR SOME-THING?
OR ARE YOU TRYING TO GET BROWNIE POINTS?
NO, NOTHING LIKE THAT.
OH.
SENSEI, CAN YOU TELL ME SOME GOOD FOODS FOR MY HAIR?
HAIR?

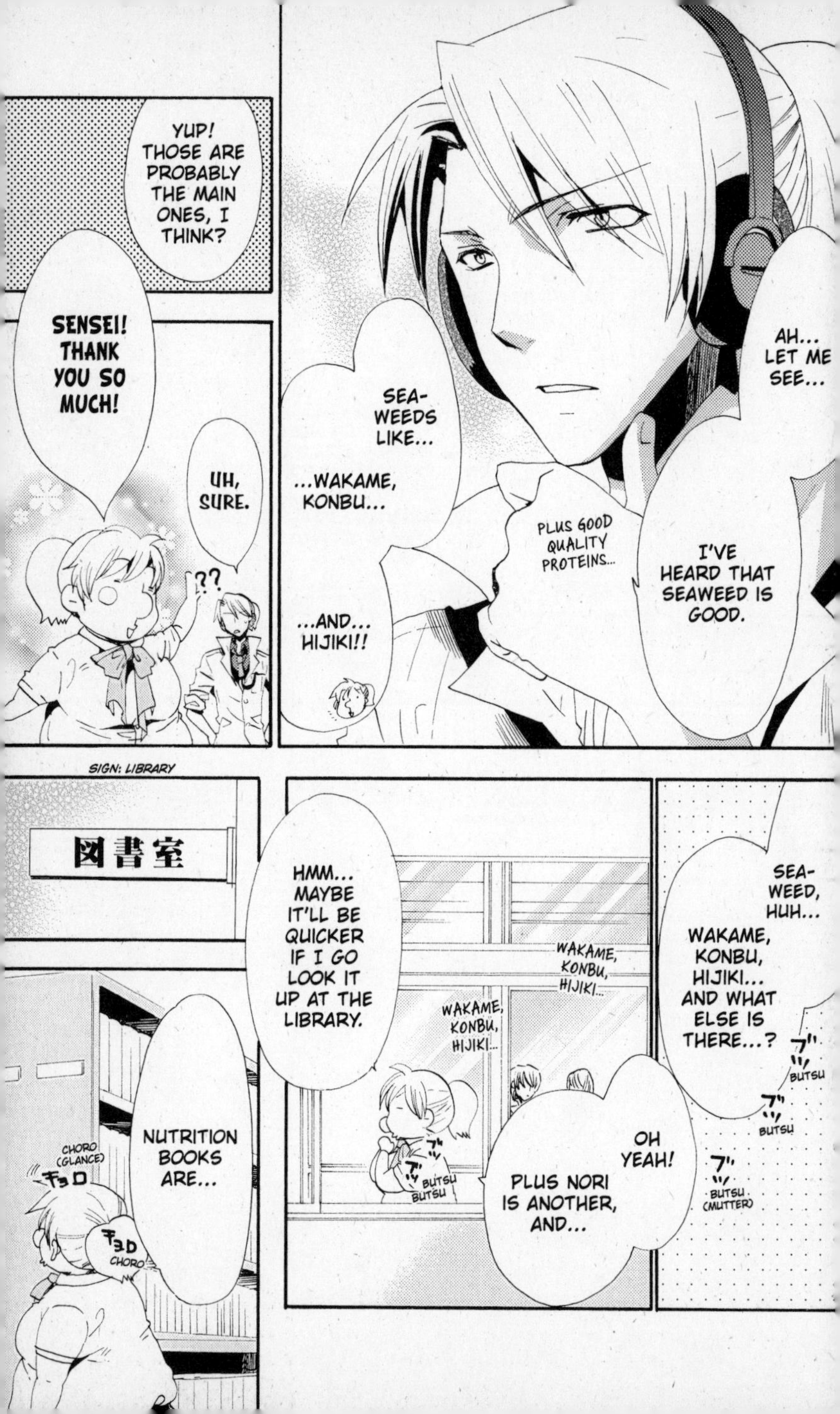
AH... LET ME SEE...
I'VE HEARD THAT SEAWEED IS GOOD.
PLUS GOOD QUALITY PROTEINS...
SEA-WEEDS LIKE...
...WAKAME, KONBU...
...AND... HIJIKI!!
YUP! THOSE ARE PROBABLY THE MAIN ONES, I THINK?
SENSEI! THANK YOU SO MUCH!
UH, SURE.
??
SEA-WEED, HUH...
WAKAME, KONBU, HIJIKI... AND WHAT ELSE IS THERE...?
ブツ BUTSU
ブツ BUTSU
ブツ BUTSU (MUTTER)
OH YEAH!
PLUS NORI IS ANOTHER, AND...
WAKAME, KONBU, HIJIKI...
WAKAME, KONBU, HIJIKI...
ブツ ブツ BUTSU BUTSU
HMM... MAYBE IT'LL BE QUICKER IF I GO LOOK IT UP AT THE LIBRARY.
SIGN: LIBRARY
図書室
NUTRITION BOOKS ARE...
チョロ CHORO (GLANCE)
チョロ CHORO

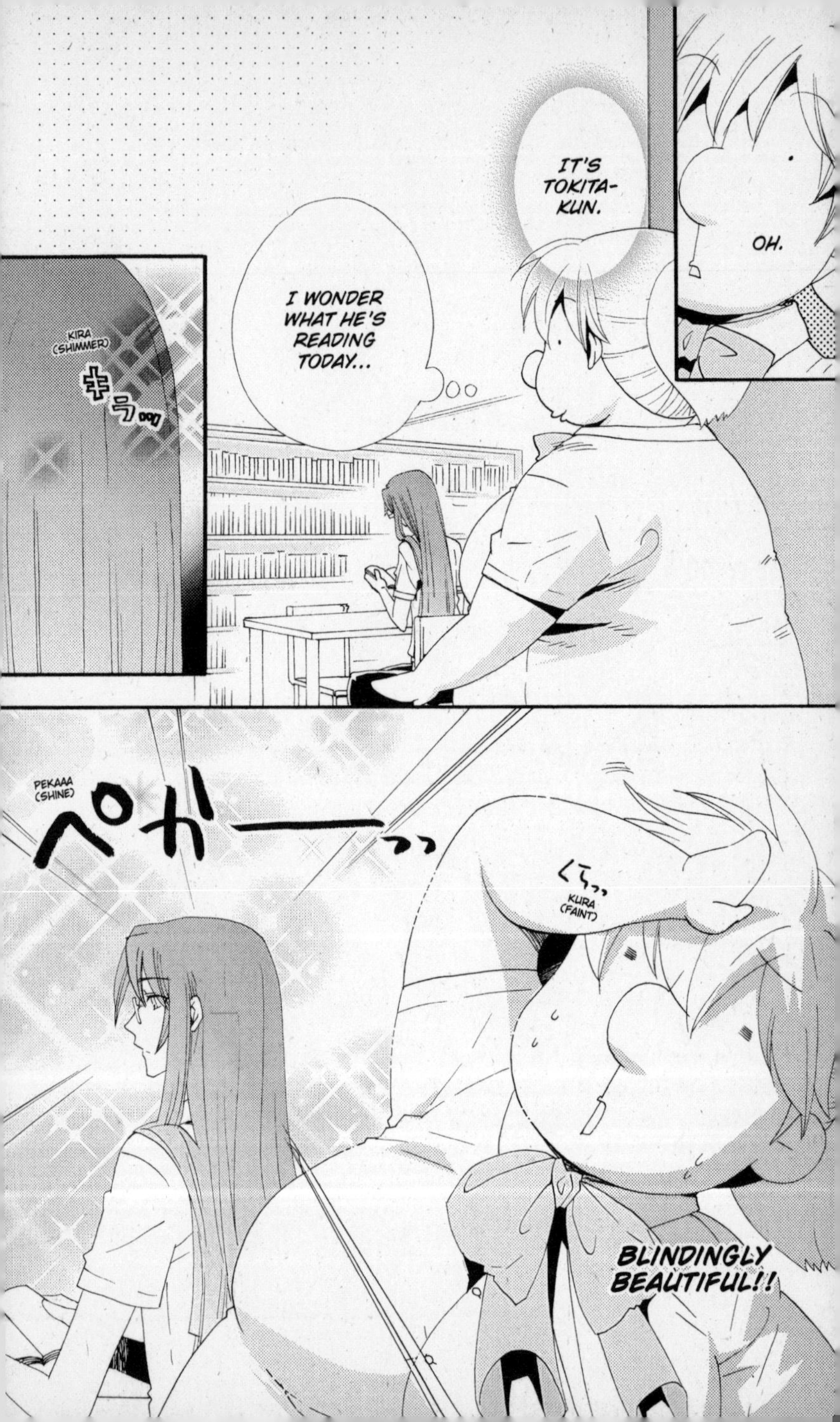
OH.
IT'S TOKITA-KUN.
I WONDER WHAT HE'S READING TODAY...
キラッ
KIRA (SHIMMER)
ペカーッ
PEKAAA (SHINE)
くらっ
KURA (FAINT)
BLINDINGLY BEAUTIFUL!!

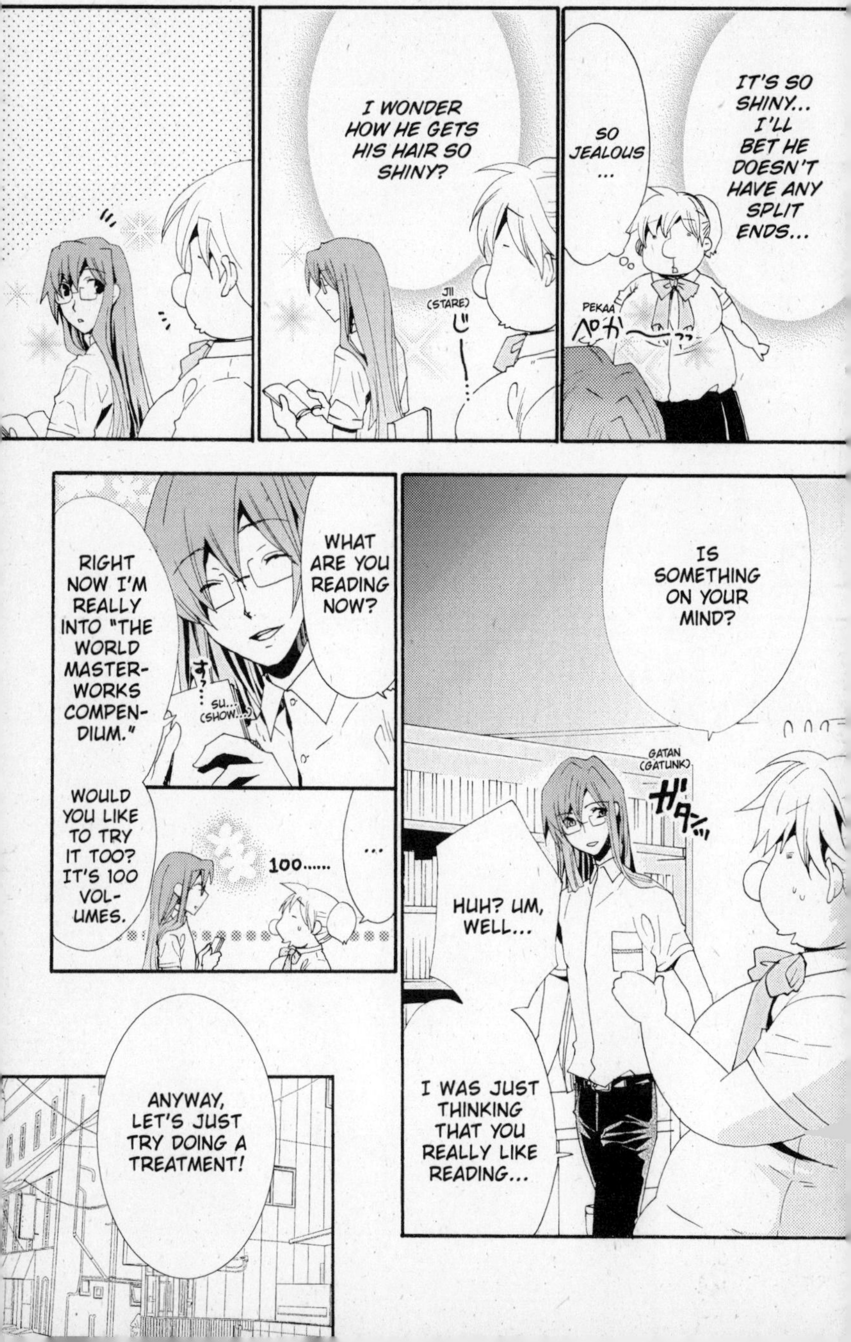
IT'S SO SHINY... I'LL BET HE DOESN'T HAVE ANY SPLIT ENDS...
SO JEALOUS...
PEKAA
I WONDER HOW HE GETS HIS HAIR SO SHINY?
JII (STARE)
IS SOMETHING ON YOUR MIND?
GATAN (GATUNK)
HUH? UM, WELL...
I WAS JUST THINKING THAT YOU REALLY LIKE READING...
WHAT ARE YOU READING NOW?
RIGHT NOW I'M REALLY INTO "THE WORLD MASTER-WORKS COMPEN-DIUM."
SU... (SHOW...)
...
100......
WOULD YOU LIKE TO TRY IT TOO? IT'S 100 VOL-UMES.
ANYWAY, LET'S JUST TRY DOING A TREATMENT!

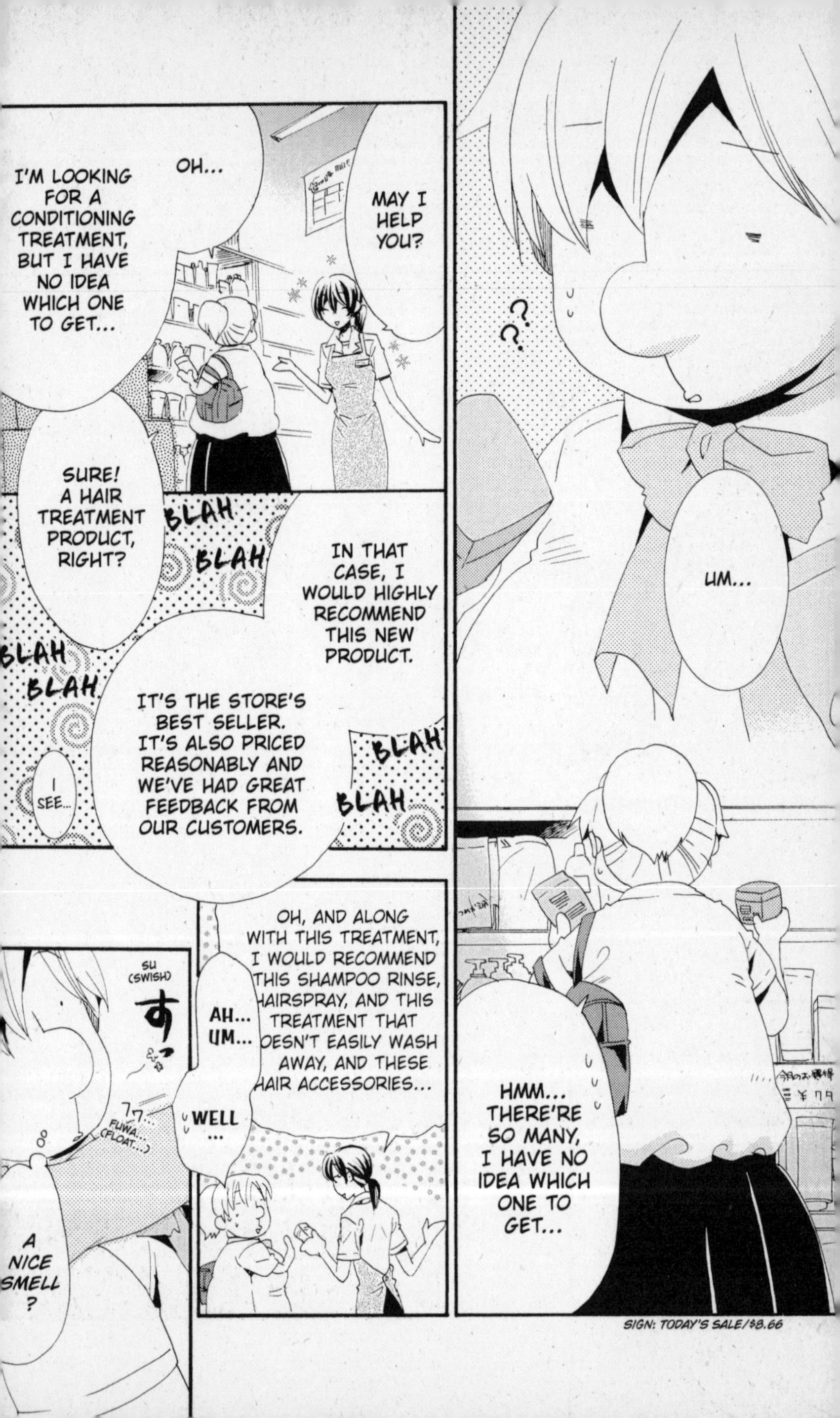
UM...
HMM... THERE'RE SO MANY, I HAVE NO IDEA WHICH ONE TO GET...
今月のお買得
MAY I HELP YOU?
OH...
I'M LOOKING FOR A CONDITIONING TREATMENT, BUT I HAVE NO IDEA WHICH ONE TO GET...
SURE! A HAIR TREATMENT PRODUCT, RIGHT?
BLAH BLAH
IN THAT CASE, I WOULD HIGHLY RECOMMEND THIS NEW PRODUCT.
BLAH BLAH
IT'S THE STORE'S BEST SELLER. IT'S ALSO PRICED REASONABLY AND WE'VE HAD GREAT FEEDBACK FROM OUR CUSTOMERS.
BLAH BLAH
I SEE...
OH, AND ALONG WITH THIS TREATMENT, I WOULD RECOMMEND THIS SHAMPOO RINSE, HAIRSPRAY, AND THIS TREATMENT THAT DOESN'T EASILY WASH AWAY, AND THESE HAIR ACCESSORIES...
AH... UM...
WELL ...
SU (SWISH)
す
フワ...
FUWA... (FLOAT...)
A NICE SMELL?
SIGN: TODAY'S SALE/$8.66

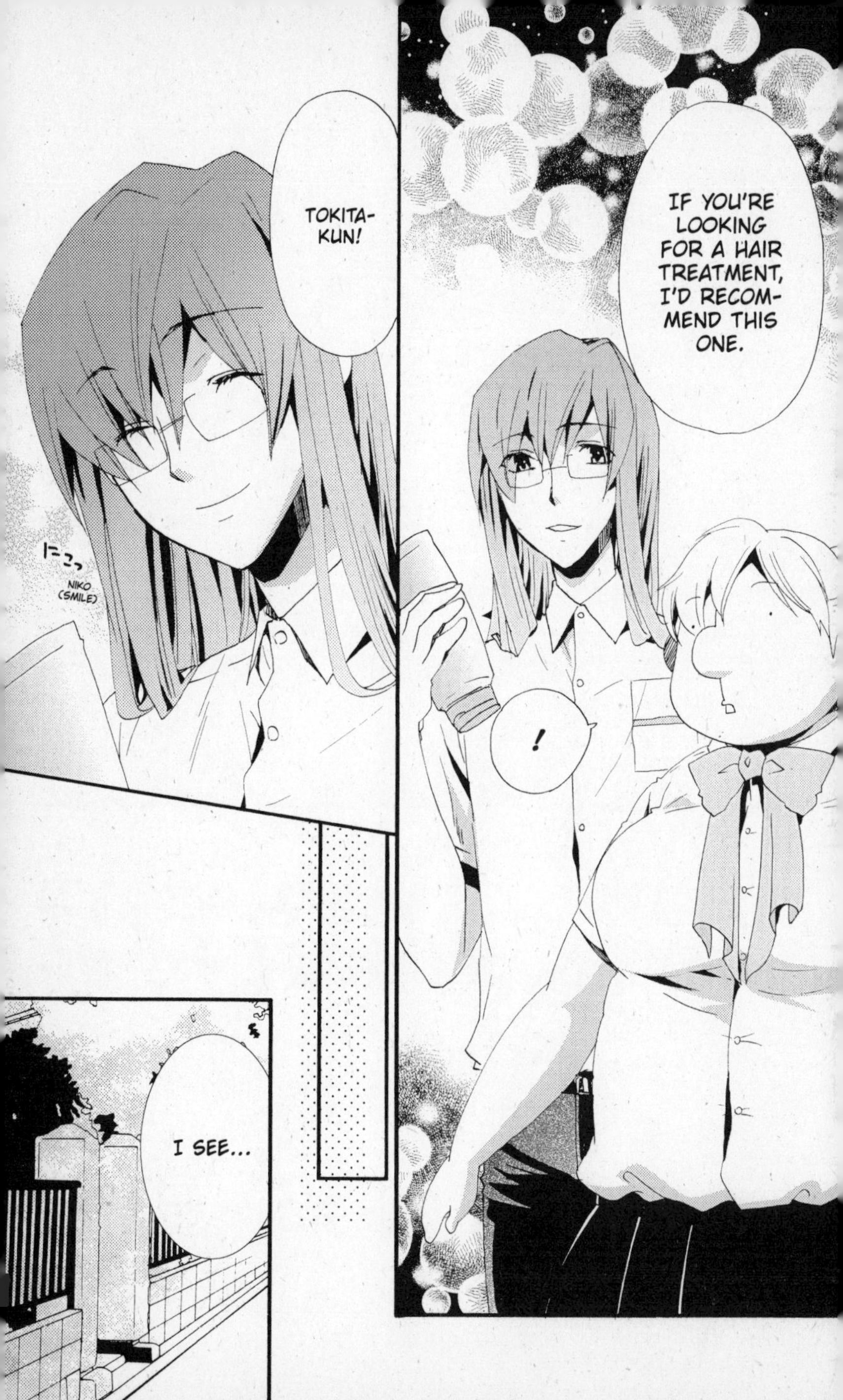
IF YOU'RE LOOKING FOR A HAIR TREATMENT, I'D RECOMMEND THIS ONE.
!
TOKITA-KUN!
にこっ
NIKO (SMILE)
I SEE...

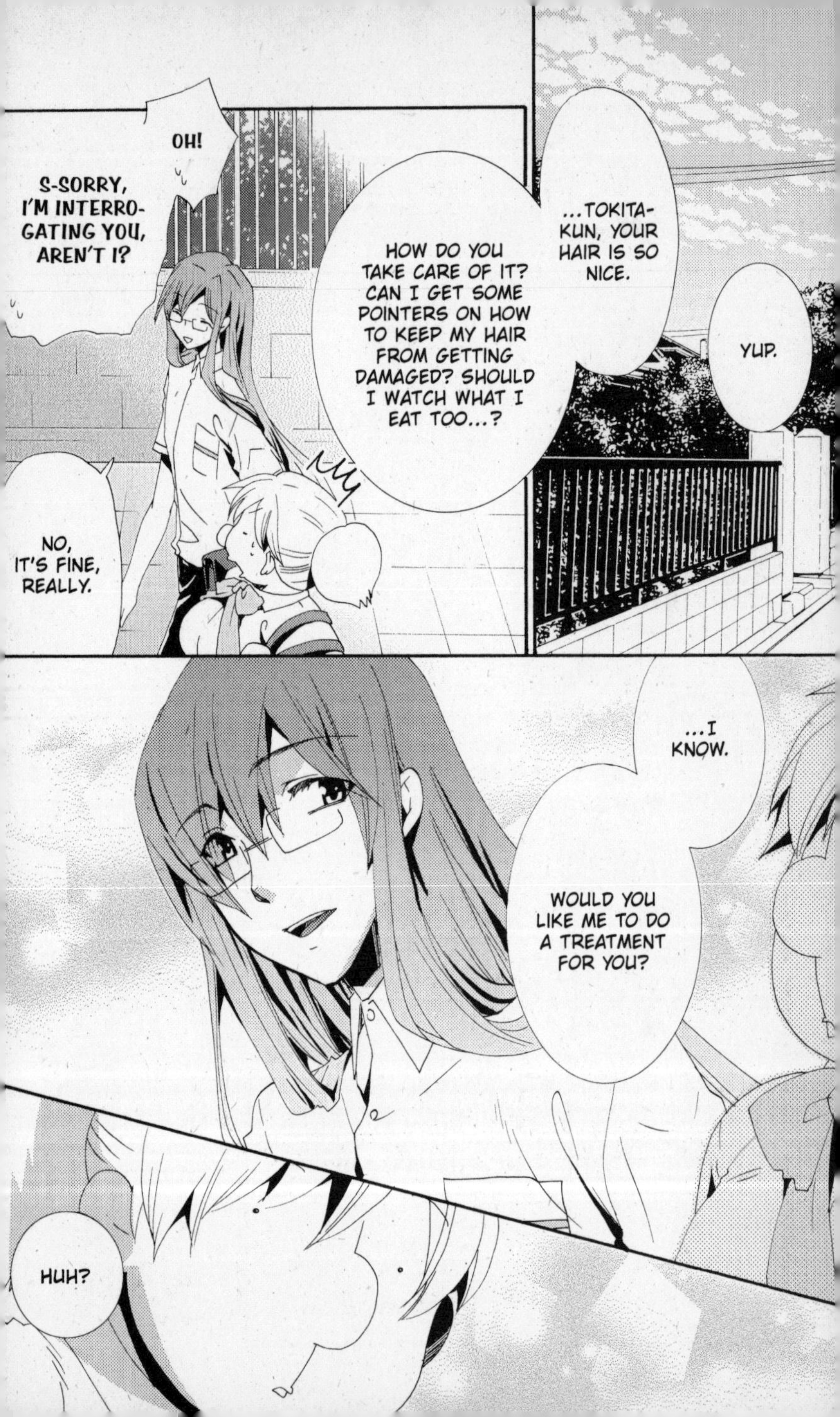
...TOKITA-KUN, YOUR HAIR IS SO NICE.
YUP.
HOW DO YOU TAKE CARE OF IT? CAN I GET SOME POINTERS ON HOW TO KEEP MY HAIR FROM GETTING DAMAGED? SHOULD I WATCH WHAT I EAT TOO...?
OH!
S-SORRY, I'M INTERRO-GATING YOU, AREN'T I?
NO, IT'S FINE, REALLY.
...I KNOW.
WOULD YOU LIKE ME TO DO A TREATMENT FOR YOU?
HUH?

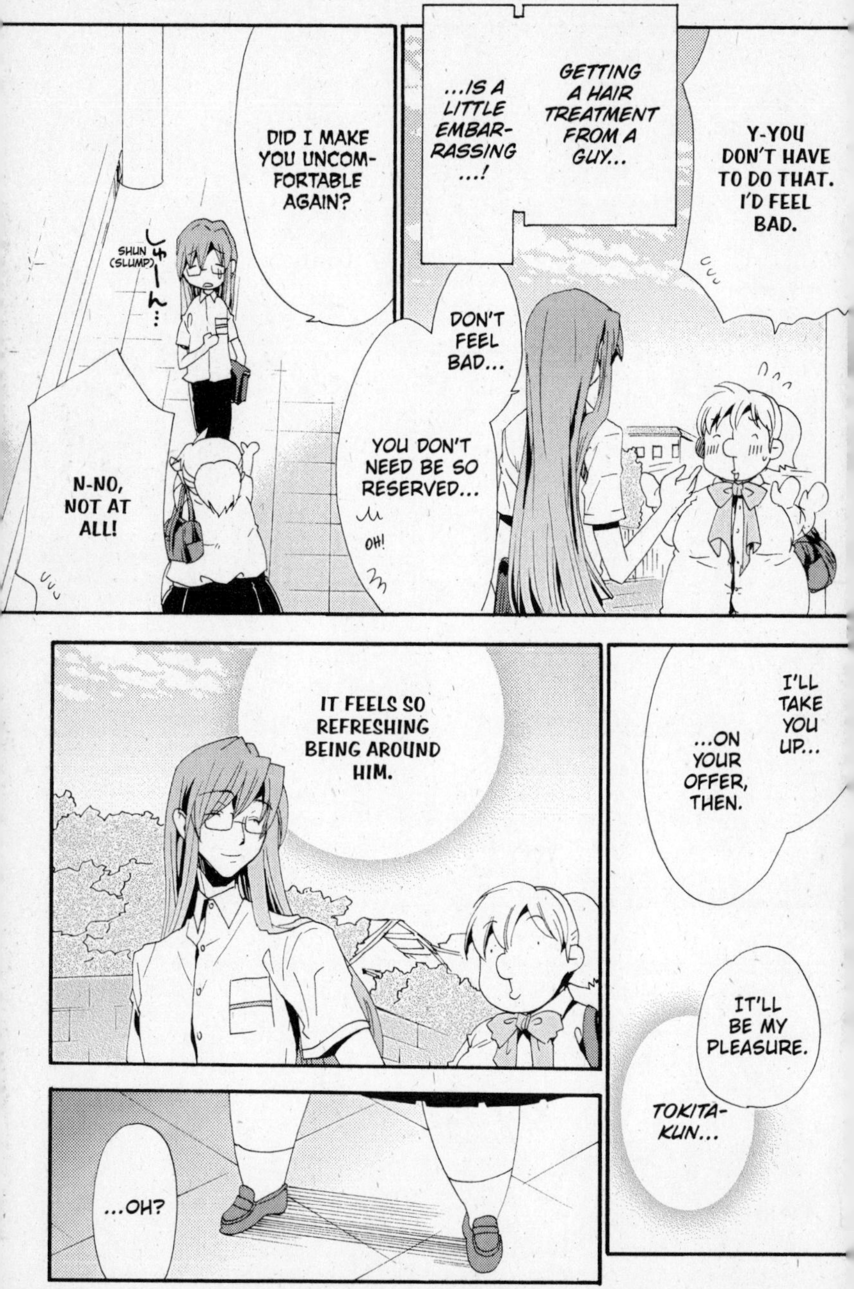
Y-YOU DON'T HAVE TO DO THAT. I'D FEEL BAD.
GETTING A HAIR TREATMENT FROM A GUY...
...IS A LITTLE EMBARRASSING...!
DON'T FEEL BAD...
YOU DON'T NEED BE SO RESERVED...
OH!
DID I MAKE YOU UNCOM-FORTABLE AGAIN?
しゅーん…
SHUN (SLUMP)
N-NO, NOT AT ALL!
I'LL TAKE YOU UP...
...ON YOUR OFFER, THEN.
IT'LL BE MY PLEASURE.
TOKITA-KUN...
IT FEELS SO REFRESHING BEING AROUND HIM.
...OH?

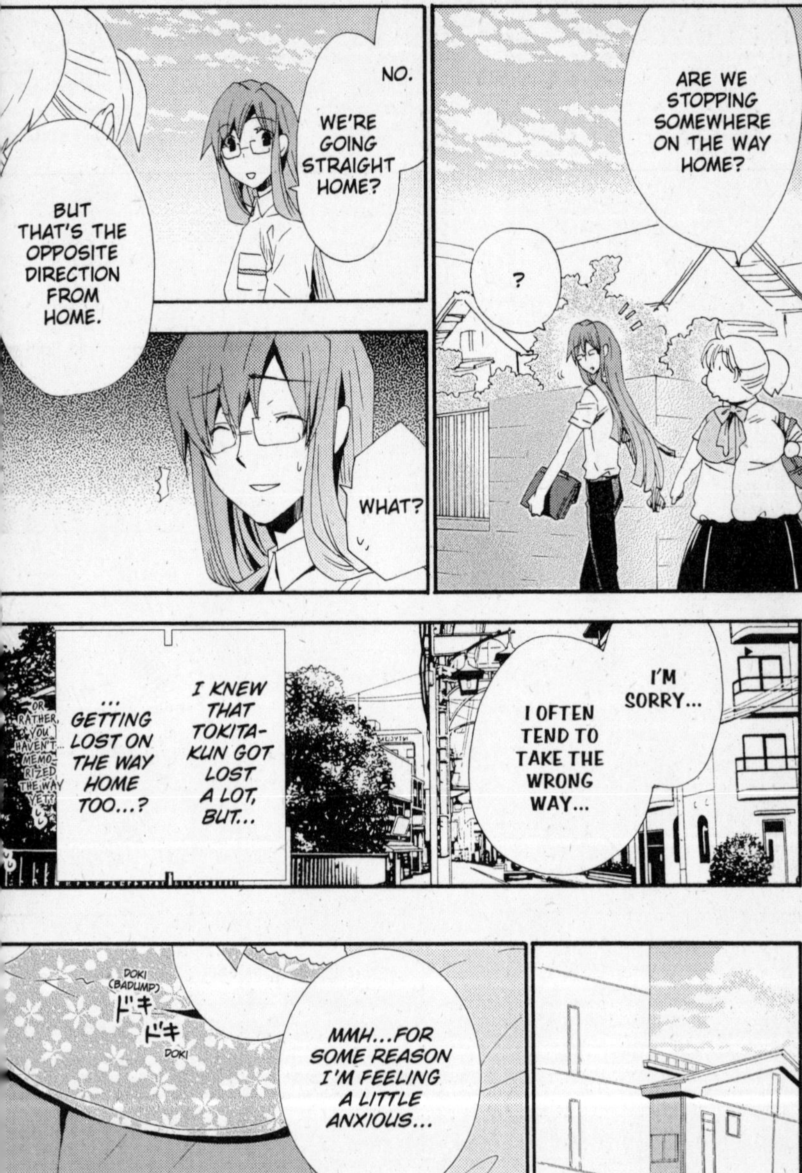
ARE WE STOPPING SOMEWHERE ON THE WAY HOME?
?
NO.
WE'RE GOING STRAIGHT HOME?
BUT THAT'S THE OPPOSITE DIRECTION FROM HOME.
WHAT?
I'M SORRY...
I OFTEN TEND TO TAKE THE WRONG WAY...
I KNEW THAT TOKITA-KUN GOT LOST A LOT, BUT...
...GETTING LOST ON THE WAY HOME TOO...?
OR RATHER, YOU HAVEN'T MEMORIZED THE WAY YET?
DOKI (BADUMP)
ドキ
ドキ
DOKI
MMH...FOR SOME REASON I'M FEELING A LITTLE ANXIOUS...

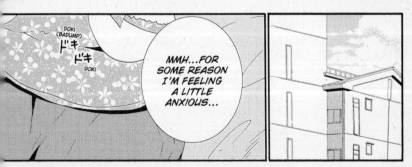

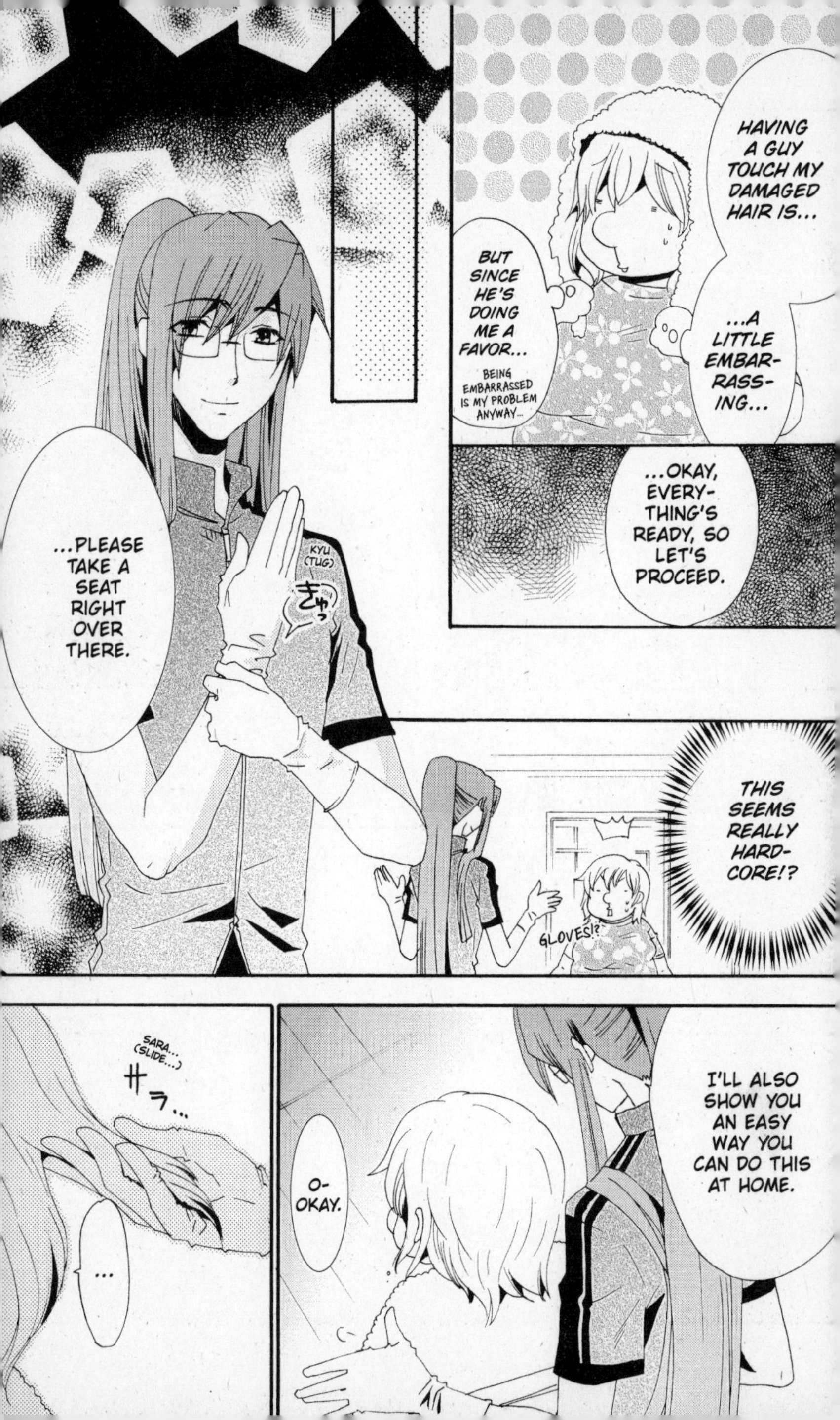
HAVING A GUY TOUCH MY DAMAGED HAIR IS...
...A LITTLE EMBAR-RASS-ING...
BUT SINCE HE'S DOING ME A FAVOR...
BEING EMBARRASSED IS MY PROBLEM ANYWAY...
...OKAY, EVERY-THING'S READY, SO LET'S PROCEED.
...PLEASE TAKE A SEAT RIGHT OVER THERE.
KYU (TUG)
きゅっ
THIS SEEMS REALLY HARD-CORE!?
GLOVES!?
I'LL ALSO SHOW YOU AN EASY WAY YOU CAN DO THIS AT HOME.
O-OKAY.
SARA... (SLIDE...)
サラ...
...

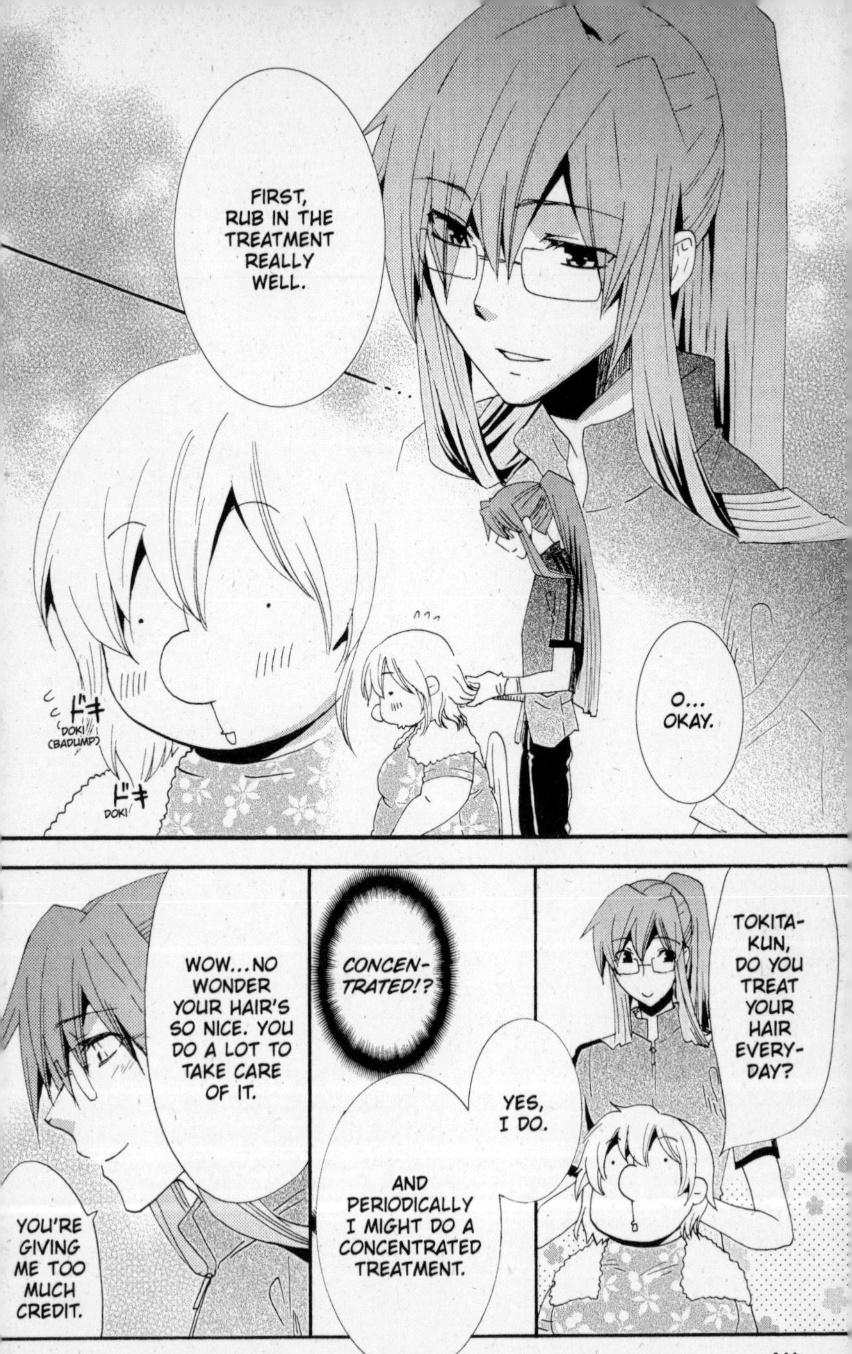
FIRST, RUB IN THE TREATMENT REALLY WELL.
O... OKAY.
ドキ (DOKI (BADUMP))
ドキ DOKI
TOKITA-KUN, DO YOU TREAT YOUR HAIR EVERY-DAY?
YES, I DO.
AND PERIODICALLY I MIGHT DO A CONCENTRATED TREATMENT.
CONCEN-TRATED!?
WOW...NO WONDER YOUR HAIR'S SO NICE. YOU DO A LOT TO TAKE CARE OF IT.
YOU'RE GIVING ME TOO MUCH CREDIT.

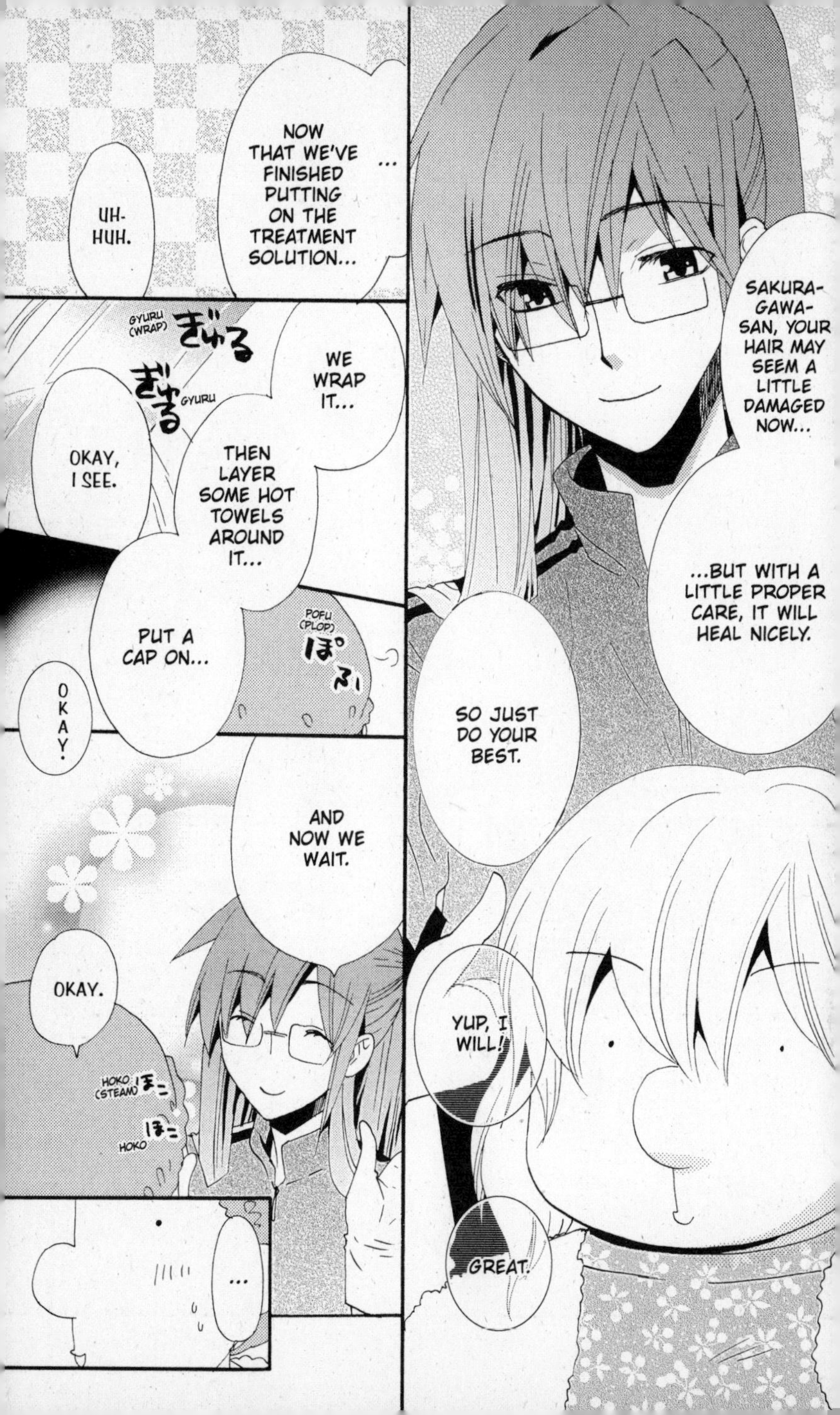
SAKURAGAWA-SAN, YOUR HAIR MAY SEEM A LITTLE DAMAGED NOW...
...BUT WITH A LITTLE PROPER CARE, IT WILL HEAL NICELY.
SO JUST DO YOUR BEST.
YUP, I WILL!
GREAT.
NOW THAT WE'VE FINISHED PUTTING ON THE TREATMENT SOLUTION...
...
UH-HUH.
GYURU (WRAP) ぎゅる
WE WRAP IT...
ぎゅる GYURU
THEN LAYER SOME HOT TOWELS AROUND IT...
OKAY, I SEE.
PUT A CAP ON...
POFU (PLOP) ぽふ
OKAY.
AND NOW WE WAIT.
OKAY.
HOKO (STEAM) ほこ
ほこ HOKO
...

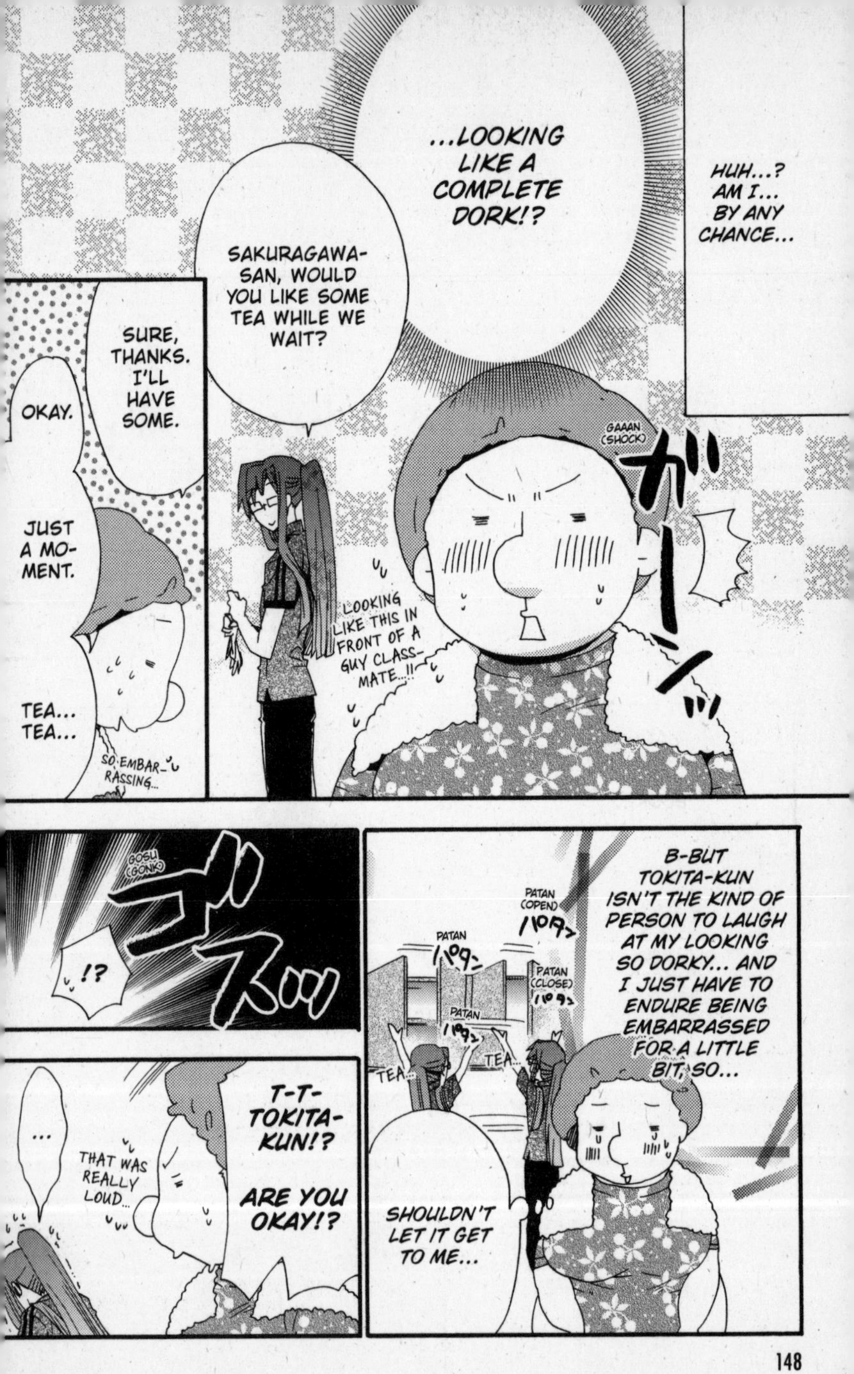
HUH...? AM I... BY ANY CHANCE...
...LOOKING LIKE A COMPLETE DORK!?
SAKURAGAWA-SAN, WOULD YOU LIKE SOME TEA WHILE WE WAIT?
GAAAN (SHOCK)
LOOKING LIKE THIS IN FRONT OF A GUY CLASS-MATE...!!
SURE, THANKS. I'LL HAVE SOME.
OKAY.
JUST A MO-MENT.
TEA... TEA...
SO EMBARRASSING...
B-BUT TOKITA-KUN ISN'T THE KIND OF PERSON TO LAUGH AT MY LOOKING SO DORKY... AND I JUST HAVE TO ENDURE BEING EMBARRASSED FOR A LITTLE BIT, SO...
PATAN (OPEN)
PATAN
PATAN (CLOSE)
PATAN
TEA...
TEA...
SHOULDN'T LET IT GET TO ME...
GOSU (GONK)
!?
T-T-TOKITA-KUN!?
ARE YOU OKAY!?
THAT WAS REALLY LOUD...
...

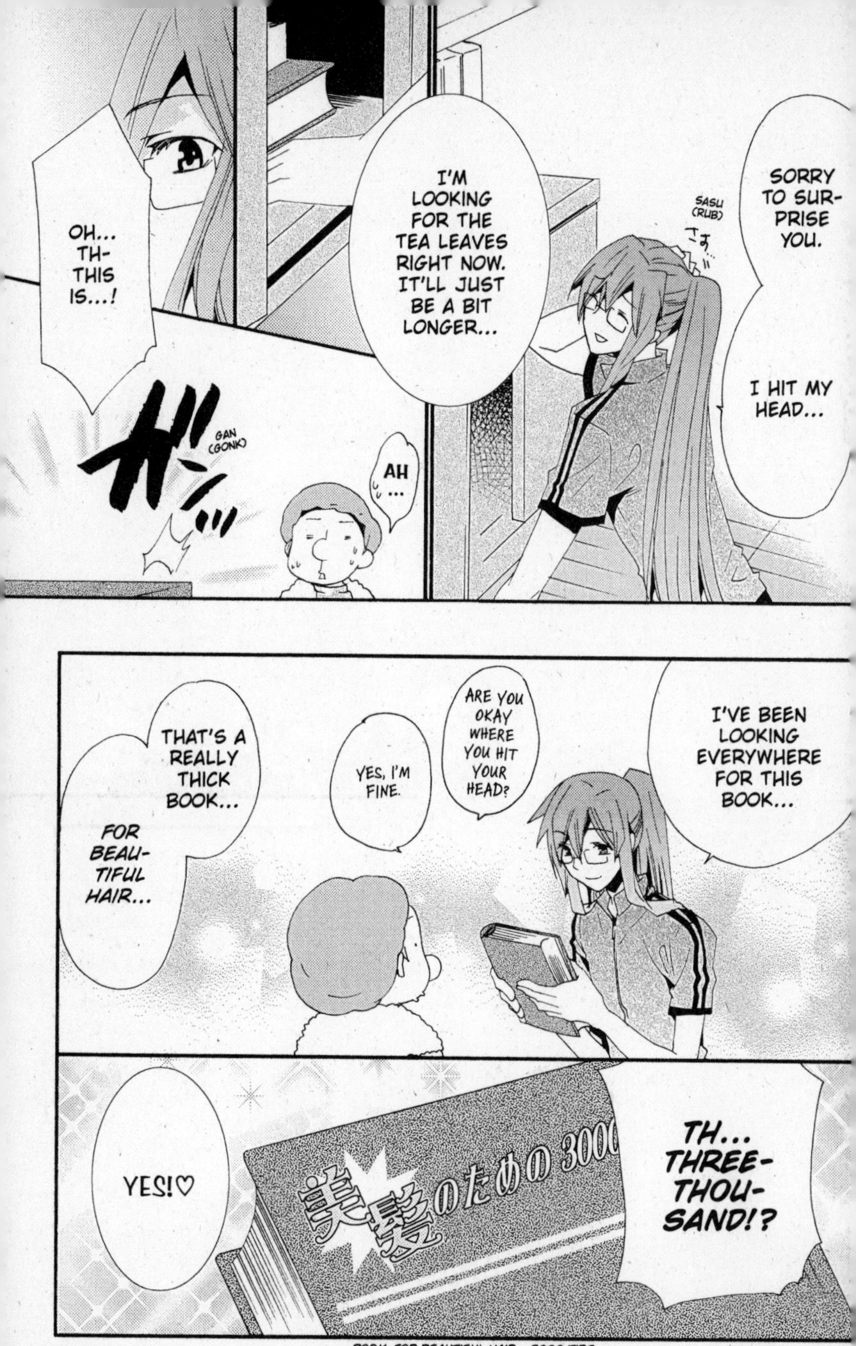
SORRY TO SURPRISE YOU.
SASU (RUB)
さす…
I HIT MY HEAD...
I'M LOOKING FOR THE TEA LEAVES RIGHT NOW. IT'LL JUST BE A BIT LONGER...
AH...
GAN (GONK)
OH... TH-THIS IS...!
I'VE BEEN LOOKING EVERYWHERE FOR THIS BOOK...
ARE YOU OKAY WHERE YOU HIT YOUR HEAD?
YES, I'M FINE.
THAT'S A REALLY THICK BOOK...
FOR BEAUTIFUL HAIR...
TH... THREE-THOUSAND!?
YES!♡
美髪のための3000

BOOK: FOR BEAUTIFUL HAIR - 3000 TIPS

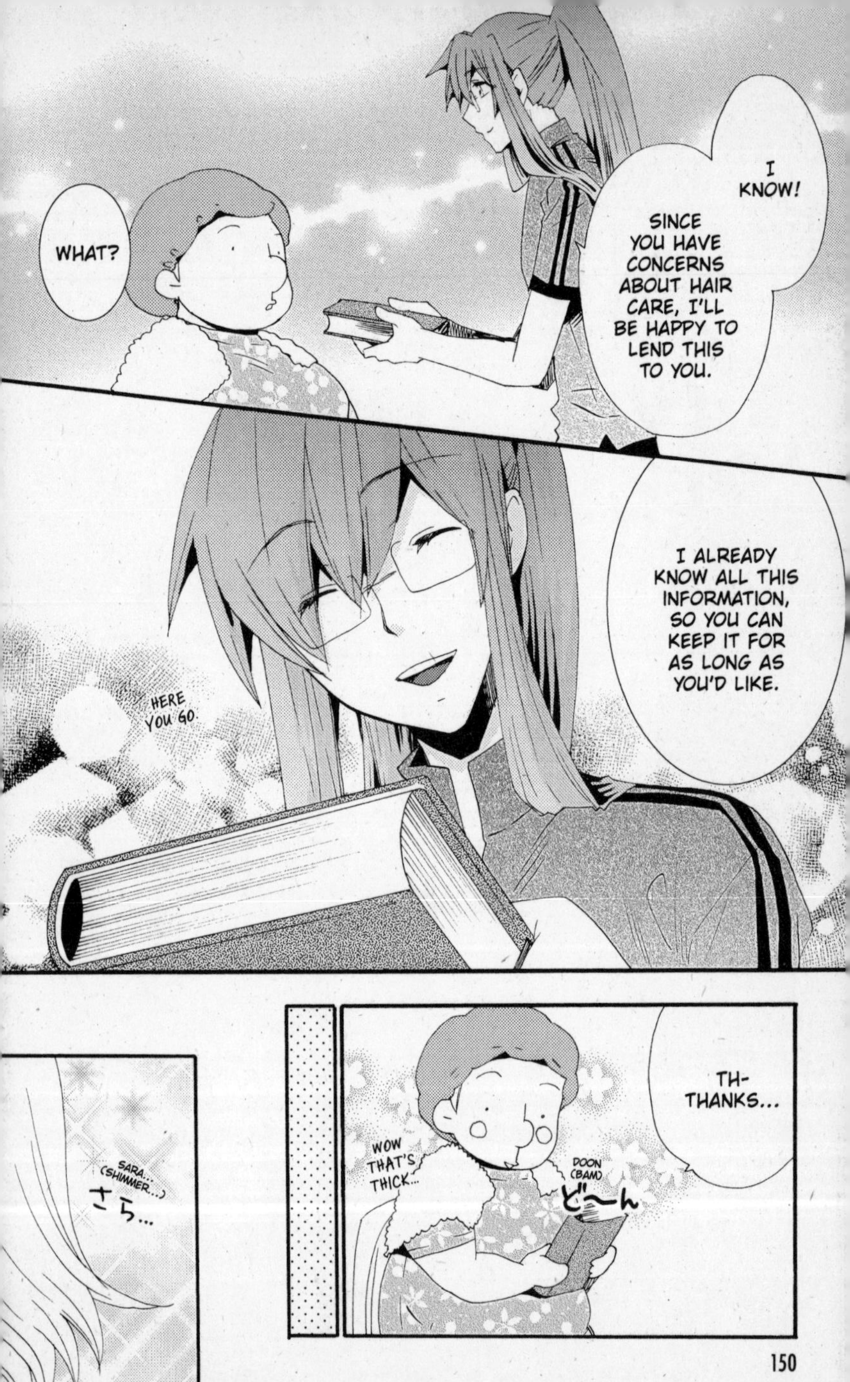
I KNOW!
SINCE YOU HAVE CONCERNS ABOUT HAIR CARE, I'LL BE HAPPY TO LEND THIS TO YOU.
WHAT?
I ALREADY KNOW ALL THIS INFORMATION, SO YOU CAN KEEP IT FOR AS LONG AS YOU'D LIKE.
HERE YOU GO.
TH- THANKS...
DOON (BAM)
ど〜ん
WOW THAT'S THICK...
SARA... (SHIMMER...)
さら...

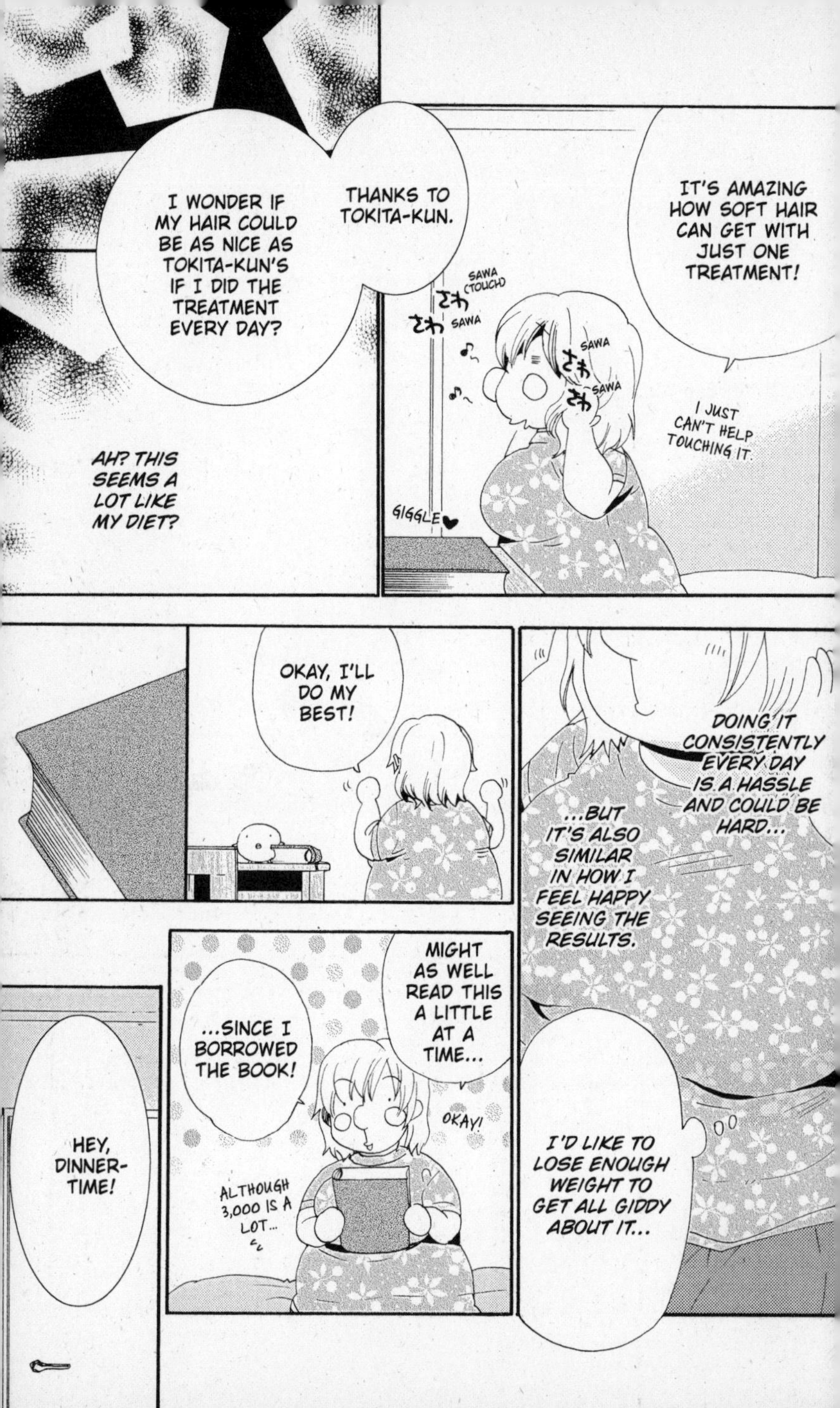

IT'S AMAZING HOW SOFT HAIR CAN GET WITH JUST ONE TREATMENT!
さわ SAWA (TOUCH)
さわ SAWA
さわ SAWA
さわ SAWA
I JUST CAN'T HELP TOUCHING IT.
GIGGLE
THANKS TO TOKITA-KUN.
I WONDER IF MY HAIR COULD BE AS NICE AS TOKITA-KUN'S IF I DID THE TREATMENT EVERY DAY?
AH? THIS SEEMS A LOT LIKE MY DIET?
DOING IT CONSISTENTLY EVERY DAY IS A HASSLE AND COULD BE HARD...
...BUT IT'S ALSO SIMILAR IN HOW I FEEL HAPPY SEEING THE RESULTS.
I'D LIKE TO LOSE ENOUGH WEIGHT TO GET ALL GIDDY ABOUT IT...
OKAY, I'LL DO MY BEST!
MIGHT AS WELL READ THIS A LITTLE AT A TIME...
...SINCE I BORROWED THE BOOK!
OKAY!
ALTHOUGH 3,000 IS A LOT...
HEY, DINNER-TIME!

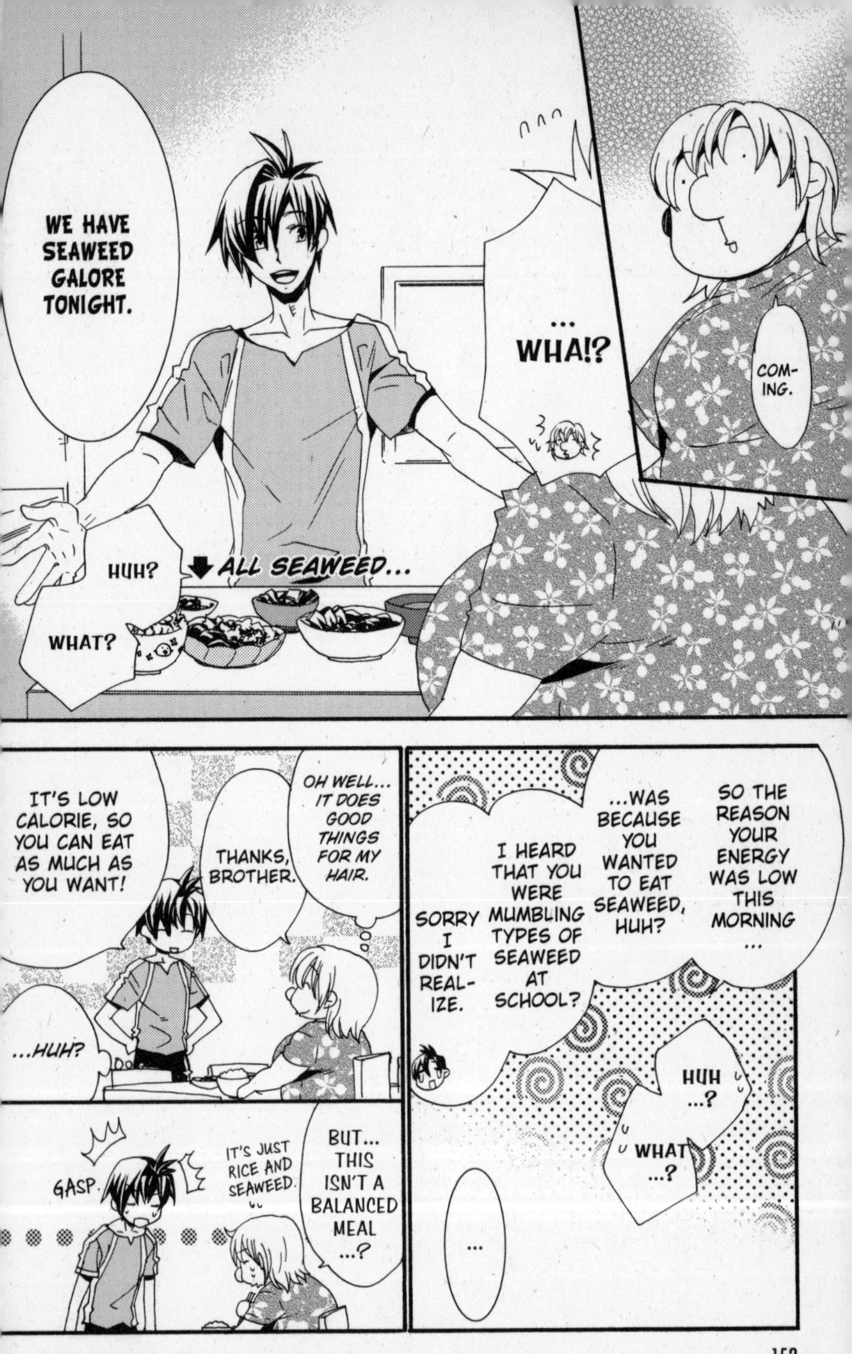

COM-ING.
... WHA!?
WE HAVE SEAWEED GALORE TONIGHT.
ALL SEAWEED...
HUH?
WHAT?
SO THE REASON YOUR ENERGY WAS LOW THIS MORNING ...
...WAS BECAUSE YOU WANTED TO EAT SEAWEED, HUH?
I HEARD THAT YOU WERE MUMBLING TYPES OF SEAWEED AT SCHOOL?
SORRY I DIDN'T REAL-IZE.
HUH ...?
WHAT ...?
...
OH WELL... IT DOES GOOD THINGS FOR MY HAIR.
THANKS, BROTHER.
IT'S LOW CALORIE, SO YOU CAN EAT AS MUCH AS YOU WANT!
...HUH?
BUT... THIS ISN'T A BALANCED MEAL ...?
IT'S JUST RICE AND SEAWEED.
GASP.

LOVEREVO!!

UGLY DUCKLING'S LOVE REVOLUTION

STORY CHARACTERS

MASAKI KAHARA

THE POPULAR LIFE OF THE PARTY IN HITOMI'S CLASS WHO CAN SEEMINGLY DO EVERYTHING. PART OF THE SOCCER TEAM AND A DOG LOVER. PRECIOUS DOG'S NAME IS STEIN.

AYATO KAMISHIRO

WITH HIS QUIET, CONTEMPLATIVE PERSONALITY, HE HAS QUITE THE FEMALE FAN BASE. PHYSI-CALLY ON THE FRAGILE SIDE, HE OCCASIONALLY HAS FAINTING SPELLS. A JUNIOR.

RYUTAROU WAKATSUKI

HITOMI'S SCHOOL'S HEALTH CLINIC DOC. A DELINQUENT OF A TEACHER, HE IS FREQUENTLY FOUND SMOKING IN THE CLINIC. AGE IS KEPT SECRET.

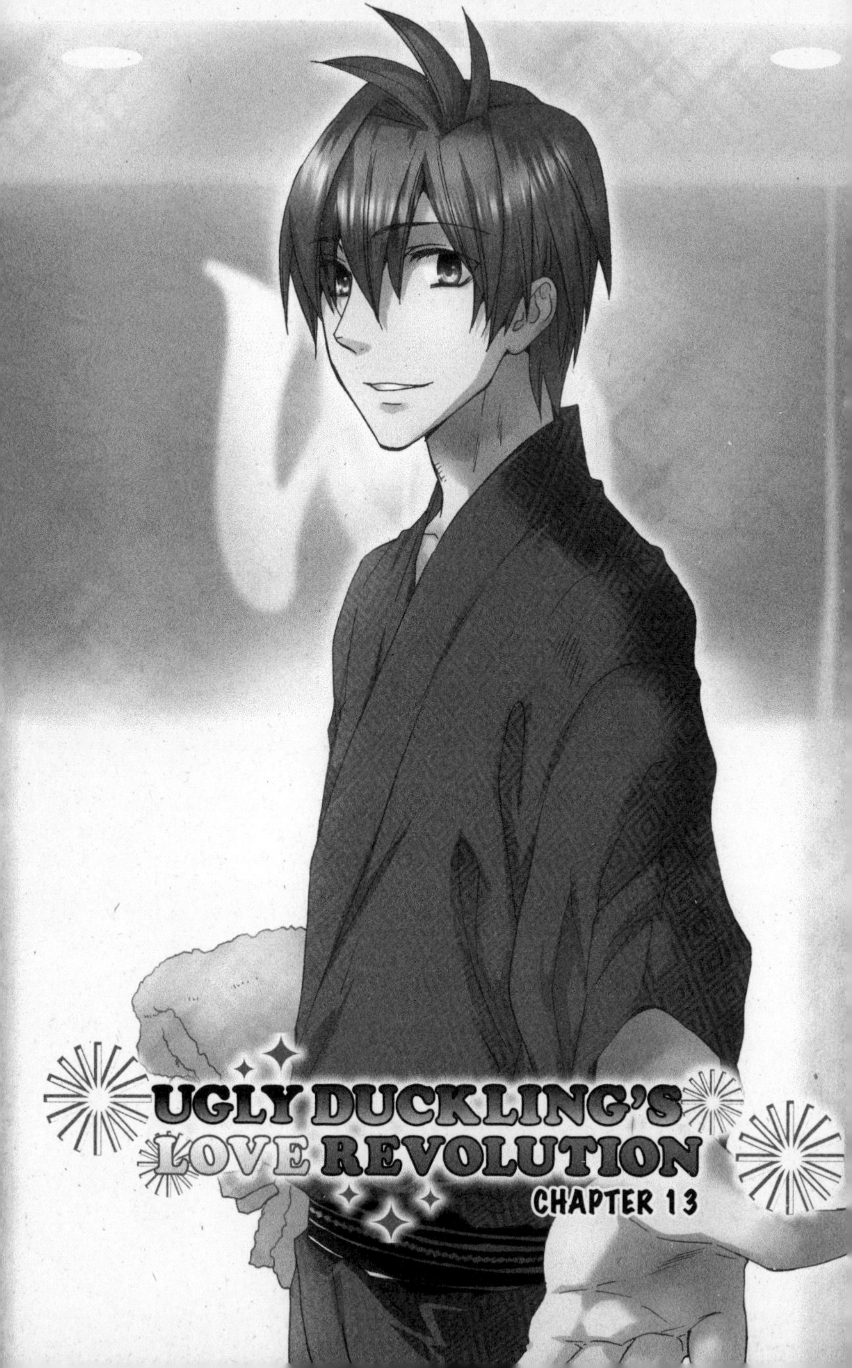
UGLY DUCKLING'S LOVE REVOLUTION
CHAPTER 13

UGLY DUCKLING'S LOVE REVOLUTION

STORY CHARACTERS

KAEDE TOKITA

THE SLIGHTLY MYSTERIOUS TRANSFER STUDENT WHO IS ALWAYS STUDYING. READING BOOKS MORE OFTEN THAN CHATTING WITH OTHERS. SOPHOMORE.

TOORU KINOMURA

A CHILDHOOD FRIEND WHOM HITOMI PLAYED WITH OFTEN SINCE THEY WERE LITTLE. INSPIRED BY THE SIGHT OF HITOMI WORKING HARD AT HER DIET, HE STARTED HIS OWN DIET. SOPHOMORE.

YURIKA TOUJOU

THE PRINCESS IN HITOMI'S CLASS. COMPLETELY DIFFERENT PERSONALITY IN FRONT OF GUYS VS. GIRLS. BECAUSE OF HER ENDLESS BITING COMMENTS, SHE IS HITOMI'S NEMESIS.

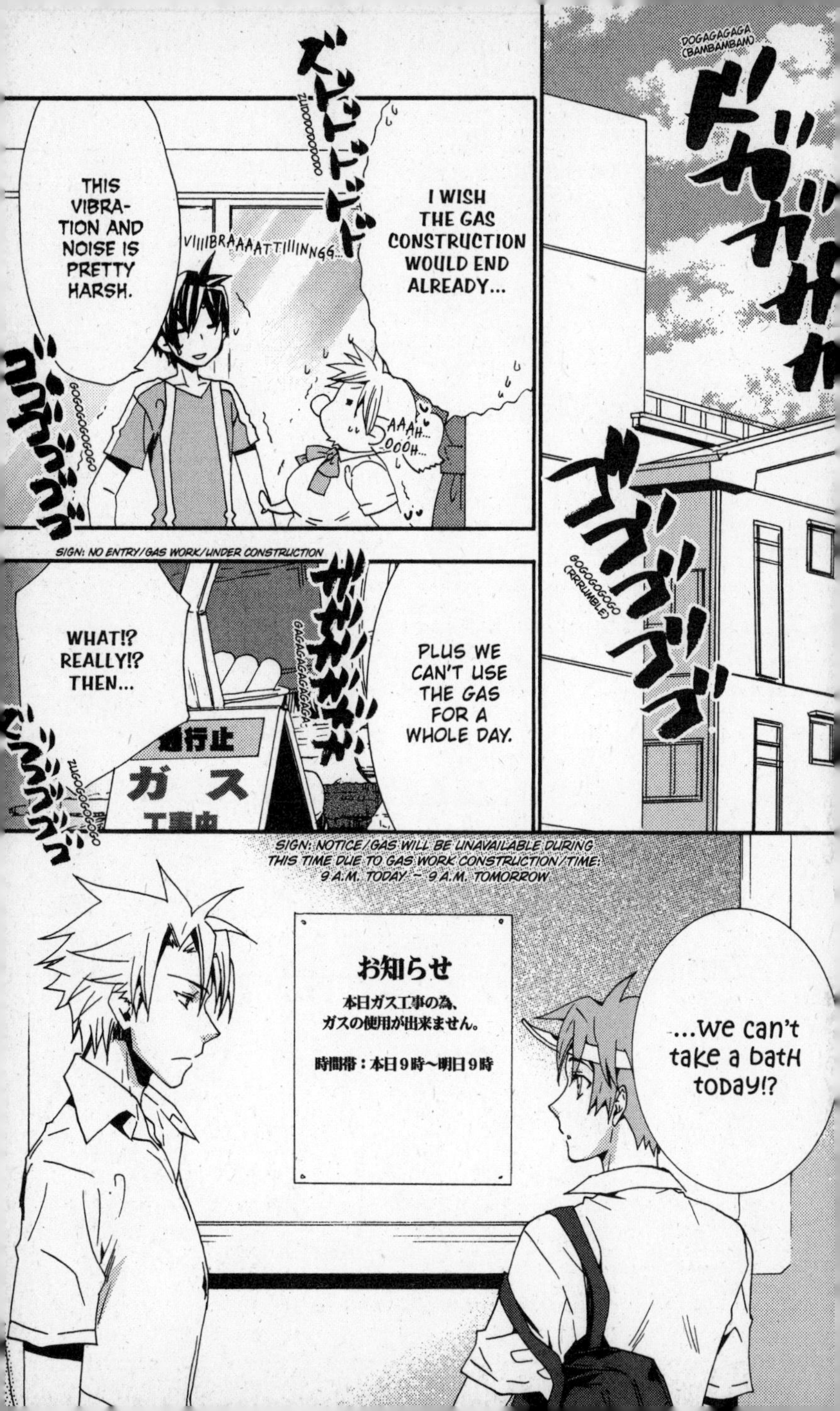
DOGAGAGAGA (BAMBAMBAM)
GOGOGOGOGO (RRRUMBLE)
ZUDODODODODO
I WISH THE GAS CONSTRUCTION WOULD END ALREADY...
VIIIIBRAAAATTIIIINNGG...
THIS VIBRATION AND NOISE IS PRETTY HARSH.
AAAH... OOOH...
GOGOGOGOGO
SIGN: NO ENTRY/GAS WORK/UNDER CONSTRUCTION
GAGAGAGAGAGA
PLUS WE CAN'T USE THE GAS FOR A WHOLE DAY.
ガス
WHAT!? REALLY!? THEN...
ZUGOGOGOGOGO
SIGN: NOTICE/GAS WILL BE UNAVAILABLE DURING THIS TIME DUE TO GAS WORK CONSTRUCTION/TIME: 9 A.M. TODAY – 9 A.M. TOMORROW
...we can't take a bath today!?
お知らせ
本日ガス工事の為、
ガスの使用が出来ません。
時間帯：本日９時～明日９時

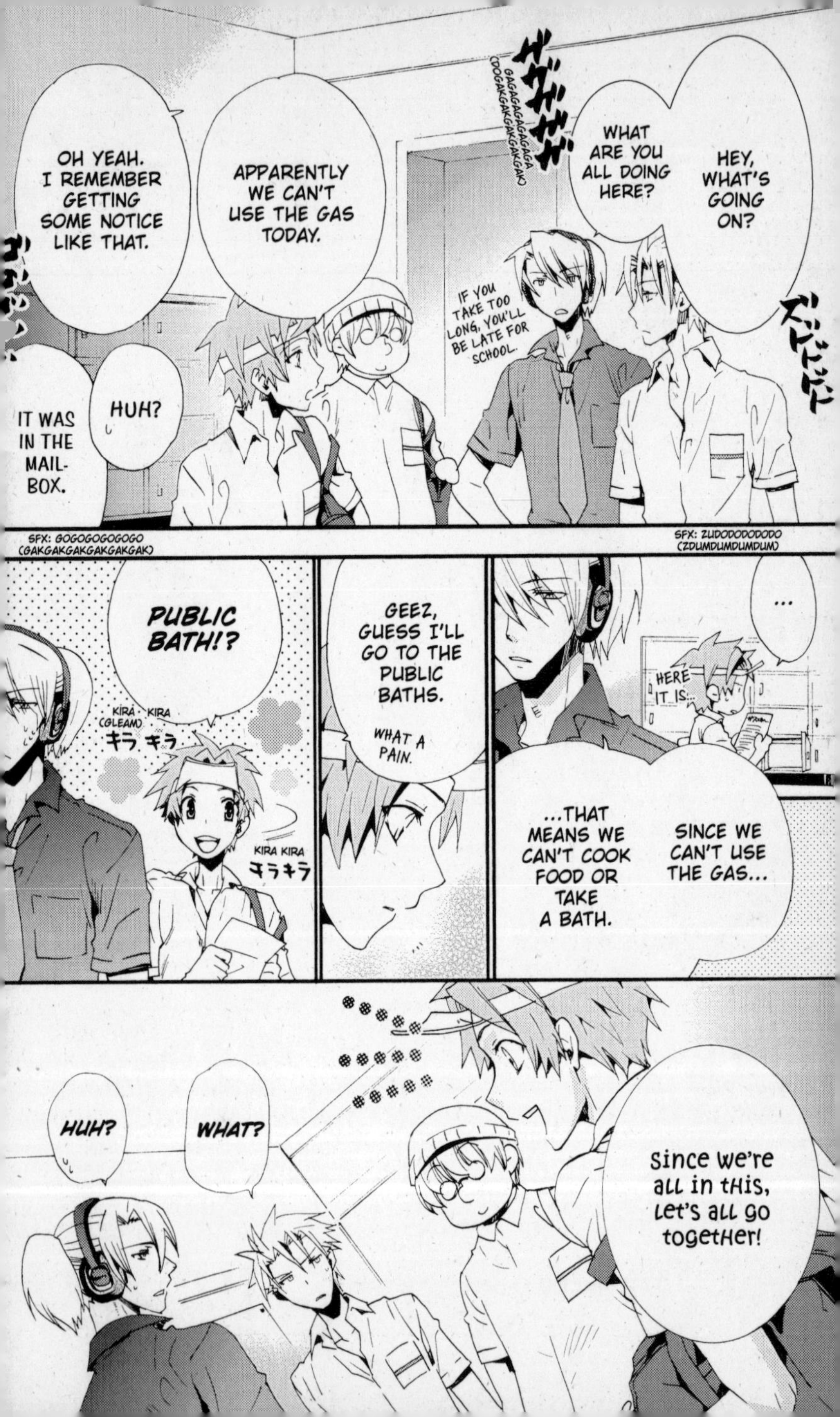
HEY, WHAT'S GOING ON?
WHAT ARE YOU ALL DOING HERE?
IF YOU TAKE TOO LONG, YOU'LL BE LATE FOR SCHOOL.
GAGAGAGAGAGA (DOGAKGAKGAKGAKGAK)
APPARENTLY WE CAN'T USE THE GAS TODAY.
OH YEAH. I REMEMBER GETTING SOME NOTICE LIKE THAT.
HUH?
IT WAS IN THE MAILBOX.
SFX: ZUDODODODODO (ZDUMDUMDUMDUM)
SFX: GOGOGOGOGOGO (GAKGAKGAKGAKGAKGAK)
...
HERE IT IS...
SINCE WE CAN'T USE THE GAS...
...THAT MEANS WE CAN'T COOK FOOD OR TAKE A BATH.
GEEZ, GUESS I'LL GO TO THE PUBLIC BATHS.
WHAT A PAIN.
PUBLIC BATH!?
KIRA KIRA (GLEAM) キラキラ
KIRA KIRA キラキラ
Since we're all in this, let's all go together!
WHAT?
HUH?

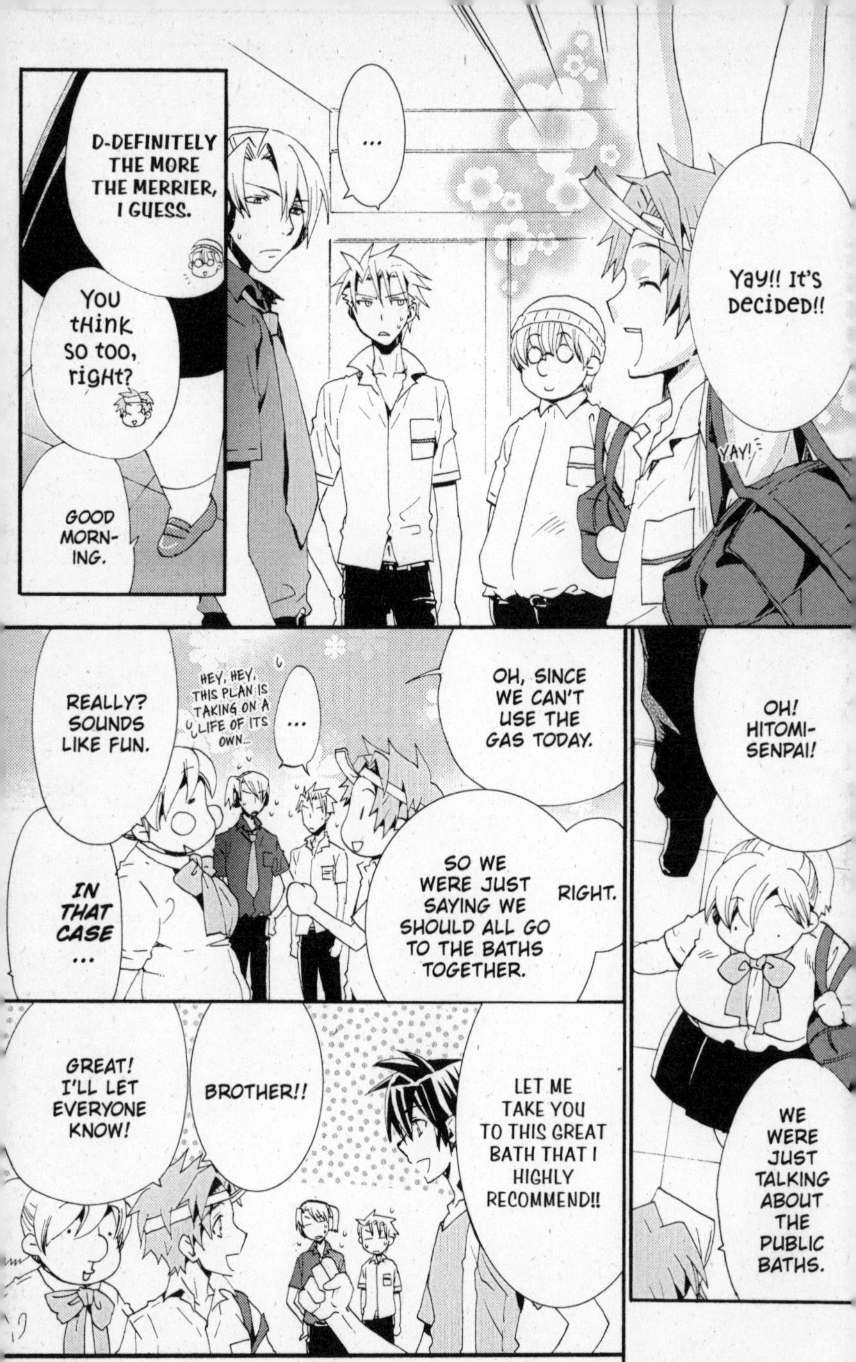
...
Yay!! It's decided!!
YAY!
D-DEFINITELY THE MORE THE MERRIER, I GUESS.
YOU think so too, right?
GOOD MORN-ING.
OH! HITOMI-SENPAI!
WE WERE JUST TALKING ABOUT THE PUBLIC BATHS.
OH, SINCE WE CAN'T USE THE GAS TODAY.
SO WE WERE JUST SAYING WE SHOULD ALL GO TO THE BATHS TOGETHER.
RIGHT.
...
HEY, HEY, THIS PLAN IS TAKING ON A LIFE OF ITS OWN...
REALLY? SOUNDS LIKE FUN.
IN THAT CASE...
LET ME TAKE YOU TO THIS GREAT BATH THAT I HIGHLY RECOMMEND!!
BROTHER!!
GREAT! I'LL LET EVERYONE KNOW!

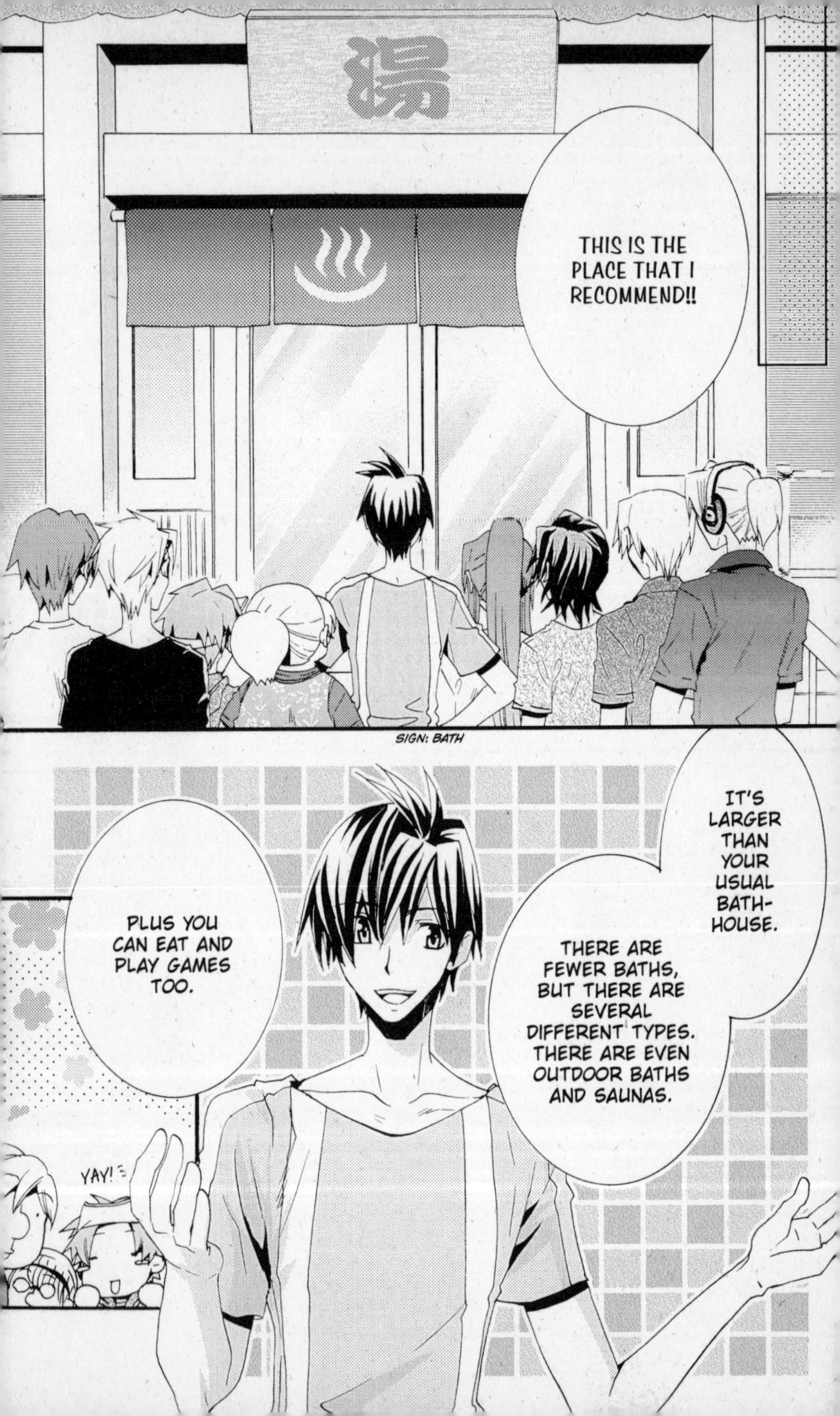
THIS IS THE PLACE THAT I RECOMMEND!!
SIGN: BATH
IT'S LARGER THAN YOUR USUAL BATH-HOUSE.
THERE ARE FEWER BATHS, BUT THERE ARE SEVERAL DIFFERENT TYPES. THERE ARE EVEN OUTDOOR BATHS AND SAUNAS.
PLUS YOU CAN EAT AND PLAY GAMES TOO.
YAY!

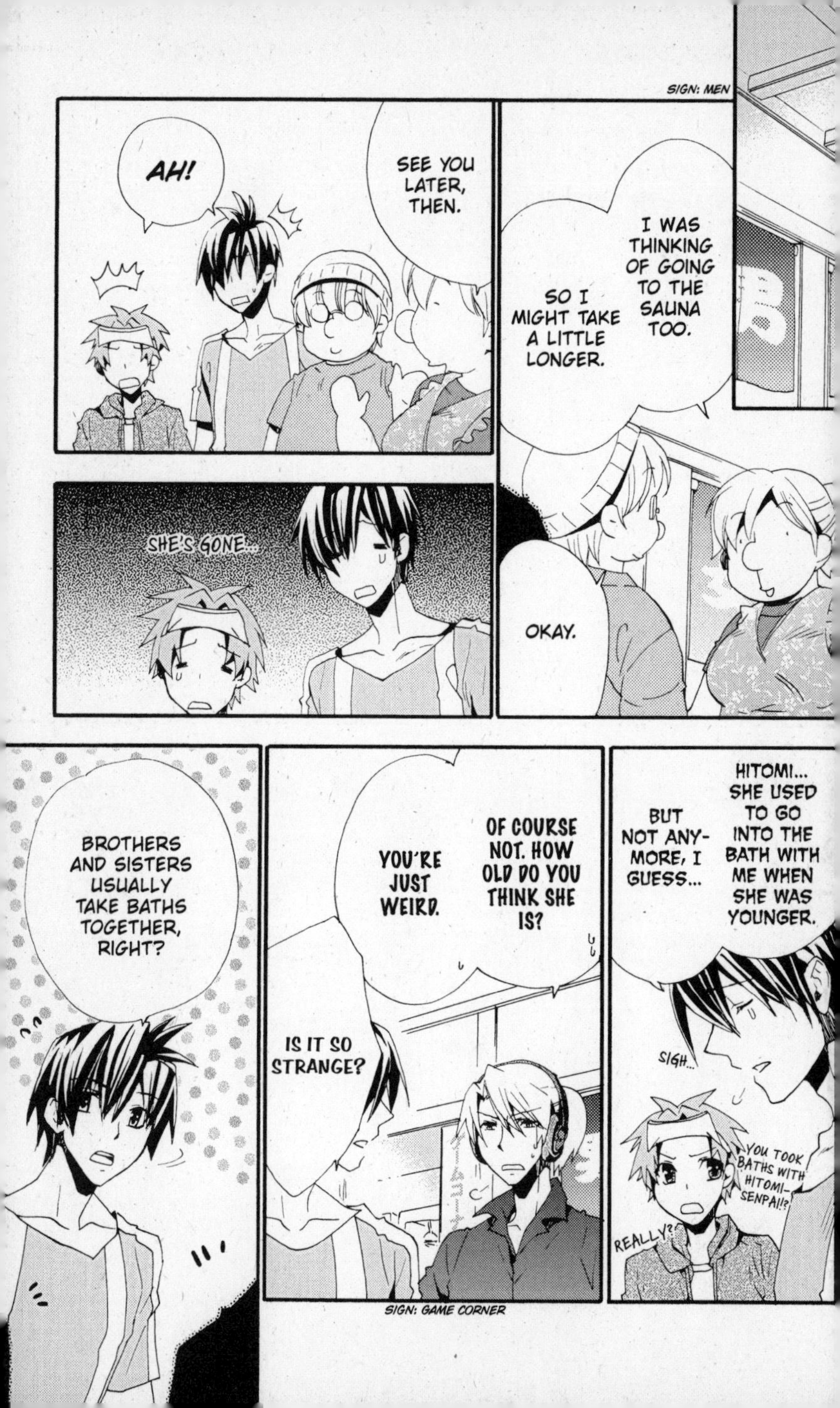
SIGN: MEN
I WAS THINKING OF GOING TO THE SAUNA TOO.
SO I MIGHT TAKE A LITTLE LONGER.
OKAY.
SEE YOU LATER, THEN.
AH!
SHE'S GONE...
HITOMI... SHE USED TO GO INTO THE BATH WITH ME WHEN SHE WAS YOUNGER.
BUT NOT ANY-MORE, I GUESS...
SIGH...
YOU TOOK BATHS WITH HITOMI-SENPAI!?
REALLY!?
OF COURSE NOT. HOW OLD DO YOU THINK SHE IS?
YOU'RE JUST WEIRD.
IS IT SO STRANGE?
SIGN: GAME CORNER
BROTHERS AND SISTERS USUALLY TAKE BATHS TOGETHER, RIGHT?

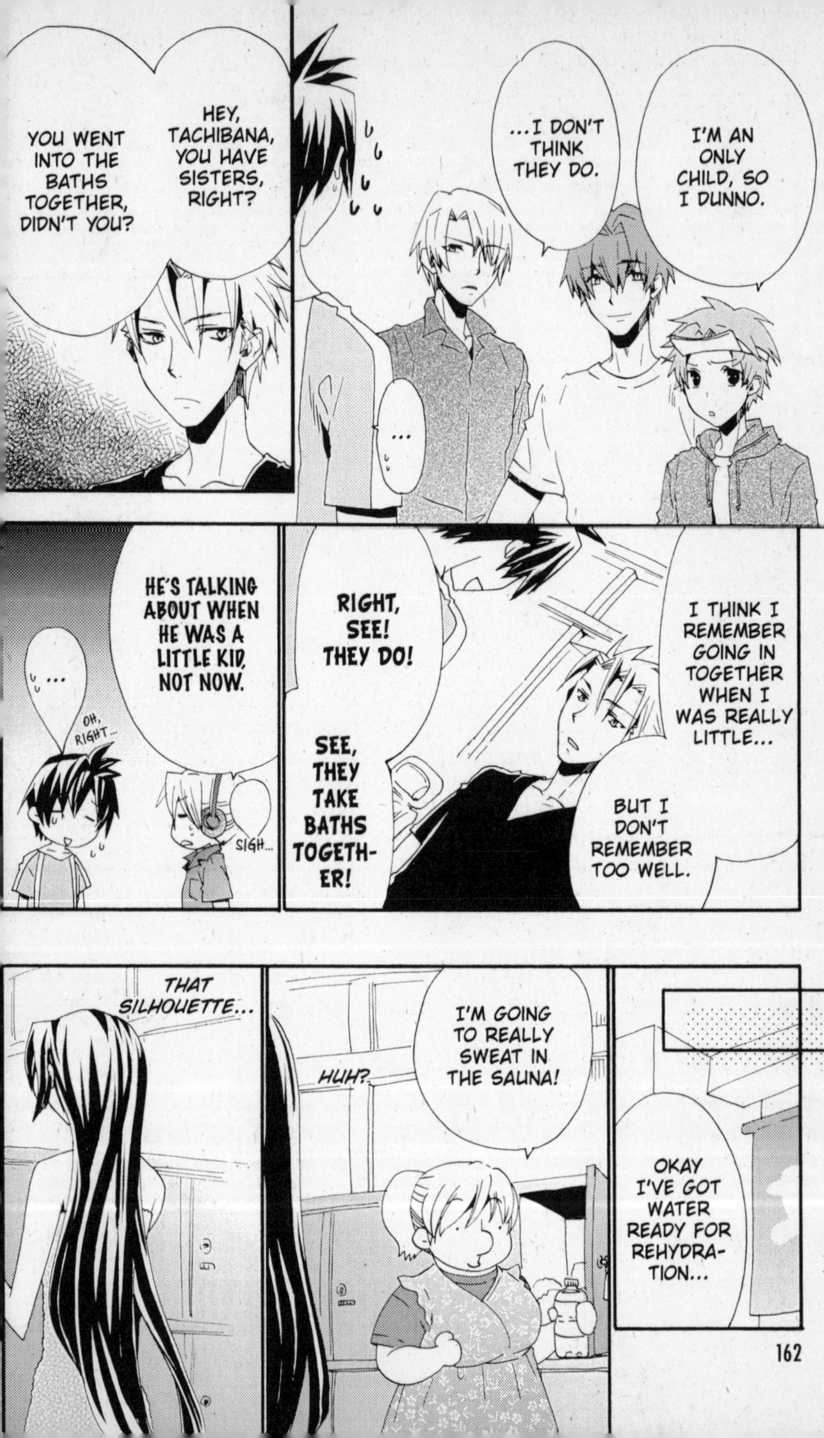
I'M AN ONLY CHILD, SO I DUNNO.
...I DON'T THINK THEY DO.
...
HEY, TACHIBANA, YOU HAVE SISTERS, RIGHT?
YOU WENT INTO THE BATHS TOGETHER, DIDN'T YOU?
I THINK I REMEMBER GOING IN TOGETHER WHEN I WAS REALLY LITTLE...
BUT I DON'T REMEMBER TOO WELL.
RIGHT, SEE! THEY DO!
SEE, THEY TAKE BATHS TOGETH-ER!
HE'S TALKING ABOUT WHEN HE WAS A LITTLE KID, NOT NOW.
SIGH...
...
OH, RIGHT...
OKAY I'VE GOT WATER READY FOR REHYDRA-TION...
I'M GOING TO REALLY SWEAT IN THE SAUNA!
HUH?
THAT SILHOUETTE...

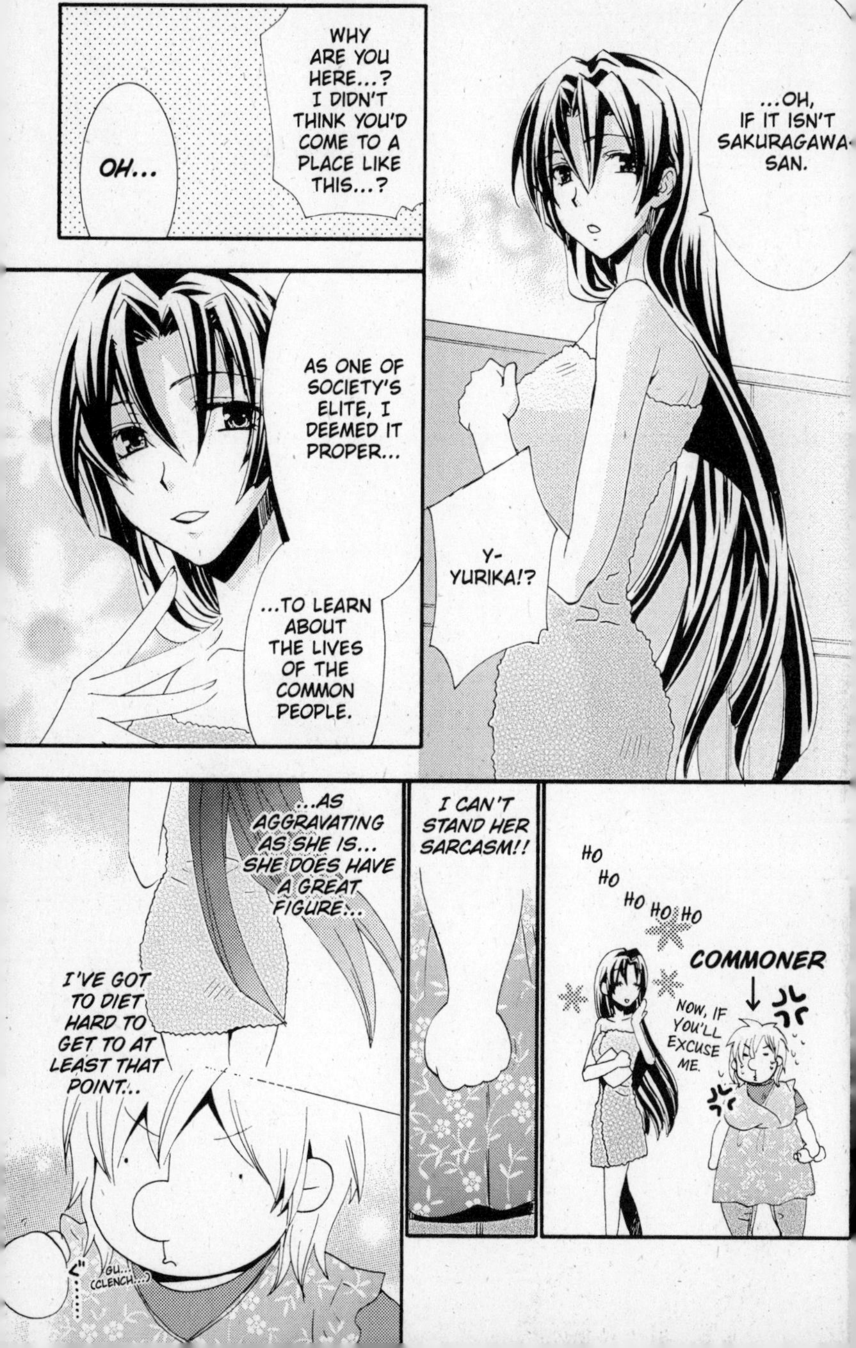
...OH, IF IT ISN'T SAKURAGAWA-SAN.
Y-YURIKA!?
WHY ARE YOU HERE...? I DIDN'T THINK YOU'D COME TO A PLACE LIKE THIS...?
OH...
AS ONE OF SOCIETY'S ELITE, I DEEMED IT PROPER...
...TO LEARN ABOUT THE LIVES OF THE COMMON PEOPLE.
HO HO HO HO HO
COMMONER
NOW, IF YOU'LL EXCUSE ME.
I CAN'T STAND HER SARCASM!!
...AS AGGRAVATING AS SHE IS... SHE DOES HAVE A GREAT FIGURE...
I'VE GOT TO DIET HARD TO GET TO AT LEAST THAT POINT...
GU... (CLENCH...)

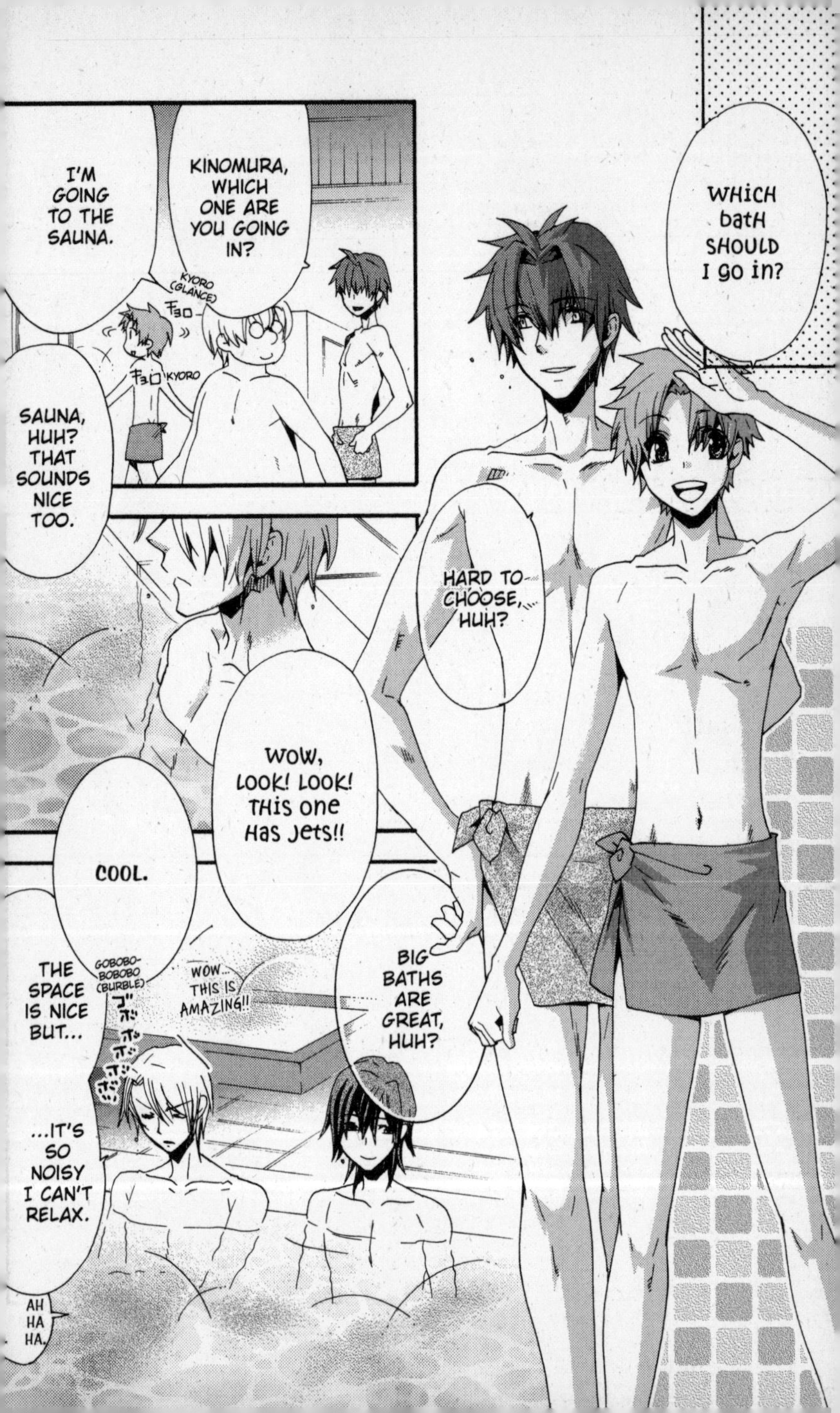
WHICH bath SHOULD I go in?
HARD TO CHOOSE, HUH?
WOW, LOOK! LOOK! THIS one Has Jets!!
BIG BATHS ARE GREAT, HUH?
KINOMURA, WHICH ONE ARE YOU GOING IN?
KYORO (GLANCE)
I'M GOING TO THE SAUNA.
KYORO
SAUNA, HUH? THAT SOUNDS NICE TOO.
COOL.
WOW... THIS IS AMAZING!!
GOBOBO-BOBOBO (BURBLE)
THE SPACE IS NICE BUT...
...IT'S SO NOISY I CAN'T RELAX.
AH HA HA.

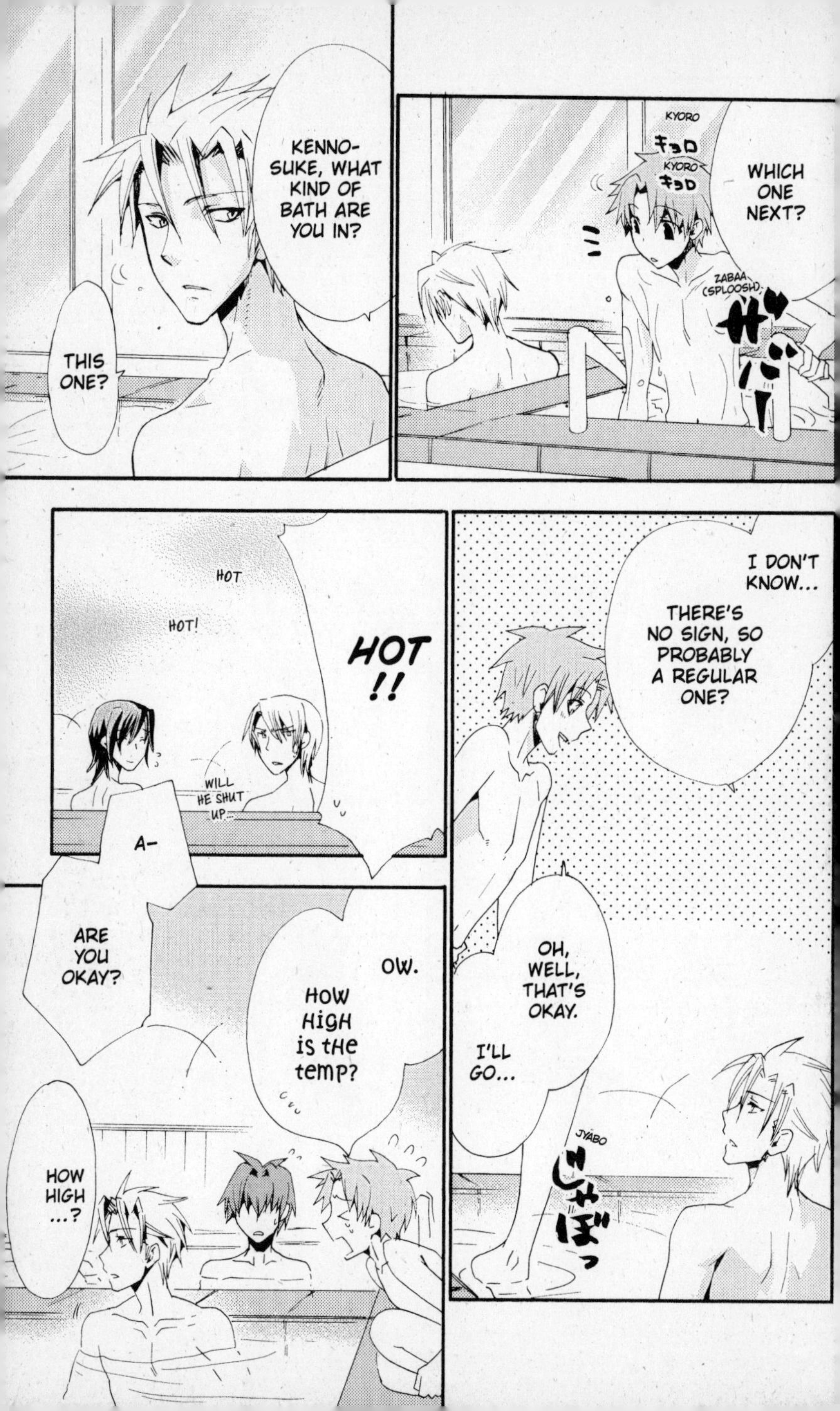
KYORO
キョロ
KYORO
キョロ
WHICH ONE NEXT?
ZABAA (SPLOOSH)
KENNO-SUKE, WHAT KIND OF BATH ARE YOU IN?
THIS ONE?
I DON'T KNOW...
THERE'S NO SIGN, SO PROBABLY A REGULAR ONE?
OH, WELL, THAT'S OKAY.
I'LL GO...
JYABO
HOT!!
HOT
HOT!
WILL HE SHUT UP...
A-
OW.
HOW HIGH IS THE TEMP?
ARE YOU OKAY?
HOW HIGH ...?

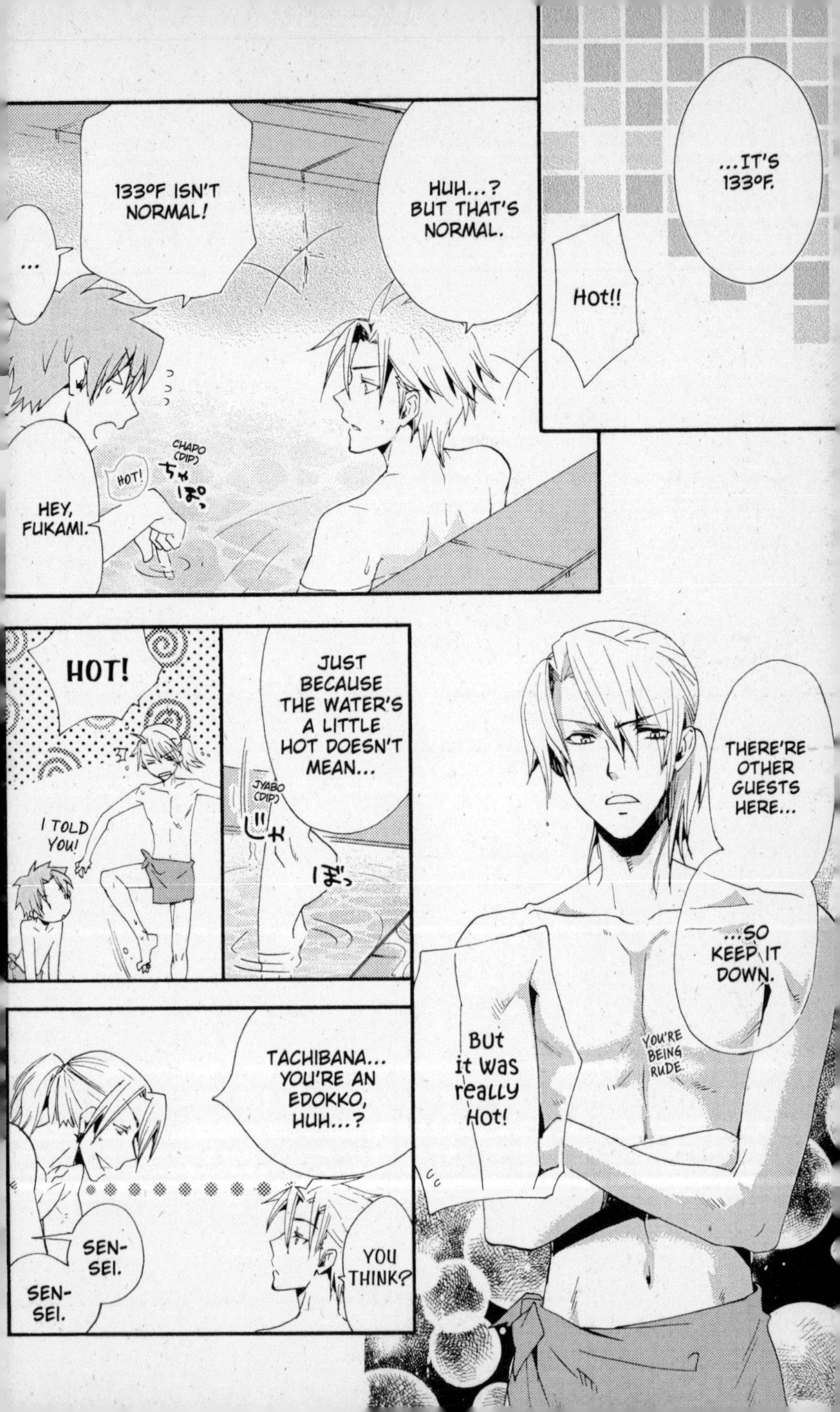
...IT'S 133°F.
Hot!!
HUH...? BUT THAT'S NORMAL.
133°F ISN'T NORMAL!
...
CHAPO (DIP)
ちゃぽっ
HOT!
HEY, FUKAMI.
THERE'RE OTHER GUESTS HERE...
...SO KEEP IT DOWN.
YOU'RE BEING RUDE.
But it was really Hot!
JUST BECAUSE THE WATER'S A LITTLE HOT DOESN'T MEAN...
JYABO (DIP)
じゃぼっ
HOT!
I TOLD YOU!
TACHIBANA... YOU'RE AN EDOKKO, HUH...?
YOU THINK?
SEN-SEI.
SEN-SEI.

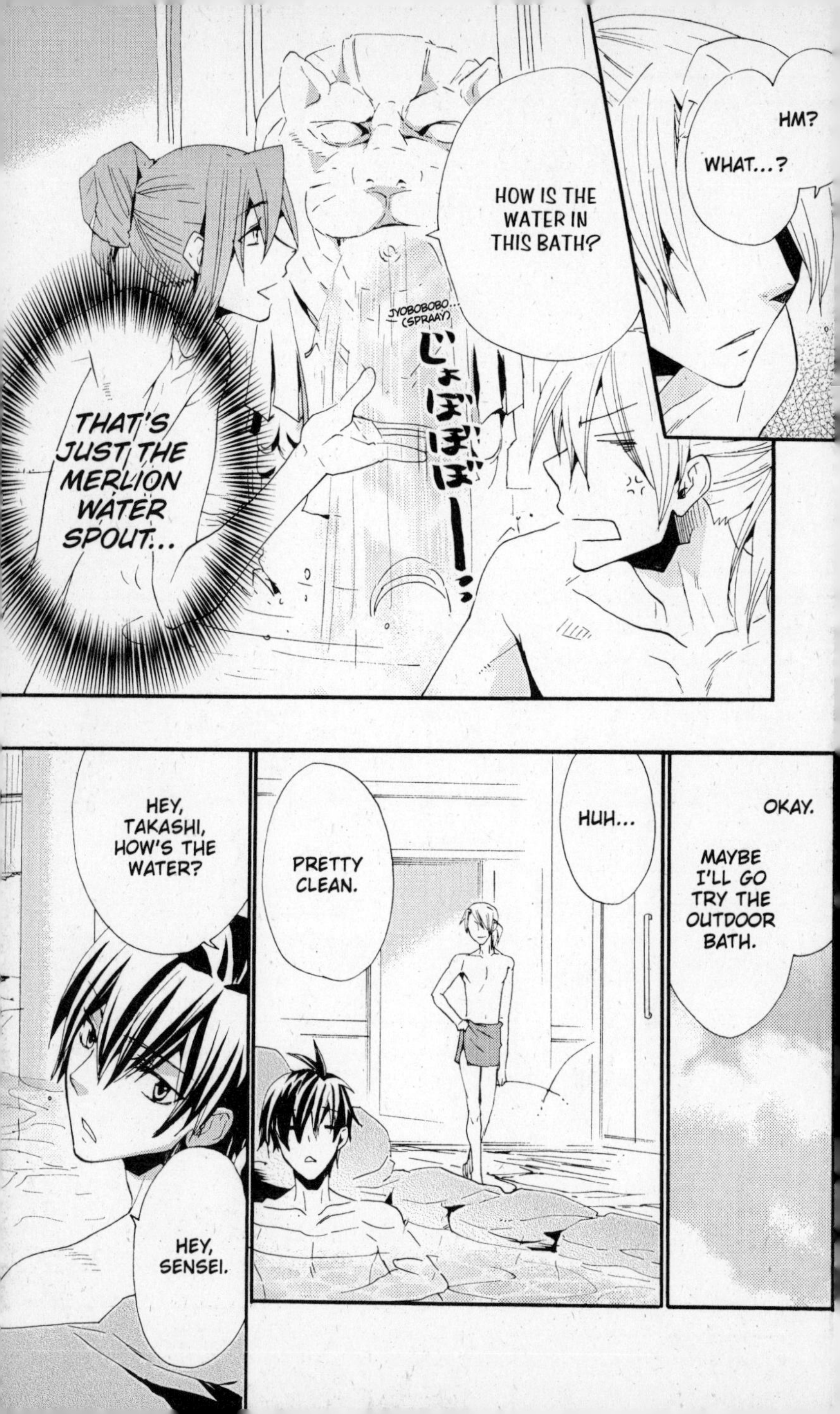
HM?
WHAT...?
HOW IS THE WATER IN THIS BATH?
JYOBOBOBO... (SPRAAY)
じょぼぼぼー
THAT'S JUST THE MERLION WATER SPOUT...
OKAY.
MAYBE I'LL GO TRY THE OUTDOOR BATH.
HUH...
PRETTY CLEAN.
HEY, TAKASHI, HOW'S THE WATER?
HEY, SENSEI.

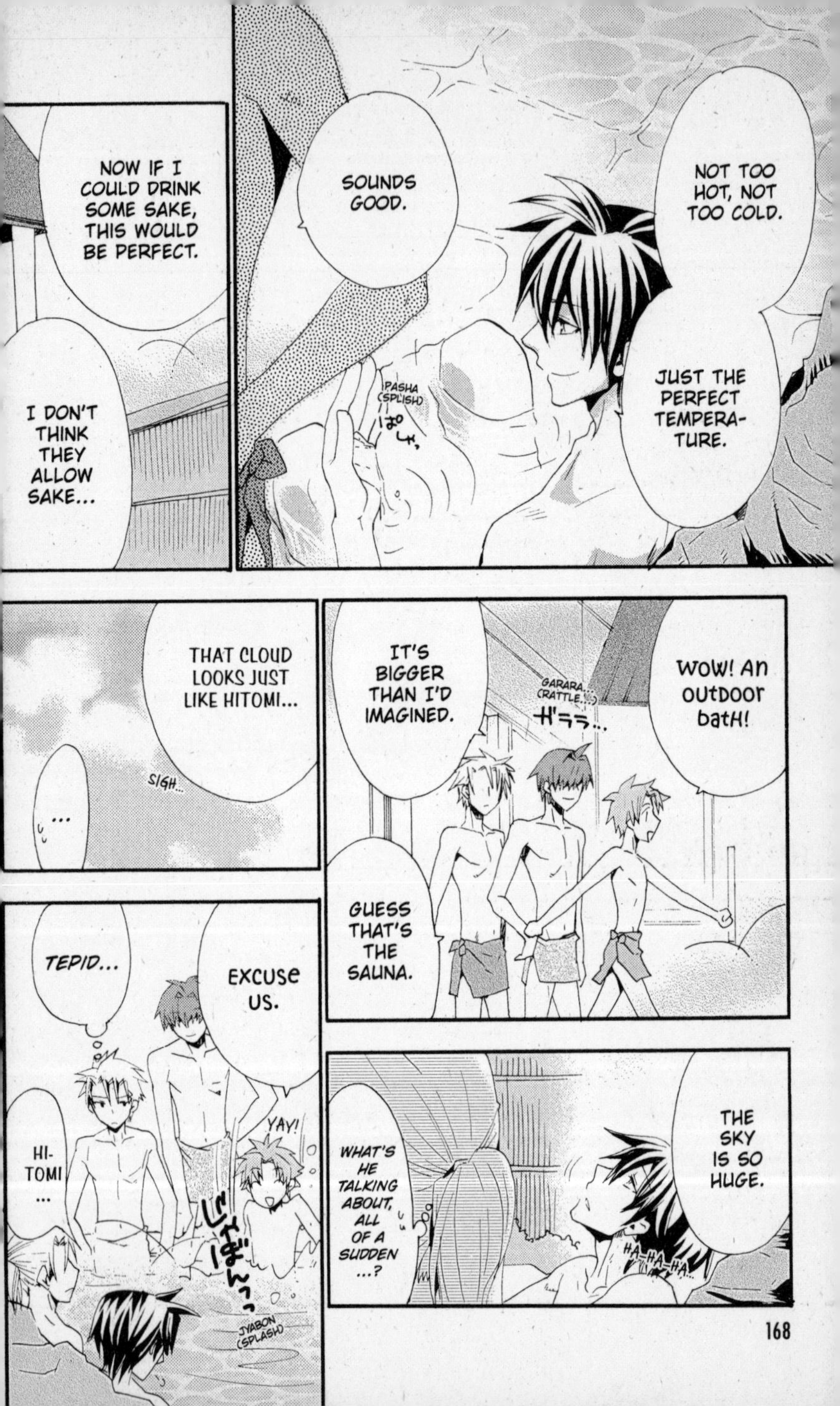
NOT TOO HOT, NOT TOO COLD.
JUST THE PERFECT TEMPERA-TURE.
PASHA (SPLISH)
ぱしゃ
SOUNDS GOOD.
NOW IF I COULD DRINK SOME SAKE, THIS WOULD BE PERFECT.
I DON'T THINK THEY ALLOW SAKE...
WOW! An outdoor bath!
GARARA... (RATTLE...)
ガラララ...
IT'S BIGGER THAN I'D IMAGINED.
GUESS THAT'S THE SAUNA.
THAT CLOUD LOOKS JUST LIKE HITOMI...
SIGH...
...
EXCUSE US.
TEPID...
YAY!
じゃぼんっ
JYABON (SPLASH)
HI-TOMI...
THE SKY IS SO HUGE.
HA-HA-HA...
WHAT'S HE TALKING ABOUT, ALL OF A SUDDEN...?

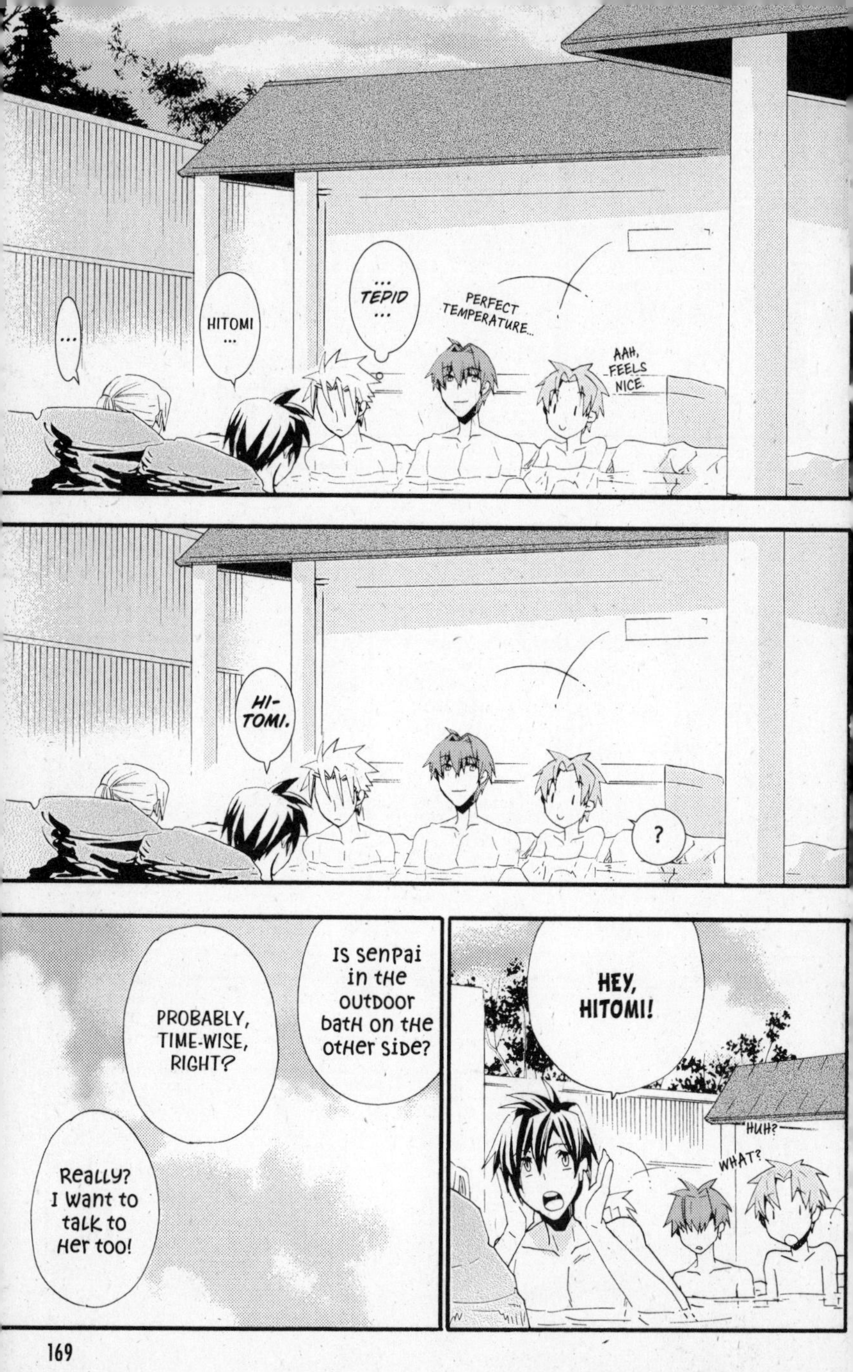
AAH, FEELS NICE.
PERFECT TEMPERATURE...
...TEPID...
HITOMI...
...
?
HI-TOMI.
HEY, HITOMI!
HUH?
WHAT?
Is senpai in the outdoor bath on the other side?
PROBABLY, TIME-WISE, RIGHT?
Really? I want to talk to her too!

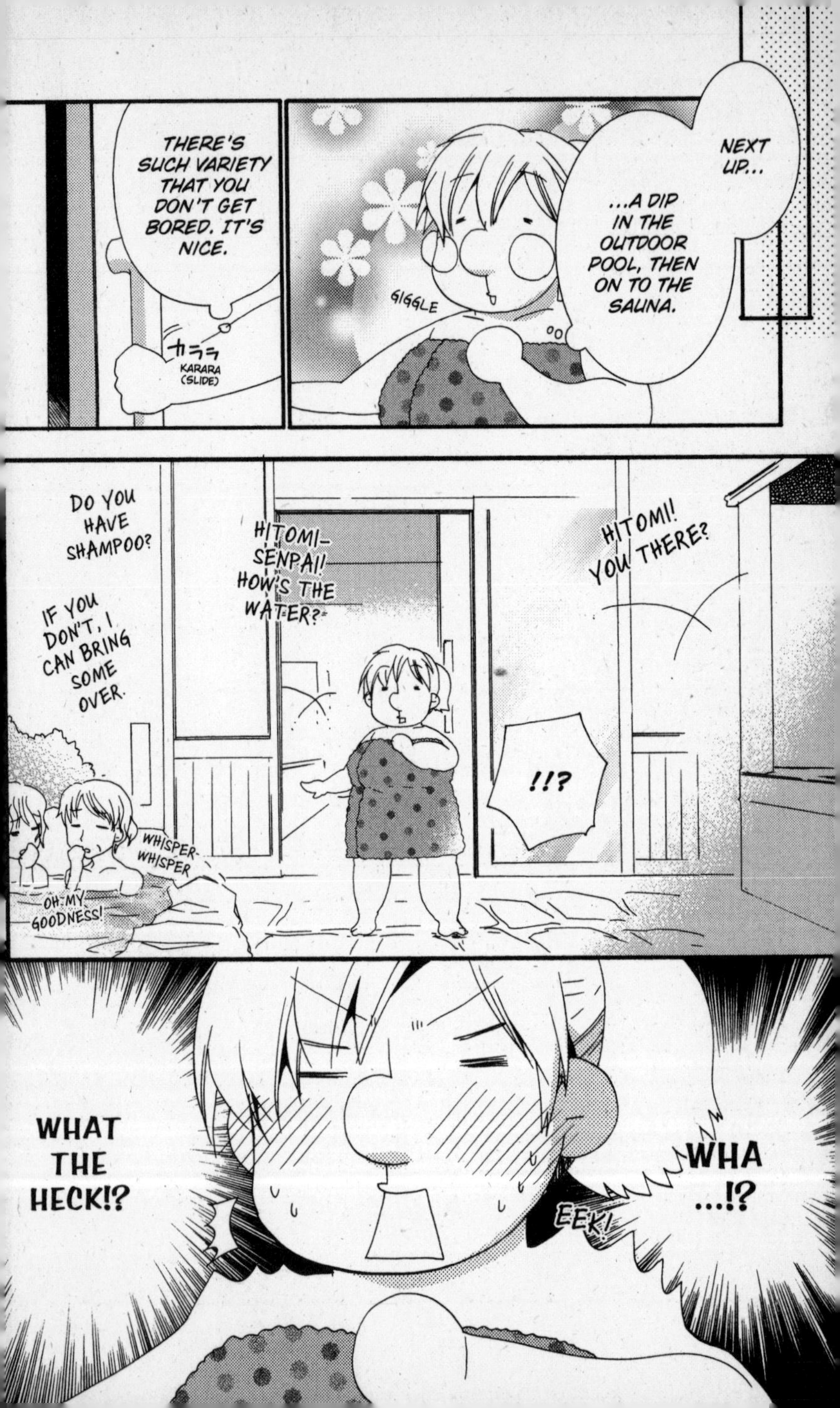

NEXT UP...
...A DIP IN THE OUTDOOR POOL, THEN ON TO THE SAUNA.
GIGGLE
THERE'S SUCH VARIETY THAT YOU DON'T GET BORED. IT'S NICE.
カララ
KARARA (SLIDE)
HITOMI! YOU THERE?
!!?
HITOMI-SENPAI! HOW'S THE WATER?
DO YOU HAVE SHAMPOO?
IF YOU DON'T, I CAN BRING SOME OVER.
WHISPER-WHISPER
OH MY GOODNESS!
WHA ...!?
EEK!
WHAT THE HECK!?

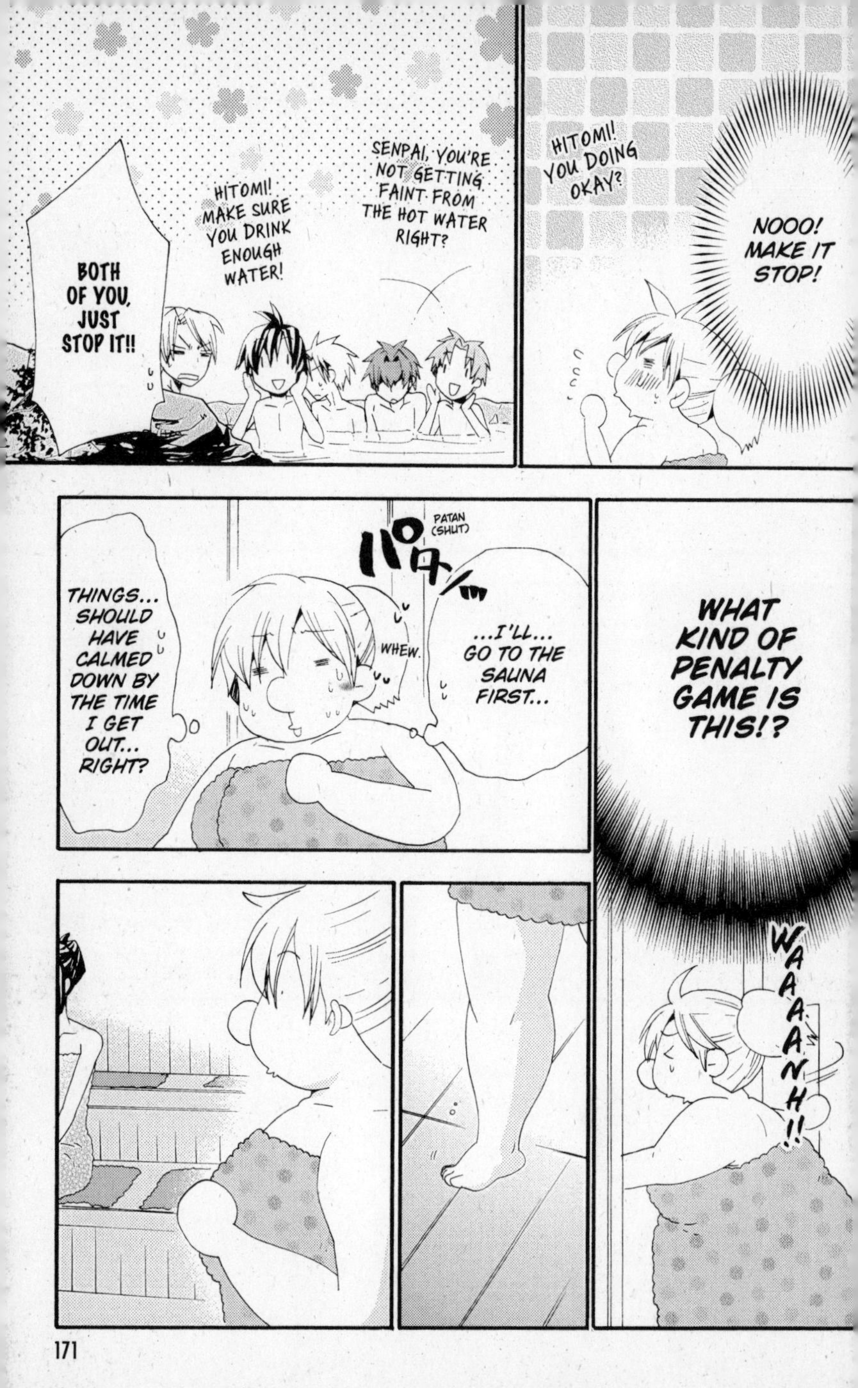
HITOMI! YOU DOING OKAY?
NOOO! MAKE IT STOP!
SENPAI, YOU'RE NOT GETTING FAINT FROM THE HOT WATER RIGHT?
HITOMI! MAKE SURE YOU DRINK ENOUGH WATER!
BOTH OF YOU, JUST STOP IT!!
WHAT KIND OF PENALTY GAME IS THIS!?
WAAAAANH!!
PATAN (SHUT)
...I'LL... GO TO THE SAUNA FIRST...
WHEW.
THINGS... SHOULD HAVE CALMED DOWN BY THE TIME I GET OUT... RIGHT?

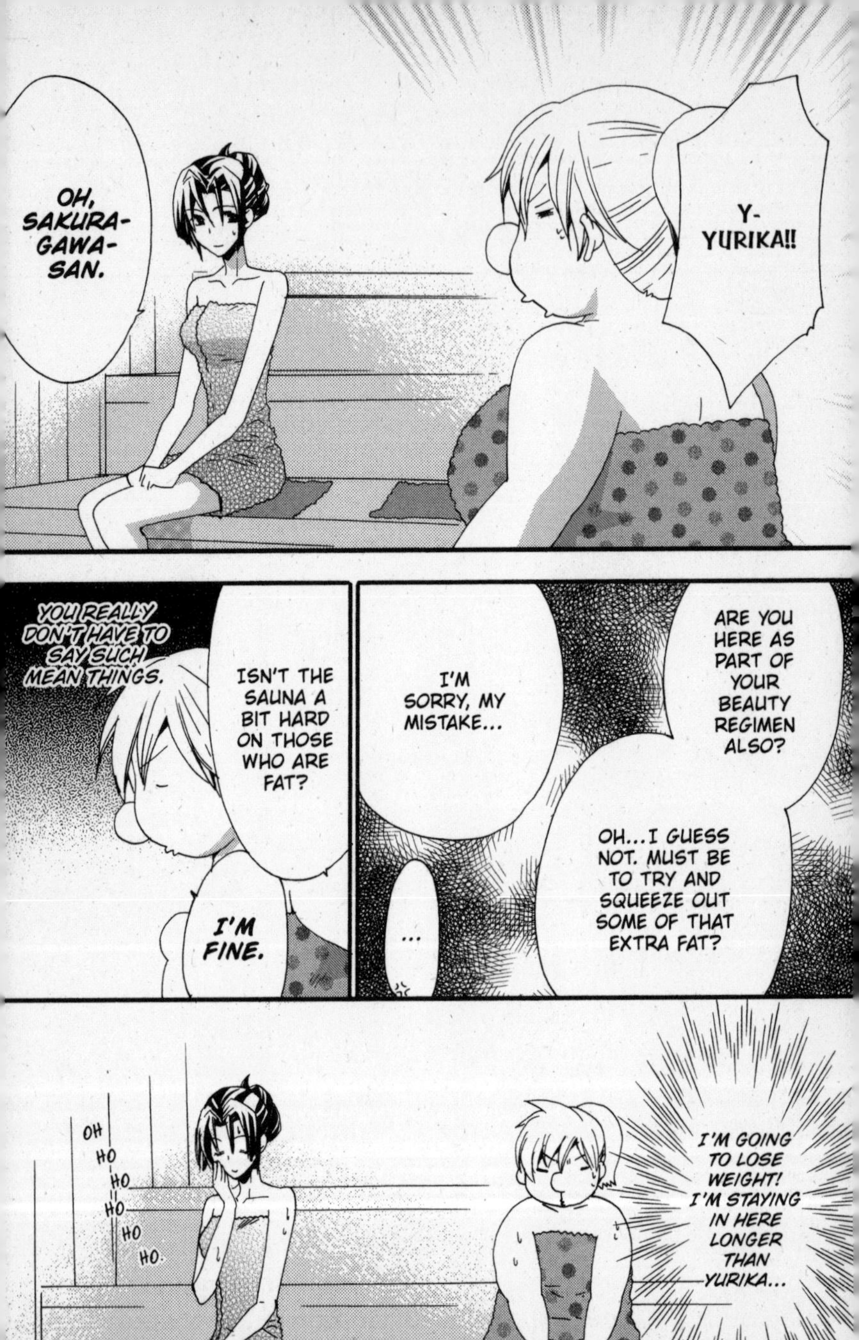
Y-YURIKA!!
OH, SAKURA-GAWA-SAN.
ARE YOU HERE AS PART OF YOUR BEAUTY REGIMEN ALSO?
I'M SORRY, MY MISTAKE...
OH...I GUESS NOT. MUST BE TO TRY AND SQUEEZE OUT SOME OF THAT EXTRA FAT?
...
ISN'T THE SAUNA A BIT HARD ON THOSE WHO ARE FAT?
YOU REALLY DON'T HAVE TO SAY SUCH MEAN THINGS.
I'M FINE.
I'M GOING TO LOSE WEIGHT! I'M STAYING IN HERE LONGER THAN YURIKA...
OH HO HO HO HO HO.

TO BE CONTINUED IN UGLY DUCKLING'S LOVE REVOLUTION 3!

LOVEREVO!!

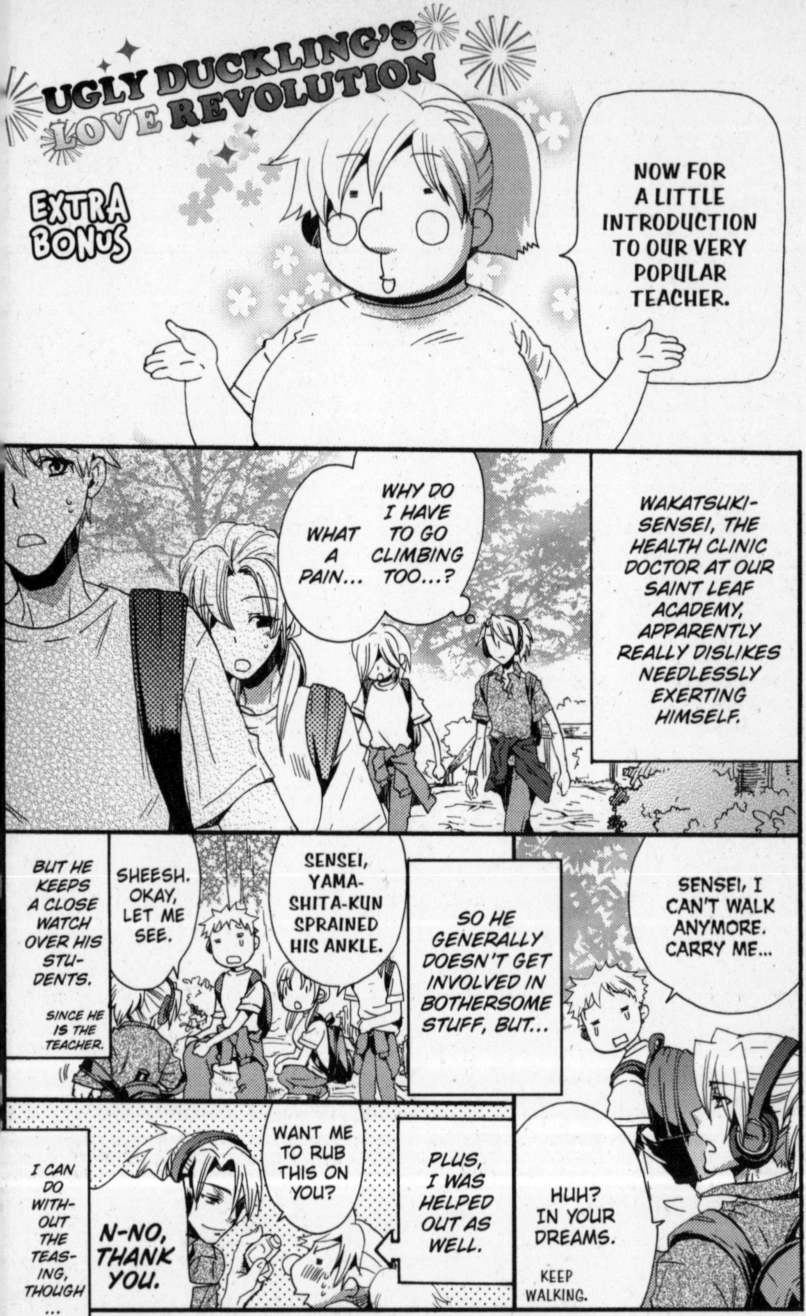
UGLY DUCKLING'S LOVE REVOLUTION
NOW FOR A LITTLE INTRODUCTION TO OUR VERY POPULAR TEACHER.
EXTRA BONUS
WAKATSUKI-SENSEI, THE HEALTH CLINIC DOCTOR AT OUR SAINT LEAF ACADEMY, APPARENTLY REALLY DISLIKES NEEDLESSLY EXERTING HIMSELF.
WHY DO I HAVE TO GO CLIMBING TOO...?
WHAT A PAIN...
SENSEI, I CAN'T WALK ANYMORE. CARRY ME...
HUH? IN YOUR DREAMS.
KEEP WALKING.
SO HE GENERALLY DOESN'T GET INVOLVED IN BOTHERSOME STUFF, BUT...
SENSEI, YAMASHITA-KUN SPRAINED HIS ANKLE.
SHEESH. OKAY, LET ME SEE.
BUT HE KEEPS A CLOSE WATCH OVER HIS STUDENTS.
SINCE HE IS THE TEACHER.
PLUS, I WAS HELPED OUT AS WELL.
WANT ME TO RUB THIS ON YOU?
N-NO, THANK YOU.
I CAN DO WITHOUT THE TEASING, THOUGH...

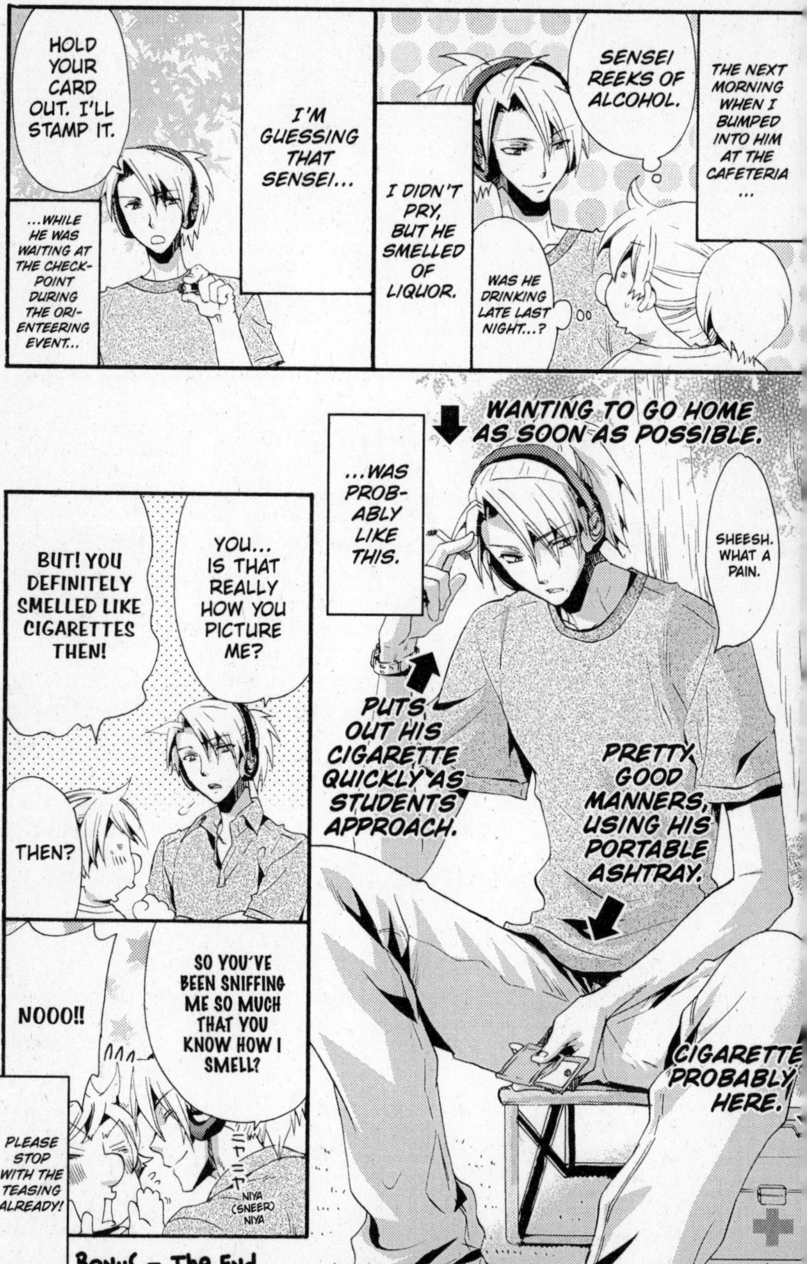
THE NEXT MORNING WHEN I BUMPED INTO HIM AT THE CAFETERIA ...
SENSEI REEKS OF ALCOHOL.
WAS HE DRINKING LATE LAST NIGHT...?
I DIDN'T PRY, BUT HE SMELLED OF LIQUOR.
I'M GUESSING THAT SENSEI...
HOLD YOUR CARD OUT. I'LL STAMP IT.
...WHILE HE WAS WAITING AT THE CHECK-POINT DURING THE ORI-ENTEERING EVENT...
...WAS PROB-ABLY LIKE THIS.
WANTING TO GO HOME AS SOON AS POSSIBLE.
SHEESH. WHAT A PAIN.
PUTS OUT HIS CIGARETTE QUICKLY AS STUDENTS APPROACH.
PRETTY GOOD MANNERS, USING HIS PORTABLE ASHTRAY.
CIGARETTE PROBABLY HERE.
YOU... IS THAT REALLY HOW YOU PICTURE ME?
BUT! YOU DEFINITELY SMELLED LIKE CIGARETTES THEN!
THEN?
SO YOU'VE BEEN SNIFFING ME SO MUCH THAT YOU KNOW HOW I SMELL?
NOOO!!
NIYA (SNEER) NIYA
PLEASE STOP WITH THE TEASING ALREADY!

Bonus - The End

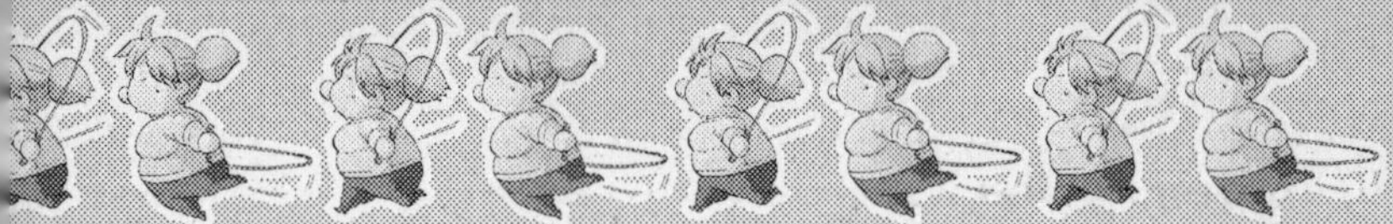

Hello! Yuuki Fujinari here. It's *Ugly Duckling's Love Revolution, Volume 2!*
The continued serialization of this story is all thanks to you, the readers! Thank you so much!
Actually, it's the first time I'm seeing a "Volume 2" next to my name, so it's quite exciting for me.

I've been trying to write a story about all the main characters and have finally touched on all of them in this volume. I love all the characters and want to write about them equally, but the two juniors didn't get much page time in volume 2. So I thought I could at least do an illustration. So here is Ren as a prince.

By the way, I know I mentioned in volume 1's afterword that I wanted to start a diet, but that hasn't happened at all. The workout gear I got for the diet is covered in dust. Every month as I draw Hitomi, hard at work at her diet, I'm pained by my own weakness.
My weight hasn't gone down at all (actually might have gained weight...), but Hitomi is still hard at work on her diet and losing weight, so please keep cheering her on.

Thank you for all your comments. I read them all, and they are very helpful.
Thank you so much!
Please let me know your thoughts on volume 2! And keep an eye out for volume 3.

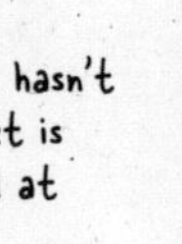

2007 Spring. Yuuki Fujinari

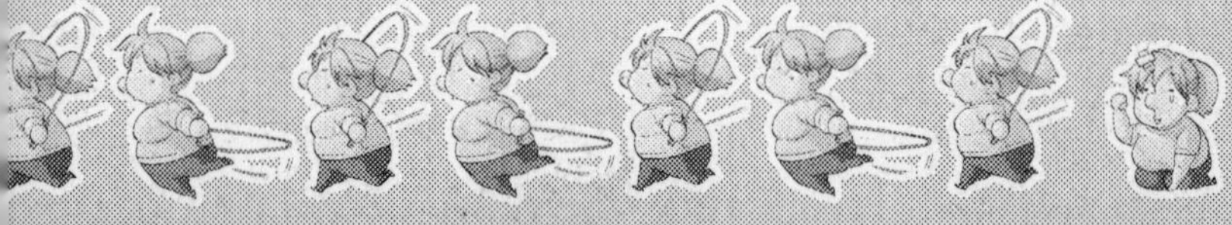

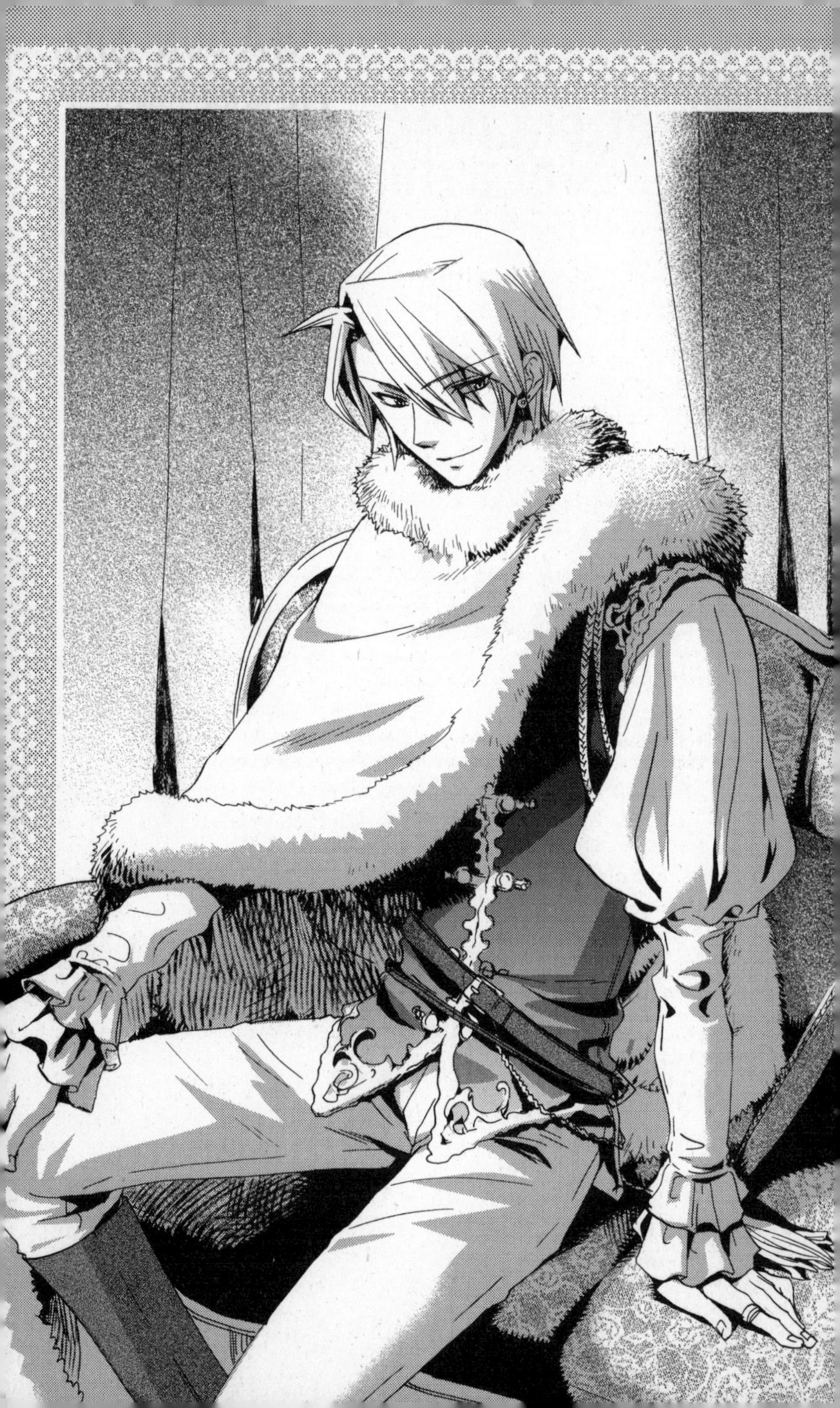

UGLY DUCKLING'S LOVE REVOLUTION ❷

YUUKI FUJINARI
GungHo Online Entertainment, Inc.

SA JUN 2013
OS MAY 2013
KR OCT 16
RJ JAN 2019
KR JUN 2020

Translation: Kaori Inoue • Lettering: Lys Blakeslee

Otometekikoikakumei★Loverevo!! Vol. 2 © 2007 YUUKI FUJINARI © 2006, 2008
GungHo Online Entertainment, Inc. / Will. All rights reserved. First published in
Japan in 2007 by ENTERBRAIN, INC., Tokyo. English translation rights arranged
with ENTERBRAIN, INC. through Tuttle-Mori Agency, Inc., Tokyo.

Translation © 2010 by Hachette Book Group, Inc.

Yen Press
Hachette Book Group
237 Park Avenue, New York, NY 10017

www.HachetteBookGroup.com
www.YenPress.com

Yen Press is an imprint of Hachette Book Group, Inc. The Yen Press name and logo
are trademarks of Hachette Book Group, Inc.

First Yen Press Edition: October 2010

ISBN: 978-0-7595-3176-5

10 9 8 7 6 5 4 3 2 1

BVG

Printed in the United States of America